The M
and America

The Marx Brothers and America

Where Film, Comedy and History Collide

ROBERT E. WEIR

McFarland & Company, Inc., Publishers

Jefferson, North Carolina

Library of Congress Cataloguing-in-Publication Data

Names: Weir, Robert E., 1952– author.
Title: The Marx Brothers and America : where film, comedy
and history collide / Robert E. Weir.
Description: Jefferson, North Carolina : McFarland & Company, Inc.,
Publishers, 2022 | Includes bibliographical references and index.
Identifiers: LCCN 2022030838 |
ISBN 9781476688954 (paperback : acid free paper) ∞
ISBN 9781476648729 (ebook)
Subjects: LCSH: Marx Brothers films—History and criticism. |
Comedy films—United States—History and criticism. | Motion pictures
and history. | BISAC: PERFORMING ARTS / Film / Genres / Comedy
Classification: LCC PN1995.9.M33 W45 2022 | DDC 791.43/6553—dc23/eng/20220714
LC record available at https://lccn.loc.gov/2022030838

British Library cataloguing data are available

ISBN (print) 978-1-4766-8895-4
ISBN (ebook) 978-1-4766-4872-9

Front cover: (left to right) Groucho, Harpo and Chico Marx
(images and design by Dominique Thiébaut)

Printed in the United States of America

*McFarland & Company, Inc., Publishers
Box 611, Jefferson, North Carolina 28640
www.mcfarlandpub.com*

For Emily, always.
My partner, organizer, editor, comrade
in Marxian humor, and guiding star.

Acknowledgments

COVID-19 shut down access to physical collections, so I'd like to give credit to the various library staff members who handled email queries, especially at the University of Massachusetts Amherst and Smith College. Thanks especially to Marlene Wong at the Werner Josten Library at Smith. A shout-out to students in my history and film courses at Bay Path University and the University of Massachusetts Amherst. They helped me refine material in this book by showing me what worked, what was clear, and what was not.

Thanks to personal friends Chris Rohmann and Jan Whitaker for sharing their expertise on theater and department stores, respectively. Thanks to Huck Gutman of the University of Vermont, who encouraged me not to apologize for past social values as if, somehow, they had been my own. Much appreciation goes to Tony Fournier and Marv Goldberg for tracking down African American entertainers whose details are often overlooked in published works on popular music. I am grateful to cartoonist Bill Griffith for allowing me to use one of his "Zippy" strips.

Much appreciation goes to colleagues at UMass Amherst who schooled me in how to think about popular culture, gave the green light to courses centered on the Marx Brothers, and/or offered cheerleading support. The UMass history department is, simply, an extraordinary group of scholars and fine individuals. Gratitude goes to Ron Story and Kathy Peiss. Ron is now retired and Kathy has moved on to the University of Pennsylvania, but they were among the first to help me think about culture in more complex ways. Thanks to Audrey Altstadt, Joye Bowman and Brian Ogilvie who, during their respective chairing of the department, gave the go-ahead for my courses, and to Margaret Leahy at Bay Path for the same courtesy. I also wish to acknowledge scintillating discussions about culture with Brian Bunk, Jennifer Fronc, David Glassberg, Marla Miller and Joel Wolfe. I had so many wide-ranging bus-ride discussions with Sigrid Schmalzer and Heidi Scott on the seven-mile trip between Northampton and Amherst that I'm sure a few of their ideas slipped into my book without specific recollection of their contributions. The same is true of the many conversations I had with Dan and Helen Horowitz during semesters when we all taught at Smith College.

A special thanks goes to my many cherished friends associated with the Northeast Popular/American Culture Association, an organization I served for many years. Among the many people who have enriched my life intellectually and on the personal level are: Kathleen Banks-Nutter, Lance Eaton, Carol-Ann Farkas, Don Gagnon, Bob Hackey, Jim Hanlan, Peter Holloran, Karen Honeycutt, Kraig Larkin,

Robert MacGregor, Mark Madigan, Tim Madigan, Andi McClanahan, Carol Mitchell, Bob Niemi, Marty Norden, Russ Pottle, Amos St. Germain, David Tanner, Jennifer Tebbe-Grossman and Mark van Ells. Apologies to anyone whose name I forgot to mention. In memoriam to Bruce Cohen, who died of COVID as I was writing this book.

Table of Contents

Preface

This is a work about how humor and history collide. I begin with a confession and rationale. My interest in the Marx Brothers began when I was a boy of ten. Groucho was always my favorite Marx Brother because he saved me from childhood thrashings. But I'm getting ahead of myself.

In the early 1960s, it wasn't hard to find Marx Brothers movies on television. There were just three networks in the pre-cable days—ABC, CBS and NBC—but if you lived in the right place, you could also pull in a Metromedia station. I grew up in Chambersburg, Pennsylvania, about a hundred miles north of Washington, D.C. A few trial-and-error twists of the rotary box that controlled the rooftop antenna allowed me to watch Metromedia WTTF in Washington. Metromedia, a loose confederation of stations from the defunct DuMont network, was a small player. It had some shows of its own, but mainly showed a lot of old movies.

"Cheap" mattered to my family as well. There were two downtown movie houses where I saw both first-run and old movies, but with two younger brothers, a construction-worker father who was often unemployed, and a mother who worked part time, money was tight. One of my earliest economic lessons was old movies because they were cheap to air.

Textbooks routinely state that by the mid–1950s virtually all households had a TV. That's flat-out wrong. First, you had to live within reception distance of an urban TV station or relay transmitter. Second, you had to be able to afford a set. We had no TV until 1962, nor did lots of my neighbors. Television was still a novelty and it was pretty exciting to plop down in front of the "small box," as TV was colloquially called. (Less charitably, it was called an "idiot box.")

I invite middle-class readers to imagine what it was like to come of age in a neighborhood that sociologists described as "working-class poor." Think of a life in which money and food had to be "stretched." Families often had to shuffle which bills could be paid and which could be delayed. Sometimes that meant your party-line phone or household electricity was cut off until payments were made. It meant eating lots of noodles, soup, Spam and pre–food-stamps "surplus food" allotments that came in unmarked cans and boxes. I recall blocks of Velveeta and tins of canned meat sitting in globs of congealed fat that had to be skimmed before eating.

Things got better when my mother started working in a grocery store, but some neighbors relied upon food stamps when they first appeared in 1964. It's likely we did too for a while, but my parents didn't talk about that. To this day, if you want to get my dander up, try to tell me that Lyndon Johnson's Great Society programs were wasteful government handouts to the lazy and undeserving. (LBJ was also the reason I got to go to college, though I had to get over being angry about his Vietnam War policies to appreciate that.)

I watched a lot of free TV in my boyhood, by which I mean *a lot* of TV. Quality didn't matter. I viewed cowboy shows such as *Bonanza* and *Wagon Train* and variety shows hosted by Jackie Gleason, Garry Moore, Red Skelton, Andy Williams and Ed Sullivan. I avidly consumed mindless tripe such as *The Beverly Hillbillies, Mister Ed, Petticoat Junction* and *Car 54, Where Are You?* Thanks to Metromedia, I also watched the classic 1950s productions *I Love Lucy, Father Knows Best* and *Leave It to Beaver*. (I couldn't relate to *Ozzie and Harriet*; I knew no one who lived like that!) Above everything stood Looney Tunes cartoons, major league baseball and Groucho Marx's *You Bet Your Life*.

Groucho fascinated me with his quips, his leer, his cigar and his rapid-fire patter. Naturally, I wanted to see his old films as well. Groucho became a personal hero by saving me from bloody noses and broken bones. My neighborhood was literally on the wrong side of the tracks. A Western Maryland Railroad line bisected the town

The author holds a signed photograph from Groucho (author's collection).

east and west, with much of the West End a repository for the working-class poor. The closer you were to the tracks, the worse things were, and I would have had to live *on* the tracks to be any closer. I grew so accustomed to rumbling trains that I often struggled to fall asleep until the late-night freight rolled by, an odd lullaby to be sure.

My neighborhood was early 1960s tough. That made it fairly tame by today's standards. There were no murderous gangs or crack dealers, and most disputes were resolved without resorting to firearms. Still, it didn't take much to find yourself on the wrong end of someone's ire. Loyalties and friendships shifted with the wind, and a wrong glance invited a beating. Someone who was mad at you might chase you down the street while brandishing a club, clods of dirt or a snake, and you knew better than to dawdle to consider the thickness of the stick, check for stones in the mudball, or identify the reptile as a venomous copperhead or a harmless garter snake. One local family was known to hurl pocketknives or darts. On occasion, African American kids from an adjacent ghetto ("Cardboard City") got into rumbles with the white kids.[1]

It was a challenging place to grow up if, like me, you never really *grew* much at all. I topped out at five foot five and one half inches and was pretty scrawny. In short—pun intended—my pugilist dreams ended after second grade. My lack of brawn made me a convenient punching bag for those having a bad day. It got worse when I reached my early teens. My junior high school threw most of the townies together and, suddenly, kids you'd never met before wanted to pummel you. Toss in raging male hormones and it was an aggressive place. I had a chronically sore left arm; a popular male ritual was to sneak up on someone and punch them with a single raised knuckle. For some reason, it was "fun" to watch the bump rise on the arm as the victim howled in pain.

In the midst of this, there was an unwritten code: You couldn't beat on someone who bested you verbally. It was dishonorable to strike someone whose insult left you sputtering. When ripostes flew, spectators became impromptu judges who determined who had been "burnt," or suffered an "in your face" verbal blow. They were the peer-pressure referees who, when I let loose a good wisecrack, admonished my tormentor: "Leave the little guy alone." Years later, I learned that I had African American youngsters from Cardboard City to thank for this ritual; it was an old custom called "playing the dozens."

Wit, not fists, got me through adolescence with just minor bruises. As often as not, "my" wit was Groucho's. No matter the time of day—midnight was a personal favorite—if a Marx Brothers film was on television, I watched it. Long before I appreciated the Marx Brothers' maniacal anarchism, I was a student of the art of insult. When a tormentor signaled his intent to boot my posterior, I'd paraphrase Groucho: "That subject covers a lot of ground. Say, you cover a lot of ground yourself. I hear they're going to tear you down and put up an office building." Or maybe, "Your parents always wanted children. Imagine their disappointment when *you* came along." I suppose I stayed up late because I needed new material.

The fights stopped when I reached senior high, but I credit Groucho for my quick tongue. It helped me gain cachet during the late '60s, when it was okay to lambaste policy-makers, authority figures and other "Establishment" members who we blamed for sundry bad decisions and injustices. It helped less in college, where my professors insisted that I offer *evidence* for my opinions! A few had the moxie to tell me I wasn't the radical I fancied myself to be. They were right. I am a Marxist, but from the school of Groucho rather than Karl.

In college, I began to see Marx Brothers films in a new light. I found their assaults on puffed-up authority figures meshed well with my working-class disdain for phonies, and I admired how they deflated egos, banished pretense and ridiculed social climbers. Sometimes they led me to brandish humor as a more deadly weapon than I intended. It astonishes me how irony-challenged contemporary Americans can be.

The Marx Brothers have been hailed as comedic geniuses, though their popularity has waxed and waned. Groucho and his siblings were such an important part of my youth that it stings to discover how many young people today have never heard of them. To be fair, the Marx Brothers' heyday, the 1920s, '30s and '40s, was a different era. That's fine by me; I became a historian, so *all* of my material belongs to a different time period. I spent my teaching career searching for "hooks" to help students connect to, and compare and contrast their experiences with, things from the past.

I often quote the English novelist L.P. Hartley: "The past is a foreign country. They do things differently there." But Hartley's statement isn't universally true. History, after all, studies human beings. Often, we discover things that looked different in bygone days yet remain burning issues in the present. Emma Goldman, an anarchist in the early 20th century, allegedly remarked, "If I can't dance, I don't want to be part of your revolution."[2] If we substitute "laugh" for dance, we have a slogan that can help get us through the trials and challenges of understanding both history and ourselves.

Speaking of Trials

A *not*-so-funny thing happened as I began to write this book: COVID-19 shut down universities, libraries and archives. Luckily, I have an entire shelf of works about and by the Marx Brothers, plus articles, clippings and other materials in my file drawers. And of course, there's always the Internet.

My approach is that of a social historian, not a film historian. What are the broad social contexts that shape what we see on the screen, and what we can we learn about American history by unraveling Marx Brothers films? This book is aimed at new and old fans of the Marx Brothers who want to know how movies embody, reflect and reveal the time period in which they first appeared. I am a fan of the "usable past," things that make us think more deeply about our current conditions. This book is, then, a look at the first half of the 20th century. I consider the 13 Marx Brothers feature films to be historical documents that lend insight into a time when nearly everyone would have known of the Marx Brothers.

There is biographical detail in this work, but this is not intended as a biography of the Marxes. As much as Groucho influenced me, I doubt I would have liked him very much as an individual. Chico and Zeppo weren't exactly candidates for humanitarian awards either. Had I known any of them, I probably would have enjoyed most conversing with the brother who didn't speak on the screen, Harpo. I certainly would have been fascinated by his intellectual pals.

Unlike much of my past scholarship, this book grounds itself in secondary research and uses the films as primary source material. I'll also draw upon memoirs, interviews and other such sources, but with caution. The Marxes were notoriously unreliable curators of their own past. They were comedians, a profession not known for letting unvarnished truth get in the way of a good line. Similarly, their offspring and inner circle were sometimes more subjective than objective.

Mostly I want to offer a way of studying pieces of 20th-century history that is fun to contemplate and research. I hope it also makes readers laugh and discover (or re-discover) Marx Brothers films. If it does, don't thank *me*. Thank Groucho.

ONE

That's Not Funny

Comedy and Context

September 3, 2009: Day One of the first time I taught "Humor and American History." As an introduction, I showed a clip from *The Cocoanuts* (1929), the Marx Brothers' first film. Beyond a few snickers, no one was laughing. Just as I had anticipated. When the clip was done, I asked, "Was this funny?" Most said no, but I really wanted them to grapple with this question: Why not? We batted that around until one young woman said, "I don't get it."

Nor could she. She was watching a 90-year-old movie by a troupe whose last member (Zeppo) died more than a decade before she was born. Most students simply

Publicity photograph from *The Cocoanuts*: **Zeppo, Groucho, Chico, Harpo (Paramount, via Wikimedia Commons).**

couldn't relate to the material. Who *were* these people on the screen? Why were they singing such corny songs? Why was the technology so clumsy? Were those dance numbers considered "good"?

Nancy Walker, a Vanderbilt University English professor, once wrote, "Humor, like all forms of communication, requires *context*: To find it amusing, the audiences must have certain knowledge, understanding and values, which are subject to evolution from one century or even one decade to the next."[1] Walker was on the money. Scholars often overestimate what they perceive to be universal qualities of humor. They forget that when comedy comes from another time period, additional background is needed to "get" a joke. The German word *Zeitgeist* is usually translated as "spirit of the times," a catchphrase for the dominant values, mindsets, morals and cultural expressions of a particular time period. It's hard to unpack numerous Marx Brothers gags without a rudimentary understanding of their *Zeitgeist*. Their films are, in essence, *historical* artifacts.

Consider this short exercise. Write down your favorite joke. Next, try to explain to someone why it's so funny that you find it superior to all others. Not so easy, is it? Take it a step further. Make note of a comedian you once thought was funny, but now you don't. How did that person become unfunny? The gags and jokes didn't change, so what did? Was it you? The *Zeitgeist*? Both?

It's important to know a few things about how humor works, but first let's meet the Marx Brothers.

Marxism Without Karl

In order of birth, the Marx Brothers were Leonard (1887–1961), Adolph—later known as Arthur (1888–1964), Julius (1890–1977), Milton (1892–1977) and Herbert (1901–1979).[2] They were better known by their stage names: Chico, Harpo, Groucho, Gummo and Zeppo. They were the offspring of Jewish immigrant parents Samuel and Mienne Schönberg Marx. Samuel (1859–1933), nicknamed "Frenchie" since he was born in Alsace, was a tailor whose skills—or lack thereof—were frequently lampooned by his sons.[3]

Mienne (1865–1929), always known as "Minnie," was—pardon the pun—cut from different cloth. She was born in Hanover before German confederation took place. Her father Levy ("Lafe") was a magician, ventriloquist and umbrella maker who later went by the name of Louis. Minnie's mother, Fannie Schönberg (*née* Salomons), yodeled and played the harp. She probably came from a well-to-do family, as harps were expensive. Fannie and Lafe performed throughout the Kingdom of Hanover. Their successes and failures were family lore, though not much is known of their lives in Europe. They immigrated to the U.S. around 1880, and two of their children caught the performing bug. That was a good thing, as neither parent spoke English and they often relied upon their children for support.[4]

Minnie's brother Abraham Eliser Adolf Schönberg (1868–1949) paved the way for family stage success. He performed in vaudeville as Al Shean and eventually partnered with Edward Gallagher. Gallagher and Shean made the jump from vaudeville to Broadway, though they apparently did not like each other. They performed from 1910 to 1914 and reunited for a stint that lasted from 1920 to 1925. Shean/

Schönberg then worked as a solo performer, but his major role in our tale is as Minnie's idol.

Minnie's ambition was enormous, but her talent and business acumen were meager. She was far more determined that her sons would become performers like their uncle Al—often with herself as part of their act—than that her sons receive formal education.[5] She once acted as their manager under the name Minnie Palmer, a subterfuge to hide her parenthood from booking agents. This allowed her to pocket the commission that would normally go to a third-party manager. She also skirted accepted boundaries, as there was an established singer and actress named Minnie Palmer.[6]

In their early days in burlesque and vaudeville, the Marxes used their birth names. Julius was the first to appear on a stage, but Minnie thought that ensemble

THE TIMES-DEMOCRAT, SUNDAY, MAY 11, 1913.

FOUR MARX BROTHERS,
In "Green's Reception," at the Greenwall.

The Marx Brothers on the vaudeville circuit, 1913. From left: Julius (Groucho), Leonard (Chico), Adolph (Harpo) and Milton (Gummo) (New Orleans *Times-Democrat*).

acts had a higher earning potential. In 1909, she uprooted the Marx clan from New York City and relocated them to Chicago in the belief that it would be easier to secure bookings in the Midwest than in New York's competitive theater scene.

Milton (Gummo) was technically the first to appear on the stage. At least we think so. A family legend holds that, in 1899, he donned a *papier-mâché* head and pretended to be a dummy in a ventriloquist's act. More substantively, in 1905, 14-year-old Julius (Groucho) debuted as a "boy singer." Under Minnie's guidance, from 1907 to 1910, he was featured in a series of musical acts: the Three Nightingales (with Milton and Mary O'Donnell), the Four Nightingales (Julius, Milton, Adolph and O'Donnell), and the Six Escorts (Julius, Milton, Adolph, Leonard, Minnie and her sister Hannah).[7]

Apparently, the act wasn't spellbinding in any configuration. Groucho later spun the story that he began to have doubts when the Nightingales hit Jacksonville, Florida, and the theater manager ran down the aisle screaming, "Stop it! Stop it! It's rotten. Hey, you fellers, you call that singing? That's terrible. The worst I ever heard. My dog can do better than that."[8]

In a better-documented incident, the Six Escorts were in Nacogdoches, Texas, in 1910, when most of the audience left the theater to watch a runaway mule gallop down the street. They returned once the excitement was over and Julius began to riff, "Nacogdoches is full of roaches.... The jack-ass is the flower of Tex-ass." Much to his surprise, patrons laughed.[9] Thus began the Marxes' transformation from a musical to a comedy act.

After 1911, the act minus Minnie and Hannah was known simply as the Marx Brothers. Perhaps you wonder why the Marxes were in a town like Nacogdoches in the first place. In 1910, its population was just 3,369. This was a measure of Minnie's misfires. Upon the move to Chicago, she signed contracts that alienated Edward F. Albee II, who controlled the Keith-Albee-Orpheum syndicate of some 1,500 stages.[10] This effectively blackballed the Marxes and relegated them to houses operated by Alexander Pantages, who had just 80 stages. His was at best the second tier of the vaudeville hierarchy, with most of his venues scattered among small towns. Performers often had to travel long distances and endure dirty boarding houses, bad food, dishonest theater managers and thieves within their own ranks.

It took time to repair Minnie's mismanagement, but comedy became the route to success. It began later in 1910, with *Fun in Hi Skule* [*sic*], a sketch that centered on an easy target; schoolroom comedy was very popular at the time. The show got decent reviews for its energy and witty repartee. Julius assumed a German accent and Arthur (formerly Adolph) was Julius' banter partner rather than Leonard, who was in the process of creating an Italian character.

The Marx Brothers appeared in several other shows, but their big break came when they scored a New York staging for their 1919 show *Home Again*. Home again, indeed! They left Chicago and moved back to New York City. In 1921, *I'll Say She Is* opened in Philadelphia, and moved to Broadway in 1923. Fame loomed on the horizon.[11]

What's in a Name?

The vaudeville years were difficult, but the Marxes slowly honed their comedic characters and adopted the names by which they are known to history. Most sources credit vaudeville monologist Art Fisher with cooking up their monikers. Fisher delighted in coming up with nicknames, and during a May 1914 poker game in Galesburg, Illinois, he decided his traveling partners needed them. At the time, there was a comic strip titled "Knocko the Monk," *monk* referencing Knocko's simian-like features. It touched off a fad of nicknames ending in the letter "o." Knocko himself had recently been rechristened as Sherlocko, a bumbling version of Sherlock Holmes.[12] Fisher suggested that Julius, Milton, Leonard and Arthur become Groucho, Gummo, Chico and Harpo.[13] (Arthur had changed his name from Adolph in 1911, not in response to the rise of Adolf Hitler, as is sometimes misreported.[14])

Why those names? It depends whose story you believe. Some have linked Groucho's moniker to his grumpy and pessimistic outlook, but a more likely explanation is that it came from the grouch bag, a small money pouch that vaudevillians wore around their necks at night to prevent fellow actors from pilfering their wages. Harpo recalled that many vaudeville performers were analogous to "gypsies and other vagrants," which made a grouch bag a good idea.[15] Groucho sometimes agreed that the grouch bag was the origin of his nickname; at other times, he maintained that it merely resembled Knocko. Groucho's character was essentially that of a secular *schnorrer*, though he was usually an unsuccessful con artist. His trademark looks also evolved in vaudeville: an oversized greasepaint mustache, bushy eyebrows, wire-rimmed glasses, leering glances and an ever-present black cigar. That prop might have begun as an homage to his grandfather Louis, but Groucho remained a cigar smoker for the rest of his life.

Chico's name was originally spelled "Chicko" and was always pronounced that way. In the parlance of his day, Leonard was a chicken-chaser (chickens or "chicks" being slang for young women). The name fit his lifestyle. He was a notorious womanizer and a problem gambler who sometimes hocked items belonging to his father or brothers to pay his debts. He remained irresponsible with money and was often broke. Before he joined the act for good in 1912, he occasionally served as an agent for his brothers. He was good at it, though he sometimes gambled away this brothers' advances. On stage, he sported an Italian accent, shabby clothing and a soft Tyrolean hat. Legend holds that his accent was so convincing that he played cards with Italian mobsters who assumed he was a *paisano* (fellow Italian). That's probably a tall tale, but Chico certainly cavorted with mobsters from time to time.[16]

Comic accents were a vaudeville staple, and some performers built their acts around parodying ethnic groups. Especially popular were faux Dutch, German, Italian, Scandinavian and Irish accents. In vaudeville, ethnicity was an acceptable parody target. For example, Gentiles often pretended to be Jews, a license for lampoon.

Chico had the added advantage of being a very good pianist, a skill he reportedly refined by playing in bars, speakeasies and houses of ill repute. His signature move was to flip his right hand and "shoot" the keys as if his index finger were a gun barrel.

Arthur probably would have been nicknamed "Harpo" even had he not been an actor. Like his maternal grandmother, he played the harp. His character was a tramp-like clown who dressed in clashing clothing, an oversized coat and a worse-for-wear top hat. But most Marx Brothers shows and movies featured a serious interlude in which he showcased his namesake abilities. What movie audiences never saw was that his curly hair was a red or blond wig. (Marx Brothers movies were in black and white.) Harpo never spoke in a Marx Brothers' film; his character was a mute trickster.

Milton's nickname Gummo was likely a nod to the popularity of detective novels, comic books, serialized newspaper stories and stage acts ("gumshoe" is slang for a detective). An alternate story holds that Milton wore rubber overshoes ("gum shoes") as a child, and still another was that he danced in rubber-soled shoes. Take your pick. By his own design, Gummo did not attain celebrity fame. He quit the act in 1918 and eventually carved out a successful career as an agent—sometimes for his brothers.

When Gummo left the act, youngest brother Herbert entered and acquired the sobriquet Zeppo. Stories differ over why he who performed straight-man roles bore such a silly name. Some have claimed it derived from the rigid gas-filled airships called zeppelins, though Harpo insisted Herbert was named for Mr. Zippo, a chimpanzee in a vaudeville act. Then again, Chico claimed Zeppo was a variant of Zeb, the Minnesotan rube equivalent of Irish stereotypes Pat and Mike.[17]

Zeppo seldom got a laugh unless involved in hijinks with one or more of his brothers. He appeared in the first five Marx Brothers films, but quit in 1933 to become an agent, engineer and inventor. His screen persona differed from his off-screen personality: Zeppo was a street tough as a youth, and then a jealous adult with an explosive temper.

What Is Humor?

To understand why the Marx Brothers are funny, let's investigate humor itself. Comedy is more complex than a belly laugh. We don't really know why one person roars at something that strikes others as unfunny. That's among the reasons why artificial intelligence (AI) is lousy at comedy. It can locate jokes in a database and detect patterns in them, but it doesn't "get" them.[18] AI's only saving grace is that human beings aren't much better at explaining humor.

Scholars from disciplines such as anthropology, biology, communications, history, linguistics, medicine, philosophy, psychology and sociology have studied humor. Likewise, those who make their living in comedy have theories about the subject. It's worthwhile to mention some of their ideas. Preview of coming attractions: No one has definitively explained comedy.

Neuroscientist Robert Provine once proclaimed that laughter is part of a "universal human vocabulary." That's probably understated. Although the vocal cords of chimpanzees and apes can't reproduce the same sounds as humans, numerous primatologists think that these animals laugh.[19] Zoologists and some psychologists speculate that humor also extends to whales, seals, otters, birds, cats, dogs and various animals whose behaviors are analogous to human play. Skeptics counter that this anthropomorphizes non-human species. Maybe they're right, but who can watch squirrels chasing each other around a tree trunk without thinking that they're pranking each other?

As for *Homo sapiens*, Dutch historian Johan Huizinga believed that all human language and culture had their origins in play.[20] Aristotle linked play and laughter to feelings of ecstasy and relief, and most physiologists, psychiatrists and psychologists agree. Even Sigmund Freud—hardly anyone's idea of a stand-up comic—thought wit and playfulness were portals between the conscious and subconscious mind.

They say "laughter is the best medicine," and it might be literally true. There is no pragmatic reason for comedy to exist unless it is somehow linked to the evolutionary development of humankind. It did not make us better hunter-gatherers, fire makers, shelter builders, water haulers, carpenters or stockbrokers. Some speculate that it aided the social evolution of humans: Once our ancestors began to live in close proximity, laughter reduced tensions that threatened group cohesion. On the individual level, Julia Watkins and Amy J. Eisenbraum make a strong case for the "physiological benefits of laughter." They claim it helps human beings cope with struggle, stress and disappointment; lowers blood pressure, lessens pain, and reduces the effects of some medical conditions and diseases.[21]

Philosopher Henri Bergson noted that laughter suppresses other emotions, perhaps a key to its medical efficacy. He even defended clowns, the *bête noire* of legions of children. In his view, clowns (and other comics) transport us to realms of imagination, creativity and shared sociability. Other philosophers, most notably Thomas Hobbes, felt that comedy exhibited humankind at its worst.[22]

My takeaway is two-fold. First, don't invite a Hobbesian to your party! Second, defining humor is like the old chestnut about obscenity: You can't define it, but you know it when you see it.

Guffaw in the U.S.A.

The Marx Brothers were born in the United States to immigrant parents. Does either of those things matter? Nineteenth-century wits such as Josh Billings, Artemus Ward and Mark Twain were among those who wrestled with whether American humor was distinct from that of other lands.

If it's hard to explain or define humor, it's more difficult to nail down *American* humor. But certain motifs do appear to be part of the collective American comic psyche.

Constance Rourke, writing in 1931, felt that whatever uniqueness American humor once had was waning by the 1890s, just before the Marx Brothers began performing in vaudeville. She did note, though, that irreverence was a favored American device made manifest in characters such as backwoods tricksters, minstrels, rowdies, Yankees and yarnspinners.[23]

In her anthology *Humor in America*, Enid Veron cited three "symbolic characters—the wise fool, the storyteller and the little soul"—as central to the American "comic imagination." She also observed that Americans are uncomfortable about lampooning themselves. In the same volume, Louis Kronenberger struck another discordant note: "Ours has been, almost entirely, a humor of release rather than reflectiveness." To put it in fancy terms, he thought American humor is more Dionysian than Apollonian; that is, non-intellectual rather than thought-provoking.[24]

Nancy Walker gave credence to English cleric H.R. Haweis' late–19th-century observation that American humorists repeatedly drew from common sources, including the "shock between Business and Piety," expressed as an amoral impulse toward making money even by unethical means. Other staples include boasting, irreverence, lawlessness, violence and the gap between theory and reality.[25]

After studying humor extensively, folklorists concluded that much of "American" humor is found in older European traditions.[26] In the 1930s, A.H. Krappe asserted, "There exists no such thing as American folklore," and by extension, no specific American character or humor. Peter Briggs added that much of what has passed for American humor began as an intentional effort to hide its English roots: "borrowed laughter" in his wordplay.[27] He suggests that "American" humor is more form than substance and, if we add inspirations from more sources than England (miming, for example, has Italian and Japanese roots), maybe it's best to downplay American uniqueness.

Peter L. Berger concentrated on how comics work. They either disrupt social norms or ridicule selected aspects of them. Comedians know the value of timing and send signals to help audiences decode the humor.[28] Most 21st-century humor scholars follow Berger's lead and look at humor in context rather than fussing over origins or national character.

American humor, like its population, is a mutt. Nineteenth-century figures such as Ward and Twain played the role of American humorist, but it was artifice, just as Ward (Charles Farrar Browne) and Twain (Samuel Clemens) were assumed identities. Twenty-first–century Americans often insist that ours is a transnational world, but it has always been thus. When Twain launched a global speaking tour in 1894, he found that audiences frequently laughed before the punchline; his jokes preceded his physical presence. That's because he lived at a time when populations were on the move. Packet boats delivering correspondence, freight and people had plied global waters since the 18th century, and Twain's United States was in the process of being remade by immigrants.[29]

Did it matter that the Marx Brothers were American-born? Yes, in the sense that they drew upon American society for source material. But their humor also transcended the American context.

By contrast, for example, Monty Python's Flying Circus induces one of two reactions in the States: Audiences either double over with laughter or they don't "get it." Sometimes it's their English accents, sometimes it's unfamiliarity with their targets, and sometimes their brand of humor fails to tickle particular sets of funny bones. Yet the same problems of framing can be leveled at American comics from the Marx Brothers to Tim Wilson and Jeff Dunham. Humor tends to be more individualistic than nationalistic. You either laugh, or you don't.

Jewish Humor?

The Marx Brothers were Jewish, but were they "Jewish comics"? This is difficult to answer. The Marxes were thoroughly secular. Scholars have considered Jewish humor more than the Marxes usually did.

Berger notes that Jewish humor has a distinctive tone that is "sharp, cutting [and] strongly intellectual." In the U.S., many Jewish jokes reflect the group's historical marginality.[30] Joseph Boskin and Joseph Dorinson point to the irreverence of Jewish humor, the preponderance of tricksters, and the use of "droll characters" such as *schnorrers, schlemiels, shlimazels* and *lumftmentschen,* Yiddish terms that, respectively, allude to cadgers, fools, hapless individuals and those so drawn to impractical things that they neglect commonplace needs.[31]

There are many excellent studies of Jewish humor, but most aren't much help in explaining what makes the Marx Brothers funny. If we ignore the Yiddish terms above, their humor is consonant with scores of non–Jewish comics. The Marxes never hid their Judaism, but neither did they dwell on it. Of the many biographies and autobiographies of the Marx Brothers, Carolyn Chandler's is one of the few that devotes an entire chapter to religion, and it's not among the more revealing sections of her study.[32]

Aside from adding their voices to those deploring fascist anti–Semitism during the World War II era, the Marx Brothers treated religion as just another thing to lampoon. Groucho often told the story of taking his daughter to a swimming pool at a Hollywood country club. He was told that the club was "restricted" (did not allow Jews). Groucho allegedly quipped, "Since my daughter is only half–Jewish, could she go in the water up to her knees?" Funny line, but is it a put-down of anti–Semitism?

Another question to ask about such anecdotes is whether they happened at all. Sometimes Groucho said the daughter was Miriam and sometimes Melinda, thus giving the tale the earmarks of a tall tale. No club is named, no date is given, and no one can definitively be said to have witnessed the event. That's the Marxes in a nutshell; if anything could be made into a good joke, by all means, use it.

The Roots of Marxian Humor

If Marx Brothers humor wasn't uniquely American or Jewish, where did it come from? Let me emphasize that American and Jewish birth *did* shape them, though it's hard to pin down exactly how. As we shall see, their humor was filled with references that resonated more deeply with American audiences than others. Likewise, they drew from Jewish vaudeville traditions forged before they ever trod the boards. Uniqueness and influence aren't the same thing. Great comics stock their jocular tool chests with whatever instruments they collect and are not always aware of (or care about) where they came from.

The Marx Brothers' most immediate influence was vaudeville, but did they know much about *commedia dell'arte*? This older performance style also contributed to the creation of ensemble acts such as theirs. This so-called "Italian comedy" developed in Europe during the 1500s in reaction to royal court comedies enjoyed solely by the upper crust. By contrast, the *commedia* generally involved amateur or plebeian acting companies of two to a dozen actors, grew more sophisticated over time, and thrived through the 17th century.

The *commedia* relied upon stock figures—recognizable generic characters—that drew upon stereotypes, broad generalizations and archetypes. Audiences laughed because the performers lampooned the human condition. Characters such as the harlequin (in a diamond-patterned suit) and Pierrot (attired in a blousy white costume with buttons running down the front) remain well known today. Harpo's son Bill observed of the *commedia*, "[Y]ou had the authoritarian figure, you had the idiot and you had the mime, and it was a proven formula that has lasted through the ages. The Marx Brothers, through hit and miss, search and destroy, you name it, accidentally came upon it, with Groucho being the authoritarian figure, Chico being the idiot, and Harpo being the mime."[33]

Harpo is essentially Pierrot, the template for mimes, dressed in rags and minus the white-painted face. Chico is a monochromatic, threadbare Harlequin, especially in his delicate balance of stupidity, guile and a capacity for mischief. Groucho is a misanthropic composite of several figures, including the witty but wily Pulcinella and the *Dottore* (doctor) whose expertise was usually a sham. Zeppo often appears as a star-crossed lover, another *commedia* staple.

Still, it's hard to pigeonhole Marx Brothers humor. To rise through the burlesque, vaudeville and Broadway musical comedy ranks required flexibility, experimentation and improvisation.[34] Today we might call their style a "mash-up."

The Elephant in the Room: "Offensive" Humor

There are things in Marx Brothers films that violate the social norms of 21st-century society. I neither condone nor condemn these things. But it is naïve to think that most humor was, is, or *can* be, nice. Berger devotes a chapter of *Redeeming Laughter* to "benign" humor, but it is singularly unconvincing.[35] There can be non-attacking humor, but what often gets labeled as inoffensive humor occurs when comedians satirize themselves.

Much of what poses as benign humor only seems that way because the audience does not feel itself the *direct* target. This is particularly true when the underlying message of a joke or parody generalizes rather than specifies. A friend telling a "dumb blonde" joke, for instance, might preface the punchline with the disclaimer that no blonde in the room is included in the stereotype. The same is true of gendered jokes told among close associates. Women often privately tell jokes about men to other women and don't bother to depersonalize, just as men satirize women in the company of other men.

Other in-group humor works the same way. A Jewish person can lampoon other Jews, but a Gentile telling the same joke risks being labeled as anti–Semitic. African Americans can use derogatory terms and stereotypes to burlesque each other, but white comics treading on such turf might be perceived as racist. The great irony, though, is that Gentiles and Caucasians in the audience laugh at forbidden humor told by others. Did the joke suddenly become funnier because they were not telling it? In a way, yes, because the potential for social and personal stress is reduced.

Most comedy *is* offensive. It is funny *because* it violates the norms of polite society. Joan Rivers once remarked, "I succeeded by saying what everyone else is thinking." There is wisdom in that remark. An old adage holds that comedy is cruel, and that's more correct than most of us would like to believe. Nearly all jokes have a "butt," even if the person telling them is engaging in self-deprecating humor. When you laugh, you derive enjoyment from another's misfortune, even when the comic is stretching the truth.

Perhaps we should just admit that aggression and comedy are soulmates. Folklorists Alan Dundes and Roger Abrahams analyzed "sick humor" and found it everywhere. Abrahams wrote extensively about African and African American humor, and was among the first to show how marginalized groups use humor as a weapon, often in coded ways. It's now well-established that the Br'er Rabbit tales originated among enslaved people lampooning their masters, with Rabbit a stand-in for bondsmen and

Fox for masters. Once you know this, many Br'er Rabbit stories are revenge fantasies that border on cruelty.[36]

In *Cracking Jokes,* Dundes went even further. There isn't much that hasn't been satirized or turned into a joke cycle, including dead babies, the Holocaust, mentally challenged individuals, sexually inept men, and virtually every ethnic group, though especially African Americans and Jews. Even things that appear to be benign are not. Take elephant jokes. As Dundes and Abrahams showed, a lot of elephant jokes are freighted with psychosexual meanings, and elephants were veiled surrogates for African Americans. In Dundes' words, "Where there is anxiety, there will be jokes to express that anxiety. ... Don't be deceived by the façade of humor. The expression, 'laughing to keep from crying,' has a great deal of merit."[37]

Orally circulated jokes and professional comedy are different, but perhaps not as much as you might think. Paul Lewis looked at humor in the aftermath of the September 11, 2001, terrorist attacks. There was respectful silence during the period of shock and mourning and, for a time, even poking fun at President George W. Bush was viewed as unpatriotic. In less than a month, though, cartoonists, *New Yorker* illustrators and stand-up comics broke the solemnity.[38]

If you think we've evolved beyond the humor discussed by Abrahams, Dundes and Lewis, think again. Professional comics have satirized everything from slasher films and torture to serial killers and ecodisaster. African American, Jewish and Muslim comics populate the stage, yet racist, anti–Semitic, and anti–Muslim jokes proliferate. There has been a positive-humor movement of sorts, but it's often viewed as banal political correctness, which itself has been the target of wits (and nitwits). If anything, humor is more politicized now than at the time of the Marx Brothers. In many cases, the answer to the question "Is it funny?" depends upon where someone is located on the political and/or socio-economic spectrum.

When we encounter problematic or offensive aspects of Marx Brothers films, we should first put things in perspective—theirs, not ours. For good reason, historians warn against "presentism"—seeing the past as an imperfect version of today. Sometimes, what appears troublesome on the surface isn't the entire story. Overall, the Marx Brothers' zaniness is more innocent than modern humor, though that's not always the case. In this book, I will address troubling issues in sections subtitled "The Elephant in the Room." Understanding the past requires considering the bad with the good. In other words, a sanitized past is a fictional land.

Humor's Guises

There's a useful glossary of comic terms at the very end of this book. We cannot adequately define humor, but I have listed its various guises in alphabetical order. It is not an exhaustive list, but it covers most of the methods the Marx Brothers used. Forms that overlap are designated by ***italicized bold*** letters so you can cross-reference them.

With all of this in mind, it's time to crack a few comedic cocoanuts, which just happens to reference the Marx Brothers' first film.

Two

The Cocoanuts (1929)

The Marx Brothers' first feature film, *The Cocoanuts*, debuted in New York City on May 23, 1929. It was a shortened and clumsy version of their hit Broadway show of the same name.

Marx Brothers movies are built around schtick and seldom involve elaborate plots. Storylines and music generally serve to segue from one sketch to the next. In *The Cocoanuts*, Groucho plays Mr. Hammer, a hotel owner who can't afford to pay his help, not that he was inclined to do so in the first place. Chico and Harpo appear as deadbeat guests—each an "idle roomer," as Hammer puns—and Zeppo is Jamison, a straight-man desk clerk.

The subplot involves aspiring architect Bob Adams (Oscar Shaw), who is in love

Lobby card for the Marx Brothers' first film, *The Cocoanuts*. Pictured: Groucho, Chico, Harpo (Wikimedia Commons).

with Polly Potter (Mary Eaton). Bob has yet to secure a commission, which makes him an unsuitable future spouse in the eyes of Polly's mother (played with patrician snootiness by Margaret Dumont). Mrs. Potter would rather have Polly tie the knot with Harvey Yates (Cyril Ring), who appears to be a dapper Bostonian. A rich widow, Mrs. Potter is pursued by Hammer. Toss in the inept but swaggering detective Hennessy (Basil Ruysdael), a seductress named Penelope (Kay Francis), a stolen necklace and (too many) song and dance numbers, and you have *The Cocoanuts*. Remember: Marx Brothers films aren't about the story; they're about the mayhem.

The Marx Brothers, Changing Tastes and Technology

Folklore holds that *The Cocoanuts* was the third feature film to have no soundless sequences. That's inaccurate, but there is no question that sound technology was in its infancy, which is why the film was a technological mess. Let's take a short detour to see why that was the case.

On October 6, 1927, moviegoers attending *The Jazz Singer* heard Al Jolson address revelers in a crowded nightclub: "Wait a minute, wait a minute. You ain't heard nothin' yet!" Those words came 17 minutes and 25 seconds into what began as a customary silent film. Jolson's spoken patter and subsequent crooning of the song "Toot Toot Tootsie" marked the beginning of "talkies," as movies with synchronized sound were popularly called.

There is considerable myth surrounding *The Jazz Singer*, including tales of audiences gasping in surprise. That was not the case. Advance promotion included speech on film, demonstrating the technological breakthrough. Thanks to this early "buzz," most people in the theater knew what was coming.

In addition, sound-on-film predated *The Jazz Singer*. Inventor Lee de Forest had been making short films with synchronous sound since 1923, and several newsreels also "talked." You could probably win a few bets by knowing that the first president to address the nation on both radio and film, Calvin Coolidge, did so in 1923 and 1924 respectively. *The Jazz Singer* was merely the first *feature-length* movie to spotlight *spoken* sound-on-film technology. This came courtesy of Warner Brothers' Vitaphone sound-on-disc system, which produced greater clarity than de Forest's Phonofilm.[1] Nonetheless, Vitaphone's capabilities remained limited, and much of Jolson's singing was lip-synched.

Another myth is that talkies were an instant hit. Like most advances, it took time before the new (talkies) drove out the old (silent films). Some industry watchers, including gossip columnist Louella Parsons and MGM production head Irving Thalberg, dismissed sound movies as a short-lived gimmick. So did Harry Warner, whose studio made *The Jazz Singer*.[2] He curtly remarked, "Who the hell wants to hear actors talk?" Just 15 of *The Jazz Singer*'s 88 minutes featured dialogue, and it wasn't until the July 8, 1928, release of *Lights of New* York that an entire feature was produced in sound. In urban areas, talkies surpassed silent films in popularity in 1929, but silent films retained popularity well into the 1930s, as it cost a lot of money to convert theaters for sound technology.[3] New silent features were made as late as 1935.[4]

"Features" were also fairly new. A handful of feature-length silent films appeared after 1906, but the first to enjoy commercial success was D.W. Griffith's *The Birth of a Nation* (1915).[5] For most movie attendees, features were less than 15 years old when the Marxes made *The Cocoanuts*.[6] The Marxes had as many doubts about feature movies as detractors held about sound films. As noted, after years of toiling in vaudeville, the Marx Brothers broke through with the revue *I'll Say She Is*.[7] It was followed by a stage production of *The Cocoanuts*, which opened in 1925 and was revived in 1927. Next came *Animal Crackers* in 1928. By then, the Marxes were making $2,000 a week, a handsome sum equivalent to nearly $32,000 in 2021 dollars.

It is certainly understandable that the Marxes would be reluctant to jeopardize their long-sought-after acclaim. Movies were no guarantee of success, and they already had an unhappy venture under their belts: In 1921, they made *Humorisk*, a silent film. They put up $4,000 of their own capital toward the $6,000 budget, and the result was a desultory project none of them liked. Nor, apparently, did anyone else. It flunked a test screening and was never again seen. *Humorisk* vanished and is now considered a lost film.[8] Groucho thought its disappearance such a blessing that he offered $50,000 for any copy that resurfaced, just to ensure it stayed lost.

It is hard to imagine that any Marx other than Harpo would translate on the silent screen, and the quick-quipping Groucho would have been totally at sea. Groucho allegedly spent his screen time making silly gestures like a pale rip-off of Charlie Chaplin. Harpo also appeared in *Too Many Kisses* (1925), a silent film in which he played a village idiot as a Peter Pan–type character. He recalled that most of his scenes never made the final cut. It too is considered a lost film.

Although the Marxes also disliked the final cut of *The Cocoanuts*, the shift to talking pictures was destined to make them worldwide celebrities. They might never had launched a movie career were it not for a con by Chico. He played Paramount Pictures producers Walter Wanger and Adolph Zukor off against each other, with Zukor's $75,000 offer suddenly turning into $100,000, an enormous sum at the time (more than $1.5 million today).[9] *The Cocoanuts* was made, but it wasn't easy. Three challenges loomed: logistical, script-related and technical.

The first logistical challenge was that the Marxes insisted on continuing to perform *Animal Crackers* on Broadway. This was possible because moviemaking had only just begun relocating to Hollywood. Paramount had a studio in the Astoria section of Queens. Hollywood became synonymous with American movies, but the bulk of silent pictures and numerous early talkies were made on the East Coast, mostly in New York City, across the Hudson River in New Jersey, or in upstate New York locations such as Ithaca. The Marxes had only to cross the East River to Manhattan to perform on Broadway.[10]

The Cocoanuts appeared on Broadway 276 times and at least 100 more times on the road, so the Marxes probably could have done their lines in their sleep.[11] Sometimes it looks as if they did. Allen Eyles is nearly alone in proclaiming that the Marxes' "first picture is certainly one of their best."[12] The script is sharp and funny, as one might expect from such time-tested material, but the word *fiasco* would not be too strong to describe attempts to turn stage comedians into film stars. No one quite knew how to film a musical comedy; *The Cocoanuts* was Paramount's first.

The idea of hanging around a set all day waiting for a scene to be shot was alien to the Marxes. When he wasn't behind a camera, Harpo ventured off to play his instrument or sleep, and Groucho often strayed from the stage to telephone his stockbroker. Finding Chico was even harder. Try a bar, pool hall, poker game or restaurant.

Harpo claimed that Walter Wanger solved the absentee problem by locking each Marx in a film jail cell until needed. Wanger allegedly placed a telephone in Chico's so he "could call his bookie any time he felt like it."[13] Other stories hold that only Chico was confined or that a different movie was involved, but director Robert Florey was doubtless correct in observing that the Marxes "really weren't disciplined. One of them was always missing.... I'd have to send assistants all over the place to look for the missing brother."[14]

Script alterations were also needed. First, a long stage show needed to be trimmed. The original show—produced by Sam Harris with music by Irving Berlin and book[15] by George S. Kaufman—was as much a musical revue as a comedy. The movie suffers from trying to recreate that.

Although the Marx Brothers were stars of the stage, theater[16] tended to give equal (if not greater) weight to producers, composers, and writers. Movies generally reversed that formula. As early as 1909, top movie billing went to actors, a trend that accelerated in the 1920s. Adapting *Cocoanuts* meant putting the Marxes front and center. If the film appears disjointed, it's because parts of the stage show were removed or truncated. Florey noted that the first cut of the film ran two hours, but distributors desirous of packing more showings into a day demanded cuts.[17] Musical numbers were the first to go. On stage, *The Cocoanuts* featured eight numbers and three reprises in Act I alone. Act II saw ten more musical numbers plus a final reprise. By contrast, the movie has eight musical numbers.

Another bit of Marxian lore centers on Irving Berlin. In 1958, Groucho dropped him a note after seeing Berlin's photograph in the *New York Times*: "I was pleased to see your face, even though you were unable to produce a song hit for *Cocoanuts*.... But since you have become a legend in our time, I'm sure this one lyrical disaster can do you no harm."[18] A standing joke between the two was that "Always," one of Berlin's signature songs, was cut from *The Cocoanuts*. It actually was written in 1925 for Berlin's bride-to-be and was never intended for any Marx Brothers production.[19] Nonetheless, Berlin scholars seldom cite *Cocoanuts* offerings such as "The Monkey Doodle Do!" or "When My Dreams Come True" as among Berlin's finest.[20]

There were other details that needed attention. On stage, Harpo was billed as Silent Sam and Chico as Willie the Wop; in the film credits, they are merely Harpo and Chico.[21] Harpo's character needed to be established for the screen; and, even in the 1920s, the term "wop" would have been offensive.[22]

The movie cast a spotlight on Margaret Dumont, whose presence in Marx Brothers films was so important that Groucho called her "practically the fifth Marx Brother." She was usually the foil for Groucho's insults and lecherous advances, though his oft-repeated assertion that she seldom got jokes made at her expense doesn't stand up to scrutiny.[23] Dumont was a skilled comic actress before, during and after her association with the Marxes. The Marxes sometimes exasperated her, but she and Groucho (Julius) were fond of each other and addressed each other by their diminutives, "Maggie" and "Julie."

The making of *The Cocoanuts* highlights the many new technical challenges that the Marxes found infuriating. Some problems were blamed on co-directors Florey and Joseph Santley, though some of them were also *ex post facto* mythmaking. Groucho claimed, "One of the two didn't understand English, the other didn't understand Harpo."[24] The French-born Florey insisted that he "did understand English" from his years of filmmaking in the U.S., that he was assigned to do *Cocoanuts* at the last minute, and that many of the film's problems stemmed from Paramount's desire to produce the film too quickly.[25] Perhaps his greatest contribution was the wisdom to know when *not* to direct the brothers and allow them to ad-lib. Now-famous scenes of Harpo drinking ink (actually Coca-Cola) and eating a (chocolate) telephone were said to be spontaneous decisions.[26]

Florey also noted ways in which the Marxes compounded technical problems. Groucho, for instance, failed to grasp the lighting challenges inherent in reflections from his greasepaint mustache, though fortunately he ignored Florey's suggestion to dispense with it. The solution was to dust the mustache with talcum powder to reduce glare. Dumont sometimes bellowed as if she was performing in an outdoor amphitheater. Co-star Shaw, a singer, looked as if he had never before *spoken* to an audience. Everyone involved in the production was guilty of missing their marks.

There were other problems inherent in the jump from stage to film. In 1929, the Broadway stage was a superior and infinitely more flexible platform than movie studios. Sound-image synchronization was cumbersome, and recording levels had to be turned up to catch dialogue. This made Eaton's vocals painfully high in places. A visually obvious adaptation was that all the paper handled on screen had to be sopping wet lest crinkling sounds drown out the voices. Watch as Groucho shows Chico the blueprints to develop Cocoanut Manor. They look like Groucho has just fished the plans from the bottom of a canal. The film's "grass" was painted wood shavings, another attempt to tamp down external sounds such as stomping feet.[27]

Panning and tracking shots were difficult to achieve, as cameras and their operators were stationed inside soundproof boxes to prevent external noise from becoming part of the soundtrack. The Marxes tried to stay within camera range, but that crimped their style and sometimes proved impossible. Even harder was making sure certain actors stayed near sound booms or microphones strategically placed out of camera sight. Watch enough older films and you will see booms at the tops of frames and actors who seem to be talking to potted plants.

Florey had five cameras, but that was not enough. Several production numbers were butchered as a result. One sequence of high-kicking chorus girls is a blurry montage of torsos, knees and shadowy legs flying through the frame. Santley was in charge of the dance numbers, but his understanding of how to shoot them was limited. It is hardly a surprise that Harpo's *silent* physical comedy filmed better than many of the sound sequences.[28]

Nothing was shot on location; "Florida" was created in a Queens studio. *The Cocoanuts* looks bad now, but it was a huge hit and saved the Marxes from the fate of the theater in the wake of the November 1929 stock market crash, which hit Groucho especially hard. It is a reminder that, for all its technical faults, *The Cocoanuts* also reveals the dark side of what is glibly labeled the Roaring Twenties.

Oh, How You Can Get Stucco: The Florida Land Boom and Bust

Hammer (Groucho), owner of the Hotel de Cocoanut, has neither guests nor money. He hatches a scheme to sell some rather questionable land he foolishly bought for an even more questionable development. As an auction for this land begins, Groucho launches into rapid-fire jokes and puns. He promises potential buyers that 800 homes will be built on the site: "Why, they are as good as built. You can have any kind of home you want. You can even get stucco. Oh, how you can get stucco.... And don't forget the guarantee—my personal guarantee. If these lots don't double in value in a year, I don't know what you can do about it."[29]

In its own twisted way, *The Cocoanuts* was a timely commentary on economic speculation and what happens when a charging bull market runs into a starving bear market. When the play was written in 1925, the Florida land boom was at its peak; by 1929, lots of people indeed "got stucco." In hindsight, Florida land (like dipping farm prices) presaged the onset of the Great Depression.

The best way to comprehend the Florida land boom is to forget everything you think know about Florida. It was in the process of *becoming* a popular destination when the play was first staged, and was struggling when *Cocoanuts* the movie was released.

When Florida entered the Union as a slave state in 1846, its population was under 60,000. It joined the Confederacy during the Civil War and was under post-war military occupation from 1868 to 1878. By 1880, Florida had grown, but still had just 269,493 residents, a population roughly that of today's Lincoln, Nebraska. Florida attracted wealthy individuals such as businesswoman Julia Tuttle and railroad executive William Chipley, but most transplants were attracted to its remoteness, not tourist delights. When Tuttle first visited in 1875, Miami was a veritable backwater. As late as 1896, there were just 343 people there, a third of whom were African Americans and Seminoles. It grew to nearly 12,000 by 1909, just 4,470 of whom were Caucasian. Tarpon fishers were among the few outsiders to venture that far south, by boat mostly, as ground transportation options were few. One writer noted that other early visitors to the future "Sunshine State" sought "rocking chair tourism."[30]

Nor was Florida a destination for college students on spring break. There were no Disney properties or other such attractions. It was rare for Major League Baseball teams to hold spring training camps in Florida until 1889, and it wasn't until 1913 that enough did so to justify exhibition matches now known as the Grapefruit League. It would be another 14 years before John Ringling made Sarasota his circus's winter headquarters.

Chipley, though, was onto something. He was among the first entrepreneurs to imagine Florida as a refuge for wealthy Northeasterners seeking relief from the winter chill. Boosters did their job well: In the peak years between 1920 and 1925, some 1.5 million people visited Florida each year. Florida's rail development was largely of the "short line" variety; that is, tracks that connected to larger systems. In 1876, Chipley moved to Pensacola to become general manager of a 45-mile spur that connected to the Louisville and Nashville Railroad.[31]

Chipley is a largely forgotten figure, as Florida's rapid growth is inextricably tied to steamship magnate Henry Plant and Standard Oil executive Henry Flagler. Plant consolidated lines that became the Atlantic Coast Line Railroad, and Flagler was the moving spirit of the Florida East Coast Railway. Wherever either man extended tracks, real estate development followed. Jacksonville was the largest city in Florida into the 1930s. Both used it as a hub, with Plant's westward lines making possible the development of Tampa, St. Petersburg, Clearwater and Fort Myers. Flagler's eastern-shore railroads provided the catalyst for the growth of Daytona, Palm Beach and, by 1896, Miami. He didn't stop until he got to Key West.

Each built a spate of luxury hotels. Most of Plant's were in the greater Tampa area. Flagler's appetite was bigger, with elaborate and well-appointed hotels following rail construction southward: the Hotel Continental in Jacksonville; the Ponce de Leon, Cordoba and Alcazar hotels in St. Augustine; Hotel Ormond near Daytona; the Royal Poinciana and the Breakers in Palm Beach, and the Royal Palm in Miami. Monied interests followed the tracks southward. Miami Beach scarcely existed until Flagler's Florida East Coast Railway arrived in Miami in 1896. Investors soon transformed Miami Beach from a sandbar into a flamboyant resort.

Carl Fisher, an automotive enthusiast and supplier, became a Biscayne Bay promoter and developer of such renown that humorist Will Rogers quipped that he "was the first man to discover that there was sand under the water that could hold up a real estate sign. He made that sign the national emblem of Florida."[32] Aviator Glenn Curtiss, who moved to Florida in 1916, was instrumental in developing Hialeah, complete with a horse-race track and a lake stocked with flamingos. George Merrick created the town of Coral Gables by cutting down many of his own orange groves. Architect brothers Addison and Wilson Mizner showcased their skills in Boca Raton. A roll call of the rich and famous with homes or rentals in Florida included politician-orator William Jennings Bryan, industrialist Andrew Carnegie, future president Warren G. Harding, and rich Philadelphia families such as the Stotesburys, the Wanamakers and the Wideners.

Tire manufacturer Harvey Firestone and auto magnate Henry Ford also had Florida homes, a reminder that the age of the automobile had arrived. Cars transformed Florida, as they did the rest of the country. In 1906, there were just 296 cars in Florida; by 1913, there were more than 15,000 registered vehicles.[33] In *Cocoanuts'* famed "Why a Duck?" sequence, Chico asks why anyone would want a Ford if they had a horse. By 1925, though, nearly everyone would have chosen a Model T. Florida had just 748 miles of paved surface in 1924, but six years later it had 3,254.[34] New roads such as the Tamiami Trail connected Tampa to Miami, and bridges connected once discrete cities such as Tampa and St. Petersburg. Above all, land was drained and water diverted into a network of canals.

In his classic work on the 1920s, editor Frederick Lewis Allen detailed the speculative fever that fueled what was dubbed "Coolidge prosperity." It was an uneven and often chimerical surge, but few of those with capital to invest during the peak boom years between 1923 and 1926 anticipated the coming catastrophe.[35] When *The Cocoanuts* was a play, one of the implied jokes was that only a bumbler like Hammer could *lose* money on Florida real estate. That fiction was blown away by a devastating hurricane that struck in September 1926. It killed hundreds and left thousands homeless. Florida had already weathered three-plus years of decline when *The Cocoanuts* opened in movie theaters. The new joke was on Florida land barons and investors who gambled on a superheated stock market. On September 19, 1929, stocks closed at a record high. Just six weeks later, the stock market plunged, a presage of the Great Depression.

Declining Florida land values and falling farm prices should have been warning signs, but many Americans ignored them. Aspects of the Roaring Twenties are on screen in *The Cocoanuts*: the whirl of society, uninhibited dancing, big bands, costumed balls, unbridled speculation. Kaufman's script and the Marxes' antics exaggerated the land boom, but not by much. It's hard to lampoon an inherently surreal phenomenon. Downtown Miami properties that sold for $4,000 in the early 1900s soared in value to as much a million in 1925; lots in Miami Beach that listed for $7,500 in June 1925, commanded more than $35,000 just 42 days later.[36]

The only thing missing from the film's auction hype was the presence of "binder boys," real estate agents who took a non-refundable down payment (binder) on a piece of property—generally around ten percent of the price—with the balance due in a month. Many agents scoured Northern cities and accepted payments from numerous investors who had no intention of ever setting foot on the land. Florida parcels were akin to buying stocks "on margin," another 1920s financial misstep. Speculators gambled on prices rising so rapidly that they could quickly unload their purchases for a tidy profit.

Michael Gannon called land agents "perspiring, fast-talking hucksters ... in golf knickers and two-toned shoes [who] swapped paper so rapidly [that] a single lot sometimes changed hands a dozen times a day."[37] Even allowing for hyperbole, the lust for land was a major reason why Miami soared in population from 29,571 in 1920 to 110,637 by decade's end. Tampa placed 300 parcels for sale in 1924; three hours later, more than $1.6 million in binders was pledged, though many of the "building" lots were still underwater. The Massachusetts Savings Bank League claimed that in 1926, some 10,000 accounts and more than $20 million had been transferred to Florida.[38]

Hammer was a piker compared to such high-powered hucksters. T.D. Allman called it a "race to attract gullible buyers" that was fueled by shameless promotions. Glenn Curtiss built jai alai frontons and threw up shoddy buildings that outwardly echoed a *faux* Arabian design inspired by Rudolph Valentino movies. In Coral Gables, George Merrick's drainage ditches were said to have evoked Venice, Italy. He reportedly spent $3 million per year in advertising and, for a time, it paid off. By 1925, the area was awash with $100 million worth of new construction.[39]

Herman Melville is credited with coining the term "ballyhoo" in 1836, to describe an unseaworthy boat. In the 1920s, it denoted hype, exaggeration and extravagance fueled by advertising and word of mouth. Abundant sunshine, beaming celebrities, bathing beauties, lavish parties and a state with no inheritance or income taxes contributed to Floridian ballyhoo. It was, if you will, a castle made of sand. The 1926 hurricane was followed by another in 1928, and stocks collapsed one year later. Many of those who made paper fortunes in land development schemes became so many Hammers unable to recoup a fraction of their investments. Carl Fisher supposedly made $50 million in the development of Miami Beach; when he died in 1939, his holdings were worth 0.1 percent of that. Addison Mizner declared bankruptcy in 1927. By one reckoning, 90 percent of those who bought Florida land during the boom lost money. In a 1928 article for *The Nation*, Henry S. Villard wrote of Miami, "Dead subdivisions line the highway, their pompous names half-obliterated on crumbling stucco gates."[40] Oh, boy, how you can get stucco!

The Monkey Doodle Do?

The first time I showed *The Cocoanuts* to a class, students laughed harder at the dancing than at the jokes. To contemporary eyes, the production numbers do look bizarre. Of course, if a director entered a club tomorrow and aimed a camera at the dancers, in a very short period of time the dances will look silly and the music will be out of fashion. There are scads of legendary movie musicals, but they tend to share qualities that make them classics, including brilliant dancers, visionary choreographers and musical scores that transcend time. Movies that rely upon what is en vogue seldom meet such criteria. Most films are products of popular culture, which is always ephemeral. By design, what is "in" at a given moment is usually "out" a short time later.

Popular music certainly follows this trajectory. Another nickname for the 1920s is "the Jazz Age." Jazz occupies a different place in American culture today than it did a century ago. Although jazz has passionate devotees, in 2018 jazz recordings of any sort—vinyl, CDs, downloads—made up just 1.1 percent of the music sold in the U.S., and it has sunk lower since.[41] In the 1920s, though, jazz was "pop" music, which is why *The Cocoanuts* unfolds to a jazz soundtrack. Jazz is easier to identify than to describe. There are many varieties of jazz, and what we hear in *The Cocoanuts* is mostly big band swing and "hot jazz." Swing emphasizes accented off-beats that syncopate the music. Hot jazz, sometimes called "Dixieland" jazz, originated in New Orleans and blends African American ragtime with European music, especially that from Sicily.[42]

Although 1920s jazz spotlighted many legendary virtuoso musicians, swing and hot jazz were favored by dancers. In Lewis Erenberg's words, "No one was sure what jazz was or even how to spell it, but the music meant that dancing would become more energetic, with even more room for body movement and personal expression. Dancers did faster foxtrots, the less inhibited ones could shimmy, and the band played them on...."[43] "The Monkey Doodle Do" is a fatuous song, but it showcases evolving gender and sensuality codes. Mary Eaton's dance hall spiels and sensual spins during the song display her body in ways that would have shocked aging Victorians.

Eaton's unveiling of her lower torso and Kay Francis' slinky gowns reveal that neither was corseted. Popular dances such as the jitterbug, Charleston, turkey trot, the breakaway, the Texas Tommy, shimmy and black bottom required relaxed dress codes and unrestrained bodies. Female "flappers" were the cultural rebels of their day. Cincinnati's *Catholic Telegraph* raised an alarm: "The music is sensuous, the embracing of partners—the female only half dressed—is absolutely indecent; and the motions—they are as such as may not be described, with any respect for propriety, in a family newspaper. Suffice it to say that there are certain houses appropriate for such dances; but those houses have been closed by law."[44]

Jazz Age styles, dance and music exuded excitement, risk and newness. To be certain, there were limits to acceptable female sexuality in an age in which double standards excused youthful male hijinks but stigmatized "loose" women. Likewise, the music of *The Cocoanuts* is a pale copy of what one would have heard in African American communities that inspired both jazz and many of the dances enjoyed by white youths. In the American South, clubs and dance halls were segregated by law; in the North they were segregated by custom. Whites knew of and visited black enclaves such as Harlem, Chicago's South Side and Detroit's Black Bottom, though usually the only African Americans in white establishments were guest performers. White choreographers freely borrowed, exaggerated or stereotyped black culture. New York's Cotton Club sported fake jungle scenes on its walls, and light-skinned black dancers called "Copper-Colored Gals" performed in burlesque tribal costumes. Sizzling "jungle" jazz was popular long before 1927, when African American musician-composer Duke Ellington dubbed his ensemble the Jungle Band. The "monkey" dancers in Mary Eaton's solo song and group dance could plausibly be viewed as a racist lampoon of African Americans, though at the time, many whites would have argued it was homage.

Several revue numbers, including one with female bellhops, are featured early in *The Cocoanuts*. We also see synchronized kicklines the likes of which are associated with the Radio City Music Hall Rockettes. The Rockettes were formed in 1925, the same year Sammy Lee assembled the stage *Cocoanuts* dance routines. Ehrenberg notes that revues "showed chorus girls acting in a world of leisure and fun. They were healthy, coy playmates fit for the realm of leisure.... They did not portray roles in the male world of business or politics [unless] it was only as humorous counterpoints."[45]

Kick lines and splashy revues owed their inspiration to Broadway's Ziegfeld Follies, which in turn borrowed from vaudeville and burlesque stages. Big production numbers became a staple of Hollywood musicals and eventually migrated to TV variety shows such as those hosted by Carol Burnett, Jackie Gleason, Dean Martin, Red Skelton and Ed Sullivan. Quite a few televised dance routines featured overhead camera shots in which bare-limbed female dancers created kaleidoscopic, flower-like patterns with their legs and arms. For all of the filming challenges of *The Cocoanuts,* its use of overhead angles and floor-bound dance figures set standards still in use.

For many viewers, the musical numbers that resonate are those that parody opera. They paved the way for the Marxes' 1935 *A Night at the Opera,* considered one of their finest films. *The Cocoanuts* features snippets of Verdi and Bizet. Opera is now considered a form of elite culture—classical music commands just one percent of yearly recording sales—but the Marxes came of age when casual knowledge of opera was commonplace. Even non-opera listeners might recognize lampoons present in the film score. That's because opera is *not* part of popular culture, thus it has a longer cultural shelf life.

In the film, Chico makes no bones about being a freeloader or a pickpocket, but it is Harpo who engages in larcenous rampages, stuffing anything that isn't nailed down into his coat pockets. Early on, we hear him whistling the "Anvil Chorus" from Giuseppe Verdi's 1853 opera *Il Trovatore.* The tune's Italian title was "Coro di Zingari," or "Gypsy Chorus," *gypsy* being a term that has been supplanted by Roma. The lyrics praise industrious gypsy blacksmiths who strike their anvils at dawn, hence its nickname. Harpo has less lofty motives: The "anvil" sound is the opening and closing of a cash register whose cash Harpo gleefully pilfers.

Gypsies also factor into the film's funniest musical sequence. Mrs. Potter throws a party to celebrate the forced (and temporary) engagement of her daughter Polly to Yates. It is a lavish and ludicrous affair in which guests wear "Latin" costumes. Harpo enters wearing an enormous sombrero and clenching a long cigarette in his teeth. The speeches bore him and he pulls numerous "gookies" (contorted funny faces). The scene's highlight occurs when he literally steals the shirt off Hennessy's back. That's the setup for Hennessy to sing "Tale of the Shirt," a truncated takeoff of two famed pieces from Georges Bizet's *Carmen*: "Haberna" and "Toréador."

Suddenly the party costumes make sense; Bizet's opera tells of the foolish love affair between a young soldier and Carmen, a sultry gypsy woman. "Haberna," whose full title is "Love Is a Rebellious Bird," is a seductive love song, and "Toréador" a bull-fighter's litany of the dangers of the bullring. Basil Ruysdael (Hennessy) actually *was* an opera singer with a fine baritone-bass voice, though his scene is a lampoon.

All three opera pieces passed into popular culture and show up in everything from Gilbert and Sullivan to Bugs Bunny cartoons and novelty songs. The film completes its unofficial gypsy theme when Chico approaches the piano to entertain the party guests. He plays Victor Herbert's "Gypsy Love Song," Herbert being a famed composer as well as a co-founder of ASCAP, the American Society of Composers, Authors and Publishers, which assures that performers and composers get royalties for their work.

There's more than meets the eye and ear in *The Cocoanuts*. Styles come and go, but despite bad camerawork, sound problems and over-the-top production numbers, *The Cocoanuts* belongs to a long and exuberant tradition of popular dance and music on film. Think of it as a key link in a chain that stretches from *The Jazz Singer* to MTV and *America's Got Talent*.

Another Elephant in the Room: Jews and the Dangerous Decades

There are things in *The Cocoanuts* that haven't worn well, including misappropriations of black culture, Harpo's pursuit of blondes, and Groucho's barrage of misogynist insults directed at Dumont. These will be addressed in future chapters, but let's take a look at one of the few times the Marxes directly alluded to Jews.

The Cocoanuts' most famous scene is its "Why a duck?" sequence, in which Hammer shows Chico the blueprints for his planned Cocoanut Manor development. The scene is filled with outrageous banter, puns, insults and tortured wordplay. It begins when Hammer points to a map and exclaims, "Now right here is the residential section."

CHICO: People live there, eh?
HAMMER: No, that's the stockyard. Now all along here—this is the riverfront—all along the river ... those are the levees.
CHICO: Thatsa the Jewish neighborhood.
HAMMER: Well, we'll pass over that.

In context, levee is a pun on Levi, a common name for Jewish males. In the Old Testament, Levi was the progenitor of one of the Twelve Tribes of Israel. The second joke, Hammer's retort, "we'll pass over that," is a snide reference to Passover, one of Judaism's most important holidays. In the Book of Exodus, ten horrible plagues are visited upon Egypt as punishment for enslaving Jews. The last of these is the death of the first-born sons of Egypt; those of Israel were spared if lamb's blood was smeared on their doors. God's wrath literally passed over them.

Groucho quickly passed over this joke as well and moved on to an exchange considered a classic bit of Marxian humor:

HAMMER: Now here's a little peninsula, and here is a viaduct leading over to the mainland.
CHICO: Why a duck?

HAMMER: I'm all right. How are you? I say, here is a little peninsula, and here's a viaduct leading over to the mainland.
CHICO: All right. Why a duck?
HAMMER: I'm not playing ask-me-another. I say, that's a viaduct.
CHICO: All right. Why a duck? Why a duck? Why-a-no-chicken?
HAMMER: I don't know why-a-no-chicken.... All I know is that's a viaduct. You try to cross over there on a chicken, and you'll find out why a duck. It's deep water, that's a viaduct.
CHICO: That's-why-a-duck?

In the routine, there is no reason to dwell upon puns related to Jewish identity, nor is witty repartee an appropriate vehicle for religious discussions. There were, however, reasons for Hammer to "pass over" Chico's remark. As noted in the last chapter, the Marxes were secular Jews. Groucho, for instance, was an agnostic who doubted the existence of an afterlife. He sometimes held Seder meals, but he also celebrated Christmas and lampooned Jewish rituals. The Marxes' religious background surfaced mostly as jokes from their Gentile friends, in response to anti–Semitic incidents directed at them, or during outbreaks of anti–Semitism.

The early 20th century was one of the latter; it simply wasn't a great time to call attention to being a Jew of any disposition. Discussions of anti–Semitism are so often linked to the rise of European fascism and the horrors of the Holocaust that they obscure outbreaks of discrimination against Jews that have occurred since the Middle Ages. Between 1870 and 1924, about three million Jews immigrated to the U.S., the majority from Eastern Europe and Russia, where they were targets of bloody pogroms. Samuel Marx and his future wife Minnie emigrated from Germany, he in 1881 and she a year earlier. Their timing was fortuitous; the Rev. Adolf Stoecker formed the overtly anti–Semitic Christian Social Party in 1878. He was not a lone crank; Stoecker was Kaiser Wilhelm I's personal chaplain, and urged him to expel Jews from Germany. When Sam Marx arrived in New York, Germany and Austria were in the throes of pogroms. Georg Ritter von Schönerer, a politician in the Austro-Hungarian Empire, adopted the title Führer, used the greeting "Heil!" and spoke of the superiority of the Aryan race, which made him a role model for Adolf Hitler, who was also Austrian by birth.

It would be nice to say that Jews found comfort in the U.S., but historical evidence does not support such optimism. The U.S. avoided full-scale pogroms, but it was no safe haven. A Jewish man was lynched in Tennessee as early as 1868, presumably by the Ku Klux Klan, and prejudice against Jews was commonplace throughout the Gilded Age (1870–1901). With Jewish immigration came a bundle of Old World stereotypes: Jews as money-hungry Shylocks, Jews as clannish and deceitful, Jews as anarchists, Jews as peddlers or bankers. The American success of businessmen such as Charles Fleischman, Adam Gimbel, Marcus Goldman, Jay Gould, Meyer Guggenheim, Solomon Loeb and Abram Rothschild had the ironic effect of fueling conspiracy theories. Several men, especially Gould and members of the Guggenheim family, were unscrupulous robber barons, but special attention was cast upon their religion and "race." Miserliness and avariciousness were so associated with Jewry that targets of working-class ire such as meat packers Philip Armour and Gustavus Swift were called Jews, though they were Methodist and Episcopal, respectively. Numerous labor unions succumbed to anti–Semitism, as did the Greenback and Populist movements, even though Jews swelled the ranks of labor and reform organizations.

Vaudeville also complicated Jewish identity. Numerous Gentiles assumed the role of Jews to burlesque them, but numerous Jews also played to stereotypes. That list included Lew Fields (half of a famed vaudeville duo with Joe Weber) and Minnie's brother Al Shean. For pure absurdity, little could top "Yonkle the Cow-boy [*sic*] Jew," a song by Will J. Harris and Harry I. Robinson, which spawned spin-offs and became a vaudeville staple.[46]

Anti-Semitism was common among American Gentiles. Renowned 19th-century writers such as Henry and Brooks Adams, William Cullen Bryant, James Fenimore Cooper, Ignatius Donnelly, Oliver Wendell Holmes, Julia Ward Howe, Henry James and Edith Wharton dropped anti–Semitic themes into their works. Similarly, numerous ministers salted their sermons with attacks on Jews.[47] Nathan Belth dubbed the years between 1915 and 1925 as the "violent decade" for American Jews, though danger signs were in place well before then.[48] A rising tide of anti–Semitism was still another phenomenon that made the Progressive Era fall short of its name.[49] The opening salvo came on July 29, 1902, when the funeral of Rabbi Jacob Joseph degenerated into a riot involving factory workers, mourners and police.[50]

Belth's violent decade was bookended by two sensational cases. In 1913, Leo Frank, president of the Atlanta chapter of B'nai B'rith, was arrested for the rape and murder of 14-year-old Mary Phagan, a factory hand in the National Pencil Factory, which Frank headed. His conviction rested upon the testimony of two men arrested for the crime, one of whom admitted to his lawyer that *he* killed Phagan. Nonetheless, angry crowds screamed for Frank to hang. Frank lost several appeals, including one before the Supreme Court, though Georgia Governor John Slayton commuted Frank's sentence from death to life imprisonment. Alas, on August 15, 1915, a mob dragged Frank from his cell and lynched him.[51]

The second case was that of Nathan Leopold Jr. and Richard Loeb, who were decidedly guilty of the murder of 14-year-old Bobby Franks. In 1924, the two intellectually gifted 24-year-old Jews sought to commit the "perfect" crime. They murdered Franks—Loeb's second cousin—by hitting him in the head with a chisel and then gagging him. Next, they mutilated his body by pouring acid over his face and genitals, sent a fake ransom note to his parents, and destroyed the typewriter they used. Their plans unraveled, they confessed their crimes, and only the intervention of famed attorney Clarence Darrow saved them from the death penalty. (Loeb was murdered by a fellow prisoner at Joliet Correctional Center in 1936. Leopold, paroled in 1958, died in 1971.)[52]

In between these two horrible events lay an unalloyed series of discriminatory acts directed at Jews. Nativist writers such as Edward A. Ross and Madison Grant provided pseudo-intellectual heft to a swelling movement to restrict immigration, with Jews often the target of their bile. Ross ran through a litany of anti–Jewish stereotypes, claiming that lust for money, criminality and an aversion to manual labor were inbred. Grant's 1916 book *The Passing of the Great Race* placed Jews at the very bottom of the immigrant hierarchy of worthiness. Grant declared marriages between Jews and Gentiles the worst imaginable form of miscegenation.[53]

Henry Ford was more influential still. He declared Communism a Jewish movement—Karl Marx was nominally Jewish—and found a platform for his views by purchasing Michigan's *Dearborn Independent* in 1919. Although Ford later disingenuously claimed to have no part in running the newspaper, he used editor W.J. Cameron as his surrogate for fanning paranoia against Jews, whom he also blamed for causing World War I. The *Independent* published a steady diet of anti–Semitic articles, much of the material cribbed from *The Protocols of the Elders of Zion*, reputedly a Jewish plan for global domination. It was actually an elaborate forgery, but it became what one Ford biographer labeled a "manual on Jew-baiting." *Protocols* material made its way into a series of *Independent* articles published under the banner "The International Jew: The World's Foremost Problem" and were collated as a 300-page book with more than 500,000 copies in print—apparently bankrolled by Ford. The auto magnate was even said to have denied that Jesus was Jewish.[54]

Ford passed his animus toward Jews to friends Firestone and Thomas Edison, but soon found himself the target of backlash from figures such as Jane Addams, Clarence Darrow, W.E.B. Du Bois, Theodore Roosevelt, William Howard Taft and Woodrow Wilson. Ford's moment of reckoning came in 1924, when Jewish lawyer and activist Aaron Sapiro sued him for slander. Ford was forced to issue an apology and paid a settlement to Sapiro in December 1927. That same month, Ford shut down the *Independent* and shifted blame to Cameron, an absurd assertion.[55]

Anti-Semitism was not limited to Ford and his circle. In 1920, Georgia's Thomas Watson entered the U.S. Senate, in great part because of the popularity he gained from leading the prosecution of Leo Frank seven years earlier. He responded to Governor Slaton's commutation of Frank's sentence by skewering Slaton as the "King of the Jews." Watson also joined others in a Congress that passed the 1924 Johnson-Reed Act, signed into law by President Calvin Coolidge. The part of the bill titled the National Origins Act set strict quotas on lands whence newcomers emigrated. Tellingly, lands from which Jews had previously emigrated were assigned shockingly low quotas. More than 86 percent of legal immigrants came from Western Europe, and very few of them were Jews.[56]

Jewish-Americans were caught in a double bind: They were said to be incapable of assimilation, yet faced discrimination for achievements on American soil. Carl Brigham's *A Study of American Intelligence* (1923) argued that those of Nordic extraction were by nature more intelligent than other "races." Not only was his use of the term "race" unscientific, his central claim was contradicted by the high levels of academic attainment reached by American Jews. Unfortunately, higher learning institutions moved to deter that. City University of New York disbanded fraternities in 1913, when university officials determined that "too many" Jews had pledged. Columbia officials reacted with similar alarm when its 1920 enrollment was 40 percent Jewish. This percentage was cut in half by 1922, and thereafter continued to spiral downward. Harvard president Amos Lawrence Lowell followed suit in setting admission quotas for Jewish students, and schools such as Cornell, Dartmouth, Duke, Princeton, Stanford, Yale and the University of Pennsylvania did likewise. Higher education leaders routinely spoke of a "Jewish problem," by which they invariably meant "too many." In many cases, Jewish quotas persisted into the 1960s.[57]

The Anti-Defamation League, an international wing of B'nai B'rith, formed an American chapter in 1913, but it often fought rear-guard actions. The 1920s saw the rebirth of the Ku Klux Klan, whose populist call for "One Hundred Percent Americanism" added Jews, Roman Catholics, Eastern European immigrants and "immoral" women to its long-standing antipathy toward African Americans. In 1920, there were 5,000 Klansmen in the country; by 1924, over five million. The Klan declined by decade's end, but not before it helped reinforce notions that Americanism was Protestant in character.

No wonder Groucho decided to "pass over" references to Judaism. Although the Marx Brothers were on the cusp of fame within a movie industry headed by Jews, they were not immune to anti–Semitism. Chico and his family found they could not stay at a Lake George, New York, hotel because of restrictions against Jews. Chico reportedly told his disappointed daughter Maxine, "Don't worry about it, kid, I wouldn't want to stay here. There are some stupid people who don't like Jews. We don't need that hotel."[58]

Unless religious differences were thrust upon them, though, the Marxes generally downplayed their Judaism in public. Like many cultural Jews, they sometimes marked rites of passage at synagogues, but all three of Groucho's wives were Gentiles and he was, in Charlotte Chandler's words, "always ready to celebrate a holiday—*anyone's* holiday: Christmas, Chanukah, Thanksgiving, St. Patrick's Day—as long as there were good things to eat." In that spirit, he and Dumont spent several Christmases together. When asked if he had a Christmas tree when growing up, he replied, "No, I had a branch." Likewise, when Chanukah came around, his favorite felicitation was, "Happy Harmonica."[59]

Harpo scarcely mentions religion in his autobiography, other than to note that his Algonquin Round Table friends occasionally made wisecracks about his Judaism. If he felt offended, he did not register it. One of his few recorded moments of religious pique occurred in 1927, when he booked a hotel room and the confirming telegram came with the comment, "Trust you are a Gentile." Harpo allegedly entered the hotel lobby dressed in mock Scottish attire, signed the register as "Harpo MacMarx" and promptly asked for directions to a synagogue. He willed his harp to the State of Israel.[60]

Groucho disliked "ethnic" humor and remarked, "The Marx Brothers didn't depend on ethnic humor. Either a joke is funny or it isn't. Making the person Polish or Italian or Jewish doesn't make it funny if it isn't."[61] His statement, though, runs counter to the fact that Chico's character was faux Italian. It also ignored two outrageous ethnic puns in *The Cocoanuts*. When Chico checks into the hotel, Hammer asks, "Would you like a suite on the third floor?" Chico replies, "No. I'll take a Polack in the basement."[62]

Perhaps Groucho's remark was a nod to the realization that ethnic humor was a remnant of vaudeville schtick that had become passé. A more likely explanation is that the Marxes had become big stars. In 1927, just 3.58 percent of the American population was Jewish, a figure destined to decline due to the National Origins Act.[63] Practically speaking, the Marxes needed to appeal to Gentiles to remain headliners. They never denied their Judaism, but they seldom called attention to it. Anti-Semitism was bad enough in the 1920s, but the 1930s would make the so-called "violent decade" seem peaceful by contrast.

Time-Bound: Jokes Within Jokes

The Cocoanuts is a better film to discuss than to watch, though Groucho's quick patter and Chico's mangling of the English language reveal new witticisms with each new viewing.[64] Some of their gags involve time-bound terms and situations that now require explanation.

- **Wage slaves:** Hammer wiggles out of paying his staff by convincing them that they don't wish to become "wage slaves." That term has fallen from grace as many consider it inappropriate to compare free and enslaved labor. In antebellum America, though, labor activists argued that poverty-stricken wage-earners were no freer than chattel slaves. Critics argued that wage-earners still owned their own bodies, whereas the enslaved did not. Labor organizers retorted that crushing poverty anchored workers to slums and jobs analogous to plantation labor. The term "wage slave" would have been known by 1929 moviegoers, and is still occasionally used by labor activists to inflame passions. Hammer's ability to convince his staff to forego wages was, thus, indirect political satire.
- **Liberty:** In the same sequence, Hammer insists, "I want you to be free. There's nothing like *Liberty*, except *Collier's* and *The Saturday Evening Post*." These were magazines filled with graphics and photographs that appealed to mass-market subscribers for both their stories and their visual impact.
- **Looks are deceiving:** Numerous Marx Brothers films involve Groucho courting Margaret Dumont. The joke is enhanced by their seeming physical differences, with Groucho short and wiry and Dumont taller and matronly in shape. Groucho was indeed shorter, but not by much; he was 5'7" and she 5'9". When Dumont played high-society figures, she often wore heels and oversized hats, whereas Groucho gained fame for his hunched-over waddling. *The Cocoanuts* contains numerous insults about Dumont's size that audiences of the day found hysterical.
- **Sophie Tucker:** Hammer tries to convince Potter that his proposed development will be "the biggest development since Sophie Tucker." Tucker, a singer-comedienne of Jewish Ukrainian ancestry, was known as "The Last of the Red-Hot Mamas." There is an adage in comedy that if you are going to take a risk, take a big one. Tucker used her plus-sized body to sing bawdy songs and make salacious jokes that thinner actresses of the day could not. Unlike the Marx Brothers, she also made jokes about being Jewish and even sang in Yiddish.
- **Alligator pears:** Groucho's joke about "alligator pears" rests upon an old nickname for avocados. Avocados were not unknown, but neither were they widely consumed at the time.
- **A dirty joke:** A subsequent comment about an eight-inch pipe is truly a dirty joke. *The Cocoanuts* was made before the Motion Picture Production Code came into effect in 1934, and such a phallic reference probably wouldn't have survived later censors.
- **Radius vs. radio:** When Hammer asks Chico if there's even "a remote possibility that you know what a radius means," he replies, "It's-a WJZ." WJZ was a New York City radio station. It had three call letters instead of four because radio was still new for many Americans. At first, stations broadcast only on the AM band, thus there was no need for more letters. FM

changed that, though some stations were allowed to retain their three-letter identification. Coincidentally, Pittsburgh's KDKA, one of the first commercial radio stations, is one of the few east of the Mississippi River whose first call letter is "K." After 1923, K was reserved for stations west of the Mississippi, and W for those to the east.

THREE

Animal Crackers (1930)

The storyline in *Animal Crackers* sometimes seems like *The Cocoanuts* with different costumes and jokes. That's partly because it too was originally a musical comedy developed for the stage and rewritten for the screen. *Animal Crackers* spotlights Groucho as Jeffrey T. Spaulding, an alleged African explorer, though he knows even less about Africa than Hammer knew about Florida real estate. Chico is a musician for hire, Signor Emmanuel Ravelli, and Harpo is simply the Professor; their main roles are those of thief and woman-chaser, respectively.

Margaret Dumont plays Mrs. Rittenhouse, who is again a widowed upper-class socialite with a marriage-aged daughter, Arabella (Lillian Roth). Arabella is in love with a man her mother thinks is beneath her, struggling painter John Parker (Hal Thompson). Roth is a better ingénue than Mary Eaton in *The Cocoanuts*, and Thompson is an upgrade from the stiff Oscar Shaw, though there is truth to Joe Adamson's dig that Roth and Thompson were handed "the thankless task of playing The Girl and Guy Nobody Cared About."[1] Adding to the sense of *déjà vu*, Zeppo is again such an afterthought that he has the same surname, Jamison, as in *The Cocoanuts*. At least he gets a first name this time: Horatio. There's also an investigator named Hennessey, another holdover surname, this time with an extra "e." And there's another lampoon of Verdi's "Anvil Chorus."

A standard Marx Brothers trope was trimming the sails of the rich and pretentious. In *Animal Crackers,* Mrs. Rittenhouse wishes to one-up her wealthy friends by opening the summer social season with a triumphant weekend party. With Spaulding, Ravelli and the Professor on the premises, that's unlikely. Not to mention that some of Rittenhouse's peers *want* things to go awry. And that several guests are not who they claim to be. Rittenhouse's doomed gala will end much the same way as the engagement party in *The Cocoanuts* and once again young love prevails. As a movie, though, *Animal Crackers* was superior technically and in content to *The Cocoanuts*. That turned out to be a very lucky thing for the Marxes.

From Stage to Screen (Again)

On Broadway, *Animal Crackers* lasted 171 performances before the 1929 stock market crash exacted its toll. Gerald Bordman noted, "[I]n theatrical terms the 1929–30 seasons represent[ed] the lowering of the curtain...."[2] During the 1929–30 season, there were 239 Broadway plays; ten years later, there were just 72, leaving an estimated 25,000 theater hands out of work.[3] Only a few Broadway shows surpassed the

Newspaper ad for the stage show of *Animal Crackers* (Paramount Pictures, via Wikimedia Commons).

success the Marx Brothers enjoyed with *The Cocoanuts*; most producers would have been overjoyed to duplicate the more modest run of *Animal Crackers*.

Movies saved the Marxes from penury. Each suffered great losses in the 1929 stock market collapse though Chico, a problem gambler, was already in debt. After *The Cocoanuts*, Groucho toyed with the idea of chucking moviemaking. That would have been disastrous; by the time *Animal Crackers* debuted as a film, he had lost $250,000 in the

Groucho and Margaret Dumont, straight woman to the anarchic Marx Brothers, *Duck Soup*, 1933 (Paramount Pictures, via Wikimedia Commons).

stock market, a sum comparable to almost $4 million today. Harpo was more than $10,000 in debt, more than $158,000 in 2021 dollars, and required rescue from an unexpected benefactor.[4] Like it or not, the Marxes once again found themselves at Paramount.

As with *The Cocoanuts*, script alterations were necessary to make the play into a movie. That job was handed to Morrie Ryskind who, in conjunction with George S. Kaufman, had written the *Animal Crackers* stage play. Some of Harpo's gags were dropped, songs disappeared, characters were reimagined, sequences were altered, different actors were hired, and the screenplay was trimmed to get the running time down to 98 minutes. To cite just one example, stage audiences saw a Napoleon and Josephine lampoon that originally appeared in their 1923–24 show *I'll Say She Is.* It would have made little sense in the film.[5]

There was also material too vulgar or too controversial to put on film. The Motion Picture Code wasn't yet strictly enforced, but there was an in-place set of standards developed in 1924 and it was dangerous to flout them too boldly. After all, in 1915 the Supreme Court ruled that free speech did not extend to movie content and a swelling number of lobby groups sought to cleanse films of objectionable content. Among the things Paramount insisted upon excising were jokes about Mussolini, a lampoon of journalist Walter Winchell, and several rather obvious sexual innuendos.[6]

Animal Crackers was the last Marx Brothers movie filmed in Astoria. The chore of *Animal Crackers* direction was handed to Victor Heerman, who was known for being a strict taskmaster. It may have been he, not Florey, who ensconced the Marxes in locked cells to ensure they would be available when needed.[7] Heerman had assistant directors shadow the Marxes, and had the moxie to tell the brothers, "This is pictures and not the theatre."[8] Groucho initially rebelled over some of Heerman's choices, but when audience-tested scenes confirmed Heerman's judgment, Groucho helped keep his brothers on task. *Animal Crackers* still came in behind schedule and over budget, but not as much as it otherwise would have been.

Heerman's film also looks much better than *The Cocoanuts*. Remarkable technical advances had taken hold in just one year, and *Animal Crackers* had instantly noticeable improvements in sound quality and camerawork. As today, it took some people longer to adjust to the quantum leaps in technology. Some of the acting remained, in Janice Anderson's observation, "terribly stagebound, cluttered ... with 'romantic' male singers and musical 'interludes,' and directed in a very ham-fisted style, [but the Marxes'] talent showed through it all...."[9]

Vive la différence!

Animal Crackers opens with a choreographed piece reminiscent of *The Cocoanuts*, though instead of hotel bellhops we see a synchronized house staff readying Rittenhouse's estate for the big party. The first V.I.P. to arrive, renowned art dealer Roscoe W. Chandler (Louis Sorin), hands over a large crate to Mrs. Rittenhouse's butler, Hives (Robert Greig). Much fuss is made over what's inside: *After the Hunt* by Beaugard, an oil painting worth $100,000—over $1.58 million in 2021 value—that Chandler acquired in Europe. Then the fun starts, and we begin to see ways in which *Animal Crackers* departs from *The Cocoanuts*.

Horatio W. Jamison (Zeppo), Captain Spaulding's field secretary, enters to sing about what it will take to convince the captain to stay, a list that includes "warm women and cold champagne." Spaulding arrives seated in a covered sedan chair borne by four "African natives." He complains about the outrageous fare of $1.85 from Africa to Long Island, and dismisses them. Spaulding launches into a song whose first line is "Hello, I must be going/ I cannot stay, I came to say/ I must be going." He turns to leave, but Jamison restrains him and Rittenhouse implores him to stay (also in song). Spaulding makes several more half-hearted attempts to flee, as Jamison informs the assembled guests—in a sing-song–like recitation—that "the captain is a very moral man," Spaulding proceeds to demonstrate he is quite the opposite. For instance, Jamison's line, "If he hears anything obscene, he'll naturally repel it," is followed by Spaulding's, "I hate a dirty joke I do / Unless it's told by someone who knows how to tell it."

Fans of British operettas will recognize the musical and lyrical style as a parody of the famed Victorian composer-lyricist team of W.S. Gilbert and Arthur Sullivan.[10] With Spaulding's morality firmly unestablished, the score jumps directly into "Hooray for Captain Spaulding." With lyrics like "Did someone call me *schnorrer*?" (a person who sponges off others), we know the captain is a fraud, and a naughty one at that. When Rittenhouse sings of his African journey, listen carefully and you'll notice an awkward cut in the soundtrack; Spaulding's "I think I'll try and make her" was removed for being too sexually suggestive.

Another thing to note is how different this number is from anything in *The Cocoanuts*. Instead of overwrought lyrical sentimentality, Groucho's opening number calls attention to his rascality. And instead of Jazz Age dancers, it's Groucho's turn in a spotlight he commands with a series of gyrations, twists and contorted jigs. In essence, *Animal Crackers* began to shed some of its Broadway skin. *The Cocoanuts* was a series of musical numbers punctuated by Marx Brothers sketches; *Animal Crackers* flipped that formula.

Not Out of Africa

After a brief bit of nonsense in which Spaulding tries to sell Rittenhouse an insurance policy and she proclaims him the bravest man she has ever known, he casts doubt on her remark by fainting when told there is a caterpillar on his jacket lapel. He is a *schnorrer* indeed; one dressed in pith helmet and billowing knickers who has never been closer to African big game than the Bronx Zoo, where he didn't even read the exhibit labels carefully. Later, he opens his adventure tales from "Africa" by claiming to have shot a polar bear who was "six-foot-seven in his stocking feet...." When Rittenhouse interrupts to exclaim she was under the impression that polar bears "lived in the frozen north," Spaulding retorts, "This bear was anemic and he couldn't stand the cold climate." He continues his ridiculous patter, including a joke about the "principal animals" of Africa: "Moose, Elks and Knights of Pythias." These are the names of popular fraternal orders and a launching platform for jokes about conventions and drinking. It also set up one of Groucho's most-quoted lines: "One morning I shot an elephant in my pajamas. How he got in my pajamas, I don't know."

The implied joke within the jokes is that, though Captain Spaulding has clearly never been to Africa, a skillful bluffer might have gotten away with the ruse because not many Americans would have been able to challenge him. Africa south of the Sahara Desert remained the "dark continent," as Henry Stanley coined it in an 1879 book of that title. Europeans had engaged in the slave trade since the late 15th century, but very few set foot in the continent's interior. Although an estimated 12.8 million captives were taken from Africa between the years 1480 and 1860, most slave traders anchored in coastal ports, loaded human cargo purchased from African middlemen, and sailed away.[11] The African heartlands remained a mystery even to most Arab and North African traders, though Muslims had been conducting trade there since the seventh century.

The slave trade was mostly over by 1860, but its barbarism gave way to imperialism's abominations. A few Europeans and Americans penetrated the African interior in the spirit of intellectual inquiry, but most who ventured there sought to extract natural resources and win souls, another way of saying that Western hegemony over Africans rested upon a foundation of soldiers and missionaries.

Rivals—especially Belgium, Britain, France, Italy, Portugal and post–1870 Germany—carved out African colonies during the 19th century, but white governance was mostly indirect.[12] Top colonial administrators and armies usually hunkered down in a Westernized outpost and carried out policies through African intermediaries, preferably those assimilated to Western values. When soldiers ventured far from their barracks to put down rebellions or assert influence over recalcitrant tribes, they did so with great trepidation. Wars between imperialist masters and Africans were bloody, with each conflict viewed by Europeans as an affirmation of African "savagery." Areas of South Africa controlled by Britain, and the Congo under Belgian rule, saw especially brutal subjugation of indigenous populations.[13]

Commodities such as diamonds, gold, minerals, palm oil, rubber and timber left

Africa, but only missionaries and explorers wandered far from safety or bothered to learn much about tribal cultures. Their stories, often greatly embellished, were retold in lecture halls, newspapers and books. Britain's Association for Promoting the Discovery of the Interior Parts of Africa, founded in 1788, begat the Royal Geographical Society (RGS) in 1830. Both pledged to advance knowledge of geography, botany, fauna and rudimentary anthropological understanding, but were decidedly the servants of imperialist values.

Explorers were usually the first Westerners to map the interior. During the years 1856 to 1860, the RGS sent Sir Richard Francis Burton and John Hanning Speke to find the source of the Nile. They did not settle that question, but their notes, maps and geographical discoveries facilitated future journeys in East Africa that, not coincidentally, helped the British maintain control of the area.[14] Belgium's *Société Belge Royale de Géographie* and the Dutch *Koninklijk Nederlandsh Aardrijkskundig Genootschap* also served imperial masters.

African lands were looted to fill Western museums. Non-Caucasian peoples and cultures were, at best, viewed as exotic; at worst as subhuman, backward and primitive. Advocates of "scientific racism" drew upon the accounts of white African explorers to advance assertions of Caucasian superiority. Rudyard Kipling was among the many popularizers of such views.

The United States was a lesser player in Africa, though much of its white population shared the values of European imperialists. Scientific racism thrived in antebellum America. Slavery apologists such as Samuel A. Cartwright and James Henry Hammond relied upon pseudoscience to assert that bondage was beneficial to the dark races. American racialist beliefs were overtly on display in Liberia. The modern nation evolved from an experiment of the American Colonization Society, which established the settlement of Monrovia in 1822, to provide a haven for freed slaves. Its logic was that free people of color could not be assimilated into American society, though fewer than 20,000 voluntarily emigrated.[15]

In 1871, the *New York Herald* sensationalized African exploration by dispatching reporter Henry Morgan Stanley to Africa in search of David Livingstone, a British doctor and explorer presumed lost somewhere in the Congo. Stanley located him near Lake Tanganyika and allegedly greeted him with the words, "Dr. Livingstone, I presume?" Or so the newspaper stories went. Livingstone, though ill from tropical diseases, was neither lost nor imperiled. Nonetheless, Stanley parlayed the embellishment into an 1872 book titled *How I Found Livingstone; Travels, Adventures and Discoveries in Central Africa*. He later became an agent for King Leopold and assisted in Belgium's subjugation of the Congo.[16]

Ota Benga, a Mbuti (Pygmy) man, was purchased by an American missionary and displayed at the 1904 World's Fair in St. Louis. When the fair closed, Benga was housed at the Bronx Zoo—in the monkey house! Public outcry secured his freedom, but despite humanitarian assistance, he led a sad life that culminated in his 1916 suicide.[17]

The racism underlying Benga's tragedy was hardly an anomaly. One often-reproduced illustration from the *Types of Mankind*, an 1854 book from American Josiah Nott and Britain's George R. Giddon, featured a "Greek" profile and skull above those of a black African, the latter shown as similar in shape and appearance to that of a chimpanzee. Eugenics movements, hate groups and casual racism similarly drew upon the Nott-Giddon worldview.[18] Even before Benga met his sad fate, America had entered its own age of imperialism, one that involved many unfortunate encounters between white- and dark-skinned peoples.

In *Animal Crackers*, Groucho's Jeffrey Spaulding is obviously an absurd figure, but what millions of Americans knew about sub–Saharan Africa came through tales as exaggerated and exoticized as Groucho's gibberish. Spaulding's sedan chair entrance is hard for modern viewers to stomach, but it would *not* have offended many white moviegoers in 1930, a reminder that values—even regrettable ones—change across space and time. Imperialist logic was among those lamentable values. Competition for empire was among the causes of World War I, but that conflict did not settle matters. When *Animal Crackers* opened in 1930, the only sovereign African nations were Egypt, Ethiopia, Liberia and South Africa.

Groucho's Strange Interludes

Several times during *Animal Crackers*, Groucho does something that is usually a movie no-no: he "breaks the frame," meaning he walks away from the story taking place behind him, looks into the camera and speaks directly to his audience. "Excuse me while I have a strange interlude," he intones. Groucho mentions playwright Eugene O'Neill, and you'd need to know a little about his plays to grasp the parody about to unfold. Why is this in the movie in the first place? The key lies with both O'Neill and a relatively new interest in psychology.

Audiences would have recognized Groucho's reference, as O'Neill won the 1928 Pulitzer Prize for his drama *Strange Interlude*. It's essentially a love pentagon involving emotionally damaged people. Its pivot is Nina Leeds, the daughter of a widowed college professor. Her fiancé was killed during World War I and his (figurative) ghost stands between Nina and three living suitors: novelist Charles Marsden, Dr. Ned Darrell and ne'er-do-well Sam Evans. The play covers 25 years of time and runs so long—over five hours—that it's sometimes staged on two successive evenings, lest it exhaust the audience physically and emotionally. It's definitely not the kind of play for a first date!

Strange Interlude delves into matters that made it controversial in its time, including marital infidelity, premarital sex, insanity, abortion, betrayal and thoughts of suicide. In one of Nina's final scenes, she declares, "Strange interludes! Yes, our lives are merely strange dark interludes in the electrical display of God the Father!!"[19] If this sounds like an unlikely source to be mined for comic material, you're right. It's not the material, but the device. Groucho-Spaulding simultaneously woos Rittenhouse (Dumont) and Mrs. Whitehead (Margaret Irving), but turns to the camera and says, "If I were Eugene O'Neill, I could tell you what I really think of you two." Instead, he tells us: "You couple of baboons, what makes you think I'd marry either of you? Strange how the wind blows tonight. It reminds me of poor old Marsden."

In this scene and several others, Groucho lampoons O'Neill's use of soliloquies, moments in plays in which actors appear to be talking to themselves while conveying characters' inner thoughts and feelings. It's not known who first used soliloquies, but Shakespeare's plays are loaded with them. We still encounter them indirectly in literature, movies and TV shows through voiceovers, writers laying bare their thoughts in letters or journal entries, and characters speaking to props. On the stage, it is called "breaking the fourth wall," the invisible wall dividing the actors and the audience.

Soliloquies are common in theater, but O'Neill's *Strange Interlude* makes them the primary way we know what anyone really thinks. Great swaths of the play are built around the gap between what is said and what is thought, with only the audience privy to the latter. Groucho's "strange interlude" is played with mock seriousness to set up jokes once the fourth wall is re-established and the narrative continues. He asks both women to marry him. When an aghast Rittenhouse blurts out, "That's bigamy," Groucho puns, "Yes, and that's big of me, too. Let's be big for a change. One woman and one man was enough for your grandmother, but who wants to marry her? Nobody. Not even your grandfather."

Shortly thereafter comes an interlude in which Groucho ridicules O'Neill's use of ornamented language: "Hideous footsteps creaking along the misty corridors of time, and in those corridors, I see figures, strange figures." Of course, his figures are different: "Steel 186, Anaconda 74, American Can 138"; that is, stock prices.[20] Movie audiences would have detected a deeper level of irony than pre–stock market crash stage show attendees would have.

As a small aside, there was a reason why Groucho often left the movie set to call his broker. Unlike today, when stocks can be bought and sold automatically and online, ticker-tape machines spat out the prices at which stocks were trading. Those wishing to buy or sell particular stocks paid close attention and then rushed to the telephone to tell their brokers what to buy and sell. Since it didn't happen instantaneously, one could only hope the transactions were advantageous.

"Strange interludes" also resonated with audiences because of another recent development in American society: psychology. In 1930, the notion that it was therapeutic to analyze hidden thoughts and emotions was of recent vintage. Although many find Sigmund Freud problematic today, his influence is hard to exaggerate. Freud was not the first to observe that the unconscious mind influenced human behavior, but it was he who systematized theories of the mind that led to the form of talk therapy known as psychoanalysis. Freud insisted that sexual desire was not just part of the human psyche but, in Frederick Lewis Allen's words, "the central and pervasive force which moved mankind." Freud's ideas—often in popularized and distilled form—found receptive audiences among 1920s youth and intellectuals wishing to overturn older moral codes.[21]

Had not World War I diverted attention, popular interest in psychology might have occurred earlier. In the 1890s, William James developed a theory of the self that slightly predated Freud, and thinkers such as Charles Peirce and John Dewey articulated forms of pragmatism sometimes called functional psychology. Such thinkers were typical of their generation in that their psychological theories were offshoots of philosophy, logic and mathematics.

G. Stanley Hall is often credited for making American psychology a stand-alone discipline. He was the first American whose Ph.D. thesis was based in psychology and the first to direct a research lab. In 1887, he founded the *American Journal of Psychology* and, five years later, the American Psychological Association. By the turn of the century, the so-called "new psychology" took its place among the social sciences rather than being regarded as a subdiscipline.

Hall's views on eugenics, neurasthenia and women's minds are now frequently cast in a negative light, but in his day, he was considered a psychological expert. In 1889, he became the first president of Clark University in Worcester, Massachusetts. In 1909, Hall invited many of the leading European psychologists to Clark to commemorate the school's 20th anniversary, including Freud and his protégé, Carl Jung.[22] Freud's lectures attracted great notice and, in some circles, notoriety.

The conference at Clark is now regarded as a milestone for American psychology, but its full impact would not be felt until the 1920s. New ways of perceiving the mind showed up in various places, including theater. O'Neill's *Strange Interlude* is filled with allusions to inner turmoil, guilt and unconstrained behaviors driven by desire. But why would Groucho make such references on stage and screen? Allen once again was on target:

> Psychology was king. Freud, Adler, Jung and Watson had their tens of thousands of votaries; intelligence-testers invaded the schools in quest of I.Q.s; psychiatrists were installed in business houses to hire and fire employees and determine advertising policies; and one had only to read the newspapers to be told with complete assurance that psychology held the key to the problems of waywardness, divorce and crime.[23]

Those seeking social capital embraced new ideas, even if they misunderstood them. To use terms of the day, they sought to be "modern" and "scientific," though the line between them and hokum was thin. Freud was all the rage, but so were Ouija boards, horoscopes and the questionable self-improvement methods of Émil Coué.[24]

Groucho's interludes seem strange now, but at the time he did what most comics do: milked humor from current trends. It probably wasn't necessary to break the frame four times to riff on O'Neill. Only the first and the last actually set up a joke. The final time is more of an aside. Groucho has just made a dumb remark about his coat, looks into the camera and remarks, "Well, all of the jokes can't be good." He's right; his quip was lame and he knew it. Telling the audience that he's self-aware is the funniest part of that sequence. With that, Groucho goes back into character as Captain Spaulding, and the Marxes return to one of the things that made them special: exposing pretense.

A Parade of Phonies

We know that Spaulding is a fraud, but the company he keeps is even worse. The holder of the famed Beaugard painting, Roscoe W. Chandler, is also a phony. He presents as an upper-class European art critic, perhaps the offspring of aristocracy. Allen Eyles labeled him "a pompous oaf," an accurate description.[25] Ravelli–Chico and The Professor–Harpo recognize him as Abe Cabiddle, a former Czechoslovakian fish peddler. They dispense with his denial by wrestling him to the ground to expose a distinctive birthmark.

Chandler tries to buy their silence—well, Ravelli's, as the Professor is mute—and this leads to sight gags such as a check that literally bounces, and another in which every time Chandler thinks he is depositing something into his trouser pocket, it ends up in Harpo's. There's also a sneaky bit of dialogue in which Chandler finally admits he was once Cabiddle. Ravelli asks, "How did you get to be Chandler?" When Chandler ripostes, "How did you get to be Italian?" Ravelli admonishes, "Whose confession is this?"

Spaulding and Chandler aren't the only poseurs in the room. Rittenhouse's rotund butler Hives hadn't always served those to the manor born; he once served four years in prison for theft. This makes him the perfect accomplice for a different kind of phony: snobs with affected airs. He agrees to help Whitehead, his former employer, to assist her sister Grace Carpenter in switching the Beaugard with an imitation she painted in art school. Whitehead's motive is pure jealousy: She wants to ruin Rittenhouse's opening of the summer social season. Ryskind's script leaves no room for sympathy for stuck-up social climbers. Dumont is also an imperious patrician, an open invitation for ridicule. In *Animal Crackers*, even her daughter Arabella is a bit overbearing.

There is also the matter of the Beaugard painting, the film's central prop. You don't need to stop the film and get out a magnifying glass to tell it's a joke in its own right. The Beaugard is an insipid, poorly rendered work that looks like a wallpaper design for a very tacky smoking room. Grace switches the real painting with her copy. Later, Arabella and Parker unwittingly switch Grace's painting with Parker's, but we can clearly see that there's no difference between either of them; each is a rotten piece of art. Even Spaulding, who doesn't know about Chandler's past, calls him an "old bluffer." Parker asks, "What does he know about art?" What indeed?

One might ask the same about music. Ravelli and the Professor are clearly nobody's version of the highbrow entertainment one would expect at a posh party. When Ravelli finally sits down at the piano, he plinks his way through endless bars of "I'm Daffy Over You," which was written by Chico and Sol Violinsky, though numerous works incorrectly list it as "Sugartime." (The melody is so similar to that 1957 McGuire Sisters hit copyrighted by Charlie Phillips and Odis Echols that one wonders why they weren't sued for copyright infringement.) The point, though, is that for a skilled pianist—and Chico was gifted in his own wacky way—the melody we hear in *Animal Crackers* is but a small step above "Chopsticks." Ravelli plays it to plant an annoying earworm so that both he and Groucho can make fun of it. Eventually Ravelli stops and says, "I'll tell you what I do. I play you one of my own compositions by Victor Herbert." Call it three jokes in one. First, he has *already* played his composition and second, the next tune is *not* by Victor Herbert; it is "Silver Threads Among the Gold," an 1873 composition by H.P. Danks and Eben Rexford. Finally, in Chico's hands, the second tune is no longer a sentimental Victorian ballad, but one showcasing his keyboard acrobatics. Ravelli's performance is high society cut down to size.

Harpo's solo, after a short echo of "I'm Daffy Over You," is more dignified. It takes place on the patio, with no one to hear it. Harpo soloed in all but two films, but his turn in *Animal Crackers* doesn't really serve much of a purpose. The same is true of the Thompson-Roth duet on "Why Am I So Romantic," a view shared by many critics. Incidentally, in 1930, Harpo was still considered a novice harpist, not one of professional caliber.[26] All of the affected personae and musical performances are digs at pretense.

Priceless Gems

Among the delights of Marx Brothers films are the filler sketches and mayhem. They are, after all, comedians, not O'Neill-like dramatic actors. *Animal Crackers* contains numerous amusing sequences and a few that are considered comedy classics.

The first is "Hooray for Captain Spaulding," soon followed by Ravelli's mirthful explanation of his musician's pay rate: $10 an hour to play, $12 an hour for *not* playing, and $15 an hour for rehearsing. As for not rehearsing, Ravelli explains, "You couldn't afford it. If we don't rehearse, we don't play. And if we don't play, that runs into money." When Spaulding inquires, "How much for running into an open manhole?" Ravelli retorts, "Just the cover charge."

The second classic scene is the aforementioned discussion of bigamy, and the third Spaulding's explanation of how inflating the nickel would solve all economic woes. For pure outrageousness, though, it's hard to beat the bridge game that pits Ravelli and the Professor against Rittenhouse and Whitehead. The inspired madness begins with Harpo befuddling Hives' attempt to set up a card table and placing a cosh on the table when Rittenhouse responds, "Well I hope so" to Ravelli's question of whether she wants to play an "honest" game. There are hysterical sight gags involving Harpo pretending to shuffle and cut the deck, licking his left thumb while drawing from the bottom of the deck with his right, showing cards to Ravelli before dealing, tearing up or tossing away cards he doesn't want, and producing an endless supply of aces. Suffice it to say, there is nothing remotely honest in any part of the game.

Even Zeppo managed to be included in a now-classic piece. When the police arrive to investigate the missing Beaugard, Spaulding demands that Jamison write a letter to his lawyers in the firm of Hungadunga, Hungadunga, Hungadunga, Hungadunga and McCormack.[27] Spaulding's dictation is utter nonsense, but Jamison plays things close to the vest. When asked to read what he took down, Jamison replies, "A lot of things you said weren't important, so I just omitted them." That turns out to be nearly everything! Spaulding feigns outrage, which sets up another round of jokes. Incidentally, Zeppo had one of his greatest moments in the spotlight during the stage show of *Animal Crackers*: When Groucho contracted appendicitis in 1930, Zeppo took over as Spaulding, complete with greasepaint mustache, and was so good that no one knew the difference.[28]

Although they fall short of being classics, *Animal Crackers*' sexual references are far more salacious than Spaulding's "I think I'll try to make her" line sliced from "Hooray for Captain Spaulding." Groucho introduces Ravelli's solo with the quip, "His first selection is 'Somewhere My Love Lies Sleeping' with a male chorus." Another bit of naughtiness comes when the power goes out at the Rittenhouse estate. When she cries out, "The lights have gone out. You can't see your hand before your face," Spaulding protests, "Well, you wouldn't get much enjoyment out of that!" And even that pales in comparison to Spaulding's admonishment that Jamison needs to "brush up on your Greek," followed by a leering, "Get a Greek and brush up on him."

The Elephant in the Room: Harpo's Sexist Interludes

Insinuation isn't the most distressing thing in *Animal Crackers*. Viewers today might be disturbed by Marxian sexism. Groucho's japes directed at Dumont are not the biggest issue; he insulted everyone, and stinging wisecracks were expected of him. Later "insult comedians" such as Don Rickles, Joan Rivers, Bernie Mac, Ricky Gervais, Louis C.K. and Lisa Lampanelli are cut from Groucho's frock coat.

In *Animal Crackers* and several other films, it's Harpo's antics that trouble us.

We know early on that he is up to no good in this film when Hives attempts to take his coat and leaves him clad only in top hat, shoes, undershirt and undershorts. However, the most problematic sexist moments are of Harpo punching Margaret Dumont in the stomach and his incessant chasing of blondes.

From today's perspective, it's probably not funny. I remind readers that comedy is often cruel. Eyles labeled Harpo's pummeling of Dumont as "the most barbaric image found in any Marx film."[29] I am tempted to agree, though Harpo's blows were, of course, slapstick, not real punches. He lifts Dumont into the air after each uppercut to the midriff, much in the way that so-called "professional wrestlers" disguise fake body blows. Harpo's pulled punches highlight a constant thorn in a comedian's side: how to end a sketch. That's precisely what it was: material that serves no purpose other than ending the otherwise brilliant card game scene. We must also remember that *Animal Crackers* material was thoroughly audience-tested, and gags that didn't work were discarded. Like it or not, viewers apparently found mirth in Harpo's assault on Dumont's midsection.

When encountering cringeworthy material, we need to explore why audiences found Harpo's fury funny. The answer, though it may not be any more palatable than the scene itself, is that American society was deeply paternalistic and sexist. Nineteen-twenties flapper culture notwithstanding, America was very much a man's world. Gender essentialism did not go unchallenged, but the battle for genuine equality was still stuck in low gear. Women had only gotten to vote in national elections a decade earlier, and women smokers were considered immoral.

An enduring myth of the 1920s is that the experience of working women during World War I opened postwar workplace doors. Actually, an estimated 95 percent of women working during the conflict were already employed when it began. As Michael Parrish explains, "Instead of being a springboard to further victories as some feminists predicted, the war proved to be a short coda to a movement that lost much of its dynamism and coherence in the next decade."[30] He also reminds us not read too much into the sexual liberation of flappers, the presence of female cultural icons, crusades for birth control access, rising numbers of companionate marriages, and the accomplishments of extraordinary women. History is too often refracted through the experiences of those who challenged barriers that took decades to collapse. Paula Fass noted, for instance, that although younger women tested Victorian sexual mores, "Even in the '20s, it was not unknown for reformers to introduce legislation that would prohibit petting and define it along with fornication as illegal, as well as immoral."[31] One Arkansas community passed an ordinance that forbade unmarried individuals "guilty of committing the act of sexual intercourse" from living within the town limits.[32]

Double standards prevailed. Unmarried flappers who got pregnant faced social ostracism, which is why many pregnant and unwed women were sent elsewhere to deliver and why so many babies were raised in orphanages. *Middletown*, the famed sociological analysis of Muncie, Indiana, published in 1929, recounted arrests for "sex crimes," a category that included both prostitution and pregnancy outside of marriage.[33] Negative sanctions against single mothers persisted well into the 1960s.

Many young women dreamed of careers, and some realized them. But there remained wide gaps in social expectations. Young men overwhelmingly expressed the view that wives should withdraw from the public realm and take on "natural" roles of homemakers and mothers. Numerous men entertained the idea of giving women greater say in finances and other domestic decisions. In Fass' words, "[B]y the 1920s, the young seemed to believe in complete equality in the home, but not outside it." It didn't help that psychologists, especially Freud, claimed that women were not just the "weaker" sex, but also incompletely developed individuals who suffered from penis envy and were prone to neuroses and hysteria.

Advice experts made questionable assertions of their own that added pseudo-scientific gravitas to norms that kept women in subordinate roles. These ran the gamut from crude theories about microbes that demanded wifely household engineers to vanquish them to ideals of child-centered families in which women bore responsibility for educational and moral instruction.[34] Outside of urban areas, where social change took root earlier, 1920s gender roles often resembled Victorianism dressed in looser clothing.

In *Animal Crackers*, Rittenhouse is an urban woman who happens to have an estate on Long Island. She is certainly not a flapper and neither are her female guests, though several have assumed the garb. Rittenhouse is a socialite, an easy target for ridicule. Her party is the epitome of frivolity, and the Marx Brothers gleefully expose it as such. Harpo's stomach blows may be hard to watch, but the Marxes correctly surmised that audiences would find an assault on a socialite amusing. The moment is an extreme turnabout of the social convention in which women slapped men for being too "fresh" and gentlemen were expected to walk away from such a confrontation. The very fact that Harpo slugged a woman made it "funny."

The idea that such a scene was even imaginable reflected the evolving but tentative position of women in American society. Such a real act could, in theory, have led to an assault charge. In practice, law enforcement often ignored such attacks in the belief that women were occasionally in need of correction administered by the allegedly superior male sex. Those assumptions persisted into the 1970s, and it was not until 1994 that the Violence Against Women Act ended casual and customary acceptance of ignoring male assault, insisted that law enforcement treat such matters as crime, and provided legal recourse for victims. Quick arithmetic reveals a 64-year gap between Harpo's antics and sanctions that made them legally un-funny.

There is also the matter of Harpo's constant chasing of blondes, a prank he pulls in several Marx Brothers films. That phenomenon has a less sinister backstory. It originated as an ad-lib from the *Cocoanuts* stage show. According to Harpo, it began as "a little surprise for Groucho" during a matinee. He pulled it because he trusted that Groucho would devise a comeback:

> [W]hile I was offstage, I selected a blonde cutie from the chorus, and asked her if she'd like a bigger part in the show. She was willing and eager. I told her all she had to do was run screaming across the stage. She did and I tore after her in full pursuit leaping and bounding and honking my horn. It broke up Groucho's scene, but when the laugh subsided, Groucho was ready to top it. "First time I ever saw a taxi hail a passenger," he said. So, I chased the chorus girl back across the stage the other way, trying to catch Groucho flat-footed. I didn't. "The 9:20's right on time…. You can always set your clocks by the Lehigh Valley."[35]

Groucho's second retort referenced the Lehigh Valley Railroad, which was mostly a freight service but also carried passengers to New York City and westward to Buffalo. Harpo also claimed that he was lucky that the actress's boyfriend wasn't in the audience, as he was none other than the gangster "Legs" Diamond, who "wanted his bimbo stashed securely in the chorus" away from the "loony actors." Harpo chose a different actress for the evening show. From there on, chasing blondes "became a running gag."[36] Harpo chased blondes because audiences laughed. It was never intended to look as ominous as it now appears.

Animal Cracker Crumbs

Here's how to decode some of the more obscure references scattered throughout the film.

- **House of David:** As the mystery of the Beaugard painting unravels, accusations fly back and forth and Parker comes under suspicion. Amidst the racket, Spaulding intones, "This program is coming to you from the House of David." This quip references a religious utopian experiment centered in Benton Harbor, Michigan, whose history rivals a Marx Brothers script for improbability. Benjamin and Mary Purnell established the House of David colony in 1903 and attracted hundreds of followers to their thousand-acre complex. That alone wasn't unusual; there were numerous communal experiments in the early 20th century. Many, including the House of David, were built around unconventional values and social practices.

  Its official name, the Israelite House of David, implies a connection with Judaism. Some Jews joined the House of David, including Orthodox believers whose male adherents grew long beards. But Christian millenarianism—signs presaging the return of Christ—was the community's guiding principle.[37] According to the Purnells, the end of the world was imminent, and they were the seventh and final "messengers" sent to prepare believers for the Apocalypse.[38]

  While waiting for the last judgment, members were supposed to renounce sex. The House of David was fodder for Groucho's gibe because it was in the news due to scandals that eventually split the movement. Benjamin Purnell was better at preaching celibacy than practicing it: Numerous teenaged girls accused him of sexual assault in the guise of religious rites. He was ousted from the community, but established a rival sect. In turn, his estranged wife created Mary's City of David, which more strictly adhered to its core tenets. In the press, though, "commune" gave way to a different descriptor: cult.

  For all of the House of David's internal difficulties, it excelled in keeping its name known through creative outreach. It had its own band, opened a public park, and sponsored sports teams. The House of David barnstorming baseball teams—often staffed with off-season Major League and Negro Leagues stars—were particularly popular. The players grew long beards, which contributed to the popular belief that they were Orthodox Jews. Most sources claim these teams disbanded after 1955, but I saw a traveling House of David team as a child in the early 1960s.[39]
- ***The Trial of Mary Dugan:*** During Spaulding's exchange of fractured crime-solving reasoning with Ravelli, they reach the conclusion that the fake Beaugard came from a southpaw painter. Spaulding remarks, "If we can find

the left-handed person, we'll have *The Trial of Mary Dugan.*" This was not a tawdry tabloid crime story. At least, not a real one. *The Trial of Mary Dugan* was a play-turned-film about a shapely showgirl accused of murdering her millionaire lover. It opened on Broadway in 1927 and was made into a 1929 movie with Norma Shearer in the title role. It was Shearer's first "talkie" after a string of successful silent movies.[40] She became one of the few actresses to win fame in both silent and sound pictures.

Like many Groucho wisecracks, the surface reference establishes a secondary inference. His witticism was aimed at the instantly recognizable Shearer, not the fictional Mary Dugan.

- *Abie's Irish Rose:* In the same sequence, Spaulding tells Ravelli that with enough evidence, they could go to court and get a writ of *habeas corpus.* Ravelli has never heard of such a thing, but he does know about "Habie's Irish Rose," mangled English for *Abie's Irish Rose.* It sounds like a whiskey brand name. It's not, but there is an Irish connection. It was a Broadway comedy about a love affair between a Jewish man and an Irish Catholic woman. Detractors thought *Abie's Irish Rose* a terrible play. Harpo dismissed it as "no worse than a bad cold."[41] The public, however, adored it. It opened in May 1922 and when it closed after nearly five and a half years, it was the longest-running play in Broadway history until *Hello Dolly!* surpassed it four decades later. Perhaps it resonated because it was a goes-down-easy comedy, or perhaps because New Yorkers in a city that was one-quarter Jewish were registering a backhanded protest against the 1924 National Origins Act. A simpler explanation is that its tale of young lovers and disapproving families held the same appeal as *Romeo and Juliet.*
- **Chic Sale:** Groucho also makes an offhand reference to Chic Sale. Who? Charles Partlow "Chic" Sale is a forgotten vaudevillian and film character actor. Groucho's reference is not flattering. In 1929, Sale wrote a play titled *The Specialist,* about a carpenter who built outhouses. Groucho used Sale's name as a synonym for an outdoor toilet. I doubt that Sale was amused by the line.
- **Harpo's hair:** Astute viewers might notice that Harpo's hair is said to be red, though it appears to be light in color. Harpo wore a curly red wig on stage, but some directors felt that that a blond wig gave more contrast, so Harpo added a few to his arsenal. If in some movies his hair looks darker or lighter, don't adjust your screen.

Getting Reel: Movies and the Marxes

Critics didn't rave over *Animal Crackers,* but most felt it was a good take on the Broadway show.[42] By 1930, though, several things were clear. First, the Great Depression had changed the economic rules of the acting game. The Marxes mused over a return to the stage, but the offers they received for stage work were not as lucrative as they had hoped. They also toyed with doing a radio serial but, as we shall see in the next chapter, another movie contract and an ocean voyage changed their thinking.

It was also increasingly clear that talking pictures were not a flash—or, as Chico would have it, a "flesh"—in the pan.[43] Talkies were here to stay and the Marxes were good at them. Paramount knew this. From then on, the Marx Brothers movies would be made in the company's Hollywood studio; their first was 1931's *Monkey Business*. Ten more West Coast productions followed.

To project even further into the future, if you wanted to watch *Animal Crackers* any time before 1979 and didn't live in Great Britain, you were probably out of luck. Under the copyright laws of the day, Paramount could have owned *Animal Crackers'* rights for 95 years, with the stipulation that it needed to renew the copyright after 28 years. It was released in 1930 and, in 1957, Paramount renewed the *picture* rights, but either forgot or didn't bother to secure the *soundtrack* rights. This meant that the latter reverted to the authors of the play, George S. Kaufman and Morrie Ryskind, and to Bert Kalmar and Harry Ruby, holders of the musical and lyrical rights.

Paramount didn't renew the soundtrack rights for *The Cocoanuts* either, but few seemed to care about that more dated work. Two unforeseen things occurred that made Paramount wish it had paid more attention. In 1950, Groucho's radio quiz show, *You Bet Your Life,* transitioned to television. Groucho's entrance occurred as the band struck up "Hooray for Captain Spaulding" from *Animal Crackers*. Groucho's TV run lasted 11 years, making the song a public earworm. The second shoe dropped when Marx Brothers films enjoyed a revival during the mid–1960s. Their blend of mayhem bordering on anarchy resonated with rebellious youth born after World War II.

Suddenly there was great demand for the entire Marx *oeuvre*, but it took 17 years of finagling before Universal, to which Paramount had sold their early film catalog, reacquired the soundtrack rights. Until then, an abridged British copy of the film was available but not the original. Prints of *Animal Crackers* re-opened to great fanfare in 1974, but one had to live near an art cinema to see it. Many theaters screened the British version into the 1980s.

In 1979, the original cut of *Animal Crackers* made its way to television. Until then, the second film the Marx Brothers made was the hardest for most people to find.[44]

FOUR

Monkey Business (1931)

The Marx Brothers are stowaways on an ocean liner headed for New York. We hear them before we see them, as they croon "Sweet Adeline" from four clustered barrels labeled "Kippered Herring." Their characters bear no names other than Chico, Harpo and Zeppo; Groucho has none at all. Once they are discovered, a mad chase ensues. They elude the ship's hapless crew members and, along the way, fall into the middle of a dispute between two gangsters: Joe Helton (Rockcliffe Fellowes) wants to get out of the rackets, and Alky Briggs (Harry Woods) needs Helton's blessing to take over his operation. The suave Helton wants no part of the thuggish Briggs. Little could make less sense than having the Marx Brothers be bodyguards for organized crime figures. That's exactly why it's funny.

Along the way, Zeppo falls for Joe's daughter Mary (Ruth Hall) and Groucho engages in dangerous flirtation with Alky's wife Lucille (Thelma Todd). All four Marxes have to figure out how to get off the boat once it docks. They do, but the Helton-Briggs power struggle continues on land. After Groucho goes on the prowl during Helton's party, Helton's thugs kidnap Mary. Zeppo battles to save her.

Joe Adamson astutely observed, "the glory of *Monkey Business* is that all four

Theater lobby card for *Monkey Business*: Harpo, Zeppo, Chico, Groucho (Paramount Pictures, via Wikimedia Commons).

[Marx Brothers] run nothing but amok."[1] It's another simple plot—once the dust settles. The real mess occurred in getting there.

Real-Life Mayhem

Speaking of messes, even though *Animal Crackers* appeared after the 1929 stock market crash, *Monkey Business* is considered the Marx Brothers' first Depression-era film. By 1931, few could predict how long the economic downturn would last. It was President Herbert Hoover's misfortune that he did dabble in prognostication. Throughout 1930 he promised that the economy was on the verge of recovery. On May 1, he told the Chamber of Commerce, "I am convinced we have passed the worst and with continued unity of effort we shall rapidly recover." Four months later, he praised the American Bankers Association for saving the nation's credit system.[2]

Hoover's were among the most infamous bad predictions in American history. Democratic National Committee Chair Charles Michelson was more realistic; he coined a term that defined the times better than the president's rosy assessment: Hooverville. It was the nickname given to instant slums, hobo camps and makeshift shelters erected by the homeless and unemployed. Soon, castoff newspapers used for warmth became "Hoover blankets" and the small animals devoured by the desperately hungry—including rats—morphed into "Hoover hogs."

Monkey Business was released on September 17, 1931. By then, few insisted that the recession would end soon. By year's end, even Hoover referred to a "great depression."[3]

Crafting *Monkey Business*

The task of creating a Marx Brothers movie from scratch fell to S.J. Perelman and Will B. Johnstone, with rewrite help from Arthur Sheekman, Nat Perrin and Bert Granet, the last two uncredited. Sidney Joseph Perelman would later be feted as a great comedy writer, but in 1930, he was considered a cartoonist, novelist and occasional magazine contributor. He had not worked with the Marx Brothers. Producer Herman Mankiewicz warned both Perelman and Johnstone, "They're mercurial, devious and ungrateful. I hate to depress you, but you'll rue the day you ever took the assignment."[4] Perhaps Perelman was disarmed by Groucho's humorous blurb for his (Perelman's) 1929 novel *Dawn Ginsbergh's Revenge*: "From the moment I picked up your book until I laid it down, I was convulsed with laughter. Someday I intend reading it."[5]

Johnstone's experience was just as thin, but at least the Marxes knew him from an aborted radio project. When Johnstone asked Groucho why he was chosen when he had never before written for radio, he was told, "Well, that's one reason. If you think of any others, call me."[6]

In the entertainment business, scripts move from idea to treatment, the latter a fleshed-out idea before characters are finalized, dialogue is written or plotlines developed. The treatment is a long way from a first draft. When the Marxes arrived in Hollywood for a first read-through of this treatment, Perelman read the 126-page draft to a room filled with 27 people and five unruly dogs. Perrin recalled that Perelman was "a rather high-strung man and ... a stutterer.... It was asking an awful lot of [the Marx Brothers] to sit there and listen for two hours."[7] When Perelman finished, Groucho growled, "It stinks. Come on." With that, the Marxes walked out and prepared for a trip to London.[8]

Sheekman, Groucho's favorite gag writer, was called upon to fix the script, and J. Carver Pusey began to work on sight pranks for Harpo.[9] Perrin also joined the creative team but was such a novice that he signed aboard for $100 per week, not realizing that others were making up to $1,500. That rewrite took five months! Granet added a few jokes.

In London, the Marxes performed a pastiche of sketches from past productions, including *I'll Say She Is, The Cocoanuts* and *Animal Crackers*. Reviews were mostly glowing, but Groucho complained that the British didn't understand some of their humor. He may have still been reeling from a 1922 visit in which that was decidedly the case.[10] Groucho didn't care for the British winter—they arrived in January—and was in a foul mood overall. He was alleged to have delayed his February 14 re-entry into the United States by listing his occupation as "smuggler," writing, "Wouldn't you like to know?" on his Declaration of Purchases form, and jokingly asking his wife Ruth if she still had any opium. Customs agents were unamused. The entire family, including their two small children, were grilled by officials before being allowed to disembark.[11]

His brothers enjoyed their ocean voyages. Groucho did not, but all four returned with ideas about how to fix the script. Not coincidentally, these involved hijinks on the high seas. *Monkey Business* emerged, and the brothers got down to work. Groucho didn't like Hollywood at first but, as Simon Louvish noted, he was there not "to make art, but money."[12] A public relations campaign preceded the film's September 17 opening. Part of it was as strange as the Marx Brothers.

I'll Say She Is, Redux

Trailers preceded the release of feature pictures to create "buzz," a term that would not have been used in 1931.[13] *Monkey Business* had two trailers. The official one ran two minutes and 22 seconds, though there are no film clips until the 40-second mark. It opens by exhorting, "You who have laughs to spread, prepare to spread them now. The funniest men in the world are on their way here." The clips were not shown in sequential order and several were early takes, sharpened before the final print.[14]

The second trailer was part of an hour-long compilation film, another phenomenon familiar to modern audiences, especially Oscar viewers. Most are montages cobbled from past films, but in 1931, Paramount released a compilation of both older and upcoming movies. Titled *The House That Shadows Built*, it spotlighted Paramount films from 1912 and 1932. Some from the silent era were used to build excitement for talkies being released in 1931 and 1932. Histrionics stoked the illusion of gravitas. An opening slide tells us, "[T]he house of modern Entertainment....... Symbol of twenty years of progress. First the shadows flickered ... then moved ... then spoke ... bringing us Romance and Adventure ... ever-changing ... ever-new...."[15]

In a five-minute segment for *Monkey Business*, Paramount promised that it will be "four times funnier than the funniest picture you have ever seen," though not a single frame of the film was shown. Instead, there is a filmed sequence from the 1924 stage show *I'll Say She Is*. You will, however, recognize some of the gags. The Marxes enter the office of a booking agent one at a time: Zeppo as Sammy Brown, Chico as Tomalio, Groucho as "a dramatic actor" and Harpo with a calling card that insults the agent. Each, except Harpo, introduces himself in rhyme and asks for a tryout, and each does a Maurice Chevalier imitation to showcase his talents. Things go haywire, cacophony ensues, and Harpo goes berserk. This material was reworked for *Monkey Business*.[16]

It's curious that Paramount featured *I'll Say She Is* rather than the same material as it appeared on the screen. Groucho claimed the movie was unfinished at the time, but Paramount certainly could have found usable footage, as evidenced by the official trailer. Chalk it up to an old proverb: "Waste not, want not."

Was Harpo Mute?

Modern viewers invariably want to know if Harpo was truly mute. Groucho claimed he was asked this more than any other question and usually said yes![17] Chico also got in on the fun of claiming that Harpo couldn't speak.[18] In truth, Harpo spoke with the same New York accent as his brothers. He even traded barbs with a company of intellectuals, the Algonquin Round Table, known for their witty repartee.

There are conflicting tales attached to Harpo's silence. The two best ones go back to the days when the Marxes were struggling vaudeville performers. Harpo was said to be a terrible singer in an age in which many successful vaudevillians fleshed out their acts with song-and-dance routines. Groucho claimed that Harpo was so bad that an Ohio theater manager docked their pay by $2 in the days when "we could have used it."[19]

Another often-repeated story concerns an incident involving Jack Wells, owner of a Bloomington, Illinois, vaudeville house. Groucho was fined $5 for ignoring the no-smoking sign. As Groucho related in a 1948 article,

> "What sign?" I said, a little puzzled. "What sign!" he roared, and pointed in the gloom, to a tiny NO SMOKING poster tacked high on the wall, almost out of sight. "Why don't you hang it in a closet?" I asked. "Then you can make sure no one'll see it." "Oh, a wise guy, eh! That crack'll cost you another five...." The more I thought about Wells and the $10, the madder I got.... I was still burning when the rehearsal was over.... Back at the hotel, I woke up the boys ... and told them what happened.... We held a council of war and decided we wouldn't go on unless Wells rescinded the fine.

They were bluffing, but Wells caved rather than refund 500 tickets. He did, however, pay each their $112.50 salary in sacks filled with pennies. As their train pulled from the station, Harpo yelled out, "Goodbye, Mr. Wells. Here's hoping your lousy theater burns down!" Such a fate allegedly occurred that very night. Groucho added, "From then on, we decided not to let Harpo talk—his conversation was too dangerous."[20]

Keep in mind that Harpo was merely a character played by Arthur Marx. As noted, Harpo had spoken and sung on the stage before he developed his pantomime routines. His muteness was just an act, as were his wig, his oversized coat, his funny faces and his blonde-chasing. Just like Chico pretended to be Italian and wore a wig.

Just like Groucho's absurd greasepaint mustache. Zeppo was the only member of the ensemble who never had to explain that he was not the same as his character. He dressed in street clothes and played the straight man, a role much appreciated by fellow comedians, though they are seldom asked if they are *really* as they appear on screen.

Film historian Richard Schickel dubbed Harpo "the last great silent comedian, supplying the Marx Brothers films with pantomime comparable to that of the silent days."[21] Charlie Chaplin once lamented to Groucho, "I wish I could talk on the screen like you."[22] Chaplin did eventually speak in movies, so was Harpo really the final link to the silent era? The answer is a qualified yes.

A ship's officer named Gibson (Tom Kennedy) informs Captain Corcoran (Ben Taggart) that there are four stowaways on board. When asked how he knew there were four, Gibson replied it was because they were singing "Sweet Adeline." That 1903 sentimental ballad became a favorite offering of barbershop *quartets, a cappella* vocalists noted their four-part close harmonies. When we hear four harmonizing voices coming from the barrels, is one of them Harpo's? Probably. He might not have been a great singer, but the opening sequence is played for laughs, not virtuosity. Barring a remarkable bit of acoustic detection, we may never know if Harpo sang; all the vocalists were hidden in barrels. Given the Marx Brothers' love of improvisation, though, Harpo might have furtively broken character. After all, he puckishly named his autobiography *Harpo Speaks!*

"Running" Gags

Captain Corcoran, Gibson and crew members search for the stowaways in the cargo hold. When they look away for a moment, Groucho pops up to bark the command to ignore the barrels. That's a temporary reprieve: When ropes are attached to hoist the barrels to the main deck, the bottoms give way to reveal the fare-dodgers and wares such as dice, teapots, books, toiletries, nail files, brushes and hats.

From this moment on, *Monkey Business* is a breakneck chase film that puts the motion into motion pictures. The Marxes must have been in the best physical condition of their lives, as they spent most of the film running, pursuing or engaging in physical pranks. Harpo even adds a wrinkle to his old gag by pedaling a bicycle to chase a blonde. They invent ways to avoid capture, such as pretending to be statues and diving under the blanket of an obese woman lying on a deck chair.

Gag after gag unfolds, which makes it puzzling why one Marx Brothers scholar claimed its title didn't have anything to do with the movie.[23] The *Oxford English Dictionary* notes that references to monkeys as deceivers appeared in print in 1767, and that "monkey business" had been a synonym for fooling around for nearly a century before the film appeared. The barrel is another tipoff. The phrase "a barrel of monkeys" was at least 35 years old at the time of the film. It implied disorderly and/or amusing mischief.[24]

Much of the monkey business involves taking down authority figures, including the staff of the ocean liner. Despite infamous tragedies involving the *Titanic* (1912), the *Lusitania* (1915), the *Princess Sophia* (1918) and the SS *Afrique* (1920), the only way for passengers to cross the Atlantic in 1931 was by ship. Ocean liners were socially stratified and mirrored dwelling patterns on dry land. Numerous songs and labor speeches featured references to shacks along the riverbank and mansions upon the hill, metaphors for how money bought dwellings further from undesirable locations such as riversides, factories, mines, rail lines and busy streets.

Analogous patterns held on ocean-going vessels: Those with means booked well-appointed cabins as far above the waterline as possible. All boats rock and pitch, but higher lodgings are smoother than those at or below the waterline, especially in rough seas. Lower berths were also smaller, corridors narrower, were closer to the ship's engines, and were Spartanly furnished. This was where engine crews, immigrants and working-class passengers were usually housed for the four- to six-day crossing.[25]

The luxury of ballrooms, lounges and dining facilities for wealthy patrons such as old-money families, parvenu industrialists, haute bourgeoisie and show business celebrities beggars the imagination, as does the lavishness of their lifestyles.[26] But wealth was not the sole determiner of status. As Gardner observed, "The crews of ocean liners imagined their own status to be superior to the passengers' social standing no matter how famous or wealthy [they] might be."[27] Garner exaggerates slightly, but a ship's upper echelon—especially the captain, officers, security chief, navigator and purser—were certainly aware of occupying prestigious positions. It was a great honor, for instance, to be invited to dine at the captain's table.

This makes Groucho's putdowns of Captain Corcoran transgressive. Armed with gloves he has taken from the captain's trunk, Groucho reduces him to sputtering by asking, "Are you the floorwalker on this ship?"[28] Groucho unleashes a string of criticisms: "Do you know who sneaked into my stateroom at three o'clock this morning?" When the captain asks, "Who did that?" Groucho replies, "Nobody, and that's my complaint.... I don't care for the way you're running this boat. Why don't you get in the back seat for a while and let your wife drive?" The captain's indignant reply that he has been in charge of the vessel for 22 years is fodder for more smart-aleck comebacks.

To add further insult to injury, Groucho and Chico rush into the captain's outer office and when he pursues them, Groucho—wearing one of the captain's hats—pushes him into his dining room. Groucho then turns to Chico and huffily remarks, "How dare you invade the sanctity of the captain's quarters?" They exchange silly badinage after ordering the captain's lunch to be sent up. Chico boasts that he comes from a family of sailors and asserts, "My father was-a partners with Columbus." When Groucho points out, "Columbus has been dead 400 years," Chico retorts, "Well, they told me it was my father." During a few rounds of verbal jousting and puns, Chico turns shortcut into "strawberry shortcut," twists *whistle* into *vessel*, and *mutinies* into *matinees*. An exasperated Groucho asks, "You suppose I could buy back my introduction to you?"

Instead, they burst into the captain's dining room and plop themselves down at the table. The captain screams, "Well, of all the colossal impudence!" Groucho and Chico pretend to be stockholders in the ship's company, but the captain recognizes them as stowaways, which necessitates locking Corcoran in a closet.

Harpo deals dignity wordless blows. We see him leaning against the sign for the MEN'S lavatory. A well-dressed gentleman enters and is immediately tossed out on his face. Then we see that Harpo's body had obscured the WO on a WOMEN'S sign. Then it's off to chase a blonde and be chased by Gibson. Harpo runs into a room where children are laughing at a Punch and Judy show, a slapstick puppet play with roots in the *commedia dell'arte*. What better setup for Harpo? He ducks to the back of the stage, pulls a gookie, places his head through to the front, and is battered by club-wielding puppets. Both and he and the children are greatly amused. Gibson and Corcoran catch on, but Harpo eludes them. The scene, which lasts just over two and a half minutes, features Harpo at his most inspired.

As if the crew hasn't suffered enough, Harpo and Chico next disguise themselves as barbers. Officers looking for them don't see through the ruse. One with an impressive mustache decides to stay for a quick trim. Just the pretext for the two "barbers" to take off his entire mustache one "snoop" at a time.

Gangsters, Cowboys and Punsters

Satirical takes on popular shows, movie genres, celebrities and trends were constants for the Marx Brothers and their writers.

By 1931, movie revenues were sagging. Paramount co-founder and producer Jesse Lasky noted that "weary and depression-ridden" Americans wanted to see "new ideas" on the screen.[29] Moviegoers yearned for respite from the grim realities outside the theater, even if the subject was someone else's misfortune. The Internet Movie Database (IMDb) lists an astonishing 1,844 titles made during 1930–31.[30] On this list, comedies, romances, musicals, domestic dramas, gangster films and Westerns proliferated.

Crime fiction and murder mysteries provided cheap thrills during the 1920s and '30s, especially those by British writers such as G.K. Chesterton, Agatha Christie and Dorothy L. Sayers. Americans Carroll John Daly, Dashiell Hammett and Damon Runyon took grittier approaches that gave rise to hardboiled detective novels in the 1930s. Part of the allure was linked to the constant news stream related to organized crime during the 1920s and '30s. Al Capone, John Dillinger, Machine Gun Kelly, Meyer Lansky, Lucky Luciano, Bugs Moran and Bugsy Siegel were household names, often for keeping Americans lubricated during Prohibition. They also ran rackets, prostitution rings and graft schemes. Atlantic City, Chicago, Miami, New York and Philadelphia saw bloody turf wars and murders.

The 1930s were a golden age for gangster pictures. Movies both reflected public fascination with crime and stimulated new interest in it. In Hollywood's defense, it did not glamorize hoodlums. The 1930 MPPDA codes established standards of how law-breaking could be depicted on the screen, and even though they were loosely enforced, most producers paid attention to guidelines on how to depict things such as murder, graphic violence, robbery, arson and the use of guns.[31] The overarching principle is embodied in a phrase coined by the FBI and popularized in Chester Gould's *Dick Tracy*: Crime doesn't pay. That was certainly the case in *Little Caesar* (1931), the box-office smash that made Edward G. Robinson a major star. His character Rico is a case study in hubris; Rico's rags-to-riches rise leads to an equally dramatic fall and violent death.

Americans devoured crime pictures in 1930–31. Titles such as *The Big House, The Criminal Code, The Doorway to Hell, Outside the Law, The Pay-Off* and *The*

Woman Racket suggest the nature of films available to audiences. *The Public Enemy* (1931) established James Cagney as a tough guy in the Robinson vein, and *Smart Money* (1931) paired them in the same movie for the only time in their careers.

Monkey Business is a parody of crime movies. Alky Briggs' swagger, his bullying of his wife Lucille, and lines that sound as if he swallowed a cliché dictionary are lampoons of tough-guy screen imagery and speech. Though Briggs was probably a composite, his rough manners evoke Al Capone. Writers Perelman and Johnstone also had a specific villain in mind for Joe Helton: Arthur Rothstein, who ran New York City's Jewish mob. He is best remembered for fixing the 1919 World Series, the infamous "Black Sox" series in which the heavily favored Chicago White Sox lost to the Cincinnati Reds. Rothstein is presented more as a savvy businessman than a wise guy. Looks were deceiving; he died at the hand of an unidentified assassin in what almost certainly was a mob hit. This was also the fate of his bodyguard, the dapper Jack "Legs" Diamond, an enforcer for mob figures before and after his association with Rothstein.[32]

Whether smooth or crude, real-life organized crime figures shared the view that irreconcilable disputes were best settled by bloodshed. This is why the idea of Helton and Briggs hiring bodyguards was not far-fetched.[33] The absurdity lies in hiring the Marxes as muscle or putting up with their guff. Groucho, for instance, is caught flirting with Lucille by Briggs. Instead of fleeing, Groucho expresses outrage and ducks into Lucille's closet. After an exchange of non sequiturs, Briggs promises, "I'm going to lay you out pretty" because he's "wise" to the situation. Don't try to match wits with Groucho! "You're wise? What's the capital of Nebraska? What's the capital of the Chase National Bank? Give up?" A frustrated Briggs pulls out a gun and sputters, "Do you see this gat?" Groucho parries, "Cute, isn't it? Did Santy Claus bring it for Christmas? I got a fire engine." Briggs knows when he's beat but decides, "I can use a guy with your nerve."

Before you can say, "You're coming with me," Groucho and Zeppo have guns in their hands and are ordered to accompany Briggs to "have it out" with Joe Helton. The guns barely make it to the door before they are unceremoniously dumped into a soapy bucket. Briggs' plan to browbeat Helton goes awry when Joe calls him a "small-time chiseler" and tells him to "scram." Just as Briggs is about to pull his gun on Joe, Harpo emerges from behind Alky with the stick end of one of his horns extended like a rifle. Briggs concludes that Helton has his "gang" with him, vows to get even later, and exits. Both Harpo and Chico are hired as *Joe's* bodyguards. They are about as useful as Groucho and Zeppo.

Shortly thereafter, Groucho approaches Helton with an offer to switch sides and be Joe's bodyguard—sort of. He explains:

> If I show you how to save 20 percent, would you be interested? Of course, you would. First, your overhead is too high and your brow is too low. Interested already, aren't you? ... Two fellows are trying to attack you ... and two fellows are trying to defend you. Now, that's 50 percent waste. Why can't you be attacked by your bodyguards? Your life will be saved, and that's a hundred percent waste.... [H]ave me, I'll attack you for nothing.

He concludes his pitch by sharing his credentials as a man who "worked his way up from nothing to a state of extreme poverty." His "protection" plan is simple: "[L]et me know when you want to be attacked and I'll be there ten minutes later to defend you." By then, the retired mobster is just as befuddled as Briggs.

Groucho takes at a swipe at another symbol of hypermasculinity: cowboys. How do cowboys factor into a plot about gangsters? Like most Marxist mayhem, the gag comes in through the back door.

After the ship has docked, Helton throws a party for Mary at his estate and Groucho is among the guests. Helton spots him and encourages him to have a good time. Groucho cracks, "Is this a party? The beer is warm, the women are cold, and I'm hot under the collar." Helton can only shake his head: "You're a funny kind of a duck but I like you. You stuck by me, and I'll stick by you." Groucho replies in an exaggerated Western drawl, "Sheriff, I ain't much on flowery sentiments, but there's something I just got to tell you. Shucks, man, I'd be nothing but a poisonous varmint and not fit to touch the hem of your pants if I didn't tell you you've treated me square, mighty square.... And I ain't forgetting. Sheriff, I ain't forgetting." With that he swipes a ten-gallon hat from a costumed guest, imitates a horse and waddles off with a cowboy's bow-legged gait. Helton and his guests laugh.

This is another Marxian poke at recent Hollywood fare. Like crime films, Westerns enjoyed great popularity. The years 1930 and 1931 saw the release of *The Arizona Kid*, *The Big Trail*, *Billy the Kid*, *The Texan* and *Under a Texan Moon*, the last of which co-starred Raquel Torres, who would soon find herself in a Marx Brothers film. Westerns were so popular that such famed directors as Michael Curtiz, Cecil B. DeMille, John Ford, King Vidor and Raoul Walsh saddled up, as it were. "Cowboy" stars emerged, including Hoot Gibson, Gabby Hayes, Buck Jones and John Wayne, but Westerns also enlisted A-list celebrities such as Mary Astor, Gary Cooper and Lupe Vélez.[34] In 1931, *Cimarron* carried off the Best Picture Oscar, the only Western to do so until *Dances with Wolves* (1990) and *Unforgiven* (1992). As Wes D. Gehring observed, "Consequently, western parody was ... very timely in 1931."[35]

Return of the Nightingales?

As previously mentioned, Minnie Marx hustled young Julius and Milton onto a vaudeville stage in a singing trio called the Nightingales. Move the clock forward to *Monkey Business*. A different kind of nightingale comes into play as the four stowaways try to sneak off the boat. They decide to steal a passport, though how all four of them intend to use just one is not explained. But that's the least of their worries; the name on the pilfered passport is Maurice Chevalier.

Chevalier was a friend of the Marxes; they met him during their ill-fated 1922 London tour. When the Marxes and Chevalier were on Broadway, Chevalier invited them onto the stage during one of his shows. They did not forget his kindness, and began to do Chevalier imitations in their act.

Chevalier's fame was as improbable as that of the Marx Brothers. He was born into a poor French family and, like the Marxes, had little formal education. He took to the stage at an early age—as an acrobat. That path was short-circuited by an injury that turned him toward the Paris café scene, though mainly he basked in the renown of his older lover, Mistinguett, a Folies Bergère musical star.

Chevalier was a prisoner of war during World War I and learned English from a British POW during confinement. After his release, he became a cabaret singer. To compensate for a so-so voice, he created a character to enhance his charm. He performed in a costume that included a bow tie, tuxedo or double-breasted jacket, straw boater and thin cane. To these he added witty repartee and oodles of urbane sophistication. Chevalier arrived in Hollywood in 1928, just in time for talkies. The next year he made an English-language musical, *Innocents in Paris,* and, in 1930, *The Big Pond.* In the latter he crooned "You Brought a New Kind of Love to Me," which became a signature song.[36] It contained the lines, "If a nightingale could sing like you / They'd sing much brighter than they do."

How does any Marx Brother hope to get off a ship using Maurice Chevalier's passport when none of them looks like him? By doing a Chevalier imitation, of course! Zeppo is first up and manages to sing "If a nightingale could sing like you…" before being told to go to the back of the line. Zeppo actually faked some of Chevalier's mannerisms pretty well, but if he couldn't get through the passport line, there's no way Groucho's New York accent or Chico's faux Italian will pass muster.

Enter Harpo, who sounds just like Chevalier, courtesy of a windup phonograph tied to his back. If only it hadn't wound down at exactly the wrong moment! But Harpo doesn't go quietly to the end of the line. Instead, he goes on a wilding spree in which he tosses anything not nailed down into the air, runs across a table, and rubber stamps the heads of flustered customs agents. All of this was a supercharged reworking of the agent scene from *I'll Say She Is.*

In the end, the Marx Brothers exit the ship by creating a diversion. When a panicked man faints, the call goes out for a medic, and "Doctor" Groucho appears to exclaim, "I can't do anything for this man. He's fainted. What he needs is an ocean voyage. In the meantime, get him off this boat and have his luggage examined." A gurney is summoned and carried down the gangway. The Marx Brothers emerge from under a blanket and run ashore.

There's My Argument: Restrict Immigration

To return briefly to Groucho and Chico in the captain's office: After several mangled-English puns from Chico, Groucho replies, "There's my argument. Restrict immigration." In Chapter Two, we saw how Jews were the targets of discrimination that included efforts to restrict their immigration into the U.S. The Immigration Act of 1924 also sought to curtail Roman Catholic and Southern European entry into the U.S.

Groucho's remark was aimed at the Italian character that Chico played. More than four million Italians immigrated to the U.S. between 1880 and 1920, but the Immigration Act of 1924 reduced their number to no more than 4,000 per year via a convoluted formula that limited the total number of immigrants from any one country to two percent of the total number that entered in 1890. It appeared fair without actually being so. As those who drafted the bill knew, the bulk of Eastern and Southern immigration took place *after* 1890.

During the first Red Scare, Italian immigrants were among the groups suspected of anarchism and criminality. Some of this was factually based, though the vast majority of those of Italian heritage were law-abiding. Alas, the Sacco and Vanzetti arrest (1920), trial, conviction (1921) and execution (1927) fanned perceptions that Italians were criminals, as did the presence of Italian-heritage mobsters during Prohibition.

Italians also suffered discrimination as Mediterranean peoples. The adjective "swarthy" was used as a code word to suggest they were not "white," a particular burden for darker-skinned Neapolitan and Sicilian Italians. They were much more likely than lighter-skinned northern Italians to be slurred as "dagos," a term thought to be a vulgarization of Diego, a common first name in Spain and Portugal. It was used to slander Mediterranean peoples broadly, though by the 20th century it was mostly brandished against Italians.

This is another example of how the American concept of race operates in arbitrary ways. The same scientific racism theories discussed in Chapter Three were applied to virtually anyone on the fringes of American society, including recent immigrants. A distressing tendency thrust newer immigrant groups to the bottom of the social-acceptance ladder. Eastern and Southern Europeans had the misfortune of being in that role when war, restriction laws and prolonged recession temporarily ended mass immigration. It would take Italians longer to be viewed as "Americans."

Work patterns complicated matters. The 1885 Alien Contract Labor Law cited Italians as "ignorant [and] brutal."[37] Coming just three years after the Chinese Exclusion Act, it was rooted in a similar fear. Contract labor frequently entailed gang hiring practices contrary to individual employment practices in the U.S. A labor contractor was paid a fee to recruit workers to immigrate to America. Their wages were stipulated in the contract and frequently undercut the prevailing rates paid to other workers. In addition, contract workers were often recruited as strike-breakers or rate-busters. The two most notorious contract workers were said to be Chinese "coolies" and those coming from Italy through *padrones* (bosses). In each case, myth outstripped truth, but each had just enough attached fact to lend credence.

Groucho's "Restrict immigration" line in *Monkey Business* was actually a holdover quip from *I'll Say She Is*. That show was written before the 1924 Immigration Act, which makes the Marxes guilty of recycling rather than insulting Italians, though some 1931 movie audiences might have read that into it. To offer some defense of the joke, Chico is a lovable doofus.

And Now a Word from Our Sponsor: Zeppo Gets the Girl

Stop the presses: In *Monkey Business*, Zeppo gets something to do![38] Groucho spends time pursuing Lucille, but Zeppo is the successful lover. He even gets to be funny. While strolling the deck arm in arm with Mary, Zeppo remarks, "You know, there's mighty pretty country around here." It's not the greatest pick-up line considering they are in the middle of the ocean, but it worked. Later he pledges to stay by her side, only to break into a full sprint when he's recognized as one of the stowaways. But he eventually honors his pledge: "Mary, I'll never leave you."

Of course, Zeppo isn't in the film to steal comedy scenes from his brothers. He is, after all, wearing a suit and tie the first time we see him. Who dresses like that when hiding in a herring barrel? Some have speculated that Zeppo played the romantic lead in *Monkey Business* to save production costs. That's feasible; neither Oscar Shaw in *The Cocoanuts* nor Hal Thompson in *Animal Crackers* was particularly memorable or romantic. As a seasoned performer, Zeppo was a logical alternative. Wes D. Gehring notes that *Monkey Business* also spoofed romance movies, though his remarks are aimed more at Groucho's pursuit of Lucille.[39] Nonetheless, Zeppo is a suave suitor.

The less said of his pugilistic skills, however, the better. Mary is kidnapped by Helton's gang and held hostage in a barn. The sequences that follow, especially the battle to save Mary, are so woodenly acted that Adamson complained they appeared an afterthought and were more suitable for the stage.[40] He has a point—Constantine Romanoff is out of his depth as Butch, Helton's henchman[41]—but the film's climactic sequence nonetheless provided additional opportunities for zaniness, puns and social observations.

In the spirit of lampooning romance movies, Chico delivers a real groaner. The lads are casing the barn in which Mary is being held under the ruse of having a "picnic." Butch orders Chico to get out of the loft, which sets up his pun, "It's better to have loft and lost than never to have loft at all." Groucho also tortures the English language with a pun so bad that he acknowledges it. During the slugfest between Zeppo and Briggs, Groucho turns to a stabled cow and remarks, "You're a mother, you understand. How would you like to have somebody steal one of your heifers? I know, heifer cow is better than none, but this is no time for puns."

The barn serves two plot purposes. First, Zeppo saves Mary by beating up Briggs. Don't expect realistic fisticuffs. There is nothing remotely convincing about what could be labeled the battle of the haystack. Zeppo's final haymaker sends Helton into a beer vat, as Harpo happily swims in an adjacent one. The beer barrels are backdoor references to the illegal alcohol trade carried on by Prohibition-era thugs like Helton, and his pummeling at the hands of Zeppo is an emasculating insult to his pretensions of toughness.

The punch-up also allows Groucho to make timely jokes about radio. What television was to the 1950s and the Internet to the late 20th and early 21st centuries, so was radio to the 1920s and 1930s. Think of it as a communications system that went viral. Wireless telegraphy had been in development since the late 19th century, but audio signals were not available until 1916, and there was no commercial broadcast station until Pittsburgh's KDKA in 1920. Humble beginnings set the stage for what has been called the first "mass audience" radio broadcast, heavyweight boxer Jack Dempsey's July 2, 1921, title defense against French challenger Georges Carpentier, allegedly heard by hundreds of thousands of listeners.[42] The next month, baseball made its radio debut.

By 1922, radio was all the rage, with radio sales topping $60 million and more than 200 radio stations on the air. In 1929, sales soared to over $842.5 million, a whopping 1400 percent increase in just seven years.[43] Sports were a staple of radio broadcasts; boxing and baseball led the way, but college football, horse racing, tennis and even golf also found audiences. The number of radio stations tripled between 1922 and 1929, and by decade's end, an estimated 60 percent of all households owned a radio set. The stock price of Radio Corporation of America (RCA) was among those investors carefully watched during the decade.

As the data suggest, the 1920s saw radio move from the domain of hobbyists and electronics wizards to a commercial juggernaut supported by advertising dollars. Radio and movies played major roles in what Michael Parrish called a "triumph of consumer culture [that] continued its conquest of America even in the face of massive unemployment and grinding poverty" during the Great Depression. With it came "standardized tastes, habits and values."[44]

Radio signals were the first thing Americans brought into their homes that did not have to be carried there physically, and it gave Americans a shared culture. A listener in Iowa could hear of a Babe Ruth homerun simultaneously with fans at New York's Yankee Stadium, or revel in the same breaking news of Charles Lindbergh's successful solo flight across the Atlantic.

Groucho's "broadcast" of the Zeppo-Helton skirmish—itself a parody of boxing broadcasts—came with this interruption: "This program comes to you courtesy of the Golden Goose Furniture Company.... Look for our advertisement in today's ash can." With this small quip, Groucho focuses attention to three salient aspects of radio: its commonality, its fixation on sports, and the centrality of advertising in promoting a culture that was inherently capitalist.

While holding a lantern as a fake microphone, Groucho peppers his fight call with clichés like those in modern sports broadcasts. "Here we are again at the ringside, and it looks like a great battle.... What a grudge fight.... Ending of the first inning. No runs, no errors, but plenty of hits.... Oh! That one hurt.... Oh, mama, if I only had my youth again.... And the crowd hurrahs." With Helton vanquished, Zeppo gets the girl.

Monkey Business was originally intended for radio. That didn't happen, but a line from the film portends what did. When Groucho first hides in Lucille's closet, he eventually emerges and plops down on her bed. The two parry a bit before Lucille hurls the barbed remark, "I didn't know you were a lawyer. You're awfully shy for a lawyer." Groucho comes back with, "You bet I'm shy. I'm a shyster lawyer." (Shyster is a slang term for a crooked individual, especially one in business or the law.) In 1932, the Marx Brothers hosted a radio program titled *Flywheel, Shyster and Flywheel.* Twenty-six episodes were broadcast in 1932–33, with Groucho and Chico heading a dodgy law firm. It was cancelled before Harpo or Zeppo appeared, but it earned the brothers $6,500 a week while in production.[45] More importantly, it was a vehicle for both past and new material, much of which made its way into subsequent movies.

Romance, Dance, and Where's Maggie?

Margaret Dumont is missing from *Monkey Business.* Rumors persist as to why the "fifth Marx Brother" didn't show up again until their fifth film, *Duck Soup.* One held that Groucho didn't want her in the film because she lacked sex appeal.[46] That's feasible, as Thelma Todd vamped in ways that would have stretched credulity for Dumont. It does not, however, explain why there was no other role for her.

Another bit of scuttlebutt is that Dumont was the victim of one too many practical jokes and wanted a break from such antics.[47] This too sounds reasonable, but how do we explain that Dumont returned just two years later and went on to make five more films with the Marxes? Dumont actually appeared in more Marx Brothers films than Zeppo.

It is easy to forget that Dumont was *not* just "the fifth Marx Brother." She made two movies before she met the Marxes and 32 more after 1939, the year of her last appearance in a Marx Brothers film. In all likelihood, she simply wasn't available for

Money Business. She landed a role in *The Girl Habit*, which debuted on June 27, 1931. *Monkey Business* was not released until September 19, but script rewrites and early filming would have overlapped with Dumont's production and post-release publicity duties.

Whatever the reason, Groucho and Todd have wonderful screen chemistry. Whereas Dumont is a foil for Groucho, Todd is a sparring partner. She tells off Alky and reminds him, "I'm young. I want gaiety, laughter, I want to ha-cha-cha." Later she scolds, "Now listen to me, Mr. Alky Briggs. You can't keep me cooped up like this." If she can tell off a gangster, she's more than a match for Groucho. It is she, in slinky satins and plunging necklines, who initiates flirtation as a way of getting back at Briggs. "Come here, brown eyes," she says before telling Groucho of what a bad "egg" her husband is and enticing Groucho to play a "ha-cha-cha" melody on a handy guitar. "From the time he got the marriage license, I've led a dog's life," says she. When Groucho quips, "Are you sure he didn't get a dog license?" she reiterates, "Alky can't make a fool of me."

Groucho is more than intrigued: "Madam, before I get through with you, you will have a clear case for divorce and so will my wife. The first thing to do is arrange for a settlement. You take the children; your husband takes the house. Junior burns the house, you take the insurance, and I take you." All of this precedes Groucho's encounter with Alky. He briefly serves as Alky's bodyguard, but it's Lucille's body that's on his mind. We later see him crawling on all fours along a banister rail meowing for Lucille. She complains anew of Alky's philandering, which prompts Groucho's well-delivered lines: "Why can't we break away from all this, just you and I, and lodge with my fleas in the hills? I mean, flee to my lodge in the hills.... Don't be afraid. You can join this lodge for a few pennies. You won't even have to take a physical examination, unless you insist on one." Lucille shoots back, "Why, I think I'd almost marry you to spite that double-crossing crook." Groucho is taken aback, but not for long! "Why, Mrs. Briggs. I've known and respected your husband Alky for many years ... and what's good enough for him is good enough for me."

As usual, Groucho's advances come to naught. In *Monkey Business,* he is indeed like a tomcat on the make. We see him doing a cheek-to-cheek rumba and later flustering Madame Swempski, a famous opera star, by pretending to be an interviewer. When photographers close in to take her photograph, he horns in and remarks, "Here's a little sex stuff for your front page.... You can say it was a real love match. We married for money." She calls him "an impudent cad," and he responds with questions that prove it. Finally, she blurts out, "I don't like this innuendo" and he volleys back with a now-classic pun: "That's what I always say, love flies out the door when money comes innuendo."

At Helton's party, Groucho flirts with every woman in sight, including a married woman already in the process of jilting her husband. He also sidles up to a complete stranger and says, "How about you and I passing out on the veranda, or would you rather pass out here?" She responds, "Sir, you have the advantage of me." He lifts an eyebrow and replies, "Not yet, but wait until I get you outside." Back inside, he dons a beanie and is surrounded by four lovely women. He tells them, "No, you're wrong, girls.... In the first place, Gary Cooper is much taller than I am."[48]

There is so much innuendo in *Monkey Business* that Groucho seems obsessed with sex. He pokes fun at his own lasciviousness when he confounds Alky with the question, "Do you think that girls think less of a boy if he lets himself be kissed? Don't you think that although girls go out with boys like me, they always marry the other kind?" Groucho had recently published *Beds* which, like Groucho's suggestive remarks, is more smoke than fire. At just 71 pages, it's really an extended pamphlet. Its title and first chapter are the only things remotely salacious about it. The title is a playful come-on, as it's about what people do in bed that isn't sex. The first chapter, on the advantages of sleeping alone, is completely blank![49]

Elephant in the Room I: Marxist Lechery

Actors are not the people they portray in movies, but some Marx Brothers routines fare poorly in post–Harvey Weinstein Hollywood. Their vaudeville days were filled with casual sex of the love-'em-and-leave-'em variety. Chico was a serial womanizer and only Harpo avoided marriage-ending infidelities. Chico divorced once, Zeppo twice, and Groucho thrice. Interviewer Charlotte Chandler asked Groucho if he deserved his reputation for lechery; he replied, "Not any more. But certainly 15 years ago, maybe a little longer.... I tried to get women into my bed," and he claimed to have been successful about half the time. Chico was another matter: "The girls were crazy about him.... We all had girls, but Chico was the one who really had something for the girls." Everything except respect.[50]

Different gender expectations and social mores prevailed. There was no whiff of coerced sex attached to any of the Marxes. They certainly took advantage of cultural norms that today would be labeled sexist, but were then accepted practice.

The blonde-chasing Harpo was the one who respected women the most. In 1936, he married former Ziegfeld actress Susan Fleming after a four-year courtship and three rejections on her part. In his autobiography, he was candid about their courtship in a chapter he titled "Cherchez la Fleming." It is followed by one called "Most Normal Man in Hollywood." When Harpo died in 1964, Fleming composed a poem for her late husband. It reads in part,

> I sing a song of joyous praise
> Of one who labored in the garden of laughter.
> A quiet man who sensed the absurd
> In all he saw and all he heard....[51]

Elephant in the Room II: Native Americans

There are three moments in the film that today would be considered unflattering to Native Americans, a subject to which I will return in Chapter Eleven. Two of them occur at Mary Helton's party. Some of the guests are in costume, though Joe, Mary, Zeppo and most of those attending are dressed in formal evening wear. The costumes are probably there to provide convenient props, such as the ten-gallon hat Groucho appropriates. Several people are wearing Great Plains–style Native headdresses. Today, such appropriations of Native American culture are considered gauche, even racist. What has been dubbed "dressing in feathers" is often viewed as comparable to Caucasians in blackface.[52]

Groucho's flirtation raises the ire of a woman's husband. As he makes his objections known, he wields a menacing tomahawk. Groucho cracks, "If you don't like this country, go back to where you came from," and the enraged husband looks at his weapon and scowls, "I should sink that right into your scalp." Groucho responds by yelling, "Run for your life! The Indians are coming!" For good measure he pulls off another man's toupee, hands it to him and says, "Put your scalp in your pocket." Groucho then whoops around the room in a mock war dance.

The final evocation of Native Americans takes place in the barn before the Zeppo-Briggs fight. Groucho and Chico ignore Butch's command to get out of the barn; they plop down in a hay mound with a basket as if they are about to have lunch. Groucho remarks, "Gosh, the picnic is off, we haven't any red ants." Chico replies, "I know an Indian who's got a couple of red aunts."

Very few non–Natives would have been offended by any of this. It had been just seven years since Congress passed the Indian Citizenship Act of 1924, which granted Natives the same legal protections as other Americans, though there remained a large gap between legal and social equality. It didn't help that Native Americans were disproportionately poor, or that some were loath to abandon traditional lifestyles or view themselves as part of the United States.[53] Even tribes that accumulated wealth, most notably the Osages in Oklahoma, were cheated out of oil revenues by unscrupulous whites who resorted to legal trickery if possible, and murder when considered necessary.[54]

As we shall see later, large obstacles remained before Native American culture was deemed worth saving, or voting rights legally protected. In 1931, the illogic of Manifest Destiny lingered, and Indians continued to be viewed as "savages" who stood in the way of "civilization," a term that almost always meant white values, culture and skins. What we see in movies may shock, but like sexism, animus toward Native Americans was a dominant value in 1931.[55] History, like comedy, is often cruel.

Banana Peels

These "banana peels" are things that would be easy to slip past a viewer.

- **Just one of the boys:** *Monkey Business* is the only Marx Brothers film in which Groucho does not hold a position of authority. He is merely a stowaway.
- **Frenchie as an extra:** Samuel "Frenchie" Marx, father of the Marx Brothers, was an extra in the picture. Those with eagle eyes can glimpse him twice. In an absurdist twist, he is seen both on the ship and greeting the ship on shore. He is easiest to spot sitting atop the luggage on the pier as his sons cast off the gurney blanket. Frenchie was paid the industry standard of $12.50 per diem for his two days on the set.
- **Harpo and Caruso?** Harpo's solo has a surreal setup: Disguised as the rear bustle of a woman's gown, he displaces a female harper. A female opera vocalist warbles "'O Sole Mio," a well-traveled love song often sung in Neapolitan dialect; the Marxes probably first encountered it in a recording from celebrated Italian tenor Enrico Caruso. In Harpo's scene, he tries to play along with the singer, but her piercing tones drive him to goofy antics such as scratching himself with a fake hand and covering his head with his coat until

the song is over. Chico tells him to play something else and hums a tune we know very well: "I'm Daffy Over You"—but soon you won't recognize it from Harpo's sensitive treatment.

- **Hello, Dali:** Speaking of surrealist touches, Harpo's antics gained him a following among the avant-garde. One of his admirers was surrealist painter Salvador Dali. The two became friends and correspondents after meeting in Paris in 1936. Dali made Harpo a namesake (and unplayable) instrument strung with barbed wire. He also drew several surrealist sketches of the Marxes and proposed a movie whose tentative title was *Giraffes on Horseback Salad*. It was never made.[56]

- **A joke that doesn't work:** Austrian-born director-actor Erich von Stroheim was another darling of European surrealists. His 1924 film *Greed* is considered a silent-era masterpiece, though his most popular was *The Merry Widow* (1925). It was a romantic drama of a nobleman in love with a dancer whom his uncle, the king, has forbidden him to marry. Instead, she marries an elderly baron, who soon dies. The prince woos her anew. This provided what is surely one of the most oblique references in any Marx Brothers film. When Groucho finishes meowing to attract Lucille, he proclaims, "Come, *Kapelmeister* [choir master]. Let the violas throb. My regiment leaves at dawn." S.J. Perelman intended to parody the affected weightiness of von Stroheim's movies. Groucho disliked the line and felt it too obscure. He was right!

- **Yonkers:** Outside of Helton's party, the woman wants Groucho to understand how unhappy she has been in her marriage: "Four years of neglect, four years of battling, four years of heartbreaks." By Groucho's reckoning, "That makes 12 years. You must have been married in rompers." His reference to a toddler's one-piece outfit is intended as a pun on the Westchester County city of Yonkers, New York. Hands up if you got that. I didn't think so!

FIVE

Horse Feathers (1932)

College hijinks, Prohibition scofflaws and the craziest football game you've ever seen. What's not to like?

Groucho is Professor Quincy Adams Wagstaff, new president of Huxley College, which hasn't won a football game since 1888. Zeppo is Frank Wagstaff, Wagstaff's son. He has been a Huxley student for 12 years and still hasn't graduated—perhaps because he's been paying more attention to Connie Bailey (Thelma Todd) than to his studies. Something has to change, and you can bet that Wagstaff will shake things up, though not in any ordinary fashion. He makes it clear that the stuffed shirts known as the faculty are part of the problem. Winning a football game is somehow vital to Huxley's vitality.

Forget anything that has the remotest relationship to sportsmanship. Gridiron success entails having good players, and where else would you find them but in a speakeasy, an illegal bar selling alcohol to Prohibition scofflaws? That's where we meet Baravelli (Chico), an ice delivery man and bootlegger. It's also where Pinky (Harpo) wreaks havoc. Wagstaff goes to the speakeasy in hopes of securing the paid services of two ringers but he gets his signals crossed and ends up with Baravelli and Pinky.

Before this madcap farce concludes, we are treated to failed seductions, a plot to steal Huxley's football signals, crooked gamblers, kidnappers and a wild gridiron match. Any resemblance between college football and the Huxley vs. Darwin College grudge match is purely coincidental.

The Marx Brothers Defeat Paramount

Before any of this unfolded, the Marx Brothers battled Paramount. Place your bets on the Marxes. By the time *Monkey Business* was released, the Great Depression had begun to take its toll on the movie industry.[1] Paramount made an $18 million profit in 1930, but lost it all in 1931.[2] As Hector Arce observed, overall movie revenues were down by 40 percent and Paramount would have been in even worse shape if not for the success of *Monkey Business*. Suddenly even what was left of vaudeville was interested in the Marx Brothers; RKO offered them $10,500 a week for a one-month tour.[3] That offer nearly led the Marxes back to New York to film *Horse Feathers* in Paramount's Astoria Studios, though it's unclear if that was serious contemplation or a bargaining chip.[4]

Paramount and the Marxes were feuding like Joe Helton and Alky Briggs.

Paramount wanted to renegotiate the $200,000 per picture deal it signed with them during better times. It was not to be. The Marx Brothers had Paramount over a monkey barrel. If Paramount broke their contract unilaterally, it would surely have lost both the lawsuit and the services of one of its few successful franchises. Any studio would have been happy to sign the Marx Brothers, and Paramount would have faced the grim prospect of paying them a settlement to make money for someone else.[5] As it was, Paramount was forced into receivership at the end of 1932.[6]

But wasn't all rosy for the Marxes. As Maxine Marx noted, "Paramount couldn't afford to give them a year off."[7] Groucho's son added that it was a "struggle to make a picture a year in Hollywood.... By the time the Marx Brothers finished making *Monkey Business* and *Horse Feathers* ... Groucho was beginning to realize that making movies wasn't the soft racket that he imagined it would be."[8] Add filmmaking to radio ventures, interviews, personal appearances and stage work, and it's easy to imagine the grind.

The Marxes could force Paramount to honor their contract, but they had little control over how Hollywood made movies. *Horse Feathers* was a wonderful romp but for various reasons it was not a pleasant film to make. Adamson notes that moviemaking in the 1930s "was the realm of the producer, and (once in a while) the star, and (almost never) the director. The producer dictated policy, made crucial time and money decisions, and supervised the aggregation of contributions into the amalgamation of a movie."[9] Producers generally steered toward homogeneity and repetition, phenomena that many modern moviegoers lament.

The Marxes, especially Groucho, argued that the *Horse Feathers* script didn't lend itself to piano and harp interludes and the final cut suggests that was correct. By 1932, though, these were viewed as being indispensable, hence they were crammed in. No wonder Groucho "had little respect for some of the producers and front office executives" and railed against directors, "who had to shoot simple scenes over and over again."[10] Paramount could have saved money by reducing the number of takes; it's not as if the Marxes were subject to direction in the first place.

The *Monkey Business* team reassembled for *Horse Feathers*. Herman Mankiewicz produced it and Norman McLeod had the dubious honor of being the first to direct two Marx Brothers films. Once again, S.J. Perelman and Will Johnstone wrote the script with assistance from Arthur Sheekman, and Bert Kalmar and Harry Ruby supplied the music and lyrics. *Horse Feathers* hit the cinemas on August 19, 1932, by which time McLeod was done with the Marxes and Perelman was ready to move on.[11] More substantively, the first seeds were cast for what turned into mutual loathing between the Marxes and Mankiewicz.

Horse Feathers is an apt title: It was used as a reaction to someone trying to pass off something dubious as true. Today we might respond to such an attempt with something along the lines of "Give me a break" or "Rubbish." In 1932, the phrase "horse feathers" was relatively new. The *Oxford English Dictionary* credits American comic strip cartoonist William DeBeck with coining the phrase in 1928. He was the influential artist who created *Barney Google*, the third-longest-running strip in cartoon history.

There are five major ways in which *Horse Feathers* captures the Zeitgeist of the 1930s: its lampoons of college football and of college life generally, its reflections on the Great Depression and Prohibition, its sharp take on crime, and its insights into gender relations.

Whatever It Is, I'm Against It

Anyone who has spent much time at a college—as a student, staff member, academic or visitor—will savor the hysterical takedown of academia in *Horse Feathers*. Huxley College's president addresses the faculty upon the occasion of stepping down after just one year on the job, the tenure of every Huxley president since 1888. His last task is to introduce his successor, Professor Wagstaff. Pan right and witness Groucho shaving in the corner, our first clue that Wagstaff is about to make life uncomfortable for the faculty. Not only is he irreverent, he's the only clean-shaven man on a stage filled with bearded or profusely whiskered peers.

Wagstaff pulls up his suspenders, dons his jacket and strides to the podium. When the outgoing president tells Wagstaff that the faculty would appreciate it if he were to throw away his cigar, Wagstaff huffs, "The faculty can keep their seats. There will be no diving for this cigar." Wagstaff's opening comment to the faculty: "I thought my razor was dull until I heard his speech." He proceeds to insult the faculty and berate the ex-president, the latter sputtering, "Professor Wagstaff, now that you've stepped into my shoes—" He can't finish his statement before Wagstaff pushes back: "Is that what I stepped in? At least you could have cleaned them."

After signaling that he intends to pay no heed to the trustees either, Wagstaff launches into a song that, I confess, used to rattle around in my brain during dull faculty meetings. "I'm Against It" includes lines such as:

> I don't know what they have to say,
>   it makes no difference anyway,
> Whatever it is, I'm against it.

Wagstaff's son Frank sings the bridge to the following song ("I Always Get My Man") and showcases a decent tenor voice in a style that was probably intended to evoke the era's most popular crooner, Bing Crosby. Wagstaff continues to humiliate the faculty. He accomplishes this through a gyrating dance, a duck waddle, a series of lap plops and beard pulls, and leading the faculty in zany chorus line maneuvers. Frank reminds his father that Huxley's line of one-year presidents corresponds with not having won a football game since 1888. Their discussion features some of Groucho's sharpest insults. Frank says, "Dad, let me congratulate me. I'm proud to be your son." That prompts the withering retort, "My boy, you took the words right out my mouth. I'm ashamed to be your father. You're a disgrace to the family name Wagstaff, if such a thing is possible." After berating Frank for spending too much time with the "college widow," he unleashes the zinger, "I married your mother because I wanted children. Imagine our disappointment when you came along."

You name them and Wagstaff skewers them: naysayers, yes men, pompous prigs, students, staff. When Wagstaff encounters two professors so obsequious they echo each other, Wagstaff informs them that Huxley can't afford both football and education so, "Start tearing down the college." They naturally ask, "But professor, where will the students sleep?" Wagstaff retorts, "Where they always sleep. In the classroom." When Wagstaff asks how much his two lackeys make, they tell him, "$5000 a year. But we've never been paid." Wagstaff counters, "Well, in that case, I'll raise you to $8000. And a bonus. Bring your dog around, and I'll give him a bonus, too."

One Marx Brothers scholar argued that the Depression meant that most faculty members were indeed as humble as Huxley yes men because they couldn't rebel in a world of pay cuts and closing colleges.[12] Actually, both enrollments and the number of accredited colleges rose slightly between 1930 and 1940. Moreover, just 2,299 individuals held a Ph.D. in 1930, with another 14,969 having a master's degree. Even had everyone with an advanced degree pursued a career in higher education, the 1,400 colleges in the U.S. would have needed to scrape to fill faculty ranks.[13] Professors, like all workers, endured wage cuts, but they were in a better position than most. Wagstaff's insults are thus aimed at professorial privilege, not vulnerability.

A particularly incisive lampoon of education takes place in the classroom. After meeting Baravelli and Pinky in a speakeasy, Wagstaff enters a biology professor's classroom with his two new pals in tow. The bearded professor (Robert Greig—*Animal Crackers'* duplicitous butler) tries to ignore antics such as Baravelli and Pinky bearing gifts of an apple and a watermelon, and sitting on the laps of young women in the front row. As Wagstaff peers into a microscope, the professor asks him what he thinks of the slide. Reply: "I think he was safe at second." The professor tries to continue his lecture on the circulatory system, but there is no way his remarks on the liver or cirrhosis will go unchallenged. Plus, he is the sort of professor who obscures basic information behind a barrage of big words. Wagstaff ripostes, "Is this stuff on the level or are you just making it up as you go along?" An outraged Greig remarks, "Everything I told you can be found in the simplest anatomy book. I'm sure my students will bear me out," Baravelli and Pinky proceed to do exactly that: They carry him out of the lecture hall.

Wagstaff takes over and delivers a fractured lesson filled with non sequiturs, puns and gags, some of which were recycled from the Marxes' stage show *Fun in Hi Skule* (1910–13). In his discussion of corpuscles, Wagstaff suddenly pivots:

> We now find ourselves among the Alps. The Alps are a very simple people living on a diet of rice and old shoes. Beyond the Alps lie more Alps, and the Lord Alps those who Alp themselves. We then come to the bloodstream. The blood rushes from the head down to the feet, gets a look at those feet and rushes back to head again. This is known as auction pinochle. Now, in studying your basic metabolism, we first listen to your hearts beat; and if your hearts beat anything other than diamonds or clubs, it's because your partner is cheating....

Matters disintegrate further. The anatomy chart disappears and is replaced by a picture of a horse, then a risqué saloon dancer. That's followed by a pea-shooter battle pitting Wagstaff against Baravelli and Pinky. What madness! What mayhem! Had my undergraduate biology class been half as much fun, I might have reconsidered my major.

Swordfish and Prohibition

In a film as irreverent as *Horse Feathers*, it shouldn't surprise that the Marxes refused to take Prohibition seriously. So many other Americans also mocked the ban on selling, buying, manufacturing and imbibing alcohol that Prohibition became a synonym for misplaced moral reform. The 18th Amendment and the 1919 Volstead Act were so spectacularly unsuccessful that they were on their way out the door by the time *Horse Feathers* was released. Franklin Roosevelt was elected president three months later and pledged to make short work of Prohibition. The 21st Amendment, which repealed the 18th, was passed by Congress in February 1933 and ratified by the states in December.[14]

Daniel Okrent writes, "In almost every respect imaginable, Prohibition was a failure."[15] This has been the judgment for so long that many Americans wonder how it happened in the first place. That decision was neither sudden nor a plot by curmudgeons bent on depriving Americans of liquid pleasure. In the decades leading up to the Civil War, far more Americans took up the cause of temperance than what now are considered more noble causes: abolitionism, women's suffrage, prison reform, workers' rights, free public education.

Temperance and prohibition are not necessarily the same thing—the first can be a form of self-control—but both had the same target: eliminating social harm associated with intoxicants. As W.J. Rorabaugh noted, by the early 19th century, America was an "alcoholic republic."[16] Note that he used the term alcoholic, not alcohol-consuming. Alcoholism was (and is) widespread, especially among men. It was/is made manifest in everything from domestic abuse and avoidable accidents to health problems and lost wages that plunge families into poverty. Long before the 18th Amendment was ratified on January 16, 1919, 28 states had experimented with "going dry," and 26 remained so before January 16, 1920, when the 18th Amendment went into effect in the remaining 22.[17] Six states remained dry even after Prohibition was repealed.[18]

Prohibition was conceived as an enlightened social reform and in its early days, an effort was made to enforce the law. It soon became apparent that there were more ways to evade the law than resources to deter scofflaws. It didn't help that a year passed between ratification of the 18th Amendment and its implementation. Wealthy individuals made sure their liquor lockers were replenished and took advantage of loopholes in the law to obtain more. Other enterprising individuals stockpiled booze in the correct belief that demand would yield great profits once existing supplies dwindled.[19]

Several other factors assured that, for every barrel of booze seized, dozens more went undetected. Other nations enacted their own prohibition laws, but these were not always concurrent with those of the United States. Canada lifted its ban in 1920 and, under its federal system, individual provinces and territories were free to regulate or not as they saw fit. By 1924, most were open for business and the rest—except for Prince Edward Island—followed suit long before the U.S. repealed Prohibition. Cross-border smuggling was especially common in northern tier states. It wasn't all that difficult, given that the boundaries were porous for those intrepid enough to fetch hidden stashes from their wooded hiding places or ply boats across watery dividing lines.[20] As for states in the South, Mexico never passed prohibition laws, nor did most Caribbean nations.

For Americans who found smuggled booze too expensive, a cheaper alternative was to make it. The fermentation process isn't that difficult; "bathtub gin," a phrase that appeared around 1920, flowed freely during Prohibition. Bathtub gin was a catch-all reference for all manner of homemade alcoholic beverages, especially those of dubious quality. If you weren't picky, beer and wine could be made at home easily enough, though special equipment was needed for distilled spirits. Some people created improvised stills, but there were plenty of underground suppliers from whom one could buy ethanol. That option came with the danger of alcohol poisoning. Unscrupulous dealers sometimes included toxins such as antifreeze, industrial alcohol or paint thinner in the mix. Those ingredients accelerated intoxication, but were deadly if not properly diluted.[21]

For the record, tales of untold thousands of Jazz Age flappers and sheiks making booze in their bathtubs are greatly exaggerated. As late as 1940, half of American households didn't even *have* a bathtub! Adulteration was more commonplace. The first time we meet Baravelli in *Horse Feathers*, he is in the back room of an illegal bar taking orders from a regular customer who wants one bottle of rye and one of Scotch. Baravelli takes out two appropriately labeled bottles and proceeds to fill them from the same jug. This is, as Eyles notes, "a satiric comment on the times," though an appropriate one.[22] Scotch, for instance, should be aged at least three years, and even that would be a very fiery drink. Most ethanol is either harsh or tasteless when first distilled, but few illicit producers or drinkers had the time or inclination to age their brews. Instead, they "improved" them by adding enhancers such as fruit juice, sugar, herbs or spices. Many added water to stretch their supply.

What was done on a small scale by individuals could be done on a massive one by organized crime. Those serving or drinking in speakeasies generally got their booze directly or indirectly from gangsters. Okrent aptly titled his chapter on their activities "Crime Pays."[23] It did, handsomely. Many of the crime figures mentioned in the previous chapter—Capone, Genovese, Kelly, Lansky, Luciano, Moran, Siegel—and scores of others grew wealthy during Prohibition. Capone reportedly accumulated as much as $100 million by 1927, a sum that would have made him a billionaire (and then some) by today's calculations.[24]

Expressed in starkest terms, mobsters had far more resources than Prohibition agents. Private yachts and speedboats filled with booze could anchor in international waters—defined as three miles from shore in the 1920s—and use lookouts to advise when it was safe to unload. Often, that wasn't necessary, as well-placed bribes led law enforcement officials to look the other way. The same was true of speakeasies; police were often on the take.

The city of Detroit provides a case study of the depth of Prohibition's failings. Its smuggling operations began as small-scale concerns outside of the control of mobsters. In 1920, the alcohol ban was aggressively enforced, but diligence soon yielded to creative ways to outwit Prohibition agents. These included the use of Belle Isle, which was perched in the Detroit River within sight of the namesake city, but located in Ontario. Rumrunners worked out a routine—aided by signalmen—in which they crossed into U.S. waters and unloaded cargo in a waterfront warehouse in less than a minute.

Hundreds on both sides of the border engaged in these operations. A story circulated of a 2000-foot pipeline that brought booze to Detroit. That may be apocryphal, but it was no less absurd than verified sightings of iceboats gliding across frozen winter waters being pursued by police officers in automobiles outfitted with tire chains. Mack Sennett's Keystone Cops of silent-film fame couldn't have appeared more ridiculous. It took until 1930 to curtail cross-border smuggling, by which time such operations weren't needed, as the city's notorious Purple Gang had taken over the task of quenching the thirsts of Detroiters through untold numbers of speakeasies.[25] It speaks volumes that Michigan was the first state to ratify the 21st Amendment.

Another measure of Prohibition's futility shows up early in *Horse Feathers*. When Frank tells his father that the services of two great football players can be purchased at the local speakeasy, Wagstaff is ready to charge out the door. Frank protests, "But you can't pick up football players in a speakeasy. It's unethical." Wagstaff replies, "It is, eh? I'll nip that in the bud. How about coming along and having a nip yourself?" Note that Wagstaff never bothers to ask how his son knows what goes on at a speakeasy, nor does either give a second thought to the ethics of such an establishment's existence in the first place.

The Marx Brothers didn't need to invent cavalier acceptance of speakeasies. By one estimate, there were as many as 100,000 of them in New York City. That number is probably inflated, but there is no question that illegal bars proliferated.[26] Whether one called them speakeasies, blind pigs, holes in the wall, barrel-houses, private clubs or blind tigers, they were places where those in the know could drink.[27] Some were lavishly furnished, some were functional, and some defined the term dive bar,[28] but getting a drink on the sly was a perverse demonstration of the economic supply-and-demand principle. Police raids periodically closed down speakeasies, but others opened to fill the void.

Prohibition is sometimes configured as either a clash between urban and rural America, or a moral struggle between modernists and traditionalists. Both views are overly simplistic. Rural drinkers lacked variety, but not opportunity. Local businesses sometimes established easy-to-disassemble bars in back rooms. Remote roadhouses sold alcohol. Mob figures set up grog shops in places where demand justified them. Illegal stills, bootleggers and moonshiners also serviced rural imbibers.

Most speakeasies tried to regulate their clientele. Passwords, secret signals and referrals were often necessary to gain entrance. The daily password provided fodder for a classic bit of Marx Brothers humor. Baravelli—I suspect his name is a pun on beer belly—is called from his task of filling telephone orders to guard the speakeasy door. None can enter unless they utter the password, "swordfish." Wagstaff raps on the speakeasy door and Baravelli informs him that he can't enter without the password. He does, however, give Wagstaff three opportunities to guess and offers a hint: "It'sa the name of a fish."

> **WAGSTAFF:** Is it Mary?
> **BARAVELLI:** ...Atsa no fish.
> **WAGSTAFF:** ...Well, she drinks like one. Let me see, is it sturgeon?
> **BARAVELLI:** Ah, you crazy. Sturgeon, he's a doctor. Cutta you open whenna you sick....
>   Now I give you one more chance.
> **WAGSTAFF:** I got it! Haddock!
> **BARAVELLI:** Atsa funny. I got a haddock too.
> **WAGSTAFF:** What do you take for a haddock?
> **BARAVELLI:** Well-a, sometimes I take-a aspirin, sometimes I take-a calomel.
> **WAGSTAFF:** Say, I'd walk a mile for a calomel.
> **BARAVELLI:** You mean chocolate calomel. I like that too, but you no guess it.... You can't
>   come in here unless you say "swordfish." Now I give you one more guess.
> **WAGSTAFF:** ... I think I got it. Is it swordfish?
> **BARAVELLI:** Atsa it. You guess it!

This routine is loaded. Wagstaff's joke about Mary drinking like a fish is a sideways reference to the drinking habits of flappers. Some women, including Mary

Louise "Texas" Guinan and Helen Morgan, even operated speakeasies of their own. The name Mary was probably coincidental in paralleling Texas Guinan's given first name, but gender was no barrier when it came to violating Prohibition laws.

Calomel sales were banned in 1948, and we should be grateful. A mercury-based concoction sold in pill or powder form, it was used to treat everything from headaches to wounds, constipation to teething pain. Wagstaff and Baravelli use it for two puns. A long-running slogan for Camel cigarettes advertised its desirability under the slogan, "I'd walk a mile for a Camel." Baravelli also twists it into a variation on caramel.

When Baravelli finally opens the door, Wagstaff pushes Baravelli aside, rushes in and slams the door. Baravelli knocks on the door and Wagstaff demands the password. Of course, Baravelli says, "Swordfish," only to be told that Wagstaff has changed it, but because he's forgotten the new password, Wagstaff joins Baravelli outside the locked door. Both wait until another client enters and crawl in behind him. Once inside, Wagstaff orders Baravelli, "Get up. That's no way to go into a speakeasy. That's how you come out."

Viewers will quickly surmise that this speakeasy is more than just a place where people drink. It has all manner of characters in it, including shady ones. This makes it a perfect venue for Harpo to run wild. Baravelli introduces Harpo's Pinky the dogcatcher as his partner, though why Baravelli, an iceman and bootlegger, has a dogcatcher partner is never explained. When a despondent man tries to bum change from Pinky with the line, "I'd like to get a cup of coffee," Pinky pulls one still steaming from his pocket and hands it to him. Harpo is so manic that Charney offers the opinion that he was "the primary comic figure among the brothers."[29] Pinky is plucky and lucky. He approaches the bar and dances a Highland fling, Baravelli's cue to tell the bartender, "He'll take a Scotch." Pinky hits the jackpot on a slot machine, again at a pay phone, and relieves a trolley conductor of the coins in his change holder. When he walks by a card game and overhears the dealer say, "Cut the cards," Pinky pulls a cleaver from his coat and slams it through the deck.

Wagstaff somehow mistakes Baravelli and Pinky for the football players that Frank intended him to hire. Before leaving, he pulls a con to avoid paying his bar tab. Wagstaff asks the bartender if he can cash a check for $15.22. The bartender counts out his change and Wagstaff rushes out the door with the promise, "As soon as I get a check, I'll send it to you."

Okrent harshly judged Prohibition:

> It encouraged criminality and institutionalized hypocrisy. It deprived the government of revenue, stripped the gears of the political system, and imposed profound limitations on individual rights. It fostered a culture of bribery, blackmail and official corruption. It also maimed and murdered, its excesses apparent in deaths by poison, by the brutality of ill-trained, improperly supervised enforcement officers, and by unfortunate proximity to gun battles.[30]

The Marx Brothers preferred satire to politics and slapstick to gunfire, but in its own inimitable way, *Horse Feathers* skewers Prohibition's flawed moral logic. Groucho recalled he was a teetotaler *before* Prohibition: "I never had a drink before January 16, 1920.... I didn't like the taste of the stuff.... But with the advent of Prohibition, I came to the conclusion that if it was illegal there must be something to it that I had never discovered."[31] Groucho never drank very much, but by 1932, he didn't need to be mirthful about Prohibition; it was a national joke.

Elephants in the Room: Women, Education and Sexism

Horse Feathers has four major settings: Huxley College, the speakeasy, a boarding house and a football stadium. A return to Huxley unveils issues of women and sexism. Wagstaff and Frank are lascivious from the start. We meet Frank with a young woman sitting on his lap and a triumphant smile on his face. Moments later, Wagstaff insults Huxley's outgoing president: "Go home to your wife. No, I'll go home to your wife. Outside of the improvement, she'll never know the difference."

Wagstaff then turns to his son. He ignores Frank's *flirtation du jour* and derides him for "fooling around with the college widow," Connie Bailey. The term "college widow" debuted around 1887, and generally has nothing to do with a deceased husband. A college widow is a young woman—though older than undergraduates—"known" to "several generations of collegians."[32] Circumstances dictated whether she was known as a mentor or in the Biblical sense of knowing. Eyles thought the latter. His take is that Connie Bailey is a "woman of rather loose morals," and there is little in Thelma Todd's dress, speech or physical carriage to suggest otherwise.[33] To use a more recent descriptor, Todd plays Bailey as a "cougar," a woman who enjoys carnal relations with younger men.

We first see her lounging in bed as Frank intercepts a tray from a servant. He enters, serves Connie her breakfast, and tells her he has been arguing with his father over her, but thinks she's "wonderful." Connie asks, "Are you making love to me?" and Frank replies, "Why not?" Given Connie's come-hither interaction with Frank, one might assume intimacy is about to occur, but that's not necessarily the case. "Making love" was used as a synonym for sexual relations, but that was not its primary meaning in 1932. An older meaning is to act in an amorous fashion, as in courting. Wooing sets up Frank's next action: singing the movie's signature song, "Ev'ryone Says I Love You." If you find the song childish and silly, know that it was a big hit for writers Kalmar and Ruby.[34]

We certainly infer that Frank and Connie had on occasion shared more than breakfast in bed. We also learn that her loose morals extend to criminality, as she is in cahoots with Jennings (David Landau), a gambler adroit at fixing sporting events. He has bet heavily on Darwin College in their upcoming game against Huxley, and Connie's job is to steal Huxley's football signals from Frank to help assure a Darwin victory. But even Jennings suspects that Bailey has acted beyond the call of duty. "I didn't ask you to fall for him," he growls.

Wagstaff doesn't know that Bailey and Jennings are using Frank, but he is intent on convincing Bailey to drop by his office to tell her to give up on Frank. He calls her to deliver that message, but his tactics change when he learns she is answering his call from her bed: "You're in bed? In that case, I'll come to your office." He arrives wearing galoshes and carrying an umbrella and makes his pitch by sitting on Bailey's lap while angling for a liaison of his own. Wagstaff's lovemaking, both rhetorical and physical, is interrupted by an endless parade of visitors dashing in and out of Bailey's apartment, including Baravelli and Pinky charging through the room with ice deliveries they toss through a window. All four Marxes try to romance Bailey, but no one sticks around long enough to get a chance. Doors open and slam from those coming in and sneaking out, as if *Horse Feathers* were a caffeinated Restoration comedy. Eventually, a suspicious Jennings bursts in to get to the bottom of the shenanigans.

Sexual inferences extend beyond scenes involving Bailey. Professor Wagstaff advises Baravelli to go to college and "get yourself a co-ed." Baravelli's puns, "I got a co-ed last week for $18, a co-ed with two pairs of pants." Wagstaff suggestively asks, "Since when has a co-ed two pairs of pants?" Baravelli replies, "Since I joined the college." Martin Gardner speculates that the two pairs of pants reference could be construed as a chastity belt, even though college women in 1932 were "more open about their sexual activities than were the coeds from the previous decade."[35]

I suspect the co-ed jokes were simply wordplay, but it's certainly the case that the script sexualizes women. As noted, Baravelli and Pinky accost young women in the biology classroom and Pinky replaces an anatomy chart with a picture of a woman that looks as if it was lifted from an 1870s Wild West saloon. When Pinky tearfully accepts blame for this action, Wagstaff points to a comely student and orders her to stay after school. When she protests that she has done nothing wrong, Wagstaff arches a painted-on eyebrow and responds, "I know, but there's no fun in keeping *him* [Pinky] after school."

We later find Professor Wagstaff lounging in the back of a boat rowed by Bailey. He strums his guitar[36] and nasally sings "Ev'ryone Says I Love You." When she finds out he has the Huxley signals in his coat, Bailey puts the moves on him in hope of picking his pocket. That plan fails when she resorts to baby talk to cajole Wagstaff into showing her the signals. She tries to grab them and is pushed into the lake.

Horse Feathers is a parody, but what was actual college life like in the 1930s? First of all, college education was rare. As late as 1940, white males averaged 8.7 years of formal education and white women 8.8 years. The numbers were much lower for people of color, just 5.4 years for men and 5.1 percent for women. As such numbers suggest, very few of America's 123 million citizens were qualified to attend, let alone graduate from, college. In 1940, a mere six percent of white males and four percent of white women obtained four-year college degrees.[37]

Horse Feathers exaggerates the number of women in the classroom for comic effect—men outnumbered women by a 6:4 ratio in the 1930s—but the existence of co-eds was indeed on the rise. Helen Horowitz notes that college women in the 19th century generally held "outsider" status unless they enrolled in women's colleges.[38] Women's colleges such as the Seven Sisters (Barnard, Bryn Mawr, Mount Holyoke, Radcliffe, Smith, Vassar and Wellesley) were more accommodating places for young women seeking higher education, but a college degree was "hardly common among women daughters [sic] of the upper middle class before 1920."[39] Horowitz adds that is proper to speak of the "upper middle class," as college education among those of lesser means was rare for either sex.

Horse Feathers does capture a moment in which increasing numbers of American women were attending colleges that had previously been entirely or overwhelmingly male. Female students were not immune to the new sexual frankness of post–World War I America. Data on sexuality are notoriously difficult to collect and this was seldom attempted until the 1930s, but anecdotal evidence suggests that at schools such as Rutgers, frank discussions of sex took place among students.[40] Similarly, sexual exploration took place, though much of it never went beyond kissing and petting.

Horse Feathers reinforces several earlier discussed points. As "sex came onto campus" in the 1920s, double standards remained firmly in place.[41] It was all well and good for young men to leer, paw and seek sexual conquests, but women needed to be more circumspect. Pregnancies generally ended a young woman's education, and "loose" women—like college widows—were held in low regard. Tellingly, a 1938 study showed that 76 percent of American women were virgins at the time of marriage, but the same was true of just 48 percent of males. Perhaps more revealing is that as late as 1947, nearly a third of female college graduates never married.[42] In *Horse Feathers* we can see the Marx Brothers as embodiments of raging male hormones and Thelma Todd that of a sexually unconventional woman.

Todd never made another Marx Brothers film. In 1935, she died at age 29. Her death remains a matter of great speculation. After she was reported missing, her body was discovered inside the garage of actress Jewel Carmen, the ex-wife of Todd's current lover, Roland West. Los Angeles detectives, the coroner and a board of inquest all declared that Todd died of suicide by carbon monoxide poisoning. Yet, the week before, Todd argued with her ex-husband Pat DiCicco, ostensibly a movie agent, though widely recognized as a member of Lucky Luciano's crime syndicate. DiCicco had a reputation for heavy drinking and explosive violence. Todd expressed a fear of mobsters, which fueled speculation that she was murdered. Did the saucy young woman who played the role of arm candy to gangsters in two Marx Brothers films become a victim of organized crime? Her death remains one of Hollywood's unsolved mysteries.[43]

Gridiron Follies

Early in the film, Wagstaff declares that Huxley College has been "neglecting football for education." That statement rings far too true in our own time. Many administrative ears burn from faculty complaints that there is always money to pump into big-time sports, but academic programs are under-funded and under-staffed. Those cries grow louder during economic downturns when campus budget offices call for reductions in spending to balance the books. Blame it on the 1920s. That's the era in which college sports became a commodity in the literal sense of the word.

Readers can probably rattle off names of colleges that are more famous for athletics than scholarship. This is the case even though football is a drain on college resources. A 2015 study indicated that just two dozen Football Bowl Subdivision programs generated profits, and in 2019, as few as 12 had athletic programs operating in the black.[44] College football and basketball have also faced charges that student athletes are not really students at all. Both are infamous for recruiting talented players who showcase their wares for professional leagues and leave school well before graduation, often a step ahead of flunking out, as many spend considerably more time in training than in the classroom. Some football programs graduate as few as 19 percent of their players.[45]

Data such as these suggest that the Marx Brothers were prescient in their take-down of college football. The problems outlined above are now a century old. Horowitz notes, "after 1920 ... larger universities, public and private, undergraduate teams, especially in football and basketball, became the training ground for professional sports."[46] Though the intent in *Horse Feathers* is to lampoon, not expose, good satire generally caricatures things familiar to audiences. Let's return to the speakeasy, which Wagstaff enters with the intention of hiring two non-students to play for Huxley. Though Wagstaff signs Baravelli and Pinky instead of intended targets Mullen and MacHardie, none of the four was college age. In 1932, Chico was 45, Harpo 44. James Pierce and Nat Pendleton, the actors playing Mullen and MacHardie, are strapping lads who at least look like football players, though Pierce was 32 and Pendleton 37. All four are "ringers," those fraudulently pretending to be eligible to play in an athletic event. That's why Wagstaff "enrolled" Baravelli and Pinky as students, though neither character is literate, let alone college material. From their speech and mannerisms, it doesn't appear as if Mullen or MacHardie are any better qualified.

As early as the mid–19th century, athletic prowess conferred status on college campuses, but the 1920s brought sports into the age of ballyhoo. Radio broadcasts increased the renown of professional athletes and even college football stars Red Grange (University of Illinois), Mike Michalske (Penn State), Bronco Nagurski (University of Minnesota) and the Four Horsemen: Jim Crowley, Elmer Layde, Don Miller and Harry Stuhldreher (Notre Dame). Radio also valorized coaches Knute Rockne (Notre Dame), Alonzo Stagg (University of Chicago) and Pop Warner (Stanford).[47]

Although schools did not, as Wagstaff suggested, tear down the college and build a stadium, the early 20th century saw numerous great and expensive stadia rise on or near college campuses: Camp Randall Stadium (Wisconsin, 1917), the Cotton Bowl (Texas, 1930), Harvard Stadium (1903), Memorial Stadium (Illinois, 1923), Notre Dame Stadium (1930), Ohio Stadium (Ohio State, 1921), the Rose Bowl (UCLA, 1922), Sanford Stadium (Georgia, 1929), the Yale Bowl (1914) and numerous others.

Hype, large crowds and public interest spelled opportunity for bettors, gamblers and fixers like Jennings. What's most remarkable is that big money could be made on a sport that was nearly abolished in 1905. College football had been around since 1869, but had become increasingly dangerous. Skills, strength and bodies developed faster than protective equipment. In *Horse Feathers*, we see numerous players being carried off the field on stretchers. That was no exaggeration; in 1905 alone, 18 young men died playing college football. President Theodore Roosevelt—hardly a shrinking violet—threatened to ban football unless dramatic changes were made to the game. Helmets and pads grew thicker and, in 1906, the organization soon to be renamed the National Collegiate Athletic Association (NCAA) drafted rule changes and safeguarded the amateur status of players. The NCAA was moderately successful in its first charge but has continually struggled with the second. Two particularly dangerous maneuvers, the flying tackle and the flying wedge, were banned. Nevertheless, seven collegians died in 1908, and at least 49 college and high school players perished in 1931.[48]

Deaths and catastrophic injuries continue to occur in scholastic football, but the popularity of the sport since the 1920s helps explain why calls to ban it were quieted. It persisted despite a 1929 Carnegie Report that savaged college football, despite educator Abraham Flexner's judgment that it was little more than "an athletic orgy ... to amuse and placate a populace."[49] Mass appeal also explains why faculty complaints over athletic department budgets fall upon deaf ears.

Horse Feathers debuted just 13 years after baseball's Black Sox scandal, but both professional and amateur sports remained tainted by suspicion that not all scores were settled on the playing field. Recruiting violations took place and "amateur" players—both stars and ringers—were sometimes paid for their performances, either directly or through dodges such as salaries for non-existent jobs.[50]

The Marx Brothers offer humorous commentary on the state of college sports in 1932. When Wagstaff learns he has hired the wrong ringers, he asks Baravelli and Pinky to kidnap them, a task for which they are even less suited than playing football. Lots of amusing dialogue ensues, including Chico's hilarious explanation of why he has a chauffeur but no car. But pipsqueaks Baravelli and Pinky have no chance against their burly targets. Our erstwhile abductors are themselves seized. They make one escape by sawing through the floor, but tumble into a room occupied by Mullen and MacHardie. This time the Darwin ringers take their clothes, lock them in a room and taunt them to listen to the game on the radio. Although Baravelli is in his union suit and Pinky his skivvies, they once again saw through the floor—what sort of kidnapper leaves saws in the room? This time they land in a roomful of shocked women. Baravelli grabs a coat, but Pinky pilfers a scarf and wraps it around his head gladiator-style. He bolts into the street and commandeers a garbage-wagon "chariot" pulled by two white horses.

Given that this film was made in Hollywood, it is tempting to think Harpo is parodying the University of Southern California Trojans. USC began playing football in 1888, and one of its grand spectacles is a male cheerleader decked out in plumed helmet, breastplate, leather leggings and a pseudo–Trojan defensive skirt (*pteruge*). He enters astride a white stallion. On occasion, USC has had its mascot arrive in a chariot of a suitably *faux* Greek style, not a garbage bucket. Sorry, but this USC football tradition was only introduced in 1961, so Harpo has no link to it.

The closest we get is that Pinky is quite fond of horses, as we see in two earlier scenes. Before we realize he is a dogcatcher, we see him plopping down to a picnic lunch that he shares with a horse. It's only fair that the horse share as well, hence Pinky nibbles on a bunch of grass, which is passed back and forth to his horse. Both ignore the honking of car horns; their lunch break takes place in the middle of traffic. Irate motorists must wait a bit longer. The camera pulls back and we notice that the horse is pulling Pinky's dogcatcher's wagon. A wayward mutt prompts Pinky to pull out a net and chase his quarry around and over waiting automobiles.

When Pinky spurs his garbage bucket into full gallop with the stolen scarf flowing behind him, he looks like Ben-Hur in underwear. That's precisely what was intended. General Lew Wallace's 1880 novel *Ben-Hur: A Tale of the Christ* was either the best- or second-best-selling novel of the 19th century[51]; literary scholars debate its ranking. But certainly *Ben-Hur* has proved irresistible for moviemakers. The first film adaptation was in 1907. It was a short, as feature films had not yet debuted in the United States.[52] MGM won raves in 1925 for its 143-minute *Ben-Hur*. It starred heartthrob Ramon Novarro and cost $3.9 million, making it *the* most expensive silent film. It would have more than recouped its cost had not MGM struck a bad deal with producer Abraham Erlanger. It would be another 25 years before MGM had a bigger box office sensation. Audiences would have instantly recognized Harpo's *Ben-Hur* spoof, especially since MGM re-released the film in 1931 with a reworked score.

Pinky and Baravelli arrive in plenty of time to play football. Adamson found similarities between the football shots in *Horse Feathers* and those of *The Freshman*, a 1925 Harold Lloyd silent.[53] He must have viewed a different version of the film than

I, as the only parallels I detected were the use of a football on an elastic band and home-team victories in each game. Actually, many of the gags were ones the Marxes rescued from *Fun in Hi Skule*, which came years before Lloyd's film.

If you think the Marxes can wreck a drawing room, wait until you see what they do to a gridiron. First, though, observe Baravelli. Players from both sides are carted off the field with bad injuries—its own commentary on why President Roosevelt wasn't crazy to entertain the idea of abolishing football—but Chico didn't need to feign his wounds. Movies are seldom shot in sequence, though the game sequences were the last to be shot in *Horse Feathers* for a reason. Chico is less present in *Horse Feathers* because an April auto accident left him with a fractured knee and ribs. For ten weeks, other scenes were shot while Chico rehabbed, but when we see him being taken *onto* the field on a stretcher, it serves both plot and necessary purposes. Watch carefully and you'll see Chico limping and moving stiffly, not exactly what a team wants from its quarterback.

You might also wonder why anyone would bother to steal Huxley's signals. Baravelli calls out each play with all the information anyone would need. For example, he announces, "Signal. Humpty Dumpty sat on a wall. Professor Wagstaff gets the ball." And why, you might ask, is the college president on the field? Wouldn't it be against the rules for him to be on the sideline chatting with people in the stands and then run onto the field to tackle a Darwin player who would otherwise score a touchdown? Any resemblance between what you see and the actual rules of football is coincidental. This includes the aforementioned ball-on-elastic trick, tackling a referee, Pinky's 80-foot warm-up jersey, playing cards in the huddle, smoking a cigar on the field, and the coup de grace that allows Huxley to win. Pinky saves the day during the game's waning moments by jumping into his makeshift chariot and crossing the goal line. He removes ball after ball from the garbage wagon and sets them down in the end zone as the scoreboard records another six points for each.

I Do (But We Wish You Hadn't)

It might have been wise to end the film right there. Instead, *Horse Feathers* concludes with a tacked-on wedding scene. We see Bailey in her bridal whites—though scarlet would have been more appropriate—with Wagstaff, Baravelli and Pinky standing beside her, each wearing a tuxedo. As the minister asks Bailey to affirm her final vow, *all* the Marxes turn their heads toward her. Her "I do" is apparently her consent to a group marriage and the Marxes tackle her and crawl over her as if the football game is still in progress.

It is a terrible ending to a funny movie and not nearly as interesting as the ones that were abandoned. One called for a victory bonfire partially fueled by Harpo shoveling books into the fire. The film would have faded with the Marxes playing cards while the college burned down in the background. Another finish had Wagstaff rush into a burning building, presumably to rescue Jennings. Instead he comes out with a diploma and hands it to Frank.[54]

Either ending would have been much better. It's not clear why they were rejected. Could it have been tense times and the rise of fascism? Perhaps, but the first book burnings in Germany did not take place until the spring of 1933. They were probably jettisoned because such black humor was out of keeping with the mirthfulness of the rest of the film. *Horse Feathers* reviews were mostly positive. It scarcely mattered as it was the box office hit Paramount so badly needed.

Horse Droppings: Miscellany

Horse Feathers has references that might be unfamiliar to some readers. Here are a few.

- **Son rise:** Early in the film, Wagstaff asks the young woman on Frank's lap "to get up so I can see the son rise." This is obvious bit of wordplay on sunrise. Less obviously, it's a backdoor reference to Ernest Hemingway's first novel, 1926's *The Sun Also Rises*. Some consider it to be his masterpiece.
- **Stick out your tongs:** When Baravelli and Pinky deliver ice to Professor Wagstaff's office, he asks, "Where are your tongs?" Baravelli and Pinky immediately thrust out their tongues. Wagstaff follows with, "Looks like a tong war." It's an amusing comeback, but references not-so-funny bloody struggles between Chinese gangs that began in the 1850s and continued into the 1920s. A tong is both a hall and a faction. Like most immigrants to America, the Chinese settled in ethnic enclaves. Tongs were set up as community centers, but some engaged in criminal activities such as prostitution, gambling, theft and the opium trade. These tongs were the Chinese equivalent of other gangster organizations, such as those run by Irish, Italians and Jews. Tongs also fought deadly gang wars, especially in West Coast cities, Chicago and New York. The tong wars ended around 1926, and most tongs today are fraternal orders, charitable organizations and benevolent associations. In 1933, though, memories of tong wars would have been fresh in people's minds.
- **Ten cents a dunce:** Wagstaff brings Baravelli and Pinky into a biology lecture and tells the lecturer, "I brought you two dunces…. Here they are, ten cents a dunce." The surface pun of dunce-dance has deeper meanings. The phrase "ten cents a dance" comes from for-hire female dance partners who worked in dance halls around the turn of the 20th century. These women, sometimes called taxi dancers, got a percentage of each dance they procured. Many had unsavory reputations. *Ten Cents a Dance* was also the name of a 1931 film starring Barbara Stanwyck.
- **Breaking the wall:** Groucho breaks the fourth wall again. When Bailey pretends to be taking singing lessons to deflect Jennings' suspicion that all the men ducking in and out of her apartment are suitors, Wagstaff remains on the couch and claims he's the plumber in case something goes wrong with Connie's "pipes." He makes a quick turn to the camera and says, "I haven't used that joke in 20 years." He does it again as Chico launches into his obligatory piano solo. This time Groucho walks toward the camera and, looking directly into it, addresses the theater audience: "I've got to stay here, but you folks can go into the lobby until it's over."
- **Lamp in the window:** A sight gag appears several times in which Wagstaff places a lamp in the window for his "wandering boy," Frank. This evokes a

mawkish song copyrighted by Henry Burr in 1903: "Where Is My Wandering Boy Tonight?"[55]

- **Fart joke:** There's a fart joke in *Horse Feathers*. It comes in the scene in which Wagstaff and Bailey are in a boat in the lake. It is set up by Wagstaff's line, "This the first time I've been in a canoe since I saw *An American Tragedy*," a 1931 film based on Theodore Dreiser's gritty 1926 novel of the same name, which involves a watery murder.[56] The passing-gas joke comes when Bailey tries to flatter Wagstaff by saying, "Professor, you're so full of whimsy." Wagstaff retorts he's always like that after eating radishes.

- **Flat bottoms and lifesavers:** When Bailey assures Wagstaff he's perfectly safe in the canoe, he replies, "I was going to get a flat bottom, but the boat girl didn't have one." Somehow, I don't think he was speaking about watercraft. When Wagstaff pushes Bailey into the lake, she asks him to throw her a lifesaver. You know what's coming, but watch the camera linger for a few seconds over the roll of Life Savers in Wagstaff's hand. Still think product placement is a new idea?

- **Zeppo robbed:** Off screen, Zeppo suffered the misfortune of being robbed twice. In August 1932, robbers stole over $37,000 worth of clothing and jewels from Zeppo and his wife Marion. In June 1933, the couple was robbed again; this time it was $30,000 worth of diamonds.[57]

- **R.I.P., "Frenchie":** The Marx Brothers lost their father Sam shortly after the film: He died on May 10, 1933.

- **Harpo abides:** To end this chapter on a light note, Harpo's famed gag of placing his leg over the outstretched arm of someone offering their hand became known as the "Harpo Handshake." A recent writer to *The New Yorker* noted it was all the rage in the offices of the *Boston Globe* during the late 1990s.[58] Harpo abides!

Six

Duck Soup (1933)

Duck Soup is my favorite Marx Brothers film. I like just about everything about it, even its silly songs. It is filled with now-classic comedy scenes, searing insults and mayhem. It flows well and doesn't pause for instrumental solos or sidetrack into tacked-on romances.

The plot is deceptively simple. The nation of Freedonia is broke, forcing officials to approach wealthy widow Gloria Teasdale (Margaret Dumont) for another loan. She won't provide it unless the prime minister resigns and Rufus Tecumseh Firefly (Groucho) is appointed in his stead. Teasdale will of course be courted by Firefly and by a rival conniver, Ambassador Trentino (Louis Calhern) from the neighboring nation of Sylvania, who would like to tap into Teasdale's fortune and annex Freedonia.

Theater poster for *Duck Soup* (Wikimedia Commons).

Chico and Harpo play Chicolini and Pinky, two Sylvanian spies of dubious loyalty. The sultry Raquel Torres is femme fatale Vera Marcal, and Edgar Kennedy is a lemonade salesman. Zeppo is Bob Roland and once again is Groucho's secretary. There's craziness and a war, all directed by Leo McCarey, the only director the Marx Brothers ever liked. The film is a tight 70 minutes.

Learning from the Opening Credits

Although history often unfolds at a snail's pace, sometimes social change is a double-time forced march. In 1933, America was again on the cusp of great change. Our first clue appears before the Marxes appear in *Duck Soup*. A logo of a stylized eagle precedes the opening credits. Though the film is in black and white, viewers of the day knew the eagle was blue. It carried a slogan, "NRA: We Do Our Part." NRA stood for the National Recovery Administration and was associated with President Franklin Delano Roosevelt, who took office on March 4, 1933.[1]

Roosevelt is often referenced by his initials, FDR, which is apt. The NRA was one of many of Roosevelt's New Deal programs identified by its abbreviation. There were so many that both supporters and critics called the New Deal an "alphabet soup."[2] FDR took office in the fourth full year of the Great Depression, and the outlook was so bleak that few observers dared predict quick economic recovery.

The NRA was officially a section of the NIRA, the National Industrial Recovery Act, which set a minimum wage, reduced work hours and established price floors on goods and services. Compliance with the NRA was voluntary, but those who did so— including movie studios—got to display the NRA blue eagle. Pressure to comply with NRA was great, as it was very popular among workers. Production increased and the NRA's minimum wage of 20 to 45 cents per hour—depending upon the job—curtailed wage cuts that would have driven workers deeper into hardship. The blue eagle came to symbolize fairness, and consumers frequently boycotted non-compliant businesses.[3]

Duck Soup also debuted when Benito Mussolini was in the eleventh year of his fascist dictatorship in Italy, Adolf Hitler was in his tenth month as chancellor of Germany, Japan was at war with China, Antonio Salazar was transforming Portugal into a repressive state, and Soviet leader Joseph Stalin was busily purging real and imagined enemies. In retrospect, 1933 seems a poor time for the Marx Brothers to release *Duck Soup*, which lampoons war. Why do so?

None of the despots mentioned above was the target of *Duck Soup*. Nor would many Americans have predicted another war in the foreseeable future. They would have viewed the Depression as the nation's enemy, not events unfolding thousands of miles away.

Though overstated in history texts, it is true that millions of Americans embraced isolationism. The Great War (1914–18), now known as World War I, had not made the world "safe for democracy," as President Wilson had promised, and postwar revelations of war profiteering further soured the public. Moreover, the bad peace treaty forged at Versailles led the U.S. Senate to reject joining the League of Nations, the centerpiece of Wilson's idealist plan to curtail international conflict. American diplomats did not withdraw from the global scene, but the politics of forging agreements were tricky. Isolationists distrusted foreign alliances and were content to let Europeans resolve their own problems. Diplomats were not highly regarded, and the Marxes lampooned them mercilessly in *Duck Soup*.

FDR is now regarded as one of the nation's greatest presidents, but few knew that would be the case in 1933. The New Deal offered hope, but would it actually benefit the nation? The 1930s were years of global unrest from which America was not immune. Whatever else the New Deal accomplished (or failed to address), it took the edge off a potentially volatile situation in which Americans on the far left and the far right flirted with radical change.[4] The Marxes' take on the turmoil of the early 1930s was that all politicians, diplomats, spies and factions were fair game for ridicule.

At Least It Wasn't Called Oo La La

The Marx Brothers appeared on the August 15, 1932, cover of *Time*, the four of them crowded into Harpo's makeshift chariot from *Horse Feathers*. At the time, they weren't certain what to do next. The radio series *Flywheel, Shyster and Flywheel* ended on May 22, 1933, after just 26 episodes. There was scuttlebutt that Marxes might perform in a Broadway revival of George Gershwin's *Of Thee I Sing*, with book by Marx collaborators George S. Kaufman and Morrie Ryskind. This came to naught. But *Duck Soup* did repurpose a few things from the Gershwin production, plus material from the radio show.

The Marxes were also embroiled in a squabble with Paramount. On March 9, 1933, execs tried anew to alter their contract, and the brothers bolted the studio. On April 3, the Marx Brothers, Inc., was formed—partly to deal with Paramount and partly to handle Chico's finances. It took until May for both parties to get down to the task of making a new film.[5]

Then came the usual pattern of script arguments, writer resignations, missed appointments, battles with agents and boorish behavior.[6] Some good came of it. Several very bad script ideas perished, along with terrible titles, such as *Cracked Ice*, *Grasshoppers* and *Oo La La*. *Duck Soup* won out, though it's not the best of titles. Duck soup, a slang phrase that appeared in 1912, means something easy to do or a person who is easy to cheat. The title was probably chosen because director Leo McCarey made a 20-minute silent Laurel and Hardy film by that name in 1927. It was a great idea to allow McCarey to direct. Two more inspired ideas occurred: the removal of screenwriter/studio head Herman Mankiewicz and the return of Margaret Dumont.

Mankiewicz could be brilliant, but he struggled with alcohol abuse, egoism and gambling. The last of these was the last thing Chico's brothers wanted, plus Groucho couldn't stand Mankiewicz. In his autobiography, Groucho used the pseudonym Delaney—as if that fooled anyone—to slam Mankiewicz as a "large, soggy man with a drooping belly, which he constantly kept pushing up with both hands as though fearful it might fall on the floor and get stepped on." He went on to say that Delaney-Mankiewicz "had a classic ignorance of the importance of a story, but he had a notion that if he bellowed instead of talked in a story conference, the sounds escaping from his face would surely make sense to someone in the room." Groucho spared no venom and asserted that Mankiewicz belched, abused writers, "ate like a pig, guzzled his booze and played the dames relentlessly. (Fortunately for the girls, in most cases unsuccessfully.)"[7]

Mankiewicz even managed to anger Harpo, which was pretty hard to do. After reading an early script, Harpo protested that he wasn't sure what his character was supposed to be. According to Joe Adamson, Mankiewicz replied, "Aw, hell, you play a middle-aged Jew who goes around picking up spit."[8] Soon thereafter, Mankiewicz was banished, and the script was whipped into shape by the battle-tested team of Bert Kalmar, Harry Ruby, Arthur Sheekman and Nat Perrin.

The Marxes also welcomed back Margaret Dumont.[9] As Maurice Charney observed, the role of Gloria Teasdale required "a certain kind of self-deprecatory humor for which Thelma Todd and any beautiful, young ingenue would be inappropriate."[10] In *Duck Soup,* Dumont is more at ease than in previous Marx Brothers films and is often the most natural actor on screen. Her sly smiles indicate that she did indeed *get* the jokes made at her expense.

Although the brothers applauded the choice of Leo McCarey to direct *Duck Soup,* the feeling was not entirely mutual. Groucho called him "the only great director we ever had" and "a good drunk," high praise from the abstemious Groucho. Chico enjoyed gambling with McCarey. "I lost a lot of bets to him," said he. Chico recalled getting even with McCarey in, of all things, a wager over who could chuck a walnut the furthest. Chico loaded his walnut with lead and collected his ill-gotten gains.[11] Maxine Marx verified the walnut story and echoed Groucho's comment that McCarey held his liquor well.[12]

Wes D. Gehring went so far as to say that *Duck Soup* was the only film for which "the team had a real auteur ... as director."[13] That's a bit rich for a director—two Oscars notwithstanding—whose major lifetime credits were silent films, screwball comedies and the romance *An Affair to Remember,* but McCarey got curmudgeonly Groucho to say that he "was a funny man. We had a lot of fun with him." McCarey must have had the right touch.[14]

That's not the same as saying he could handle the Marxes, though he had the moxie to give them a dose of their own medicine. The Marxes had a contract stipulation that they would not begin shooting a scene after six p.m. This clashed with McCarey's habit of musing upon a scene before shooting, and he grew annoyed when they walked off the set on the dot of six like factory workers punching a time clock. He one-upped them by waiting until late in the afternoon, handing directorial reins to an assistant, and telling the Marxes he needed to take a phone call. Instead, he went home as the Marxes worked late into the night. They were miffed to learn that McCarey was asleep in his bed, but it was a lesson delivered and received.[15]

McCarey also had the wisdom to adhere to the spirit of a script rather than its letter. As Adamson colorfully put it, "McCarey shared the viewpoint that a script for the Marx Brothers was about as definite as a treaty for the Indians."[16] McCarey was undoubtedly a key reason why *Duck Soup* flows so well. In Woody Allen's words, "*Duck Soup* has practically no dead spots in it," which, in his estimation, made it a film that surpassed classics from Charlie Chaplin and Buster Keaton.[17]

McCarey turned Harpo loose to wield a pair of shears, jump barefooted into a lemonade vat, light cigars with a blowtorch, and engage in other acts of havoc. Harpo was the director's favorite Marx, as his pantomime resonated with McCarey's own early experience in making silent pictures. McCarey also secured the talents of Edgar

Kennedy, a silent-film veteran whose performance as a heavy sparkled in *Duck Soup*. According to McCarey,

> The most surprising thing about this film was that I succeeded in not going crazy, for I really did not want to work with them; they were completely mad.... Yes, they were the four battiest people I ever met, which didn't stop me from taking great pleasure in the shooting of several scenes in the film.... But this wasn't the ideal film for me. In fact, it was the only time in my career ... that I made the humor rest with the dialogue: With Groucho, it was the only humor you could get.[18]

His comments were slightly uncharitable, given that Groucho was also a superb physical comedian, but we can also see McCarey's handprints on now-classic sketches, including several that were wordless.

Mirror, Mirror on the Wall

Duck Soup contains scenes now regarded as among the sharpest in the history of comedy. Several sketches were not original to the Marx Brothers, though their takes on them are considered definitive. The best of all involves a broken mirror.

Before they switch loyalties to Freedonia, Chicolini and Pinky try to steal Freedonia's war plans at the behest of Sylvanian ambassador Trentino. Trentino has planted Vera Marcal as a houseguest at Teasdale's house. He knows that Teasdale has the plans, but not where they are. Chicolini and Pinky are sent to find them and must be very quiet, as Firefly is also a houseguest. They gain entrance via a doorbell-ringing routine that echoes *Horse Feathers'* speakeasy scene. Once inside, Pinky sets off an alarm clock, opens a music box, plucks the inside of a piano, and makes enough noise to raise the dead!

Somehow, they manage to avoid detection long enough to pick up an extension phone and overhear Teasdale beg Firefly to stop by her room, as she can't sleep until the plans are back in his hands. Chicolini sneaks into Firefly's room and locks him away. He then slaps on a greasepaint mustache, grabs a cigar, dresses in sleepwear identical to Firefly's, and makes his way to Teasdale's room. When asked why he is talking so oddly, he tells her, "Maybe some time I go to Italy and I'm practicin' the language." She gives him the combination for the downstairs safe. Too easy, right?

It is. There's another knock on the door, Chicolini dives under the bed and Pinky, who has the same idea and costume, enters. By this time, Firefly has broken out and he too enters the room, prompting both Chicolini and Pinky to sneak away. Pinky makes even more noise downstairs, including turning on a radio blaring "Stars and Stripes Forever." Firefly orders guards to surround the house. Pinky runs into a mirror as he tries to flee. Firefly comes downstairs and gazes toward the mirror frame, where he sees an image that looks like him, though something's not right and he can't figure out what it is.

What comes next is a magical silent gag in which everything Firefly does, no matter how silly or unlikely, is copied by Pinky on the other side of the frame. Firefly is so mesmerized that he doesn't flinch when a hat is dropped and politely handed back, or when the routine goes three-dimensional and Firefly circles his own "image" trying to unravel the mystery. The scene ends when a similarly dressed Chicolini shows up. Chicolini is captured.

The mirror routine has been copied by everyone from Bugs Bunny to Lucille Ball, who gave it a workout in a 1955 episode of *I Love Lucy* with none other than 66-year-old Harpo. But no matter who did it, the mirror routine was never as funny as in *Duck Soup*. The idea was adapted from an old vaudeville routine sometimes credited to the Schwarz Brothers. Little is known of that act, though it was probably that of Tobias and Isaac Schwartz, who show up in a 1909 lawsuit against the Grand Union Vaudeville Company.[19]

Whether or not the Schwarzes invented the gag, there were certainly mirror routines before the Marx Brothers. Roy Blount Jr. unearthed several, all of which are available on YouTube. Charlie Chaplin gave the routine a quick nod in *The Floorwalker* (1916), though it's a stretch, as Chaplin knows that it's a man who looks like him. The closest parallel is found in the 1921 film *Seven Years Bad Luck*, expertly played by Max Linder in a routine that's much longer than the Marxes'.[20] How ironic that the Marxes' routine done in the age of sound is the best version of this piece of silent schtick.

Hats Off

The Marx Brothers also borrowed vaudeville's hat-switch routine. On the surface, it's a simple gag. Hats are knocked off two or more characters. When retrieved, they go onto the wrong heads and a well-timed shuffle ensues in which it takes ages for everyone to end up with the correct chapeau. Often, one individual grows so frustrated that, though the correct hat is on his head, he angrily takes it off and places it on another's head, an effective device to keep the visual joke alive.

The origin of the hat swap gag is uncertain. Laurel and Hardy resorted to it several times, including in their 1927 silent short *Do Detectives Think?* McCarey was its supervising director and it was probably he who suggested it for *Duck Soup*.

The first hat gag lasts just over four minutes. Chicolini operates a peanut stand beneath Firefly's window and adjacent to Edgar Kennedy's lemonade cart. Pinky arrives on the scene, swipes a handful of peanuts, and then snips off the end of the hot dog Chicolini was about to bite into. That's pretext for a mock fistfight gag in which the only blows landed are kicks to Chicolini's rear end. A frustrated Chicolini shoves Pinky, sending him into Kennedy and one of his customers. The enterprising Pinky attempts to pick the customer's pocket with his left hand and Kennedy's pocket with his right. The latter is naturally upset and grows angrier when Pinky scissors off his pocket.

Kennedy's confrontation with Pinky grows more frustrating. His approach on Pinky leads to the "Harpo handshake," his leg over Kennedy's outstretched hand. Pinky wards off a blow, but Kennedy's own painful handshake unseats both his hat and Pinky's. They don each other's headgear, and the hat swap gag is on. Pinky keeps knocking Kennedy's hat to the ground and eventually Chicolini places it atop his own hat for a three-way swap that leaves Kennedy flustered. As he chases Chicolini, Harpo loads his horn with lemonade that is sprayed in Kennedy's face. Kennedy pretends to laugh it off, then squirts lemonade down Pinky's trousers. Kennedy should have left it there, as his hat ends up in flames.

That's only part one. Later, Chicolini leaves Pinky in charge of his peanut stand

and Kennedy senses a revenge opportunity. He walks to the stand wearing his new straw boater, grabs a bag of peanuts, and slathers mustard on Pinky's outstretched hand instead of paying him. Pinky silently laughs, wipes his hand on Kennedy's sash, snips it off, and slams the peanuts to the ground. Kennedy grabs another packet, but loses his hat. I'll bet you can guess where it ends up! The sight of another blazing hat causes Kennedy to upend the peanut cart, but that doesn't settle matters. Seconds later, Kennedy's customers flee, as a bare-legged and bare-footed Pinky is splashing away in the lemonade tank. All Kennedy can do is sigh, the only "dialogue" in this 90-second scene.

The hat swap routine was also an old gag by the time Harpo and Chico used it, but they again set the standard. Samuel Beckett used the prank in his 1953 play *Waiting for Godot,* and it has been used in most adaptations since.[21] McCarey liked the hat switcheroo so much that it appeared in a different Laurel and Hardy film he directed, 1928's *We Faw Down,* and was also a centerpiece of *The Awful Truth* (1937).

Harpo is a *tour de force* in *Duck Soup.* You name it and Pinky's scissors snip it: Firefly's quill pen, Trentino's coattails, cigars, the plumes of military helmets, Bob Roland's hat while it's on his head! We watch Pinky "answer" the phone without uttering a word; he lets his arsenal of horns do the talking. Another running gag has Pinky show up with a motorcycle and sidecar each time Firefly needs to go somewhere, then drives off without him. Firefly's comment, "This is the fifth trip I've made today and I haven't been anywhere yet," sums up Pinky's chauffeur skills.

Word Play and Other Shenanigans

Duck Soup is also flavored with outstanding verbal humor, especially insults and self-deprecating remarks. In *Duck Soup* the wisecracks, puns and zingers fly early and often. As in most movies, they serve to segue from one scene to another.

When Firefly makes his grand entrance, Mrs. Teasdale proclaims, "I welcome you with open arms." Firefly retorts, "How late do you stay open?" When she hails him as the "most able statesman in all Freedonia," he replies, "That covers a lot of ground. Say, you cover a lot of ground yourself. You better beat it. I hear they're going to tear you down and put up an office building." Even flirtation is grounds for zingers:

FIREFLY: Where is your husband?
TEASDALE: Why ... he's dead.
FIREFLY: I'll bet he's using that as an excuse.
TEASDALE: I was with him 'til the very end.
FIREFLY: No wonder he passed away.
TEASDALE: I held him in my arms and kissed him.
FIREFLY: I see. Then it was murder!

As if this exchange isn't loaded enough, when Teasdale reminds him, "Notables from every country are gathered in your honor. This is a gala day for you," Firefly puns, "A gal a day is enough for me. I don't think I could handle any more."

Firefly's idea of romance is a sentimental line followed by a blistering zinger. He proposes marriage by promising Gloria Teasdale, "You take me and I'll take a vacation. I'll need a vacation if we're going to get married. Married! I can see you bending over a hot stove. But I can't see the stove! ... Oh, I suppose you'll think me a sentimental old fluff, but would you mind giving me a lock of your hair? ... I'm letting you off easy. I was going to ask for the whole wig."

One of Groucho's snarkiest insults is heard during the war with Sylvania. He tries to rally the troops by pointing to Teasdale, who is frightened and faint. "Remember, you're fighting for this woman's honor," he yells, "which is probably more than she ever did."

Chicolini gets plenty of zany lines as well. He delivers his initial spy report to Trentino, who wants to know if he and Pinky have been snooping on Firefly:

> Have we been trailing Firefly! My partner here's got a nose just like a bloodhound.... And the rest of his face don't look so good either. We find out all about this Firefly.... Remember, you gave us a picture and said "Follow him"? ... We get on the job right away. In one hour, less than one hour ... we lose-a the picture. That's-a pretty quick work."

An exasperated Trentino asks if they brought him Firefly's "record," and Pinky extracts a record from his pocket. Trentino is beside himself. The record is hurled across the room, Pinky pulls out a gun and blasts it to pieces. Chicolini rewards him with one of Trentino's cigars. Only then does Chicolini continue his report.

> **CHICOLINI:** Monday, we watch Firefly's house, but he no come out. He wasn't home. Tuesday, we go to the ball game, but he fool us. He no show up. Wednesday, he go to the ball game, but we fool him! We no show up. Thursday was a doubleheader, nobody show up. Friday, it rained all day. There was no ball game. We listened over the radio.
> **TRENTINO:** You didn't shadow Firefly!
> **CHICOLINI:** Sure, we shadow him all day.
> **TRENTINO:** What day was that?
> **CHICOLINI:** Shadderday! That's-a some joke, huh, boss?
> **TRENTINO:** Will you tell me, what happened Saturday?
> **CHICOLINI:** I'm glad you asked me. We follow this man to a roadhouse. He meet a married lady.
> **TRENTINO:** A married lady?
> **CHICOLINI:** Yeah, I think it was his wife.
> **TRENTINO:** Firefly has no wife!
> **CHICOLINI:** No? ... You know what I think? I think we followed the wrong man.

As Chicolini and Pinky lay waste to the spy business, Firefly busies himself with lowering leadership to new depths. Firefly is handed the treasury department report by a flunky who hopes Firefly will find it clear. "Clear? Why, a four-year-old child could understand this report." He then turns to Roland and commands, "Go out and find me a four-year-old child. I can't make head or tail out of it."

Next, Firefly hears from his labor secretary: "The workers of Freedonia are demanding shorter hours." His Excellency has an answer for that: "We'll give them shorter hours by cutting their lunch hour to 20 minutes." Another secretary complains, "I give my time to my duties and what do I get?" Certainly not sympathy: "You get awfully tiresome." When the angry official blurts out, "Sir, you try my patience," Firefly also has a comeback for that: "You must come over and try mine some time." By the time Firefly is done with his cabinet, Chicolini is his new secretary of war.

We know that Chicolini is actually working for Trentino. When he is captured after the mirror scene, he is put on trial for treason. Firefly has as little patience for the solemnity of a courtroom as he does for the formalities of government ministers. He presides over Chicolini's trial and makes a hash of it.

FIREFLY: Chicolini, I'll bet you eight to one we find you guilty.

CHICOLINI: That's-a no good. I can get ten to one at the barbershop.

PROSECUTOR: Chicolini, you're charged with high treason. If found guilty, you'll be shot.

CHICOLINI: I object.

PROSECUTOR: You object? On what grounds?

CHICOLINI: I couldn't think of anything else to say.

FIREFLY: Objection sustained.

PROSECUTOR: You sustained the objection?

FIREFLY: I couldn't think of anything else to say either.

PROSECUTOR: When were you born?

CHICOLINI: I don't remember. I was just a little baby.

PROSECUTOR: Isn't it true you tried to sell Freedonia's secret war code and plans?

CHICOLINI: Sure, I sold a code and two pair of plans....

FIREFLY: Now I'll bet you 20 to one we find you guilty.

With that remark, Firefly abandons his role as leader of Freedonia and acts as defense attorney.

FIREFLY: Look at Chicolini. He sits there alone, an abject figure.

CHICOLINI: I abject!

FIREFLY: I say, look at Chicolini. He sits there alone, a pitiable object. Let's see you get out of that one. Surrounded by a sea of unfriendly faces. Chicolini, give me a number from one to ten.

CHICOLINI: Eleven.

FIREFLY: Gentlemen, Chicolini here may talk like an idiot and look like an idiot. But don't let that fool you. He really is an idiot. I implore you: Send him back to his father and brothers who are waiting for him with open arms in the penitentiary.

Chicolini's trial is interrupted by news that Freedonia and Sylvania are at war. The war took place because Firefly's diplomatic skills lack an essential ingredient: diplomacy. He and Trentino had numerous insult exchanges that finally drove Trentino to mobilize his troops. The camel's back broke at a garden party, where Firefly and Trentino were allegedly mending fences until Trentino made the mistake of reminding Firefly that he once called him an "upstart." An enraged Firefly whipped out a glove and slapped Trentino. This spark ignited the fires of war. It is reminiscent of the preventable blunders that led to World War I.

Soldiers vs. Farmers

The absurdity of war as depicted in *Duck Soup* prompted Roy Blount Jr. to call it the "greatest war movie ever made."[22] He would get arguments from fans of films such as *Paths of Glory, Johnny Got His Gun, Dr. Strangelove, The Mouse That Roared, Apocalypse Now* and many others, but it's a safe bet that *Duck Soup* will never be used for military recruiting purposes. Eyles calls it a "comment on all wars: that they are pointless, tending to arise from trivialities to be rejoiced in by men as a kind of super-game and won by chance and luck."[23] Before delving into this, let's revisit the impact World War I had on the Marx Brothers.

As we have seen, Minnie Marx did whatever was necessary to assure her sons' success. The move to Chicago didn't lead to elite vaudeville house bookings, but as war approached, good fortune arrived in an unexpected way. Like many European-born Jews, neither Minnie nor Sam had much love for the military. They knew that for many young men, joining or being conscripted into the military was a lifelong sentence. If either parent held any illusions that military life was good for Jews, they were shattered by outbreaks of anti–Semitism in Sam's native France occasioned by the Dreyfus Affair (1894–1906).[24]

Minnie had already tinkered with her sons' birthdates so she could keep booking them as "boy" acts, and this paid dividends during World War I.[25] So did a temporary occupational change. The 1917 Selective Service Act required all males between the ages of 21 and 45 to register for a potential draft, but a section of the bill provided exemptions for "persons engaged in industries, including agriculture, found to be necessary to the maintenance of the Military Establishment or the effective operation of the military forces or the maintenance of national interest during the emergency...."[26] Minnie promptly purchased land in La Grange, Illinois, about 25 miles outside of Chicago. On August 17, 1917, the brothers took time off from the vaudeville circuit to make their way to the state capital in Springfield to register as "farmers."[27]

The very idea of the Marxes as farmers is absurd enough to *be* a Marx Brothers movie. Groucho recalled, "The first morning on the farm, we got up at five. The following morning, we dawdled in bed until six. By the end of the week, we were getting up at noon, which was just enough time for us to get dressed to catch the 1:07 to Wrigley Field, where the Chicago Cubs played." As noted earlier, about the only thing they produced on the farm was Herbert's character name of Zeppo.[28] Simon Louvish correctly labeled the Marx agricultural enterprise a "flimflam." Several hundred chickens were purchased, but their eggs were devoured by rats. No matter: "When buyers came for eggs, the new farmers had to rush to the store to buy some to put under the chickens. The buyers were amazed to see Rhode Island Reds, which laid brown eggs, produce white ones, by Marxian mutation."[29]

The subterfuge worked. Only Milton (Gummo) entered the military—less than two weeks before the armistice—and it altered the course of Zeppo's life. As Zeppo recalled, "My mother called me up to tell me Gummo was leaving for the army.... She insisted I join the act and that's what I did."[30] It is sobering to consider what might have happened if the Marxes hadn't become "farmers." Groucho's poor eyesight probably would have exempted him from the military, but could the brotherly partnership survive? Would Chico have survived financially? Would there have been a place for Harpo's pantomime as the silent-film era wound down?

What's in a Name?

Despite Teasdale's insistence that Freedonia needs "a progressive" leader, Rufus T. Firefly is a petty tyrant. His song "These Are the Rules of My Administration" is a grab bag of arbitrary restrictions on liberty. The same peculiar governing style surfaces in the slash-and-burn interactions with his cabinet. Freedonia, in short, is no better or worse than Sylvania, which is cast as the villain.

If Freedonia is freedom-challenged, why the name? Is the phrase "land of the brave and free" in its national anthem a veiled putdown of the United States? Probably not. "The Star-Spangled Banner" was only designated as the official U.S. national song in 1931. Some claim the name came from a failed attempt by Texas to secede from Mexico in 1826–27 in which rebels proclaimed a small section of east-central Texas the Republic of Freedonia. The poorly educated Marxes were unlikely to have known much about that, though its short-lived capital was Nacogdoches, the town in Marxian lore where the Marxes transitioned from a musical act that did some comedy to a comedy ensemble with occasional music.[31]

Freedonia was probably chosen for ironic purposes; Freedonia isn't "free." The quick view we get of Freedonia immediately after the credits indicates that Texas wasn't on anyone's mind. There are turreted castles, gambrel rooftops and stone-arched bridges, a mash-up of something Dutch, something German and something from a theme park.

Incidentally, Sylvania was the name of a fictional nation in *The Love Parade*, a 1929 Maurice Chevalier film. Sylvania means forest or woodlands, though we have no idea of what Sylvania looks like. The film tells us only that it is Freedonia's larger neighbor.

Duck Soup's writers may have had the Balkan wars in mind. The Balkan wars began in 1912 and set off reactions that were among the events that precipitated World War I. Today, the term "balkanization" is a synonym for fragmentation, which was precisely what occurred in the early 20th century when cultural, ethnic and religious groups sought self-determination. A series of crises in Greece, Montenegro and Serbia toppled precariously balanced alliance systems that sent powers such as Great Britain, France and Russia to war with Germany, the Ottoman Empire (Turkey) and the Austro-Hungarian Empire. The assassination of Archduke Franz Ferdinand, heir to the Austro-Hungarian Empire, is generally considered the immediate cause of global conflict. It took place in Sarajevo, the capital of Bosnia, but the assassin was a Bosnian Serb.

Freedonia Goes to War!

Notice how those awaiting Firefly's inauguration look as if they came from a time before the Jazz Age. Viewers of the day would have recalled how small conflicts in the Balkans sparked a larger war. Historians have long viewed World War I as the product of unstable alliance systems, militarism, nationalism, imperialism and misguided leaders. They don't get much more misguided than Firefly or Trentino.

Martin Gardner opines that corruption plaguing the administration of President Warren G. Harding and New York Mayor Jimmy Walker provided fodder for *Duck Soup*.[32] That might be so, but President Woodrow Wilson better fits the bill. When Wilson donned a top hat and morning coat, he looked the part of a college president or diplomat. He had been the first, but largely failed as the latter. A bit like Groucho, actually![33]

Wilson was reelected to the presidency in 1916 with a pledge to keep America out of the ongoing European conflict. A month after his second inauguration, America went to war. Wilson's pledge had less gravitas than Firefly's wisecrack that it was too late to prevent a war: "I've already paid a month's rent on the battlefield." Because the decision for war was not universally popular, the Committee on Public Information was ordered to convince a skeptical public to support the conflict. Likewise, legislation such as the Espionage Act (1917) and Sedition Act (1918) clamped down on domestic dissent—at the expense of civil liberties.

Duck Soup incisively parodies how easily public opinion can be changed. Cocktail parties, diplomatic intrigue and courting give way to orgiastic nationalistic frenzies. The scene of Freedonians celebrating the coming conflict is humorous, but frightening, the latter for the way in which reason is so easily derailed. Officials and military leaders leap out of their seats, horns blare and Firefly yells, "Then it's war!" Several characters appear simian-like as they sing "Freedonia's going to war/ Each son will grab a gun/ And run away to war/ At last we're going to war." The lavish production is like a perverse opera. War mania is interrupted only by the incongruous sight of Pinky entering like a marching band drum major, followed by soldiers in plumed hats, on which Firefly, Chicolini, and Roland play as if the soldiers are a marching-in-place xylophone. What comes next could be viewed as deeply disturbing. "To war, to war/ Freedonia's going to war" echoes throughout a hall filled with individuals behaving as if they are attending a bacchanal. Or perhaps a "revival meeting," as Glenn Mitchell describes it.[34]

The appropriation of the African American spiritual "All God's Chillun Got Wings" enhances war fervor. We see bent-over figures singing "Hi-de, hi-de, hi-de, hi-de, hi-de, hi-de ho," but to whom or what are they kowtowing? Some levity remains, such as the Marxes leading all assembled in kicking their legs in the air behind them like a barn full of jackasses. The Marxes also don cheesy grins for a

Freedonia's going to war in this *Duck Soup* still featuring Zeppo, Groucho and Chico (Wikimedia Commons).

minstrel routine, but listen to what they sing: "They got guns, we got guns/ All God's chillun got guns/ We're gonna walk all over the battlefield/ 'Cause all God's chillun got guns." The tension cools slightly when the brothers offer a touch of "Oh! Susanna" and turn the room into a hoedown. But the scene ends with a coda of "To war, to war, to war," and "Until the judgment day/ We'll rally 'round the flag/ The flag, the flag, the flag...."

The Absurdity of War

As for the conflict, very little escapes satirical treatment. Pinky rides off Paul Revere–style to alert Freedonians, though his antics tarnish Revere's patriotic sheen. His bugle calls rouse the citizenry, until he stops at a home in which a woman has stripped down to her slip in preparation for taking a bath. What ensues suggests that she and Pinky are not strangers. When she spies her husband—none other than the much-abused lemonade vendor—coming home, she quickly pushes Pinky into the bathroom. She meets her husband at the door, hands him a gun, and tells him Freedonia has gone to war. He promptly hands it back and gruffly declares, "I'm gonna take a bath," and immerses himself in a soapy tub. He hears a honk and eventually "Reveille," as a water-soaked Pinky rises from the foam, gestures and runs out the door. Pinky finishes his midnight run by galloping up to another home where a woman blows him a kiss. Pinky rides into the house. Cut to a floor-level shot of a pair of women's shoes, Pinky's boots, and a set of horseshoes. The camera pans up and we see the woman in bed alone; Pinky is asleep with the horse!

If the call to arms is a chaotic mess, imagine the fiasco of the battlefield. Officers inside the command station are dressed in uniforms evocative of World War I, and Firefly is dressed as a Civil War Union general. Firefly orders a radio operator to call for reinforcements, "collect," then hands money to a subordinate to purchase neck-high, ready-made trenches so Freedonia's soldiers won't need trousers. When advised that one of his generals has reported a gas attack, Firefly responds that should he take a teaspoon of bicarbonate of soda in half a glass of water.

Bombs fly through a window, the building begins to crumble, and so does sanity. At one point, Firefly accidentally opens fire on his own troops. Pinky walks the battlefield with a sandwich sign bearing the message "Join the Army, See the Navy." Firefly is next seen wearing a Confederate general's uniform, and Secretary of War Chicolini arrives and punches a time clock. There is stock footage of World War I tanks—the set-up for a Chicolini pun—and suddenly Firefly is wearing a Boy Scout outfit. Uniforms change nearly every scene. Pinky is dressed in Napoleonic garb; Firefly is a Hussar, then wears a coonskin hat.

Things look so bad for Freedonia that Pinky tacks up a "Help Wanted" sign. Luckily, help is on the way: stock footage of firefighters rushing from a station house; motorcycle cops speeding down a highway; track stars, rowers and swimmers making haste; baboons running across a wooden bridge; elephants charging; dolphins leaping out of the water.

When a large water pitcher gets stuck on Firefly's head, what can be done except paint a Groucho face on it? The surrealism heightens when the pitcher is safely removed by inserting a dynamite charge. Freedonia is finally saved when Trentino gets his head stuck in a door and the Marxes hurl fruit at him until he surrenders. The remaining fruit is aimed at Teasdale when she sings, in screeching soprano, "Hail, hail Freedonia / Land of the brave and free." Why is there a noose hanging to her left? Beats me.

Postwar Disillusionment

Films like *Duck Soup* are generally made in periods marked by anti-authority sentiment. One can debate the necessity of some wars, but *Duck Soup* hews to a time-proven reality: nations never exit a war in the same condition in which they enter it. Witness the U.S. after the World War I armistice. In his 1920 novel *This Side of Paradise*, Ernest Hemingway famously wrote, "Here was a new generation ... dedicated more than the last to the fear of poverty and the worship of success; grown up to find all gods dead, all wars fought, and all faith in mankind shaken...." As Gardner put it, *Duck Soup* touched upon a truism, "War is illogical and bizarre; its glory is an illusion."[35]

When Hemingway wrote, nations were coming to grips with the devastation of the Great War: a staggering death toll, monstrous injuries, millions of homeless refugees, unfathomable levels of property damage, failed postwar diplomacy, an influenza pandemic. In the 14 years between the end of the war and the release of *Duck Soup*, America buried 675,000 flu victims and experienced anarchist bombings, a Red scare, assaults on labor unions, the imposition of Prohibition laws and the ravages of a depression.

Duck Soup captured the disillusionment of a generation that had dared hope that the Great War would be "the war to end war."[36]

Elephant in the Room: Racist Moments

There is a joke in *Duck Soup* that isn't funny now and probably wasn't considered so in 1933 either. Teasdale tries to convince Firefly to reconsider his decision to go to war against Sylvania. His reply shocks modern ears: "Well, maybe I am a little headstrong. I come by it honestly. My father was a little Headstrong. My mother was a little Armstrong. The Headstrongs married the Armstrongs and that's why darkies were born."

The joke was a pop culture reference. In 1931, white radio star Kate Smith released a song titled "That's Why Darkies Were Born." Its lyrics are even more distressing than Groucho's snide remark. It notes that someone had to pick cotton and corn, be enslaved, sing and laugh at troubles, and has stanzas punctuated by the unsettling line Groucho sought to lampoon, "That's why darkies were born."

The song was written for the show *George White's Scandals*, in which it was sung by a white baritone in blackface, thereby adding another level of distress. In its day, the song enjoyed widespread popularity. Smith's was the second recording of it and was a hit, even though African Americans of the day denounced it. Ironically, black activist Paul Robeson also recorded the song in 1931.

This doesn't excuse the joke. Charlotte Chandler asked the elderly Groucho if it ever surprised him when his audiences laughed at a joke that he didn't think was funny. He responded, "You try different things, and if one thing doesn't go, you take it out and try something else until you get something the audience laughs at."[37] His was a stock show business response, but insofar as I can tell, Groucho never again used the Headstrong-Armstrong quip.

Another objectionable sequence in *Duck Soup* is the appropriation of "All God's Chillun Got Wings," especially the Marxes' whiteface parody of minstrelsy. Although Gardner is correct that it serves the purpose of being a "last burst of jingoism" leading to war,[38] it is hard to imagine that 1933 audiences would have reacted well to a grinning, strutting burlesque of "A Mighty Fortress Is Our God." The spoof of a black spiritual is another example of casual 1930s-style racism.

Tepid Soup: Leaving Paramount

A legend holds that *Duck Soup* bombed at the box office. Not so. The film made a decent if not spectacular profit, but it was not the powerhouse *Horse Feathers* had been. To go from Paramount's top-grossing film in 1932 to middle of the pack one year later—merely Paramount's fifth highest grossing film—hastened a decision already in the offing.[39] *Duck Soup* marked the end of the Marx Brothers' five-picture deal with Paramount and each side was sick of the other. The split ended the disputes that nearly scuttled *Duck Soup* before shooting began.

Many film historians share my view that *Duck Soup* is the best film the Marxes ever made, so why didn't it do better at the box office? First, reviews were mixed.[40] *Duck Soup* was cut from the same musical comedy cloth as their previous films. Groucho's musical entrance in *Duck Soup* is similar to those made in *The Cocoanuts*, *Animal Crackers* and *Horse Feathers*. Likewise, the fractured exchanges between Groucho and Chico resemble earlier efforts and, though it wasn't noted much at the time, Harpo's blonde-chasing routine had grown shopworn. As one reviewer put it, "Every indication points to the Marx Brothers being through with movies for the time being. They played the game for what it was worth, but the screen is relentless on comedians. It's their duty to be funnier in in each succeeding picture, and ... the same tricks can't be worked over and over...."[41]

Other factors came into play, including *Duck Soup*'s shared thematic elements with *Million Dollar Legs*, a W.C. Fields comedy released a year earlier. Gardner adds that *Duck Soup* was too critical of government at a time in which Americans wanted Roosevelt to succeed: "They were inflamed about *Duck Soup* because it went beyond their tolerance for criticism of a federal government that was trying to help them during the Depression."[42] This may have swayed some, though I doubt anyone confused FDR with Rufus T. Firefly.

Others, including Mitchell, speculate that *Duck Soup* was poorly timed with troubling developments in Europe making a war parody both a downbeat and inappropriate topic. This strikes me as reading history from front to back. Most historians agree that Roosevelt was inching the nation away from isolationism by the time of his re-election in 1936, but in 1933, there was little Freedonia-like clamor for another war. As Michael Parrish notes, 1934 and 1935 were peak years for American isolationism.[43] If anything, Americans were primed for a film like *Duck Soup*. In response to prevailing sentiment, Congress passed five separate neutrality acts between 1935 and 1939, and Roosevelt reiterated U.S. neutrality as late as 1940. In the latter year, the America First Committee was founded and swelled to more than 800,000 members.

A simpler explanation for *Duck Soup*'s box office drop is that 1933 hit Hollywood hard. Ticket sales of $2.1 million—an adjusted $84.4 million—made *Duck Soup* the 18th most profitable film of the year, as its costs were relatively low. That's not bad considering that 152 films were released in 1933, and 65 of them failed to crack the million-dollar mark, let alone two million. *King Kong* was top banana with receipts of $9.1 million, but just 14 films sold more than $3 million worth of tickets.[44] To be sure, *Duck Soup*'s box office was less than half of *Horse Feathers*' $4.3 million take— an adjusted $177.5 million—but you could argue that beggars should not be choosers. Paramount, like RKO and Fox, went into receivership later in 1933.

Duck Soup's reception certainly dispirited the Marxes. Groucho continued to feel that they were sharper on stage than on film. Maxine Marx put forth a similar view: "A vital link in the chemistry of the team had been ignored: the live audience. Working in front of the camera made for a tremendous gulf between performer and audience.... Their best routines were shaped on the road. But this kind of metamorphosis was not available to them in films."[45]

The Marxes weren't alone in their dissatisfaction with the movie industry. As the filming of *Duck Soup* was finishing, numerous actors turned their backs on the Academy of Motion Picture Arts and Sciences and created the Screen Actors Guild (SAG). SAG went on to become an important voice in advocating for the rights of movie actors but in 1933, it was considered a renegade labor union. SAG split Hollywood; the Academy was by invitation only, and those on the inside were reluctant to risk their status, especially since most producers refused to bargain with SAG.

The Marx Brothers were not members of the Academy and cast their lot with SAG partly because it opposed multi-year, multi-picture contracts like the one that bound the Marxes to Paramount. The New Deal's 1935 National Labor Relations Act safeguarded SAG's collective bargaining rights, but it took two more years before producers agreed to negotiate with SAG. Groucho served as SAG's first treasurer, but he had little stomach for labor battles. He claimed that after SAG's first meeting, he and two other actors went to a brothel, as "[i]t was the only safe place to go."[46]

In March 1934, Groucho and Chico tried another radio comedy. In *The Marx of Time,* Groucho and Chico satirically discussed the news, usually with heavy doses of puns. It could be considered a predecessor to the "Weekend Update" segment of TV's *Saturday Night Live. The Marx of Time* lasted just eight weeks.[47] Still another proposed Broadway show fizzled, as did Groucho's premature plan to write an autobiography. Zeppo and Harpo were destined to make the biggest post–*Duck Soup* splashes.

Zeppo and Harpo: Agent and Secret Agent

In March 1934, Zeppo put an end to Minnie's dream of the Four Marx Brothers. To Groucho, he wrote, "I'm sick and tired of being a stooge. You know that anybody else would have done as well in the act.... I only stayed ... because I knew that you, Chico and Harpo wanted me to. But I am sure you understand why I have joined Frank Orsatti in his theatrical agency and that you forgive my action."[48]

Zeppo was more than a stooge, but he was understandably tired of underwritten roles. Straight men tend to be better in duo acts: Dean Martin to Jerry Lewis, Dick Smothers to his brother Tommy, Bud Abbott to Lou Costello, Carl Reiner to Mel Brooks. But the Marx Brothers already had the perfect straight partner: Margaret Dumont. In addition, Groucho and Chico often traded gag man–straight man roles, often within the same sketch.

Later in life, Zeppo recalled helping his brothers come up with gags, but added, "I don't think I was one of the main contributors.... I didn't feel I did too much, either as an actor or a supporter.... [I]t wasn't what I wanted to do." By contrast, in the agency business, "I came into my own." Harboring no hard feelings, he added, "I think they were actually relieved because it meant more money for them, but I ... don't know that. But I know they didn't put up a big fight about it!"[49] Only once did Zeppo act as an agent for his brothers; his firm represented them for *Room Service* (1938). He found them difficult.

When Zeppo died in 1979, accolades poured forth. He was certainly a decent singer and could fool an audience by subbing for Groucho, but I doubt he would have seconded the praise for his straight-man skills.

He might have smiled to learn that one of my students adored him above all of his brothers.

Harpo as a secret agent? Yes, a real one, not a movie role. For a guy with almost no formal education, Harpo had fancy friends. He could also hold his own with critics, essayists, playwrights, journalists and poets such as Robert Benchley, Heywood Broun, George S. Kaufman, Dorothy Parker, Robert Sherwood, James Thurber and Estelle Winwood. The Algonquin Round Table group was nicknamed the "Vicious Circle" and, surprisingly, Groucho found them *too* vicious for his taste. Not so Harpo, and that had much to do with Alexander Woollcott, lifelong bachelor, critic, essayist, playwright, editor, occasional actor and larger-than-life personality. "Alec" was Harpo's best friend, croquet foe and fellow prankster. Harpo named two of his sons after Alec: Alexander Marx and William Woollcott Marx.

Woollcott insisted that

Alexander Woollcott, Harpo's friend and fellow Algonquin Round Table member (photograph by Carl Van Vechten, Library of Congress).

Harpo should be the first American performer to visit the Soviet Union (USSR) after President Franklin Roosevelt recognized it on November 16, 1933. "Recognition" is a formal diplomatic action in which one nation acknowledges the legitimacy of another and cultivates political and trade relations with said nation. FDR's recognition of the Communist Soviet Union (USSR) and Harpo's journey there have long provided fodder for right-wing conspiracy theorists; hence a few words are in order.

The Bolshevik revolution that installed a Communist government in Russia and several adjacent regions commenced in 1917, during World War I. When guiding star V.I. Lenin died in 1924, Joseph Stalin assumed power in the USSR. Stalin died in 1953, by which time America was in the midst of a second Red Scare and Stalin was identified as a mass murderer on par with Hitler and Mussolini. That is true, but it was not known 20 years earlier. Numerous intellectuals, industrialists and wage earners viewed the Soviet Union as a beacon of hope, a workers' revolution that toppled plutocrats and turned the social-class system upside down. Auto magnate Henry Ford traveled to the USSR in 1929. Labor leaders Victor and Walter Reuther lived and worked there for nearly two years during their travels abroad (1931–35).

It made sense, given a global recession and the downward spiral of the U.S. economy after the Stock Market crash. By contrast, the Soviet Union seemed to be unscathed. As the Great Depression deepened, quite a few individuals moved leftward politically and sympathized with socialist and Communist movements. Roosevelt had strategic motives for recognizing the USSR, but in 1933 it was possible for workers to view the Soviet Union as an experiment in working-class utopianism.

Woollcott pushed Harpo to visit, the original plan being for Alec to join him. That didn't pan out, but Woollcott wrangled an invitation from Soviet Foreign Minister Maxim Litvinov on Harpo's behalf. By Harpo's admission, the USSR "was as much of a mystery to me as the other side of the moon," but he sailed from New York on November 14, 1933.[50] His ship docked in Hamburg and his glance at Germany made him hasten to Moscow:

> In Hamburg I saw the most frightening, most depressing sight I had ever seen—a row of stores with the Star of David and the word *Jude* painted on them, and inside, behind half-empty counters, people in a daze, cringing like they didn't know what hit them and didn't know where the next blow would come from. Hitler had been in power only six months, and his boycott was already in full effect. I hadn't been so wholly conscious of being a Jew since my *bar mitzvah*. It was the first time since I'd had the measles that I was too sick to eat. I got across Germany as fast as I could go.[51]

In Poland, he was hoodwinked by an American who convinced him to exchange dollars for rubles, only to find out the Russians would have given him a much better exchange rate. He had trouble explaining his props to skeptical Russian border control agents. He was first booked into a very shabby hotel, found Moscow "all gray," and was shocked see women working in men's clothes with their feet swaddled "in burlap tied with strips of rags." He also discovered why even the early Russian winter required one to dress like a bear, Russia's symbol.[52]

Harpo eventually connected with the correct advance team and was treated well. He was a hit, even though his solo act was at first puzzling. Russian theater personnel, for example, did not understand pantomime without a script, so they wrote one for him; Harpo jocularly called his writers "George S. Kaufmanski and Morrie

Ryskindov." He had no idea what any of the Russian actors were saying, but in his words, "I'll be a son of a bitch if [the act] didn't knock them out of their seats."[53]

Harpo went on to wow audiences in Moscow and Leningrad. He marveled at the art in Leningrad's Winter Palace, was feted inside the Kremlin, shared laughs with fellow troupers, and located several Russian vaudevillians who shared his love of poker. Soon, he joked with journalists that he was related to Karl Marx and got along with handlers and officials so well that he was even the target of a practical joke. Litvinov delivered a formal thank you for bringing "precious moments of pleasure," and "held forth his hand. I shook it. A cascade of steel knives tumbled out of his sleeve and clanked to the stage."[54]

What happened next made Harpo sweat bullets. Or should I say Bullitts? He was summoned to the U.S. Embassy, where William Bullitt, America's ambassador to Russia, asked him to carry a packet of letters out of Russia. The packet was strapped to his leg. As the time approached to leave the USSR, he began to ponder the consequences were his bundle discovered. His panic levels rose when a Russian colonel asked him to come to his headquarters. Luckily, it was for an impromptu farewell dinner. On the trip home, Harpo was further startled when a knock upon his cabin door revealed "[t]wo hulking, stony-faced bruisers." They announced, "Marx, you have something we want." Imagine his relief when they flashed their Secret Service badges. Harpo later joked about being a spy and dubbed himself "Exapno Mapcase." He added, "I was a Secret Agent who didn't know what his Secret was." Harpo never learned what was in the smuggled packet.[55]

Harpo did not return to the United States with starry-eyed admiration for the Soviet Union. He liked the Russian people, but was astutely aware of the contradictions of a land in which there was a wide gulf between the rhetoric of public ownership and the make-do realities of the average Russian. He later suspected that his glamorous-seeming guide probably went from staying in the luxury hotel to a hovel once he left the country.

Duck Eggs

- **Antiwar?** Mussolini settled the question of whether *Duck Soup* was an antiwar film by banning it from Italian theaters. Hitler also banned it in Germany, along with *all* Marx Brothers films. The Marxes were Jewish, hence their films were considered degenerate art.
- **No solos:** There are no harp or piano interludes in *Duck Soup*. However, the hoedown scene of "Freedonia's Going to War" is the only time in which all four brothers played an instrument—banjos—on film at the same time.
- **Paisano pooch:** It's easy to miss, but Chicolini's dog in the vendor scene bears a suitably Italian name: Pastrami.
- **Maine attraction:** Groucho fulfilled his desire to get back on the stage, but without his brothers and in an unlikely place: Skowhegan, Maine. Groucho did a summer stock stint in *Twentieth Century*, a play written by Ben Hecht and Charles MacArthur that had debuted on Broadway on December 29, 1932. "Twentieth Century" refers to a train from Chicago to New York. Groucho

played Oscar Jaffe, an autocratic producer. His was perhaps another indirect swipe at Herman Mankiewicz, as Groucho's Jaffe was quite different from that of John Barrymore in the 1934 film adaptation. The movie emphasized humor, and is now widely viewed as a foundational screwball comedy. Groucho also penned a humorous letter to *Variety* about its lack of coverage of his Maine debut.[56]

- **Philly Follies:** When Firefly interviews Chicolini for a job in the Freedonian government, he poses a nonsense riddle: "What is it that has four pairs of pants, lives in Philadelphia, and it never rains but it pours?" It's an odd non sequitur. Apologies to Pennsylvanian readers, but the humor lies in the word "Philadelphia."

    This piece of vaudeville schtick is often credited to W.C. Fields, who told *Vanity Fair* that he wanted his gravestone to say, "Here lives W.C. Fields. I would rather be living in Philadelphia." Fields was from Philadelphia, but he and other vaudevillians often used the city as the butt of jokes suggesting that it, in Charles Mires' words, "would [only] be slightly preferable to the grave." The city had a reputation as being both dull and corrupt, but mainly it wasn't New York or Chicago, which were equated with success.[57]

- **The mayor protests:** The mayor of Freedonia, New York, wrote a letter to Paramount complaining of the film's use of his town's name. Groucho replied and suggested that the New York town change its name.

- ***Freedonia Gazette:*** A Marx Brothers Study Group formed within the National Film Society in 1978. Its 20-page magazine dedicated to all things Marx took its title from a newspaper that flashed upon the screen to announce that Rufus T. Firefly had come into power: the *Freedonia Gazette.*[58] It stopped publishing in 1994, though there is frequent scuttlebutt it will resume. Its editor, Paul Wesolowski, lives in New Hope, Pennsylvania, just 40 miles from an old vaudeville joke: Philadelphia.

Duck Soup Reheated

Many sublime American films have only been considered great in retrospect. Most famously, *Citizen Kane*, which many film scholars consider to be the *very best*, was lightly regarded when it was released in 1941. Even films that are now universally admired barely made budget when released, a list that contains surprising titles such as *The Wizard of Oz* (1939), *It's a Wonderful Life* (1946) and *Harold and Maude* (1971). The same can be said of films released since 1980 that critics now rate highly: *Blade Runner* (1982), *The Shawshank Redemption* (1994), *Fight Club* (1999), *Mulholland Drive* (2001) and *Children of Men* (2016).

Wide gaps between films that audiences like and those critics hail are common; *Duck Soup* is a rare case in which both critics and audience changed their minds. It is now regarded as one of the top American comedies of all time. It is number seven on Rotten Tomatoes' list of essential American comedies, and number five on a comparable list compiled by the venerable American Film Institute.

What caused such a reassessment? First and foremost, a new generation decided that it really *was* an antiwar film, and one that resonated with how legions of young people viewed the Vietnam conflict. Groucho gave his stamp of approval to those who concluded that the Vietnam War was as absurd as the one between Freedonia and Sylvania: "It would be different if we were fighting a just war, if there is any such thing.... If I were a youngster, I wouldn't march into the firing lines with any bravado. I would go to Canada or Sweden or hide or go to jail. If I had a son 20 years old, I'd encourage him to evade the war."[59]

If you want to add intellectual heft, New Wave auteurs François Truffaut and Jean Renoir also hailed *Duck Soup* an antiwar masterpiece. Truffaut declared that it might be the only true antiwar film, as "war films, even pacifist, even the best, willingly or not, glorify war and render it in some way attractive...."[60] Henri Langlois, co-founder of the *Cinémathèque Française*, was another *Duck Soup* fan. In accented English, he told Groucho, "I see *Duck Soup* many times in my life. But in 1940, just after the end of the French war and invasion, I go to the South of France and I see *Duck Soup*. Fantastic! It was exactly like a documentary of the time. I was a soldier in France. It was absolutely mad. So, if you want to know what happened in France between May to June 1940, you must see *Duck Soup*."[61] In topsy-turvy times, absurdity begins to make sense.

SEVEN

A Night at the Opera (1935)

Many have crowned *Duck Soup* as the Marx Brothers' best film, but in their day that honor fell to *A Night at the Opera*. It really does focus on opera. Why such a film in the middle of the Great Depression? A lot had changed in both the country and for the Marxes since their last film. The time was ripe for a lampoon of snobbery.

A Night at the Opera was directed by Sam Wood and produced by Irving G. Thalberg. Groucho is Otis B. Driftwood, who has one thing to do and isn't doing it well: getting the widowed Mrs. Claypool (Margaret Dumont) into high society. Her patience is wearing thin. Driftwood hits upon the idea of making her a patron of the New York City Opera. He calculates that if he can bring a top talent to New York on Claypool's dime, she will be the belle of society and he can stay on her payroll, perhaps even marry her.

The film opens in Milan, where we meet Rodolfo Lassparri (Walter Woolf King), a world-renowned tenor and egotistical bully. Harpo is Lassparri's long-suffering assistant Tomasso, and Chico is Fiorello, an unemployed hustler. New York opera impresario Herman Gottlieb (Sig Rumann) is nearly as pompous as Lassparri and is Driftwood's rival for Claypool's hand and money. Driftwood also faces another obstacle: He doesn't know a divo from a casino. He falls for Fiorello's claim that he represents the world's greatest tenor and signs Ricardo Baroni (Allan Jones), thinking he is Lassparri. Baroni is in love with opera diva Rosa Castaldi (Kitty Carlisle), and the feeling is mutual. But Lassparri pursues her.

The entire ensemble boards a ship bound for New York, with Ricardo, Fiorello and Tomasso as stowaways. In New York, a well-intentioned plan of uniting Ricardo and Rosa leads the Marxes to turn *Il Trovatore* into an opéra bouffe, a comic opera. That is a respected operatic form, but *Il Trovatore*—also lampooned in *The Cocoanuts*—is a tragic work, so it must be shredded. Some critics panned *A Night at the Opera* as a descent into sentimentality, but their voices were drowned in praise for the film.

Thalberg's Boys? The Making of *A Night at the Opera*

During the summer of 1934, the Marxes worried that *Duck Soup* reviewers were correct and they were washed up. Maxine remembered that her father (Chico) was so depressed that he spent his days at the track, on the golf course, and "moping around the house." There was an aborted discussion of an independent project with producer Sam Goldwyn, and the brothers considered dissolving the act. Maxine recalls

Poster for the 1948 re-release of 1935's *A Night at the Opera* **(Al Hirschfeld, via Wikimedia Commons)**

a phone call between Harpo and Chico. It's probably not a verbatim account, but the gist rings true:

> **HARPO:** I'm sick of waiting around waiting for something to break. I'm getting out of this lousy profession.
> **CHICO:** Hey, if anybody quits, I'm the oldest and I get to quit first.
> **HARPO:** That's good. You go and break the ice.
> **CHICO:** Ma would have wanted it that way.
> **HARPO:** Right. It's been a pleasure working with you.
> **CHICO:** You're swell, too, but a bit noisy.[1]

Against odds, in the fall of 1934, the Marxes got a nibble from MGM, an industry giant formed by the combination of several film production companies. Metro Pictures was the name of Marcus Loew's company. It was he who bought Louis B. Mayer's thriving movie production business and placed him in charge of the merged studios. Loew then purchased Goldwyn Pictures, which led to the official creation of MGM.[2] When Loew died in 1927, Mayer became the titan of MGM.

When Harpo spoke to Goldwyn, his was an independent production unit with no affiliation with any particular studio. This often causes confusion. In 1923, a year before Loew bought Goldwyn Pictures, Goldwyn formed Samuel Goldwyn Productions, which produced films but did not distribute them. Loew and Mayer owned Goldwyn Pictures, from its name to Leo, the trademark lion that roars at the start of an MGM picture. Harpo courted Goldwyn as head of Samuel Goldwyn Productions, hoping he'd underwrite a Marx Brothers movie he could sell to another studio, such as United Artists, with whom Goldwyn had a solid relationship. A Goldwyn production with the Marxes would have been an independent film, even if distributed by a major studio.

In the 1930s, a "studio" film was one in which production and distribution were both done "in house." A deal with MGM tied the Marxes to MGM for as long as their contracts stipulated. It might seem odd that the Marxes ultimately jumped from one studio to another after their many battles with Paramount. This occurred because Chico met Irving Thalberg at—where else?—a card game, and convinced him that the Marxes were still bankable. Were it not for Thalberg, it's unlikely the Marxes would have gone to MGM; Mayer didn't want them and Groucho loathed Mayer.[3] Most people, including Thalberg, felt that way about Mayer. Mayer had jettisoned Thalberg from his role as MGM production head, prompting Thalberg to set up his own unit within MGM but outside of Mayer's control.[4]

The initial meeting between Thalberg and Groucho began badly. Thalberg said that *Monkey Business* and *Horse Feathers* were "not bad. Not good, either." Groucho was gobsmacked. Thalberg admitted they were funny, but added,

> The trouble was, they had no stories. It's better to be not so funny and have a story the audience is interested in. I don't agree with the principle "anything for a laugh." ... [C]omedy scenes have to further the plot. They have to be helping someone who is a sympathetic character. With a sound story, your pictures would be twice as good and you'd gross three times as much.

When Thalberg opined that *Duck Soup* was "just like the others," Groucho shot back, "I didn't come here to be insulted. If you just want to knock our pictures, I'd rather have lunch by myself, somewhere else."[5]

Upon further discussion, Groucho came away from the first meeting enthused about Thalberg's filmmaking theories. Then things soured again when Thalberg left the Marxes sitting outside his office for two and a half hours. They retaliated by pushing a desk piled high with filing cabinets outside his door. It took Thalberg an hour to extricate himself and he never again kept them waiting.[6]

Despite shaky beginnings, the Marxes came to believe that Thalberg deserved the "boy genius" label that the 36-year-old producer had acquired. It didn't hurt that Chico negotiated a three-picture deal that included 15 percent of the gross, or that Thalberg backed off the idea that their salary should be reduced because Zeppo was no longer on the team. Groucho made the uncharitable remark, "Without Zeppo, we're twice as funny," and the Marxes got their money.[7]

Everything about MGM seemed an upgrade over Paramount. The Marxes hobnobbed with Hollywood royalty, including Lionel Barrymore, Joan Crawford, Clark Gable, Greta Garbo, Jean Harlow and Thalberg's wife, Norma Shearer.

Thalberg further endeared himself by sending the Marxes on tour to test their material before filming. Martin Gardner called this a form of "vaudeville reborn" akin to "market testing," though it didn't quite have that magic.[8] Their road material was not analogous to a vaudeville show. Instead of being a finished product and working from a script that could be edited, they presented out-of-context scenes from competing scripts. Arthur Marx notes that when their six-week tour opened in Seattle, it "laid one of the biggest eggs in the history of the Marx Brothers."[9] As they moved on to Portland, Salt Lake City and San Francisco, the material got sharper. Thalberg intervened to save two of the best scenes that didn't go down well on the road: a contract deal between Driftwood and Fiorello, and one set in Driftwood's ocean liner stateroom. The biggest impact of the Marxes' April–May sojourn shows up in how easily things flowed, especially how the actors anticipated each other's actions. Watch Dumont's face as she moves from a smile to scornful disapproval at the drop of a Groucho insult.

Thalberg also realized that James Kevin McGuinness' story was a dud and assented to Groucho's suggestion that George S. Kaufman and Morrie Ryskind perform major script surgery. It cost MGM $100,000 to convince Kaufman to do another Marx Brothers film.[10] Gag writer Al Boasberg also came aboard and, for once, the Marxes weren't the only mercurial personalities. When Thalberg tried to rush him on a section of the script, Boasberg told him to pick it up at his office after hours. Thalberg arrived to find dialogue scissored from the script and taped to the ceiling like pieces of a jigsaw puzzle.[11]

The Marxes were unimpressed with Sam Wood, whom Groucho called "a lousy director." He also claimed that Thalberg "was really the director." Thalberg reviewed each day's rushes and, "[i]f he didn't like it, Wood would shoot the scenes all over again."[12] In later years, Groucho labeled Wood a "fascist," a response to Wood's extreme conservatism and his testimony against Hollywood insiders accused of Communist subversion.[13]

On the plus side, the Marxes got along very well with Jones, Carlisle and Rumann. Jones recalled, "I never thought I was coming on as Zeppo's replacement. I knew they had to have a love interest and they brought me on to do it. But I knew I was going on to other things. I often saw Zeppo at parties in Las Vegas ... but we never discussed the fact that I'd taken his place." Groucho greeted Jones on the set by calling him "Sloucho."[14]

Carlisle was lured by Thalberg with the promise she could sing legitimate opera. She admitted having reservations about being in a Marx Brothers movie but was surprised by how "very seriously" they behaved on the set. Off the set, though, Groucho gave her the Marxian treatment. His best prank was sending roses C.O.D. to her dressing room with a card signed "Allan Jones."[15] Groucho found the German-born Rumann, who played Herman Gottlieb, an excellent heavy who helped make *A Night at the Opera* Groucho's favorite Marx Brothers film.[16]

And Again, the World Turned

A Night at the Opera was in production by June 1935, wrapped in mid–August, and premiered on November 15. Once again, a Marx Brothers film debuted to an industry and world in transition. Movie studios were reeling from the effects of the Depression and from tightened control over content. Robert Sklar commented that *Duck Soup* was "as thorough a satire on politics and patriotism as any film before *Dr. Strangelove.*"[17] It was fortunate that it came out in 1933, as it might not have made it past censors in 1935. By then, the Motion Picture Production Code of 1930 put strict limits on what could and could not be shown. The Code had hitherto been loosely observed.

The path to enforcement was twisty. Moviemakers and censors have battled since the first silent films flickered. The earliest American films attracted working-class and immigrant audiences, and their content frequently dismayed social elites. Erotic films were sometimes shown, as were European movies in which nude bodies appeared. Actress Audrey Munson was seen naked in the 1915 film *Inspiration* and others followed as late as 1934. Even star actress Theda Bara was practically nude in *Cleopatra* (1917).

Sex wasn't the only thing that distressed moralists: Depictions of crime, violence, misuse of patriotic symbols and disrespect for clerics were among others. Calls to prohibit objectionable material faced uphill battles as long as audiences overwhelmingly came from the working classes.[18] The National Board of Review was founded in 1909 to address immorality in films. Its greatest success came via threats of revoking exhibitor licenses, but the definition of "objectionable" remained vague.[19]

As movie production gravitated to Hollywood and more members of the middle class attended movies, pressure mounted for movies to conform to bourgeois values. In 1922, the Motion Picture Producers and Distributors of America (MPPDA) hired William Harrison Hays as the in-house censor for movie production. Hays, often vilified as a prude, actually opposed forced censorship and was more bothered by tariffs on films, dodgy financing and labor unions. He piloted the industry past the shoals of the infamous 1922 Fatty Arbuckle scandal,[20] which intensified demand for external regulations on movies. The MPPDA convinced studios to place "moral turpitude" clauses in actor contracts, but directors and studios pushed back on sex. A compromise allowed sensuality that did not cast negative light on the family or "public order."[21]

Internal regulation is frequently form over function, but Hollywood tried twice more to make movies more respectable. The MPPDA unveiled a 1927 code that forbade things such as displaying naked children, "licentious or suggestive nudity," mentions of venereal disease, miscegenation, graphic childbirth, "ridicule of clergy" and blasphemous language. It also urged caution on the use of flags, rape, cruelty to animals or children, depictions of crime and scenes of men and women in bed.

When this left too much wiggle room, the MPPDA responded in 1930 with an extensive update that established principles governing plots, plot material and how that material could be applied. On paper, prohibitions were specific and broad. Crime and "evil" could not be "presented alluringly," conventional codes of right and wrong could not be called into doubt or "fogged," adultery could never be justified or "weaken respect for marriage," seduction or rape had to be "essential to the plot," no scenes of actors undressing could be shown, religion could not be ridiculed, patriotism could not be impugned, and there could no sympathy for "sin, crime, wrong-doing or evil." Drinking could only be shown in ways that were "legal," which it wasn't until 1933, and sexuality was broken into the "pure love of a man and a woman ... permitted by the law of God," and "impure love," which was everything else including "perversion," a code word for homosexuality.[22]

In theory, *Horse Feathers* should not have passed muster in 1932, as it lampooned Prohibition. *Duck Soup* was more problematic still, as it skewered the military, hyper-patriotism and conventional sexual morality by including two scenes of women undressing. Very few Marx Brothers films adhered to how sexuality was supposed to be treated. A leering Groucho, a blonde-chasing Harpo, Thelma Todd cavorting in costumes on the verge of falling off—these all violated 1930 standards that held that none of these things was suitable for comedic treatment. They all went to the screen because standards were seldom compelled. That's why films from the period between 1929 and 1934 are dubbed "pre–Code," even though extensive guidelines existed. In 1934, though, the 1930 document became "The Code."

This was due largely to Roman Catholic Church efforts spearheaded by Martin Quigley and Father Daniel Lord. The National League of Decency, established in 1933, lobbied hard against movie immorality. In 1934, the League and Vatican officials called for boycotts of films deemed unacceptable. Given sinking revenues, few producers could afford to oppose the League, and it would have been difficult to find theaters willing to risk showing objectionable movies. Radio priest Charles Coughlin was at the height of his popularity with his free-ranging Radio League of the Little Flower allegedly reaching 30 million listeners. A negative word from Coughlin could torpedo a big-budget film.

This time, Hollywood bowed to pressure. Hays and the MPPDA entrusted Joseph Breen to enforce the Code, and he zealously did so. As Sklar put it, the Breen Office induced a "shift in values" and "a deliberate turning away from reality and controversy...."[23] Producers like Thalberg had to balance entertainment and imposed standards. Leftist thinkers—who endured endless criticism from Coughlin—soon complained that movies had become homogenized, "ignored 'regional [and] ethnic differences,'" and promoted economic disparities that divided social classes.[24]

A Night at the Opera was a stroke of genius. Hardcore fans decried the "softening" of the Marx Brothers, though both Thalberg and the Marxes faced uncertainty of how the Code would be applied.[25] They also needed to negotiate a political climate in which Roosevelt's New Deal was popular among the working classes, but denounced by both elites and the radical left. Writers, Thalberg and the Marxes hit upon a topic that was a soft target for lampoon: opera.

The Code had holes through which verbal comics such as Groucho, Mae West and W.C. Fields maneuvered. They used misdirection, double entendres, metaphors and behaviors so outrageous that no one could imagine a serious attempt to undermine American morality. Often, they were indeed seeking to subvert it. *A Night at the Opera* appeared to be a movie without politics. It wasn't!

Snobs and Commoners

It was wise to steer clear of direct political commentary in 1935. Harpo was acutely aware of the need for caution after his trip to the Soviet Union. As Louvish noted, "any hint of more left-leaning sympathies could alienate the mainstream audience." There were also minor rifts among the brothers, with Groucho and Harpo expressing liberal values and Chico verbalizing disapproval over labor strikes, a view he kept into the 1940s.[26]

Most performers tried to thread the political needle. Uncompromisingly principled stands generally ended as quixotic crusades. Journalist Eugene Lyons coined the phrase "the Red Decade" to describe the attempt of the American Communist Party to radicalize workers.[27] As it played out, the period was more "pink" than red. Roosevelt's New Deal programs were extensive, but not radical. Most were a mélange of early 20th century Progressive Era ideals and liberal notions of how to restore and reform the American economy, leavened with just enough rhetoric from the left to siphon all but its most doctrinaire supporters. Roosevelt likewise proved adroit at incorporating some of the hard right's views on segregation, squeamishness over handouts, and distaste for continued collective farm experiments. A 1934 *Harper's* magazine article asserted firmly, "the New Deal is not a revolution."[28]

The effectiveness of the New Deal is debatable, but Roosevelt presented himself as in charge and on the side of working people. Even perennial Socialist Party presidential candidate Norman Thomas admitted, "The change made by Roosevelt's inauguration and his first hundred days in office was extraordinary. He brought back hope and confidence. The people responded to his own ebullience and his pragmatic program." Thomas complained that the "Machiavellian" FDR had the goal of "saving capitalism," but grudgingly observed, "between 1933 and the validation of the Wagner Labor Act by the Supreme Court in 1937, [FDR] securely laid the foundation of our present welfare state."[29]

Historians have divided views over why America did not move sharply left or right in the midst of economic collapse. Some view the New Deal as anodyne while others cite complex ideological explanations. Melvyn Dubofsky sagely noted the difference between "turbulent" times and a "revolutionary situation." The years 1934 and 1937 were among the most strike-prone years in American history, but they occurred when "hope, profits, employment and wages all revived," that is, during years of hope rather than despair. Strikes also involved just seven percent of the workforce, which prompted Dubofsky's deceptively simple question, "What was the other 93 percent of the labor force doing during the great strike wave of 1934 and 1937?"[30]

What indeed? The answer is that tens of millions voted for Roosevelt and his New Deal, not just the NRA and its 1935 successor, the National Labor Relations Act of 1935; but also programs that targeted (white) farmers such as the Agricultural

Adjustment Act (1933) and the Rural Electrification Administration (1935); and work relief programs like the Civilian Conservation Corps (1933) and the Works Progress Administration (1935). Conservatives attacked New Deal on all fronts, and lost. The Works Progress Administration (WPA) was challenged in the courts, and the Republican Party paid a heavy price for opposing a program that put 8.5 million people to work—including an estimated 250,000 African Americans—and built more than 650,000 miles of roadway and 125,100 public buildings.

The lopsided 1936 election saw Roosevelt garner nearly 61 percent of the popular vote and all of the electoral votes except those from Maine and Vermont. The Republican Party barely had a presence in the new Congress; the House of Representatives held 334 Democrats to 88 Republicans. The Senate figures stood at 74 Democrats, two independents aligned with them, and only 17 Republicans. However one views the New Deal in retrospect, the perspective from 1936 was clear.

Still, why a Marx Brothers film about opera? To understand this, we must look at the influence of the idealism of the American left on culture. As William Stott observed, the 1930s challenged views that "culture" and "art" were "strictly European in nature." Increasing numbers of Americans discovered their own "primitive, folk and popular art." New Deal projects brought "the American artist and the American public face to face."[31]

The impact of these changes was profound. The WPA had five "projects" in addition to its work relief component: the Federal Art Project, the Federal Music Project, the Federal Theatre Project, the Federal Writers' Project and the Federal Records Survey. The national government paid talented individuals to produce public art, offer classes, create mass-appeal music, perform free concerts, write and stage plays celebrating working people, write state guidebooks and preserve historical records.

Although it wasn't written until 1942, the title of composer Aaron Copland's suite *Fanfare for the Common Man* encapsulates the thematic thrust of 1930s art. In the 1930 and '40s, commoners were in and snobs were out. This is reflected in political cartoons that hailed FDR as the champion of working people and farmers, very different from bloated, disgruntled businessmen and bankers. The same divide can be viewed in the politically charged murals of Thomas Hart Benton and Diego Rivera; in the virtue of ordinary people shown on canvas by Charles Kassler, Frances Hodgkins, Ben Shahn and Grant Wood; and in the Dust Bowl paintings of Alexander Hogue and Otis Dozier. The idea was expressed in essays and exposés by Malcolm Crowley, Meridel LeSueur and Thomas Minehan; in Luis Buñuel's documentary film *Land Without Bread*; in WPA "living newspaper" plays; and in poetry and movie newsreels. In novels, the 1930s was the era of "proletarian literature" as penned by Jack Conroy, Erskine Caldwell, John Dos Passos, James Farrell, Mike Gold, Josephine Hebst, Grace Lumpkin, Henry Roth, John Steinbeck, Richard Wright and scores of others.

Nowhere was the documentation of ordinary people during the Great Depression more visible than in photographs. Some of the most iconic images in American history were captured by the lenses of luminaries Margaret Bourke-White, Walker Evans, Dorothea Lange, Russell Lee, Arthur Rothstein, Marion Post Wolcott *et al*. Many of their greatest works came in the employ of Federal Emergency Relief Administration and, after 1937, the Farm Security Administration.

A Night at the Opera: Curtain Down on Snobs

Given the social and political context outlined above, *A Night at the Opera* chose its victims with care. Mark Twain once described opera as "incoherent noise which always reminds me of the time the orphan asylum burned down." He was more on the money, so to speak, when he remarked, "Of all the noises known to man, opera is the most expensive." It's unclear if either phrase was a Twain original; the second is sometimes attributed to the 17th-century French playwright Molière. But Twain never tired of poking fun at opera.

It's not a slam to say that opera belongs to the elite realms of culture challenged during the 1930s. This, as Lawrence Levine reveals, was by design, and had been so since the 19th century. Opera was part of the "sacralization of culture" imagined as a repository of "high" culture associated with refined taste. Not coincidentally, its structure, dress codes and expensive ticket prices served as safeguards to insulate the well-heeled from the unwashed. For a time, even Italian opera was deemed déclassé.[32] The music of *A Night at the Opera* is Italian, but all the operatic trappings highlight the divide between elites and the lower classes.

Class differences emerge from the outset. Mrs. Claypool sits miffed at a table in a fancy restaurant where she is to meet Driftwood. He's been sitting behind her the entire time, dining with an attractive woman whom he promptly sticks with the bill. Claypool chides Driftwood for inattention to his duties: "Mr. Driftwood, three months ago you promised to put me into society. In all that time, you've done nothing but draw a handsome salary." Driftwood replies with remarks appropriate for the time period: "You think that's nothing? How many men do you think draw a handsome salary? You can count them on the fingers of one hand, my good woman." Claypool indignantly protests, "I am not your good woman!" Driftwood ripostes, "I don't care what your past has been," his entrée into a round of wooing and insult. The conversation shifts when Driftwood points to Herman Gottlieb of the New York Opera Company and spills his plan: "Don't you see? You'll be a patron of the opera. You'll get into society. You can marry me, and they'll kick you out of society."

Driftwood is crass, but Claypool is a frivolous social climber willing to spend a fortune to gain entry into society at a time in which one-fifth of the U.S. populace was unemployed and the per capita income was $474 per year. Driftwood is a con man, but at least he knows it and recognizes the trait in others. After a funny round of *faux* polite introductions, Gottlieb kisses Claypool's hand. Driftwood promptly examines it and cracks, "I just wanted to see if your rings are still there." In essence, Gottlieb is in the same racket as Driftwood, he's just pursuing bigger game. Gottlieb dangles a large fish that he hopes to reel in, Rodolfo Lassparri, whom Claypool proclaims "the greatest tenor since Caruso."

Backstage at the famed La Scala opera house in Milan,[33] we find Tomasso (Harpo) playfully wearing one of Lassparri's opera costumes. The vain Lassparri is outraged to discover his humble dresser adorned in one of his costumes. Every time Lassparri demands that Tomasso take off a costume, he is wearing another beneath it, including a peasant girl's dress. Lassparri unleashes a hail of blows and dismisses Tomasso. Rosa witnesses the exchange and Lassparri tries to save face by pretending there was no incident. Rosa knows a tyrannical egoist when she sees one; moments later, she tosses flowers sent by Lassparri into the trash.

Rosa's true love, Ricardo, is also an opera singer but he's in the chorus, not the limelight. We also learn that though Ricardo now sings highbrow music, he and Fiorello were once in the circus together. The two are bonded by mutual affection, not divided by culture or status. Fiorello offers to become Ricardo's manager. He protests, "But you wouldn't make any money at it." Fiorello replies, "I'll break even. Just as long as I no lose nothing."

A quick cut back to Driftwood reminds us that his interest in opera is purely pecuniary. Riding in a carriage, he asks the driver, "Is the opera over yet?" When told not quite, Driftwood is indignant: "I told you to slow those horses down. On account of you, I nearly heard the opera. Once around the park, and drive slowly." When the driver asks, "You no like opera, signor?" Driftwood replies, "Like it? The night Caruso sang 'Bohème' at the Metropolitan, I cried like a baby. I was at the dentist's having a tooth pulled.'" Arriving just as the curtain falls, Driftwood goes backstage to sign the world's greatest tenor, though he doesn't know Lassparri from lasagna and interrupts him as he is again abusing Tomasso.

Lassparri and Gottlieb are *A Night at the Opera*'s fall guys, a decision that had Thalberg's fingerprints all over it. When Lassparri hits Tomasso or hits on Rosa, we are repulsed. Likewise, Gottlieb's humiliation of Driftwood is mean-spirited rather than one mountebank upping another. As Thalberg explained his theories on comedy to Groucho, he remarked, "Hit a fellow in old clothes with a snowball, and it won't mean a thing. But dress a man up in tails and a silk hat, and then knock his hat off with a snowball, and you get a laugh."[34]

In the age of the common man, we expect to see pride brought low, and we do. The opera company members board a ship bound for New York. On the dock, Lassparri refuses to sing for admirers, many of whom look unlikely to be La Scala patrons. He claims he has a slight case of laryngitis, though he tells Gottlieb, "Why should I sing to them when I'm not being paid for it?" Rosa steps up to the ship's railing to sing for the crowd and Ricardo joins her from his place on the dock.

As the boat sails, we catch Driftwood atop trunks being wheeled to his stateroom. Driftwood feigns reaching into his pocket to tip the steward and asks if he has two five-dollar bills, presumably to make change as $5 was the customary tip for on-board baggage handling. When the answer is in the affirmative, Driftwood replies, "Well, then, you won't need the ten cents I was going to give you."[35] Perhaps it's just as well; to say Driftwood's cabin was not what he expected is an understatement. It is little more than a janitor's closet with a bunk, but more on that later. As in *Monkey Business*, we encounter a stratified ship with social markers in place: an arrogant captain, a privileged staff, posh digs for those with wealth, below-decks lodging for those like Driftwood, grand dining for elites, steerage and open-air dining for immigrants, and Driftwood's steamer trunk for stowaways Ricardo, Fiorello and Tomasso.

Lassparri's sense of entitlement reappears later when Rosa's rebuffs his advances in favor of Ricardo, and he dumps her as the opera's leading lady. The fugitive stowaways offer to surrender if Rosa is reinstated, but Gottlieb and Lassparri refuse and the chase for all three is transferred from sea to shore, with Detective Henderson (Robert Emmett O'Connor) aiding pursuit.

Driftwood is humbled when he is fired from his post at the opera. He goes to his office in a private elevator and sees his name being scraped off the office door. His visit to Gottlieb portends worse trouble. When Driftwood leaves, he is booted down the stairs by the formerly deferential elevator operator.

Eyles remarked, "All this humiliation has the effect of making the Marx Brothers more sympathetic...."[36] The question of whether we want them to be sympathetic is washed aside by the current of class consciousness flowing through *A Night at the Opera.* Gottlieb and Lassparri should have taken the offer of surrender, as both will receive their comeuppances. Lassparri is knocked out of commission long enough for Ricardo and Rosa to save the opera, and Lassparri is booed off the stage during a vainglorious attempt to sing an encore. As the fruit flies, a deflated Lassparri cries, "They threw an apple at me." Driftwood's line "Watermelons are out of season" completes Lassparri's humiliation. Those familiar with Depression-era films might compare Rosa's triumph to Ruby Keeler's rise to the top in *42nd Street.*

The Party of the First Part: Classic Scenes

There are fewer Groucho insults in *A Night at the Opera*, due partly to the Code and partly to Thalberg's desire to tame the Marxes. Still, there are several choice barbs and at least four scenes considered classics.

Scene One: **Contract negotiations.** Driftwood negotiates with Fiorello, thinking he represents Lassparri. Both rest their shoes on the knocked-out Lassparri as if he were a barroom foot railing. An exchange of nonsensical small talk precedes the contract signing.

> **DRIFTWOOD:** I want to sign him up for the New York Opera Company. Do you know that America is waiting to hear him sing?
> **FIORELLO:** He can sing loud, but he can't sing that loud.
> **DRIFTWOOD:** I think I can get America to meet him halfway. Could he sail tomorrow?
> **FIORELLO:** You pay him enough money, he could sail yesterday.

Once money is mentioned, the two discuss negotiation fees, agent percentages, money to send home to his mother, income taxes, state taxes, city taxes, street taxes and sewer taxes until Driftwood exclaims, "I figure if he doesn't sing too often, he can break even." Of course, Fiorello accepts the terms.

Then comes the part that will warm the heart of anyone who has ever tried to read a legal contract. Long pieces of paper appear, filled with clauses that lampoon legal jargon. Confusion begins with, "The party of the first part shall be known in this contract as the party of the first part." Fiorello is troubled by this, and the two agree to tear it out of the contract. "The party of the second part" goes no better, and on it goes. At one point, Driftwood tells Fiorello, "I've got something you're bound to like," which is rejected before it's even read! The contract shrinks inch by inch. They make it to the party of the ninth part, decide to skip it, and proceed to the signing. But then Fiorello divulges, "I forgot to tell you, I can't write." "That's all right, there's no ink in the pen," replies Driftwood. There's no way Fiorello will agree to the contract's sanity clause: "You can't fool me. There ain't no Sanity Claus." I have often wondered how many lawyers have had that line thrown back at them.

Scene Two: **Driftwood's stateroom.** If two's company and three's a crowd, what's 15 or more people and a giant steamer trunk crammed into a four-foot by four-foot ship cabin designed for one?[37] Answer: One of the funniest sight gags in movie history and a lesson in trusting comedic intuition instead of test marketing. The scene takes place inside Driftwood's cabin. Driftwood takes one look at his "birdcage" and asks, "Wouldn't it be simpler if you just put the stateroom in the trunk?" Once his trunk is wedged inside, imagine his surprise when his clothes are gone and Fiorello and Baroni emerge from the trunk.

A snoring Tomasso is in the bottom drawer, where Driftwood hoped to find a clean shirt. Fiorello explains, "He's got insomnia [and] he's sleeping it off." Nothing rouses him, but Driftwood insists all three interlopers must leave because he has a date with Claypool in a few minutes. Whenever Chico is in a tight spot, he demands to be fed before he does anything. What ensues is an amusing food-ordering sequence in which the comatose Tomasso manages to honk his horn to add two more hard-boiled eggs (and one duck egg) to Driftwood's ever-expanding order.

More visitors come knocking on the door. An engineer and his assistant appear to turn off the heat, a manicurist enters with her tools, a woman looking for her Aunt Minnie squeezes in, as does a housekeeper with her mop and bucket. Also a parade of stewards bearing domed trays of food. You couldn't possibly cram another canary into this birdcage. When Claypool opens the door, everyone tumbles out like a row of dominoes knocked over.

This Al Boasberg sketch tested badly on the road. Accounts differ whether Groucho or Thalberg made the call, but the push to cut the scene from the script was overruled.[38] In retrospect, it is easy to see why it might have baffled stage audiences; without the setup to provide context, it probably looked like little more than a tumbling act gone wrong. Thalberg correctly calculated that the routine would look different on the screen. Jones added the insight that the gag got funnier as the stateroom got smaller. Plus, ad libs such as Harpo's egg-ordering honks added flourishes that had audiences snickering "before the pandemonium began."[39] How serendipitous is it that hunches saved one of comedy's greatest sight gags?

The Marxes were probably not the first to milk comedy from cramming too many people into a confined space, but variants of the stateroom gag definitely followed. Jones was right; smaller was funnier. Stick very tall clowns in a kiddie car and laughter ensues, which is why the Cole Brothers Circus added that routine to its performances in the 1950s and why it's been a staple for Shriners ever since. In the late 1950s and early 1960s, a fad of stuffing as many people as possible into a telephone booth was all the rage on college campuses, as was squeezing college women into hollow trees.[40] Television's animated series *The Simpsons* opens with too many people attempting to cram onto a couch. These Dionysian moments might rank low on an intellectual scale, but they tickle funny bones.

Scene Three: **Cute kids.** If you want to make characters sympathetic, posing them with photogenic kids is a hackneyed but surefire way of doing so. Chico and Harpo find themselves on a lower deck with Italian immigrant families. Chico sits at the piano and begins playing "All I Do Is Dream of You," a Nacio Herb Brown tune. His dramatic and silly gestures delight the children, especially his shoot-the-keys maneuver and penchant for playing a tune slowly before jocularly ratcheting up the pace.

Chico charms the appreciative children, though unlike Harpo, he's not a natural among them. Harpo's encounter with children is reminiscent of *Monkey Business'* puppet scene in that he instantly inspires gales of delight and laughter. He sits at the piano after clowning with a spinning stool, then launching what is at first an impressive spray of notes. As his face gets more serious, he slides into atonality for comedic effect. The kids squeal with amusement as he feigns slamming his hand in the keyboard lid, leaving him limp-wristed and floppy-handed. When he repeats the gags, the kids are putty in his hands. Harpo takes up his namesake instrument to play another Nacio Herb Brown tune, "Alone." It's not exactly children's fare and Harpo's treatment sounds more calypso than Italian, but he has won young hearts. The kids are enthralled by Harpo and cheer enthusiastically as he finishes. It's a sweet interlude amidst the film's themes of disruption and disorder, one that stands in marked contrast to what Harpo will do to the opera *Il Trovatore.* And for once, the instrumental solos are threaded into the plot.

Scene Four: **How to drive a detective crazy.** Ricardo, Fiorello and Tomasso need a place to hide out. Where do they go? Driftwood's hotel room, of course; it has room service! Driftwood is again forced to feed them, but he wants them gone because he knows Henderson is on their tail and has no desire to join them in jail. Of course, the vagabonds eat everything in sight, including Driftwood's breakfast and cigar. Tomasso is on such a binge that Driftwood casually remarks, "I'm glad I didn't bring my vest." Fiorello confesses, "I forgot to tell you. He ate your vest last night for dessert."

A rap at the door alerts them that Henderson has caught up with the desperados. They dash through a door to an adjoining room, thus setting in motion a madcap farce in which Henderson goes through one door or window and the fugitives duck through another. Driftwood, who is not a wanted man, provides wisecracking misdirection. For instance, when Henderson overhears a conversation and asks who he's talking to, Driftwood replies, "I was talking to myself and there's nothing you can do about it. I've had three of the best doctors in the east."

People running between rooms, fleeing onto balconies or escaping through windows has long been a staple of farce. Roman playwright Plautus (254–184 BC) is often acknowledged as Western society's first master of farce, a genre with various subcategories, including those involving mistaken identity and more risqué bedroom-sex farces. Seventeenth-century English Restoration comedies burlesqued social manners by depicting suitors and Lotharios making hasty exits. The same was true of Italian *commedia dell'arte* plays. Less bawdy farce relies more heavily upon rapid pacing and visual artistry than scandal. The in-one-door-out-the-other technique, if expertly timed, is hilarious.[41]

A Night at the Opera amps up the farce by driving the pursuer crazy. As Henderson dashes from room to room, things slowly change. There are four beds in the adjoining bedroom, then three with one in the sitting-dining room that Driftwood has never vacated. Each time Henderson returns to the bedroom, another bed has gone through the window and into the sitting room, and Driftwood pretends not to notice anything amiss. Soon, the bedroom has become the sitting room and vice versa. A blanket is thrown over Fiorello to turn him into a "rocking chair" occupied by Tomasso posing as an old woman knitting. Driftwood has been transformed into a whiskered man reading a newspaper, and Ricardo has ducked out of sight. Henderson concludes he has the wrong room and leaves, flustered and no wiser.

Scene Five: **How to ruin an opera.** Martin Gardner writes, "*A Night at the*

Opera did not disturb opera lovers to complain about the Brothers' symbolic act of the destruction of opening night at the New York Opera Company."[42] True enough, but those attending the opening of the opera season were probably not attending the debut of a Marx Brothers film. It's clear that *A Night at the Opera* is intended as a blistering satirical critique. To reiterate, hierarchy—from social climbers, opera company managers and lawyers to ship officers, hotel detectives and opera patrons— takes it on the chin.

Driftwood drops a hat he stole from Gottlieb over the theater box railing and barks to a patron on the orchestra level, "Shorty, will you toss up that kelly?" He further demeans Gottlieb by tossing the man a coin to "get yourself a stogie." Even Driftwood's use of the term "kelly" is loaded, as it usually references a straw boater or a derby worn by working-class men, not a silk top hat. Driftwood proceeds to deliver an absurd impromptu speech because Claypool is terrified to address those whose attention she craves. Leave it to Driftwood to tell everyone that Lassparri's father was the "first man to stuff spaghetti with bicarbonate of soda, thus causing and curing indigestion at the same time." Or to proclaim, "Let there be dancing in the streets, drinking in the saloons and necking in the parlor."

The Marxes level devastation upon *Il Trovatore* that surpasses *The Cocoanuts'* "Tale of the Shirt" lampoon. There are fleeting references to "The Anvil Chorus," and a moment when the lead gypsy vocalist's facial expressions make Harpo's gookie look tame by comparison. The disruption of *Il Trovatore* unites Rosa and Ricardo, but "anarchy" best describes what happens beforehand.

The Marxes do everything to the opera except spit out the scenery they've chewed. Tomasso initiates a swordfight in the orchestra pit, he and the conductor doing battle with violin bows. He also replaces the opera score with "Take Me Out to the Ballgame," while he and Fiorello stage an impromptu game using instruments as sporting goods, while Driftwood walks among the audience hawking peanuts. And what could be sillier than the beefy Gottlieb, Henderson and policemen dressed as peasants wending their way through the chorus in an effort to nab Ricardo, Fiorello and Tomasso? Picture Chico and Harpo dressed as gypsy women. Imagine Harpo's reaction when Lassparri, in character, cracks a whip on the stage. On cue, Lassparri rips the outer dress from a dancer, but Tomasso strips her to her briefs. (How did that survive the Code?)

You name it and it's done, including Harpo's wrestling match with Lassparri, lighting a match on Lassparri's armpit, and mugging between a dancer's legs. Tomasso turns half-chimpanzee, half–trapeze artist as he is pursued backstage. He swings from catwalk to catwalk using ropes securing backdrops. Lassparri desperately tries to hold the audience's attention as the painted scenery changes every few seconds, revealing woodland tents, train cars, a fruit vendor's cart and a battleship! To humiliate Lassparri even more, Tomasso swoops down and snatches his wig, smashes through a backdrop, tumbles through a ripping screen, and shimmies back up. The lunacy ends only after Tomasso trapezes his way to an electrical junction box and darkens the theater. We hear a squawk and it's lights out for Lassparri as well.

Harpo's physical schtick is amazing, but respect for opera it's not. Tomasso is a free-spirited imp seeking revenge on the cruel Lassparri, but he also enjoys wrecking the opera. During his rampage, Tommaso's face is filled with glee, not anger.

Groucho Tamed?

The only Marx Thalberg actually tamed was Groucho. Driftwood is transformed from self-seeker to sentimental matchmaker. *A Night at the Opera*, as Thalberg wished, had far fewer jokes and less dialogue, most coming at Groucho's expense as the most verbal of the brothers.

Nonetheless, Groucho delivers several zingers, a couple of which skirted Code boundaries. What does he mean when he tells Claypool, "There's something about me that brings out the business in all women?" Does "the business" imply chicanery, and double-dealing, or the inference that Claypool is not Driftwood's first attempted amorous conquest? We can't be certain what Driftwood intends, and neither could Code enforcers.

Groucho's lechery shifted from obvious to innuendo, though it doesn't take much imagination to decode what Driftwood means inside of Claypool's stateroom: He proclaims, "Twin beds! You little rascal, you." He plops down on one of them, much to Claypool's chagrin: "Mr. Driftwood, will you please get off the bed? What would people say?" Driftwood's response: "They'd say you're a very lucky woman."

Groucho's zingers come at Dumont's expense, though they are not as cutting as in the past. "Mrs. Claypool isn't as big a sap as she looks" is a backhanded insult. More direct is Groucho's admonition that Gottlieb should "nix the lovemaking because I saw Mrs. Claypool first. Of course, her mother really saw her first, but why bring the Civil War into this?" Driftwood tells Claypool that once she becomes the opera's underwriter, "All New York will be at your feet," but can't resist adding, "There's plenty of room."

A Night at the Opera was a funny film, but it was not Groucho's finest hour. His sharp barbs were filed to rounded edges that seem more like paper cuts than slashes to the jugular vein. Plus, once the opera begins, he recedes into the background. Driftwood reappears at the conclusion, but he is on good behavior. As forced as the ending of *Horse Feathers* was, it is more like Groucho to crawl all over Thelma Todd than to coo over the loving bliss of two opera singers.

We Forgot the Airplane

Ricardo, Tomasso and Fiorello pose as Russian aviator brothers to sneak off the ship, with Tomasso having tied them to their beds and cut off their beards. The poseurs hadn't planned on giving a speech when they deboarded in New York, though this was expected at a time in which air travel remained a rare and dangerous novelty.

For most readers, there have always been jet planes that fly from New York to Paris in seven and a half hours or so. But when *A Night at the Opera* was made, there would be no transatlantic passenger service by plane for another four years, via a seaplane that took 29 hours to travel from Newfoundland to Ireland. The Marx Brothers are once again on a ship, the average crossing time of which between the U.S. and Europe was four and a half days, but it was far safer.

As many of us learned in elementary school, Orville and Wilbur Wright made the first successful air flight near Kitty Hawk, North Carolina, on December 17, 1903. Their ascent lasted but 12 seconds, but it inspired tinkerers and engineers to greater heights. Flying, though, remained dangerous. In 1908, Thomas Selfridge became the first person to die in an airplane crash. Over the next two and a half decades, the carnage from air disasters made human flight among the riskiest things anyone could undertake.

The Wright brothers held aerial demonstrations between 1909 and 1911, but stopped when six of their nine team members were killed in accidents. Several famous Americans also died in air accidents, including Harriet Quimby (1912), the first licensed female pilot; aviation pioneer Charles Franklin Niles (1916); and John Purroy Mitchel (1919), a former New York City mayor for whom a Long Island airfield was posthumously named. Britain's Sir John Alcock and Arthur Whitten Brown made the first successful west-to-east transatlantic flight in 1919; Alcock died in a solo flight later that year.

You might notice that Alcock and Brown crossed the Atlantic eight years before Charles Lindbergh, whose 33½-hour flight in the monoplane *Spirit of St. Louis* from New York to Paris in May 1927 gained him hero status. He was indeed "Lucky Lindy," as several competitors died or disappeared, including two attempting a west-to-east flight that no solo pilot successfully completed until 1932. Numerous pilots had made transatlantic flights by 1927, but never without a crew and usually after several refueling stops along the way.[43] Lindbergh's achievement was significant, but his instant celebrity was 1920s-style ballyhoo also boosted by the those who followed his progress through radio broadcast updates.[44]

Lindbergh was a mail pilot prior to his famed flight; delivery services and air shows were the primary uses of airplanes until the 1920s. Even then, commercial passenger flights took place in small planes with capacities of about six people. Most were short or had multiple legs; carrying fuel for long flights proved challenging. Trains remained more popular for long-distance travel, because they were safer. Between 1920 and 1935, at least 188 people died in airplane crashes, a toll that included Arctic explorer Roald Edmundson (1928), football coach Knute Rockne (1931) and aviation pioneer Wiley Post (1935).[45]

This is why intrepid aviators were feted in the 1930s. The joke within a joke in *A Night at the Opera* is that Chico, Harpo and Jones pose as Russian aviators; in 1935, no Russian had yet crossed the Atlantic by plane. In 1934, a team of Russian test pilots flew 7,700 miles from Moscow to Kharkov, Ukraine, though it took four stages and 75 air hours. We don't know how many pilots perished during Russia's flight pioneering days; that sort of information was controlled by Soviet officials. We can ascertain that no Russian plane made it across the ocean until June 20, 1937, when a three-man crew led by pilot Valery Chkalov made a 63-hour, 23-minute flight from Leningrad (St. Petersburg) to Vancouver, Washington.[46] The next year, Chkalov perished in a crash.

Add aviation to the list of the things burlesqued in *A Night at the Opera*. With glued-on whiskers, Fiorello is forced to give a speech outside of New York's City Hall. No one seems to notice that his "Russian" accent sounds Italian, but those in the VIP bleachers certainly wondered about the content of his oration, beginning with his claim that the first time they tried, they ran out of gas halfway across the ocean and had to go back. The second time, "I take twice as much gasoline. This time we were just about to land ... when, what do you think, we run out of gasoline again. Back we go and get more gas. We get halfway over, when what do you think happened? We forgot the airplane.... Then I get the great idea: We no take gasoline. We no take the airplane. We take steamship. And that, friends, is how we fly across the ocean."

The perplexed mayor turns to Tomasso with the admonition, "I would suggest you make your speech a little more direct than your brother's." Good luck with that, since Harpo doesn't speak. He stalls by drinking glass after glass of water, but the overflow runs down his beard, loosens the glue and exposes the fraud. Tomasso, Fiorello and Ricardo create havoc in prison and escape during the confusion. So much for the pioneers of flight.

More Italian Elephants in the Room

In his 1978 book *Orientalism*, Columbia Professor Edward Said explored the ways in which Western cultures interpreted the Middle East, including through romanticized and exoticized images.[47] His work renewed awareness of how a stereotype is a stereotype whether intended to belittle or flatter. This is because they are based upon superiority-inferiority relationships between those doing the labeling and the labeled.

By extension, there is a shipboard sequence that could be considered as insulting to Italian immigrants. Since *A Night at the Opera* opens in Milan, we infer that Tomasso and Fiorello are Italian. Presumably this is true also of Ricardo Baroni, as he too is in line for deportation if caught. Shipboard hunger sends all three on the prowl for food. Their eyes pop out when they gaze down at a lower deck where a grand feast is taking place. As Gardner observes, the partiers "appear to be Italian peasants [but] they are not typical steerage passengers traveling to America.... They are a happy lot ... singing, dancing, laughing and playing music."[48]

They certainly don't like the immigrants that photographer Lewis Hine captured arriving at Ellis Island; they look more like a folkloric ensemble. Their appearance is also anachronistic; their attire looks as if it came from Italian costume museums. Note the number of pristine white aprons, laced bodices, gaily patterned skirts and head scarves among the females. The men sport artful mustaches, blousy shirts, neat vests, neck scarves and hats. Everyone is singing "Santa Lucia," a 19th-century Neapolitan song that's about as stereotypical as Italian music gets. There's also a more ominous anachronism at play. Remember that a major aim of the Immigration Act of 1924 was to curtail immigration from Southern and Eastern Europe. In 1934, just 4,374 Italians came to America. Apparently, most of them were on the same ship as the Marx Brothers.

The stowaways make for the food line and their plates are piled high with mounds of spaghetti, zeppelin-shaped loaves of bread and (strangely) entire pineapples, which are not native to Italy. Baroni repays their hosts' kindness by singing "Così Cosà," though with an affected accent that makes Chico's sound genuine. The title translates to so-so/this-that, an ambiguous answer to song questions such as, "If a lady should ask you if you care / You don't have to start an affair / It's proper to say Così Cosà." Everyone joins in to sing: "Così Cosà! / It's a wonderful world / Tra la la...."

This song was written for the film by Bronisaw Kaper, Walter Jurmann and Ned Washington. Jones later put it on an album titled *The Donkey Serenade* and it passed into popular culture. The Xavier Cugat Orchestra recorded it in 1935; Italian American opera and film star Mario Lanza did so in 1948. But no matter who sings it, it's no more Italian than Italian dressing.[49]

Is the food scene offensive? I see it as light-hearted fluff designed to integrate solos from Jones, Chico and Harpo, but the answer depends upon where one draws the line between dressing in costume and cultural appropriation. The view of Italians is so exaggerated and situationally unlikely that it could be viewed as innocent. If we draw the cultural appropriation line too narrowly, most costumed operas also descend into stereotyping. Apparently, those living on the Apennine Peninsula agree that no harm was done, as *A Night at the Opera* has been dubbed in Italian. So perhaps we should, as "Così Cosà" suggests, "Get together and sing tra la la la."

Coda: References Needing More Context

- **Trailer:** The first *Night at the Opera* trailer had Groucho and Chico roaring alongside Leo the Lion. (Harpo tried his best!) Leo soloed for the theatrical release. It's too bad MGM was so protective of its signature trademark, as the rejected trailer is funny![50]
- **Again a widow:** Dumont was again cast as a wealthy widow, a role that paralleled real life. In 1910, she married sugar refinery industrialist John Moller Jr. Alas, he died during the 1918 flu pandemic. Dumont lived until 1965, but never remarried. (She also burned through her inheritance.)
- **Duplicates?** In the legal contract scene, Driftwood hands Fiorello a "duplicate" of the original. Fiorello is baffled, so Driftwood asks, "Don't you know what duplicates are?" Fiorello replies, "Sure, those five kids up in Canada." The reference is to the Dionne quintuplets born in Ontario on May 28, 1934. It was a sensational human-interest story. The birth was unusual in that all five girls were identical. They were taken from their parents at the advice of Dr. Allan Roy Dafoe and Father Daniel Routhier and put on display, including at the 1934 Chicago World's Fair. The Dionnes had second thoughts, which led to custody battles. Eventually, the Province of Ontario assumed guardianship and turned the girls' care over to the Red Cross, though the girls were supposed to remain wards of the province until they turned 18. In 1943, they were returned to their parents and raised in a 20-room home financed by special funds and earnings from the children's "appearances," including three forgettable Hollywood films. All five lived into adulthood and, as of 2021, two remained alive.
- **Minnie the Moocher:** Driftwood is thunderstruck when told Lassparri could command $1,000 a night for singing: "You can get a phonograph record of 'Minnie the Moocher' for 75 cents." The reference is to a 1931 hit song from Cab Calloway. He was a flamboyant hot jazz and scat singer, dancer and orchestra leader who helped jazz great Dizzy Gillespie get his start. Calloway was a prototype for rock 'n' roller Little Richard.

  "Minnie the Moocher" sold over a million copies. Minnie is a "red-hot hootchie-coocher," meaning she performed a risqué dance. The song is loaded with drug and alcohol allusions. It's amazing that Groucho's reference made it past Code watchers, as "cootchie" is black slang term for female genitalia. Plus, what did censors think they were hearing in Groucho's line, "For a buck and a quarter, you can get Minnie."

- **Suspenders:** When Driftwood introduces Gottlieb to Claypool, it is with an endless series of "Mrs. Claypool, Mr. Gottlieb; Mr. Gottlieb, Mrs. Claypool" salutations. Each time, Driftwood bows and Gottlieb follows suit. Driftwood finally breaks the pattern by announcing, "I could go on all night, but it's tough on my suspenders." Gardner observed that the joke was dated, as very few men wore suspenders in 1935. He is correct, though suspenders have followed the usual in-out-in-again pattern of other fashion trends. They made a return in the 1960s with the counterculture and, most famously, spawned a short-lived trend among women after the 1977 film *Annie Hall.* They also gained cachet on Wall Street and with CNN's Larry King.[51]
- **I want to be alone:** Henderson is searching Driftwood's room and Driftwood wants him to leave. He leans against the frame as if about to faint and proclaims, "I want to be alone." This is a Hollywood in-joke. "I want to be alone" was the signature phrase of Swedish-born actress Greta Garbo, who often played glamorous but aloof characters. She first used variations of the phrase in 1929's *The Single Standard* and 1931's *Inspiration* and *Mata Hari,* and the exact phrase in 1932's *Grand Hotel.* Lampoons of it proliferated, and Garbo—who was a recluse in life—engaged in self-parody by declaring her desire or fate to be alone in at least three other movies.[52]

Box Office and Beyond

Ticket sales proved Thalberg was right about the Marx Brothers. *A Night at the Opera* raked in $3.3 million to *Duck Soup*'s $2.1 million. It's possible that some of this can be attributed to the fact that the economy was better in 1935 than in 1933.

Audiences and (most) critics liked *A Night at the Opera.* Louvish reckons the enthusiastic response had to do with it being "the only film in which the Marx Brothers' manic energy co-exists with a more humane pathos, a sense that the romance and sentiment are not just tacked on for appeasement's sake." Years later, Hollywood director Mike Nichols astounded Groucho by confessing that he had seen *A Night at the Opera* 17 times. It wasn't the gags that drew Nichols in: "I just couldn't get over that love story between Allan Jones and Kitty Carlisle," said he.[53]

New Republic critic Otis Ferguson saw it as a shameless mishmash of stolen material, clowning, and "bad jokes I've laughed myself nearly sick over." According to Adamson, "*A Night at the Opera* was greeted with waves of applause and roars of laughter deafening to the ear and to other organs as well. Critics, knowing in their hearts they had missed [the Marx Brothers] the season before, now recalled their old movies with a misty-eyed fondness…. The movie was hailed as a beautiful desecration of civilization's most claustrophobic art form … and one of the funniest comedies ever made." Never mind that not he, legendary film critic Pauline Kael, Wes D. Gehring, nor I agree with that assessment.[54] The American Film Institute ranks it the 12th-greatest comedy ever made. I like it a lot, but I take solace in the fact that *Duck Soup* remains seven slots higher.

EIGHT

A Day at the Races (1937)

The difference between the Marx Brothers' previous film and their next was the difference between night and day. That is, *A Night at the Opera* begat *A Day at the Races*. Parts of *A Day at the Races* are funnier than its predecessor, though Joe Adamson was correct that *Opera* left "a legacy of rules to follow."[1] This extended to character development, relationships, structure and the handling of musical interludes. *A Day at the Races* is generally viewed as the Marx Brothers' last great film. In my view, as a musical comedy, it's their best.

The picture opens in Sparkling Springs, a resort town that's a cross between Saratoga Springs, New York, and Kentucky's Churchill Downs.[2] Tony (Chico) is trying to drum up business for Standish Sanitarium, whose owner Judy (Maureen O'Sullivan) faces crippling debt now that the more modern Morgan Hotel is siphoning business from her spa. Morgan (Douglass Dumbrille) is willing to buy her out, and Judy's business manager Whitmore (Leonard Ceeley) urges her to accept the offer. Whitmore is actually in cahoots with Morgan; the latter is a gambler who plans to turn Standish Sanitarium into a casino. In an echo of Lassparri in *A Night at the Opera*, Morgan beats his jockey Stuffy (Harpo), who won a race he was supposed to throw.

Judy also has boyfriend woes: Gil Stewart (Allan Jones) has just spent his life savings, which were set aside to advance his music career, to buy Hi-Hat, a racehorse he hopes can win a big race (he can then retire Judy's debts). Her best hope is to borrow money from wealthy hypochondriac Emily Upjohn (Margaret Dumont), but Upjohn is in the process of moving to Morgan's hotel because Standish's doctors have pronounced her perfectly healthy, and she insists she's not.

Tony overhears Upjohn proclaim that Judy needs a doctor like Hugo Z. Hackenbush to head her medical staff. Tony runs outside and tells the porters to reverse course with Upjohn's suitcases. As they march back in, Tony pretends that lots of guests are checking in now that Dr. Hackenbush is taking charge. Upjohn is delighted and decides to stay. Tony now needs to find Hackenbush and bring him to Sparkling Springs.

Cut to Hackenbush (Groucho), who is actually a Florida veterinarian; he once met Upjohn and hoodwinked her into believing he was a medical doctor. He's a huckster, but we know he's got a good heart when he dons his jacket and there's a cute puppy in the sleeve. If an "awww!" moment doesn't foreshadow a good guy, I don't what does. Tony convinces Hackenbush to come north, and he arrives in time to defer the sanitarium's sale. Whitmore is determined to discredit Hackenbush to get his cut of Morgan's business deal.

All of this is framework for various subplots. Gil is penniless and owes $150 in feed bills for Hi-Hat, whom the sheriff (Robert Middlemass), another Morgan flunky,

Lobby card for *A Day at the Races* (MGM, via Wikimedia Commons).

threatens to seize unless Gil coughs up the dough. How do you play hide-and-seek with a horse? Observe and learn. Hi-Hat also has some horse sense: He goes haywire every time he hears Morgan's voice.

Hackenbush faces several dilemmas. If he is unmasked, the sheriff will throw him in jail. The sanitarium's medical staff has doubts about their new chief, and Whitmore has procured Dr. Leopold X. Steinberg (Sig Ruhmann) from Vienna to grill Hackenbush about his credentials. Steinberg is astounded by Hackenbush's diagnosis that Upjohn has the world's only known case of "double blood pressure," high blood on the right side of her body and low on the left. Finally, Hackenbush must also be saved from the clutches of Flo Marlowe (Esther Muir), still another Morgan plant. Adamson archly described Muir as "a quick-frozen Thelma Todd."[3]

Can the sanitarium be saved? Will Gil and Judy bury their differences? Does Hackenbush avoid jail? Will Hi-Hat win his big race? If you remember that Irving Thalberg thought women moviegoers wanted romance stories and sympathetic Marxes, you've got your answers. The film often plays like a wag-and-nag version of *A Night at the Opera*, but despite its faults, it's funnier because Groucho has more to do, his tongue is sharper, and rascality suits him.

Death Comes Early, and Other Obstacles

At 109 minutes, *A Day at the Races* was the Marx Brothers' longest film. Whether it needed to be that long is debatable. It was indeed cut from the same cloth as *A Night at the Opera,* but that was not the original intent. Its working title was *Peace and Quiet.* If only! It went through 18 scripts and numerous rewrites. The final version emerged as much out of exhaustion as revision. To make matters more difficult, filming took place against backdrops of tragedy and discord.

A Night at the Opera had scarcely debuted before pressure mounted for a new Marx Brothers movie. Much to the Marxes' chagrin, Sam Wood was retained to direct, though they were certain that producer Thalberg would take charge. Thalberg controlled his production unit, but he did not have an unlimited budget and could not deflect MGM's decision to hire George Oppenheimer instead of George S. Kaufman and Morrie Ryskind as writers. It wasn't a bad call; Oppenheimer had worked on the radio show *Flywheel, Shyster and Flywheel.* He went on to become a respected screenwriter, though in 1937 he lacked the clout of Kaufman and Ryskind and was more accustomed to writing screwball comedies. After two scripts that both Thalberg and the Marxes hated, Thalberg took Groucho's suggestion and pulled in Robert Pirosh and George Seaton, who had written for the Marxes before.

Consulting and writing are not the same thing. Pirosh came to Hollywood via advertising. In 1949, he won an Oscar and several other awards for his *Battleground* screenplay, and later enjoyed success writing for television. He had no such gravitas in 1937. Seaton also went on to screenwriting fame, most notably for 1947's *Miracle on 34th Street.* In 1937, though, he was better known as an actor; he was the original Lone Ranger on radio, but had a scanty writing résumé.

After several more desultory scripts, Thalberg approached Kaufman. He was

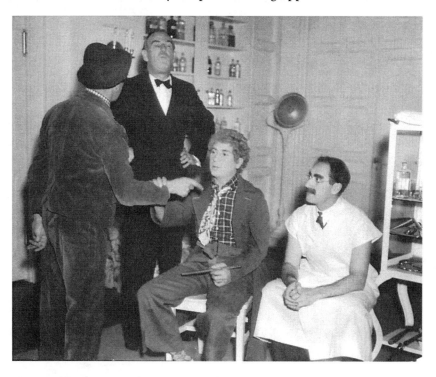

Sam Wood misdirects the Marx Brothers (Chico, Harpo, Groucho) on the *Day at the Races* set (*Minneapolis Star Tribune,* via Wikimedia Commons).

busy at the time, but agreed to take a look at the material. He is sometimes credited with suggesting the film's focus on horseracing. Kaufman pocketed substantial fees and was listed as having produced the screenplay in conjunction with Carey Wilson. Leon Gordon and Al Boasberg came aboard to punch up the script, making MGM's attempt at parsimony a costly failure.[4]

It was, though, money well spent if we consider rejected ideas such as placing Harpo on a Russian collective farm, or a scene involving drunk driving that would have been difficult to get past Code enforcers.[5] Groucho's character was originally named Dr. Quackenbush, but that had to be changed as there were 37 American doctors with that surname.[6] Seaton acknowledged that, after 18 complete scripts, help was needed. Bringing in Kaufman, said he, "was a very good idea.... I learned an awful lot from him, and so did Bob [Pirosh]."[7] Kaufman is said to have restored a physical examination of Dumont that is one of the movie's highlights.

Thalberg still wasn't happy, so he again sent the Marxes on the road to test the material. After several weeks of rehearsal, the Marxes embarked on a tour that began in Duluth, Minnesota, on July 18, 1936, and ended in San Francisco on August 18. Thalberg need not have worried, since "from the first night [it] had audiences in stitches," even when Groucho underplayed his role.[8] The material was introduced by film trailers that grounded patrons in the basic story, and 30,000 ballot cards were distributed to test 175 gags, 75 of which made the movie's final cut.

One road tale held that Harpo was displeased with one of the props. When he decided to forego it, a prop man protested that such a costly item should not be discarded. Groucho intervened to say, "He's right, Harpo. You can't waste money like that. Have it silver-plated and then throw it out."[9] Pirosh compared the tour to a Broadway show and praised the concept of audience-testing. By the time *A Day at the Races* hit the screen, it was nothing like any of the 18 scripts.[10]

The month-long tour delighted everyone except an audience in Cleveland, and Thalberg. The problem in Ohio was that the theater lacked a sound system and attendees couldn't hear the jokes. The perfectionist Thalberg was a different matter; he asked for three weeks of revisions before the movie went into production on September 3.

Tragedy struck 11 days later: Thalberg died of pneumonia at the age of 37. Director Sam Wood's insensitive announcement, "The little brown fellow just died," intensified Groucho's loathing of him. Louvish speculates that Wood may have intended it as an anti–Semitic remark.[11]

The Marxes were shattered by Thalberg's passing and wept openly at his funeral. Chico and his wife Betty were especially stricken, as they were friendly with Norma Shearer, Thalberg's widow. Groucho's son Arthur said his father "was really broken up—more so than I've ever seen him...." Groucho said simply, "After Thalberg's death, my interest in the movies waned."[12] Production shut down until December. Lawrence Weingarten, Thalberg's brother-in-law, was appointed the new producer, though by the time the film opened, it was billed as a Sam Wood Production. That was not a good thing for the Marxes.

Thalberg's death unleashed a power play inside of MGM in which there could be only one winner: the mercurial Louis B. Mayer, who promptly dismantled Thalberg's production unit and consolidated control. He was not a Marx Brothers fan, and quickly showed his hand. Per Thalberg's initiative, Harry Ruby and Bert Kalmar were at work on a different Marx Brothers script, a comic Western; Mayer ordered them to cease work on it.[13] Groucho believed that Mayer wanted them to bomb, but that Thalberg had laid down such a firm foundation that *A Day at the Races* succeeded despite the incompetence of Weingarten, Mayer and Wood.[14]

Wood was left to his own devices, which wasn't good for the picture or the bottom line. The film was supposed to wrap on March 12, 1937, but it took another five weeks as Wood insisted on reshooting scenes that were fine as they were. Pirosh echoed Groucho's opinion that Wood was no comic genius: "If Thalberg had two on a scale of 10 in sense of humor, Sam Wood had minus seven…. Why he should have directed a Marx Brothers picture, I'll never know."[15] When Groucho improvised on the set to sharpen his lines, Wood barked, "You can't make an actor out of clay." Groucho shot back, "Nor a director out of Wood." Groucho later complained to Hector Arce that Wood "never had an original idea in his life."[16] His endless takes grated on the brothers; a messy wallpapering scene was shot 20 times. Pirosh politely speculated that Wood liked "to see people get smeared in paste."[17] A less charitable view is that he liked seeing *the Marx Brothers* covered in paste.

There are continuity errors in the film that would have been unthinkable with Thalberg at the helm.[18] About the only good thing that came from Wood's direction was a decision to downplay an Allan Jones solo, "A Message from the Man in the Moon," though he inexplicably cut "Dr. Hackenbush," Groucho's entrance piece, which Groucho later delighted in singing on stage. If Mayer really did wish the Marxes to fail, he failed miserably. MGM ultimately negotiated a new three-picture deal based upon the large box office return of *A Day at the Races*.

It's amazing the film plays as well as it does. In addition to the death of Thalberg and personality conflicts, Groucho was deep into marital woes. Although he did not divorce Ruth (Johnson) Marx until 1942, he was constantly angry with her, most recently for an insult to Chico's wife Betty. At a dance, Ruth remarked, "What a pretty necklace, Betty. Did you just get it out of hock?"[19] Those were fighting words; the brothers could insult each other, but they were fiercely loyal when anyone else did. Groucho was also smitten with Maureen O'Sullivan, and admitted, "I was crazy about her. I didn't like her husband. He was a mean man."[20] O'Sullivan thought quite differently. She married John Farrow in 1936 and stayed with him until his death in 1963. They raised seven children, including actresses Mia and Tisa Farrow. Groucho's lust clearly exceeded his reason, as the Irish-born O'Sullivan was a serious Roman Catholic who only married Farrow after he converted. She knew that Groucho "had a crush" on her, but insisted, "There was nothing between us. But even if John wasn't around, Groucho was not the type I'd be interested in. I don't like funny men … that crack jokes all the time. Groucho never stopped…. I was tired of it after the third day."[21]

A Day at the Races opened on June 11, 1937, soon after a few more monkey wrenches were tossed into the works. The various writers battled over how they would be listed. When it was finally decreed that the credits would read, "Original Screenplay by Robert Pirosh, George Seaton and George Oppenheimer," with Al Boasberg's credit relegated to the *Academy Bulletin*, Boasberg directed his lawyers to force MGM to remove his name altogether.[22] That suited Mayer just fine, but tragedy struck again. Six days after the film opened, the 44-year-old Boasberg suffered a fatal heart attack, and the Marxes once again grieved.

"How about that big, strong, sick woman?"

Despite it all, *A Day at the Races* is a wonderful satire. Doctors were among its targets. The state of American medical care in 1937 was very different from that of today. There was, as yet, no vaccine against hepatitis B, influenza, polio, measles, mumps, tetanus or numerous other diseases. There were no pacemakers, production of penicillin was limited, and only rudimentary treatment for tuberculosis existed.

Tony calls Upjohn a "big, strong, sick woman," a garbled but apt description. Despite what Standish doctors say, Upjohn insists she's "on the verge of a nervous collapse." She's actually a hypochondriac in need of a psychologist, not a team of medical doctors. Oddly, though, her choice to stay at what is essentially a resort makes more sense than the zany script suggests.

The American Medical Association (AMA) was founded in 1895 to professionalize medical care, and the 1906 Pure Food and Drug Act began the process of weeding out harmful and ineffective medicines. But standards for doctors, medication, and treatment varied enormously. Even before Hackenbush arrives, there's something amiss with the Standish medical staff. Hackenbush puts his finger on it. Doctors hand him a set of X-rays that reputedly show "nothing wrong" with Upjohn. Hackenbush's quip, "Who are you gonna believe, me or those crooked x-rays?" is on the mark. X-rays, though discovered in 1895, were not widely used in the U.S. until the 1920s, after which they widely *mis*used.[23] As we know, X-rays reveal only structural problems with the body and would be of no use in treating a chemical imbalance or nervous condition.

In their pioneering work on women's health, Barbara Ehrenreich and Deirdre English noted that "science" was often simply a buzz word appropriated by self-proclaimed "experts" whose advice was egregiously wrong for women. Local doctors frequently had only second-hand information about hard science, and the AMA and other such organizations concentrated as much on eliminating competition as on acting in the patient's best interests. There was, for instance, the AMA's effort to abolish midwifery and make childbirth the sole domain of those trained in obstetrics and gynecology.[24]

Care was especially questionable when, like Emily Upjohn, a woman had psychological conditions. Matters had certainly improved since the days in which bed rest and isolation were prescribed for women suffering from scientific-sounding but medically suspect diagnoses such as dyspepsia, hysteria and neurasthenia. Well into the 20th century, there was an outbreak of what Harvey Green called the "new American nervousness."[25] Many Americans, especially women, turned to residential care programs such as those offered by sanitariums rather than entrust their care to individual doctors. Such facilities were on the wane in the 1930s, but persisted in a women's health vacuum.

American medical care was not yet completely professionalized—if, indeed, it can be said to be in such a pure state at present.[26] Coca-Cola, originally a patent medicine, lost its mildly psychotropic coca leaf alkaloids in 1903 or 1929 (sources differ). Most "snake oil" medicines claiming to be panaceas made patients feel better because of high levels of alcohol and/or opium were taken off the market after 1906, as were those containing arsenic. Still, concoctions with questionable efficacy—including Lydia Pinkham's Vegetable Compound—remained in use, as did radium "cures."

It did not help the medical profession's reputation that quacks such as the infamous "Doctor" John R. Brinkley continued to practice. (His title deserves quotation marks, as he bought his degree.) Beginning in 1918 and continuing into the 1930s, Brinkley transplanted goat glands into the testicles of adult men in the name of curing impotence and increasing virility. Though at least 42 patients died, Brinkley amassed a fortune, got nearly 30 percent of the vote in the 1930 Kansas gubernatorial election, and operated a string of hospitals before he was discredited in 1939.[27]

In such a climate, genteel facilities such as Judy Standish's held more appeal for those of means, even when staffed by men inclined to diagnosis women's complaints as endemic among females. It's a gag, but when Hackenbush meets his staff at Standish Sanitarium ("Johnson, Bellevue Hospital … Franco, Johns Hopkins … Wilderming, Mayo brothers"), he is singularly unimpressed and replies, "Dodge brothers, late."[28]

He has no time all for the oily Whitmore. When Whitmore presses him to elaborate on his medical background, Hackenbush unleashes a volley of absurdities. He begins by saying that he worked at a drug store at the age of 15 and filled prescriptions. It goes downhill from there.

> WHITMORE: Don't you have to be 21 to fill prescriptions?
> HACKENBUSH: Well, that's for grown-ups. I only filled them for children.
> WHITMORE: … [W]here did you get your training as a physician?
> HACKENBUSH: … [W]ell to begin with, I took four years at Vassar.
> UPJOHN: Vassar? But that's a girls' college.
> HACKENBUSH: I found that out the third year. I'd have been there yet but I went out for the swimming team.
> WHITMORE: The doctor seems reluctant to discuss his medical experiences.
> HACKENBUSH: Well, medically, my experiences have been most unexciting except during the flu epidemic.
> WHITMORE: Ah, what happened?
> HACKENBUSH: I got the flu.

We get a prelude of things to come when Hackenbush examines Stuffy. Tony promises Stuffy ice cream and a big steak if he lets Hackenbush examine him, though he tries to bolt when spinach is mentioned. Stuffy calms down when apple pie and a nurse enter the equation. When Hackenbush takes Stuffy's pulse, he shakes his head and says, "Either he's dead or my watch has stopped." An attempt to listen to Stuffy's heart is an excuse for Harpo's balloon-in-mouth trick. There are other disruptions, including an attempt to drink poison. The topper comes when Hackenbush thinks he's examining Stuffy through his head mirror. Hackenbush declares, "The last time I saw a head like that was in a bottle of formaldehyde," and declares Stuffy as "the crummy, moronic type…[and] the most gruesome piece of blubber I've ever peered at." Tony notices, though, that Hackenbush has his mirror turned backward and has been peering at himself. Tony discovers that Hackenbush is actually a "horse doctor" and, because Tony wants to help Judy, he blackmails Hackenbush into continuing his artifice.

Hackenbush is certainly a quack, but Whitmore and Steinberg are not exactly pillars of the medical community either. Hackenbush is instantly dismissive of Dr. Steinberg, whom Whitmore hired to discredit him. When Tony and Stuffy pose as Hackenbush's assistants—wearing "medical gowns" that say "Joe's Service Station" and "Brakes Aligned"—Hackenbush introduces them as also bearing the name Dr. Steinberg. He then accuses the actual Steinberg of not washing his hands and proceeds to dunk his own arms into the sink while still wearing his watch. Hackenbush removes it, but when Steinberg gets too close, Hackenbush throws it back into the water with a curt, "I'd rather have it rusty than missing" and admonishes, "[D]on't point that beard at me. It might go off." When Steinberg proclaims that Upjohn is healthy, it's the cue for an examination whose madness must be seen to be fully appreciated.

Water, Water Everywhere

Overall, the medical profession's androcentric approach to women's health invited those of means to seek alternative care offered by special facilities. In the 19th century, upper- and middle-class women began checking into health resorts, especially in places such as Saratoga Springs; Standish Sanitarium also bears some resemblance to its Gideon Putnam Hotel. Standish Sanitarium is essentially a mineral spring spa/rest home/resort modeled on those near the famed waters found in Saratoga Springs and other places in the U.S. Many of them had in-house medical staff, presumably of greater competency than Hackenbush, Whitmore and Steinberg.[29] Standish also has elements of European-style spas such as Aix-les-Bains, France; Baden-Baden, Germany; Saint-Moritz, Switzerland, and Spa, Belgium.[30]

Mineral spring resorts offered a variety of treatments, some beneficial and some dubious. "Water cures"—also known as balneopathy, hydropathy and hydrotherapy—involved bathing in hot and cold tubs of mineral waters, which were sometimes roiled by high-pressure water jets.[31] Treatments might also include being wrapped in sheets, undergoing hot and cold showers, and drinking lots of mineral water. Recreation and exercise were prescribed, as was a careful diet, usually one high in fruit and vegetables and devoid of stimulants such as alcohol, coffee and tea.[32] No doubt many women did feel better after a spa vacation, and a hypochondriac such as Upjohn might have fared better at such facilities than under the care of a brusque oaf like Steinberg. They would have done well, though, to avoid more questionable practices such as drinking radium water, bathing in galvanic (electric current) waters, and submitting to mild electric shock treatments that had little or no medical benefit. Some spas administered dangerous shocks.

Water is good for the body, but not necessarily as it's used in *A Day at the Races*. Whitmore demands to examine the giant pill Hackenbush gives to Upjohn and exclaims, "Isn't that awfully large for a pill?" Hackenbush's reply, "It was too small for a basketball, and I didn't know what else to do with it," prompts Whitmore to proclaim, "It must take a lot of water to swallow that." When Hackenbush replies that it would only take five gallons, a flabbergasted Whitmore exclaims, "Isn't that a lot of water for a patient to take?" Hackenbush's comeback does little to deflect suspicion: "Not if the patient has a bridge in her mouth. The water flows under the bridge and the patient walks over and meets the pill on the other side."

Water also factors prominently in the scene in which Upjohn is "examined" in the presence of Whitmore and Steinberg. In an attempt to stall, Hackenbush, Tony and Stuffy endlessly wash their hands under the guise of sterilizing them.

Hackenbush and Tony croon the 1910 song "Down by the Old Mill Stream," a staple of vaudeville, movies, barbershop quartets and recording stars. The Marxes avoid their exam room dilemma by setting off the water sprinklers, flooding the room, and riding off on Hi-Hat, who bursts through the door.

Place Your Bets

As the title suggests, *A Day at the Races* also involves horseracing. Let's look at the activity sometimes called the "king of sports," which is a flip of the original "sport of kings," which dates at least as far back as 17th-century England. Blame journalist Lincoln Steffens for the inversion, one he made in 1937, the year *A Day at the Races* was made.[33] Perhaps, though, horseracing should be dubbed the "sport for those who dream of being kings." Aristocratic trappings notwithstanding, American horseracing has a checkered past associated more with bookies, pool halls, bars, gamblers and organized crime than tea with royalty.

Horseracing was popular in Colonial America and emerged as an organized sport at the dawn of the 19th century. Almost immediately, New York State moved to ban it as immoral. In theory, horseracing was illegal between 1803 and 1821, though high-stakes gamblers circumvented the law by forming private associations and by convincing politicians to look the other way when a big race was planned. According to Elliott Gorn and Warren Goldstein, "Horse races became America's first nationwide sports spectacle when ... meets pitting Northern horses against Southern ones galvanized attention."[34]

The sport declined during the Panic of 1837 and did not recover vigor until during the Civil War. Saratoga began racing in 1863. Its founder, casino owner and former boxer John Morrissey, was later elected to Congress. In 1865, the American Jockey Club was formed.[35] Despite the label, jockey clubs seldom had much to do with those who rode horses; they were consortiums of track owners, breeders and members of the upper crust. New York's group was spearheaded by well-connected individuals such as Democratic National Party Committee chair August Belmont and Wall Street lawyer William Travers, for whom a famed thoroughbred race held in Saratoga is named. As Steven Riess notes, most tracks found it useful to forge such "political connections."[36]

Links to the Democratic Party proved very useful in New York State. In 1887, the state legislature passed the Ives Anti-Poolroom Law to curtail off-track betting in establishments frequented by bookies and punters.[37] This law was short-circuited by building proprietary tracks or by moving high-stakes races across the Hudson River to New Jersey. In 1894, Anthony Comstock's Society for the Suppression of Vice pushed for a renewed ban on racing. It was deflected by a back room deal in which a racing commission was established to "regulate" the sport. Its head was none other than August Belmont Jr., who inherited his father's love for racing and wagering. He donated the land and money for New York City's Belmont Park, the site of the third leg of thoroughbred racing's Triple Crown.

Politicians shielded racetrack and horse owners, though the sport has never completely shaken the suspicion that races are not always on the level. In 1901, New York Governor Charles Even Hughes succeeded in passing a ban on off-track betting and made track owners responsible for policing the law. Most tracks closed until 1913, when courts ruled that owners could be sanctioned only if they *knowingly* allowed bookies to operate, a high standard of evidence nearly impossible to prove. The futility of the attempt to stymie betting was evident when, in 1902, voters sent Tammany Hall politician Timothy D. Sullivan to Congress despite his involvement in a gambling syndicate that raked in an estimated $3.6 million annually in illegal boxing and horserace betting.

By the end of World War I, horseracing was again thriving. In 1926, some 11,477 races took place and nearly $14 million in prize money went to owners. Numerous states that had prohibited racing reversed course.[38] The popularization of thoroughbred's Triple Crown for three-year-old horses boosted racing's profile just in time to help the sport weather the Great Depression.[39] Racing took a hit when the economy worsened, but dreams of instant riches kept bigger tracks afloat.[40] Hype also gave it a boost. Three Triple Crown winners—Gallant Fox (1930), Omaha (1935) and War Admiral (1937)—shed positive light on horseracing. Although it occurred after the release of *A Day at the Races*, a 1938 challenge match between War Admiral and Seabiscuit attracted even greater attention. Seabiscuit won, much to the joy of millions who saw the undersized Seabiscuit as a four-legged version of the common man.

There are three types of horseracing upon which bets are placed. Harness racing is the most genteel form. It is sometimes called trotting or pacing, as the horses must maintain a gait in which a specified number of the horse's legs must remain in contact with the track when the others stride to propel a seated jockey cart (sulkie) around a track.

Trotting is absent from *A Day at the Races*, but we do see thoroughbred and steeplechase racing. The latter is a combination of speed racing and jumping over obstacles. Generally run over a course of two to three miles, it became popular in the U.S. toward the end of the 19th century. Saratoga had steeplechase racing as early as 1868.

In *A Day at the Races*, Morgan beats Stuffy for winning a race atop one of his own steeds. There are legitimate reasons not to push a horse to win, especially if a horse is recovering from an injury or training for a more important race. Sometimes, though, gamblers like Morgan collude to "fix" a race. Races at pari-mutuel tracks pay winning bets according to race-time odds. Pari-mutuel betting helps tracks—and many are held by mutual stock companies—protect the bottom line. The venue is guaranteed a certain percentage of each bet, thus odds can change right up until post time. For example, a horse might initially be listed as having 5:1 odds to win, meaning that every two dollars wagered returns $10 if one bets the horse will win. If, however, a surge of bettors wager on that horse, the odds might drop to 3:1.[41] Morgan is crooked, so we can assume that Stuffy was supposed to lose the race because Morgan had bet on another horse with longer odds.

Gil is a different sort of gambler. He's not a penny-ante wagerer, as he came up with $1,500—more than $27,000 in today's money—to *buy* a racehorse. Still, he is a small player in a sport where it helps to have a king's resources. Thoroughbreds are expensive to own and maintain. Gil can't afford Hi-Hat's feed bill and has essentially bet all he has that his undernourished horse will win his first race. Gil represents the worst kind of gambler: one who bets what he doesn't have on an all-or-nothing wager. If Hi-Hat loses his race, Gil will have to sell the horse at a loss and would still be responsible for arrears on stable fees and his feed bill. Judy will also probably lose Standish Sanitarium.

"Get your tootsie-fruitsie ice cream!"

Hackenbush's first visit to the track leads to an encounter with Tony posing as a "tootsie-fruitsie" ice cream vendor, a revered Marx Brothers routine. "Tootsie-fruitsie" is Chico's contortion of tutti-frutti, Italian for all fruit. It might seem odd that someone pretending to be Italian mispronounces tutti-frutti, but the fruit-and-nut ice cream flavor of that name isn't Italian. Insofar as we can tell, tutti-frutti originated in England and later migrated to the Apennine Peninsula. Besides, the tootsie-fruitsie scene isn't really about ice cream.

Hackenbush reminds us that for all its thrills, horseracing is indeed about gambling. He also shows how easy it is to get fleeced. It's spelled ZVB X RPL. Hackenbush plans to bet two dollars that Sun-Up will win the next race, but Tony talks him out of it. Tony confesses that his ice cream cart is a dodge to keep away the police, and that he actually sells tips on races.

> TONY: ... Sun-Up is the worst horse on the track.
> HACKENBUSH: I notice he wins all the time.
> TONY: Aw, that's just because he comes in first.
> HACKENBUSH: Well, I don't want him any better than first.
> TONY: ... Suppose you bet on Sun-Up. What you gonna get for your money? Two-to-one
>   odds. One dollar and you remember me for the rest of your life.
> HACKENBUSH: That's the most nauseating proposition I've ever had.
> TONY: Come on.... You look like a sport.

Against his better judgment, Hackenbush forks over a dollar and is handed a slip of paper with the letters ZVBXRPL. The perplexed Hackenbush exclaims, "I had the same horse when I had my eyes examined." Tony explains that that Hackenbush needs the code book to get the name. Luckily, it's free; just a one-dollar printing charge. There goes Hackenbush's two dollars. It gets worse. Hackenbush needs a "master code" book to decipher the code book, and guess who happens to have one in his ice cream cart? No printing charge—just a two-dollar delivery charge. When Hackenbush points out he's standing right next to him, Tony agrees to reduce the price to one dollar. "Couldn't I move over here and make it 50 cents?" asks Hackenbush. "Yes," Tony replies, "but I'd move over here and make it one dollar just the same." And, of course, he will need a five-volume breeder's guide to unravel everything. Just five dollars for the set.

Hackenbush also needs a one-dollar jockey guide to finalize everything. All Hackenbush has is a $10 bill. Tony claims he has no change and gives Hackenbush nine more books instead. Books are tucked under his arms and between his legs, but he does learn that ZVBXRPL stands for Burns, the jockey riding Rosie, with 40:1 odds. As Hackenbush fiddles with all his books, Tony slaps down a bet on Sun-Up. Before Hackenbush can waddle over to the window, Sun-Up has won the race. Tony is happy and Hackenbush drifts away with a cart full of books yelling, "Get your tootsie-fruitsie ice cream ... nice tootsie-fruitsie ice cream...."

Tony's winnings aren't enough to get Gil out of hock, though he discovers that

Hi-Hat runs faster whenever he hears Morgan's voice, an implication that he mistreated the horse. Gil also discovers that Hi-Hat's slow practice times are because he's actually a steeplechase jumper, not a sprinter. Gil is about to enter the horse in a premium steeplechase event when the sheriff seizes Hi-Hat. Morgan commands the sheriff to make sure the horse is hidden away and cannot compete.

Gil, Judy, Hackenbush, Tony and Stuffy need to find Hi-Hat, which means delaying post time until he is located. The Marxes demolish track decorum with the same aplomb with which they wrecked the opera. A series of gags stitched together assures that Hi-Hat will make it to the track: soap under the saddles, hats and cars on the track, moved railings, and more. The Marxes and Jones manage to elude the sheriff, rows of police, and Morgan and his henchmen. Hi-Hat is found, wins the race, the sanatorium is saved, and true love triumphs.

Anarchists Horsing Around?

The utter mayhem of *Duck Soup*, *A Night at the Opera* and *A Day at the Races* cemented the future reputation of the Marx Brothers as an embodiment of anarchist energy. Mitchell notes that Groucho came to view critics' evocations of Karl Marx tiresome, and anyone who types "anarchism" and "Marx Brothers" into a search engine understands why he felt that way.[42] In life, Groucho and Harpo were liberals, not anarchists. Chico certainly spent enough time and money on horse races to be seen as a connoisseur of them, not a wrecker. Art unleashed upon the public, though, is often perceived independently of its creators. Martin Gardner uses the term "anti-establishment" rather than anarchic to describe the Marxes' satirical thrust.[43]

Those eager to view the brothers through anarchist lenses can find ammunition in the scene dear to Sam Wood's heart, the infamous wallpaper paste mess. When all else fails, Whitmore plans to get Hackenbush fired from the sanitarium by exposing him *in flagrante delicto* with his planted seductress, Flo Marlowe. Muir lacks Thelma Todd's sex appeal, but she's sultry enough for Hackenbush, who readily agrees to a tryst.

Stuffy overhears the plot and tries to alert Tony, lest Hackenbush be disgraced and Judy ruined. How does a mute convey such information? He could write it down, but Stuffy whistles and mimes like he's playing a game of madcap charades. It takes a sword substitute assaulting a hedge to get Tony to understand that Hackenbush is the subject. His miming of a woman's figure at first confounds Tony, who thinks Hackenbush has a snake or an apple dumpling before he realizes there's a woman involved. Stuffy has to grab a photo, knock out the picture, and peer through what's left before Tony realizes that she plans to frame Hackenbush.

Not that Hackenbush is the world's smoothest Lothario. The corsage is wrong, endless thank you–thank you exchanges take place, he tosses Marlowe's fur on the floor, and a gigantic table centerpiece stands between them. Just as the conquest is about to unfold, Tony bursts in and climbs all over Marlowe. He tries to warn Hackenbush he's being set up, but Hackenbush is willing to take his chances. Stuffy enters and joins the groping, causing Marlowe to cry out, "I've never been so insulted in my life!" Hackenbush's frustrated retort: "Well, it's early yet."

Tony re-enters, wearing an oversized fake mustache, dangling keys, and claiming to be O'Reilly, the house detective. Stuffy trails behind wearing a deerstalker cap and leading a team of bloodhounds.[44] Hackenbush dispenses with them by throwing his steak dinner out the door. The hungry hounds pull both Tony and Stuffy outside as they pursue the tasty treat.

Hackenbush finally has Marlowe to himself, or so he imagines. They begin to snuggle and Marlowe's exhortation, "[H]old me closer. Closer. Closer," prompts another nifty Groucho retort: "If I hold you any closer, I'll be in back of you." Tony and Stuffy charge in again, this time posing as wallpaper hangers. As Hackenbush fires off non-stop quips, they paper everything in sight. That's a lucky thing. When Whitmore and Upjohn arrive, with Whitmore promising to expose Hackenbush as a two-timer, Marlowe is nowhere to be seen, nor is Hackenbush. When enough debris is cleared to reveal the good doctor, he is sitting on the wallpapered sofa reading. Upjohn asks him what he's doing and Hackenbush lies, "I'm having the place done over. It will make a lovely honeymoon suite." She departs, upbraiding the trailing Whitmore. Once they clear out, the cushions come off the sofa to reveal a paste-covered, sputtering Marlowe. Moments later, Hackenbush takes advantage of Upjohn's repentance and convinces her to assume Judy's debts. It's a hysterical bit.

People mired in a mess is a slapstick staple. Whether it is pie, mud, fruit, oil, garbage, whipped cream or a food fight, people getting slimed seldom fails to induce laughter. The wallpaper scene is not original to the Marx Brothers; everyone from Charlie Chaplin to the Three Stooges and Abbott and Costello have made a mess with wallpaper. A 1925 Laurel and Hardy silent film was probably the inspiration for the wallpaper mayhem of *A Day at the* Races. Once again, though, the Marxes did it so well that many post–1937 movie depictions riff off them.

Elephant in the Room: All God's Chillun

For modern viewers, *A Day at the Races* contains the most problematic scene in any Marx Brothers film, one in which Groucho, Chico and Harpo blacken their faces and join a group of African American dancers. When viewed from a 21st-century perspective, three white comedians in blackface are overtly racist. Not that the 21st century has been much better. African American film director Spike Lee has compiled an extensive set of film and TV clips from the 21st century that contain whites in blackface.[45]

What do we make of the Marx Brothers doing so in 1937? Glenn Mitchell offers two paths, one helpful and one not. His scene-by-scene commentary for the 2004 DVD version of the film doesn't mention problematic aspects of race at all.[46] In *The Marx Brothers Encyclopedia*, he notes that some Marx Brothers scenes are "embarrassing today" and several are "undoubtedly patronizing." Mitchell qualifies this with the remark that race "was not as sensitive an issue at the time...."[47]

He is correct to note that white people in the past viewed race quite differently. That's an accurate portrayal of white presumptions of Caucasian superiority. Movie audiences in 1937 were just 60 years removed from the end of Reconstruction, which placed them closer to the Civil War era than we are to the release of *A Day at the Races*.[48] In our time, the quest for racial justice is an ongoing process; in 1937, legal segregation of African Americans prevailed south of the Mason-Dixon line and was customary in the North. If we put ourselves into the mindset of 1937, the imagery from *A Day at the Races* is more comprehensible and some is surprisingly enlightened for its time.

A Day at the Races is simultaneously a comedy, a romance and a musical. There are two splashy production numbers, starting with the water carnival. Its rationale for being in the film are for Gil to earn money to feed Hi-Hat by singing, and to provide room for instrumental solos from Chico and Harpo. It opens with a rather cheesy dance number. Dozens of women garbed in yards of white tulle traipse about the stage in what looks to be ballet fused with misbegotten modern dance. There is, inexplicably, a marimba band dressed in elaborate costumes playing alongside the orchestra. Vivien Fay emerges from behind the fabric and performs an *en pointe* dance that resembles ballet, if one ignores histrionic gestures, falling flower petals and a chorus of gowned singers and their mirrored reflections.[49]

This segues to couples dancing, an excuse for Hackenbush to shuttle between Upjohn and Marlowe. Jones then croons "Blue Venetian Waters," delivered standing in a tulip boat afloat in a fake lagoon. In the background, several women play ukuleles. Before this overlong scene is exhausted, Chico plays the piano and Harpo wrecks one before his harp solo.

The water carnival—complete with an erupting fountain—is better filmed than *The Cocoanuts'* stilted song-and-dance sequences, but seems just as dated. Much of it is stitched into the film clumsily, possibly a post–Thalberg continuity error. It stands in stark contrast to what happens when African Americans come onto the screen later in the film.

The carnival sashays with sterile propriety; the black production numbers jump, shout and shake foundations: Gil has wooed himself back into Judy's good graces. As Gil serenades with "Tomorrow Is Another Day," he and Judy observe a black community behind the stable, its own subtle commentary on segregation. Stuffy appears with a pennywhistle and impish grin, and proceeds to toot and dance to timpani beats. Black children gather 'round and follow Stuffy in a Pied Piper–like procession. He's not the Pied Piper. As we learn from the song "Who Dat Man?" Stuffy is analogous to Gabriel, and his pennywhistle a stand-in for the archangel's horn.

Gabriel was a staple in African American spirituals, his guardianship of Israel transferred to enslaved and post-freedom black communities. Gabriel's horn is often associated with the second coming of Jesus and, by extension, a conclusive liberation of people of color. In 1934, just three years before *A Day at the Races,* the Cole Porter musical *Anything Goes* began its long Broadway run. It included Porter's "Blow, Gabriel, Blow," a variant of an older black gospel song, "Blow Gable [*sic*] Blow." There were so many spirituals, shout songs, gospel offerings and folk songs employing this sort of imagery that, in her exhaustive study of African American music, Eileen Southern titled sections dealing with the years 1867 to 1919 "Blow Ye Trumpet."[50]

Pinky leads the children—part of a real-life group called the Crinoline Choir—past a cabin. Inside, an extended family is engaged in a domesticity-meets-evangelicalism moment: They sing "Nobody Knows the Trouble I've Seen," a well-known spiritual. Pinky blows six notes on his whistle and "Who Dat Man?" reprises.

Adults join the kids in a parade that passes a juke joint where dancers and musicians sway to such a hot tempo that the place is literally rocking. The horn players are members of Duke Ellington's Band and Ivie Anderson, Ellington's lead vocalist, makes the first of two appearances. Pinky-as-Gabriel gives another toot on his pennywhistle and these people follow him as well. Christopher Smith observes that as they move in an interweaving circle, their dancing, hand clapping and singing are evocative of a ring shout, a shuffle and religious ceremony that blended Christian rituals with West African traditions that was often surreptitiously practiced during slavery.[51]

Anderson reappears, this time to sing "All God's Chillun Got Rhythm." Smith contends that Anderson's choreography, bent arms, curved back and lacquered hair are borrowed from famed African American expatriate Josephine Baker.[52] That's probably correct, though one should note that "All God's Chillun" is not a traditional black song; it was penned for the film by Gus Kahn, Walter Jurmann and Bronislaw Kaper.[53] Anderson uses it as a lead-in for a hold-the-push dance with John "Tiny" Bunch, a 6'4", 350-pound bundle of flexibility. Ellington's band sizzles, then the floor is given over to Herbert "Whitey" White's Lindy Hoppers for maneuvers, twists and jumps that would put competitive gymnasts to shame. This troupe, which sometimes contained future stars of stage and screen Dorothy Dandridge, Sammy Davis, Jr., and Ethel Waters, was the brainchild of White, an African American who had once been a bouncer and singing waiter. The Marxes met the Lindy Hoppers in California, and *A Day at the Races* was their film debut. They parlayed it into eight more films and several Broadway appearances before disbanding in 1942.

A jubilant Pinky grabs a pitchfork and leads everyone into the main part of the barn in a combination drum major/cakewalk. Hackenbush and Tony join the fun. This was risky in 1937, as blacks and whites were not supposed to be shown dancing together. There is no physical touching, which allowed the Marxes to satisfy the Code, but it is worth noting that Whitey's Lindy Hoppers had two white members, Ruthie Rheingold and Harry Rosenberg. (Neither is in the film.)

Within all of the joy, there remain moments that ruffle contemporary feathers, such as bug-eyed faces, exaggerated lingo and the idea of blacks following a white Gabriel. What happens next is even more troubling. The sheriff and his men appear outside the barn door, which causes Hackenbush, Tony and Pinky to dive under a wagon, "black up" with axle grease and rejoin the party. It's not a very thorough job, especially since Pinky forgot to cover half of his face, and the scene ends when a pop-eyed black actor yells, "It's the sheriff!" What astonishes modern viewers is seeing the Marxes in blackface. Their alarm is understandable; blackface is now denounced as racist and for the most part, only foolish whites or those deliberately seeking to be provocative black up.

Face to Face with Blackface

I won't defend this sequence, but I will mention ongoing debates over the meaning of blackface. Minstrelsy began in the 1830s as a burlesque of black dance, song and mannerisms. Most minstrels were whites using a darkening agent such as burnt cork as blackface. It was usually a grotesque mask that left some whiteness showing, especially around the eyes or lips; in essence, a clown's face. Eileen Southern noted that its roots lay in plantation performances that were "entertainment for the planters."[54]

In 1848, Frederick Douglass took to the pages of the abolitionist newspaper *The North Star* to denounce blackface acts such as Dan Emmett's Virginia Minstrels and Christy's Minstrels as "the filthy scum of white society, who have stolen from us a complexion denied to them by nature ... to make money, and pander to the corrupt taste of their white fellow-citizens."[55] Minstrelsy nonetheless persisted and was popular both on its own and on the vaudeville stage. Blackface remained vital when the Marx Brothers blacked up in 1937. Its lure was such that even African American performers donned blackface and some—Billy Kersands, Wallace King, Pigmeat Markham, Flournoy Miller and Bert Williams—achieved fame. Williams was among the few black performers in blackface who tried to present African American culture in its complexity, but even he sometimes performed in stereotypical ways.

The list of those donning blackface is long, surprising, and in need of constant updating.[56] Insofar as I know, the Marx Brothers did not don burnt cork on the vaudeville stage, but the same cannot be said for contemporaries George Burns, W.C. Fields, George Jessel, Al Jolson, Buster Keaton and Sophie Tucker. Jolson performed in blackface in Hollywood's first talkie, 1927's *The Jazz Singer.* White actors such as Fay Bainter, Ethel Barrymore, Eddie Cantor and Jimmy Durante appeared on screen in blackface before the Marx Brothers did so.[57]

Debate continues over whether Douglass was correct, or if imitation of African Americans was sometimes a form of respect. A substantial amount of scholarship argues for nuanced views of minstrelsy. Most scholars acknowledge that lampooned images of African Americans are troubling, but they also note that racial boundaries were more fluid than is generally appreciated. Eric Lott's *Love and Theft* remains one of the better studies, its thesis embedded in the title. He saw minstrelsy as a "counterfeit" Northern view of black culture, but also one that paved the way for black culture to enter mainstream culture through the back door. It provided working-class white males with masks through which they could assert themselves, even though "interracial solidarity" was intermittent and brief.[58]

W. T. Lhamon agrees that blackface was an incomplete "identification of whites with black[ness]," a delicate balance of understanding and belittlement. For the white underclasses, though, posing as black was a radical act of self-empowerment. The impact upon youth culture has been profound, especially in music, whose black influences can be seen in jazz, rock 'n' roll and especially in white attraction to hip-hop.[59] Hip-hop became a focus for studies such as Lhamon's.[60]

Confession: I am skeptical of white empowerment claims. Douglass' assertion that appropriating black culture was at core a market decision resonates. Some whites perhaps used blackface as a form of self-assertion, but this is a characteristic of all masks. Like Chico as an Italian, for instance. Blackface, though, occurs within rigidly defined hierarchies rooted in systemic racism. Too often, outward admiration for black culture has been self-expression without black bodies.

To reverse the equation, the earliest known incident of a black actor appearing in *whiteface* was when Canada Lee did so in a 1947 stage production of *The Duchess of Malfi.* We did not see a movie inversion until 1970, when African American actor Godfrey Cambridge "whited up" for *Watermelon Man,* a comedy of a racist white man who awoke one day to find he had turned black.[61]

In my eyes, *A Day at the Races*' blackface sequence is disrespectful, but the overall sequence celebrates black culture. Michael Rogin cautioned there were cracks in the cultural lines between black and white skins. Jews were among the co-founders of the National Association for the Advancement of Colored People and—as we have seen—"whiteness" often functioned independently of external physical attributes. European Jews had to attain whiteness in society's eyes, an incomplete process in 1937. Rogin argues that appearing in blackface was one way to "transfer identities from immigrant Jew to American."[62]

But what kind of an "American"? Daniel Lieberfeld and Judith Sanders assert that the Marxes excelled a playing "ethnic outsiders trespassing the preserves of Gentile elites. They are gauche, lower-class gate crashers who don't know the rules of polite society and furthermore, don't care.... Because the Jewish content of their work was largely covert, they could obey the letter of Hollywood's unwritten law while trashing its spirit."[63]

To return to the contrast between the water carnival and the barn scenes, the first now seems insipid and nearly unwatchable, whereas the second remains a heart-pounding thrill. Audiences in 1937 agreed. Ellington's orchestra, Ivie Anderson's singing, Whitey's Lindy Hoppers and Harpo's procession were the biggest hits of the film. Dave Gould was Oscar-nominated for the dance direction. Those looking for racism 1937-style would do well to look less at the Marxes blacking up and more at the fact that the *entire* sequence was excised from the film before it was screened in numerous Jim Crow locales because it showed blacks and whites dancing together.[64] In other words, the Marxes violated racial barriers rather than reinforcing them.

Nor should we overlook the film's ending. Hi-Hat has just triumphed, Gil has won Judy's hand, and they, Hackenbush, Tony, Stuffy and the black community sing and dance their way down the track. It's not an ending many 1937 films would have attempted. I doubt the transgressive Marx Brothers were much bothered by that.

Cleaning Out the Stable: Odds and Ends

- **Mayer in a bind:** Although the *Day at the Races* reviews were not as glowing as those of *A Night at the Opera*, most critics liked it. It raked in $6.4 million, a modern equivalent of over $224 million. The Marxes got $600,000 in royalties and Louis B. Mayer faced the dilemma of needing to negotiate a new deal with individuals he didn't like and who didn't like him.
- **Lawsuits:** The film's success was marred by three plagiarism lawsuits against the Marxes, MGM and the scriptwriters. One was dismissed because Al Boasberg was dead and there was no way to prove the allegations. A $250,000 suit against Robert Pirosh was also dismissed. That left a $26,000 lawsuit asserting that the film lifted material from a rejected script for a 1936 radio broadcast. Carroll and Garrett Graham had already collected a $7,500 out-of-court settlement, but Groucho and Chico were found guilty of a misdemeanor and each had to pay $1,000 fines. Groucho was incensed and vigorously denied the allegations.[65]
- **Ubangis?** When Hackenbush examines Stuffy, a bubble appears in Stuffy's mouth. Tony remarks, "I think he's a Ubangi." Ubangi is the name of a river and region in the African Congo. It is also a misused term for various peoples in eastern and central Africa who wore lip plates that stretched their mouths

into elongated shapes. In some cases, the lip was cut away from the face and hung free when the plate was removed, similar to how some tribes (and some in the West) use plugs to stretch their ear lobes. There was no Ubangi tribe. Ringling Brothers and Barnum and Bailey Circus began displaying African women as Ubangi around 1930 to exoticize them.

- **Frank Buck:** In the same sketch, Stuffy's curly head is mistaken for a "hairy fungus." When Hackenbush is told it's actually Stuffy's head, he declares, "I can't do anything for him. That's a case for Frank Buck." Buck was a celebrity big game hunter known for procuring live animals for circus and zoo display. Buck became the first director of the San Diego Zoo in 1923. He was fired after a year, following allegations that he abused some of the animals. Much of what Buck did is questionable by today's standards. At the time, though, he remained in high demand on the lecture circuit, penned eight books, and appeared in eight films between 1932 and 1949.
- **Scat:** In Ivie Anderson's rendition of "All God's Chillun Got Rhythm," she demonstrates superb scat singing, a vocal style often found in jazz. It uses nonsense and onomatopoetic syllables that allow singers to improvise or to convey humor. Scat is not confined to jazz, nor did jazz musicians invent it. In Scotland, *puirt à beul*—generally translated as mouth music—is ancient and was often substituted for instruments when none were available for dances. The Irish version is called lilting. Numerous other cultures have their own versions of mouth music.
- **Crunger mystery:** The term "crunger" is used in the film, but no one seems to know what it means.

NINE

Room Service (1938)

Is there a difference between "a Marx Brothers film" and one that just happens to have the Marxes in it? *Room Service* is often reviled by Marx Brothers purists. It's not really a bad film, just a middling effort with the Marxes tied to a script that overly constrained their talents. Viewing it now casts light on the theater culture of the 1930s.

Room Service is a drawing-room farce set in a hotel and its immediate environs. Gordon Miller (Groucho) is a theater producer whose entire cast has been staying at the Hotel White Way, in whose auditorium he hopes to debut a new play, *Hail and Farewell*. Miller is broke and desperate to find a backer. The only reason the cast isn't out on the street is that Gordon's brother-in-law, Joe Gribble (Cliff Dunstan),

Lobby card for *Room Service*, a box office bomb. Pictured: Chico, Harpo, Groucho, Frank Albertson (RKO, via Wikimedia Commons).

manages the hotel. Chico is Harry Binelli, the putative director of the play, and Harpo is business manager Faker Englund. Gribble lives in constant fear that upper management will discover that he has a horde of non-paying guests in the hotel. That possibility arises when hotel inspector Gregory Wagner (Donald MacBride) arrives to "get to the bottom" of discrepancies in the hotel's books.

As Miller prepares to vamoose, his room gets more crowded when both Binelli and Englund move in and Leo Davis, the play's author, arrives from Oswego, having burned all his bridges behind him. He even owes money on his typewriter. Rescue seems possible when Simon Jenkins (Philip Wood) appears, representing an anonymous wealthy investor. Miller must stall for time and keep body and soul together until the deal is finalized. The room's famished occupants only eat when Miller convinces Russian émigré waiter Sasha Smirinoff (Alexander Asro) to divert a large food order to his room with the vague promise of an acting try-out.

Subplots include Leo's instant attraction to Hilda Manney (Ann Miller), the futile attempts of the We Never Sleep Collection Agency to repossess Leo's typewriter, and the moonlighting acting of office worker Christine Marlowe (Lucille Ball); she's Miller's sister and has $250 invested in the play. There's a sequence involving a "live" turkey—clearly a stuffed bird on strings—and several gags central to the plot, such as attempts to pass off Leo as too ill to move, a doctor's examination, a scene in which the gangly Jenkins is driven to the point of madness, a tongue-in-cheek funeral service for Davis, and Englund's fake suicide.

Fast forward: The play will happen. It will be a hit, Sasha is a revelation, and Wagner faints at the sight of a not-dead Leo. If only that pesky box office perked up like Leo!

Putting the Fuse in the Box Office Bomb

An adage traced to the sixth-century Greek storyteller Aesop warns, "Be careful what you wish for, you might get it." Recent history includes examples of entertainers who worry so much about being pigeonholed that they take on projects that divert from what brought them success. Think, for example, of rock stars who make holiday albums, veteran stage actors in big-budget action pictures, rappers seeking to write formal poetry, and crooners covering pop songs. In some cases, the crossovers go surprisingly well; others become cautionary Peter Principle tales.[1] Mostly, such efforts yield mixed results.

The Marx Brothers' long flirtation with bringing George Gershwin's 1931 musical *Of Thee I Sing* to the screen remained a pipe dream. Groucho, though, continued to yearn to be more than just a funny man. Unlike Harpo, who treated his intellectual associates as friends and didn't try to compete with them, Groucho spent much of his life communicating with those whose academic credentials surpassed his own in the hope that some of their highbrow luster would rub off.

In 1938, the Marxes got a chance to stretch themselves. Written by Allen Boretz and John Murray, *Room Service* had just closed on Broadway after 500 performances. It was a farce, but one whose humor derived from situations rather than funny characters. In retrospect, *Room Service* wasn't really what the Marxes did best, which is why Joe Adamson dismissed it as an "intermission" in their film oeuvre.[2] Post–1938 revivals of *Room Service* mostly make one wonder why it lasted so long on Broadway. The Marxes later called it their "worst" movie. I don't agree, but it didn't distinguish them.[3]

"I had misgivings."

The above words were spoken by Morrie Ryskind, who transformed the stage script of *Room Service* into a screenplay. The project came on the heels of *A Day at the Races,* a smash for MGM. *Room Service,* though, was made for RKO (Radio-Keith-Orpheum), a spin-off of the vaudeville booking circuit of Keith-Albee-Orpheum, in collaboration with RCA (Radio Corporation of America).[4]

A Day at the Races marked the end of the Marxes' three-picture contract with MGM. Its success piqued Louis Mayer's desire to re-sign the Marxes, but mutual antagonism prevailed. Mayer tried to entice them by promising to underwrite a new radio series, but the Marxes distrusted him. In the interim, Zeppo, now an agent, negotiated a contract with RKO that paid his brothers $250,000 plus residuals and a promise of two more films. Groucho fumed they should have gotten more money, and Mayer was furious.[5] MGM began to lure away RKO stars, which touched off a brief tit-for-tat battle.

Mayer next tried appealing to the Marxes' professional vanity. Their success spawned trio comedy imitators, most notably the Ritz Brothers (20th Century–Fox) and the Three Stooges (Columbia). Mayer threatened to assemble his own trio if the Marxes didn't return to the fold. In retrospect, they should have called Mayer's bluff. His proposed trio was to be Buddy Ebsen, Buster Keaton and Ted Healy. Those familiar with their careers recognize that each had talents—especially Keaton—but an attempt by Mayer to create copycat versions of Groucho, Chico and Harpo held little promise.

In 1937, Ebsen was known almost exclusively as a dancer. He went on to do comedy, mostly not with MGM, with whom he, too, feuded. Today he is best remembered for his TV roles of Jed Clampett in *The Beverly Hillbillies* and in the title role of *Barnaby Jones.*[6] In short, Ebsen's comedic chops were not yet well developed.

By contrast, Keaton's golden years lay in the past. Keaton made only a partial transition to the sound era. He was signed by MGM, but his most memorable post–1933 appearances were cameo roles. Healy was even more problematic. He was the founder of the act that became the Three Stooges, but was also reputed to be an abusive alcoholic. At best, he would have been a stopgap Marx clone; the 41-year-old Healy died on December 21, 1937.

MGM and RKO settled their dispute when MGM agreed to "lend" the Marxes to RKO in exchange for three more MGM Marx Brothers features and the go-ahead for RKO to cast the Marxes in a *Three Musketeers* parody at some future date. The latter film was never made. All of this rigmarole took place as the Marxes and the writers of *A Day at the Races* battled the plagiarism allegations discussed in the previous chapter.

Chico faced an additional lawsuit filed by Patricia O'Neil Bruneman, the widow of Los Angeles mobster George "Les" Bruneman, who was rubbed out in a café shooting. Found in his pocket was a $2,000 check from Chico that had not yet cleared, and Mrs. Bruneman wanted him to pay up. Chico countersued for the return of the check. Their mutual suits were settled when Chico gave her $257 in cash.[7]

Chico's financial woes coincided with domestic battles that culminated in divorce in 1940. He attracted women the way he attracted gamblers, and was having an affair with Ann Roth, the younger sister of actress Lillian Roth. She was just 24 and Chico was 50. His daughter Maxine blasted him as "a singularly selfish man," though she implied that her mother was unstable, and that her father had an addictive personality. Chico told her, "I'm not very good about women…. And I know how hard it's been on your mother, but I can't help myself." Maxine charitably came to realize that his incessant gambling "was a sickness," though Groucho (of all people!) blasted Chico for his affair with Ann Roth. Both he and Harpo were "unsympathetic" to his gambling problems.[8]

Simon Louvish notes that by 1937, the Marx Brothers had been performing for 30 years, "an astonishing time for siblings to remain on speaking terms, let alone close."[9] They were beginning to age visibly; Chico was 50, Harpo 49 and Groucho 47. Groucho's own marriage was in no better shape than Chico's. He admitted that he spent the "the last five or eight years" of his marriage sleeping with various women.[10] Only Harpo, who married actress Susan Fleming the previous year, displayed the expected maturity that accompanies aging.

Clouded judgment prevailed across the board. You'd never know it from watching the film, but *Room Service* cost $1.5 million—the modern equivalent of more than $28 million—at a time in which just 35 films sank more than $1 million into production. It was reportedly an all-time high budget for a comedy.[11] Not much of that money is visible on the screen. About a third of the outlay went to securing the play rights and paying the Marxes' salaries. Overall, it was a lot of money for RKO, which was considered a second-tier studio.[12] The film itself was certainly second-tier; almost all of it was filmed inside a hotel, much of it in a single room.[13]

Louvish snidely remarked that Ryskind "hacked out" a script from what "had been a hit play."[14] In Ryskind's defense, more was involved than just filming a play. There was, for example, no role suitable for a mute Harpo in the original, and this necessitated rewriting the part of Faker Englund. In the play, Harry Binion is the director of the doomed production. In order for Chico to stay in character, his surname was changed to Binelli and he is merely part of producer Gordon Miller's team. Ryskind correctly judged that few viewers would buy Chico as a Broadway director. He also expressed profound "misgivings" about the entire project: "I felt that the only good things for the team were those things written expressly for them. I told them I wasn't sure if I could shape the play to their characters…. I knew that when an audience came to see the Marx Brothers, it was them [that] they came to see, not a film."[15] Ryskind did his best, but a popular play, a revised script and famous actors were no guarantee of a good movie.

The director, William Seiter, was a veteran professional that the Marxes didn't have time to hate. Groucho recalled that the entire movie was filmed in four weeks and that Howard Hughes was running RKO at the time. He misremembered; the production took five weeks and Hughes did not buy RKO until 1948.[16] But the quick production schedule begs the question of why it was so expensive. It was released on September 30, 1938, and bombed. *Room Service* reportedly lost more than $330,000 (roughly $5.6 million in 2021).

Miscasting the Cast

Ryskind correctly surmised that audiences wanted to see the Marxes in character, not out of it. *Room Service* was overly mannered, though there were flashes of Marxian spark. Groucho's subsequent denunciation of *Room Service* overlooks the fact that he initially liked it and thought it stretched him as an actor. Moreover, his complaint that he had wearied of playing Groucho begs the question of why he appeared in his trademark greasepaint mustache. Chico occasionally wears his pointed Tyrolean hat in the film, but mostly we see him wearing suits—not very attractive ones, but everything matches. Groucho and Chico mostly played it straight. Louvish claims that, for once, Chico was "not an idiot, but the fixer he was in real life."[17] I disagree that Chico is an "idiot" in Marx Brothers films, but the point is taken that both Groucho and Chico were detrimentally inhibited.

Harpo is another matter. Why must he be silent? The Marxes had made jokes about him not being able to speak for decades but by 1938, Harpo had done numerous interviews and few moviegoers imagined he was actually mute. The attempt to adapt *Room Service* to Harpo the character was, at best, a forced fit. Once he donned a red wig and began miming, even when nattily attired, the script's metaphorical waistband had to be let out for Harpo to be Harpo. There is no harp solo, so space needed to be created for silent clowning. Overall, though, Harpo's role is diminished in *Room Service*. Harpo remained silent because Ryskind was correct: Audiences came to see the Marx Brothers. Once an actor breaks a created character, it is hard to revive it.

Room Service flowed better than most Marx Brothers films because of the play's story arc, but its structure hemmed the Marxes in rather than freeing them. Ryskind's screenplay was based on treatments developed by veteran screenwriter Glenn Tyron and actor Philip Loeb, who played Harry Bunion on Broadway. In the film, Loeb played the part of milquetoast collection agent Timothy Hogarth. In total, four Broadway cast members appeared in the film: Loeb, Wood, Asro and MacBride, the last three reprising their original roles. Loeb and Wood adapted better than MacBride or Asro, who over-emoted as if they were still performing on stage.

Asro does make a convincing Russian, as one might expect of one who spent his childhood and formative years in what is now Lithuania. His overly forceful gestures and voice can be overlooked, as his was a bit role. It is intriguing to ponder, though, how a speaking Harpo would have played Sasha, a character that also did some clowning. Asro only appeared in one more film, *Comrade X* (1940), then returned to the stage, which was more attuned to his acting style.[18]

MacBride was histrionic, though the script is probably to blame. He appeared in some 140 films, as well as plays and early television, usually in character roles. His part in *Room Service* has elements of a hotel detective crossed with an accountant, but his main role is that of screen hysteric. At various places in *Room Service*, MacBride's Wagner puffs himself up to the verge of apoplexy and screams, "Jumping butterballs!" That's actually the most interesting thing about his performance, as it reminds us that the Code worked in odd ways. Its intent was clear: Religion could not be ridiculed. But, as we have seen, there was frequently an ambiguous gap between general principles and specific content. Producer Pandro S. Berman took no chances with *Room Service*. On the stage, Miller produced a show titled *Godspeed*; for the movie, it was changed to *Hail and Farewell*. If such an innocent title was changed, one can rest assured that Wagner's propensity for swearing had no chance of jumping from stage to screen. "Jumping butterballs" was the 1938 equivalent of jeezum crow, jeez Louise, or jeepers creepers; that is, a euphemism for Jesus Christ, Wagner's exclamation of choice in the play.[19]

Three other performances should be noted. Women don't have much to do in *Room Service,* and this is decidedly so for Ann Miller and Lucille Ball. Miller was primarily a dancer. She lied about her age and began dancing in a San Francisco club when she was just 13, and was actually only 15 when she appeared as love interest Hilda Manney in *Room Service.* RKO either believed she was older or conveniently chose to ignore her real age. Miller replaced Betty Field, who portrayed Hilda on Broadway and would have been a more appropriate age 25 when the film opened. There was, however, nothing untoward about Miller's performance, as she is barely in the film and in her longest shot sits demurely on a park bench with Leo.

Miller was allegedly discovered by Lucille Ball, who was 27 in 1938. Her TV sitcom *I Love Lucy* (1951–57) did much to establish the reputation of television in post–World War II America. In 1938, though, she was not an A-list actress, her movie résumé was thin, and there were few hints of her comedic talent in *Room Service.* Groucho was often asked about her, and all he recalled about her from the film was that she was "very attractive." He later ventured this opinion: "She's an actress, not a comedienne. There's a difference. I've never found Lucille Ball to be funny on her own. She's always needed a script."[20]

Perhaps the most unwatchable performance in *Room Service* is that of Frank Albertson, who played the part of Leo Davis, rather than Eddie Albert, who tackled the role on Broadway. Albert was busy in 1938, as both the lead in a Broadway musical and in his film debut in *Brother Rat.* Albertson later had moderate success in supporting roles, but in *Room Service* he is dopey and inordinately stiff. At times it's almost as if he is trying (and failing) to channel the hayseed charm of James Stewart, who scored big in Frank Capra's *You Can't Take It with You,* which was released several weeks before *Room Service.*

Almost no one was cast in roles that fit any better than one of Chico's suits. Because *Room Service* was an established play, there was no tour to test audience responses and precious little room for ad-libbing. Groucho was "softer and more vulnerable," which was not his best look. Louvish is no doubt right that audiences wanted him to play only one role, that of Groucho. Chico chimed in, "It was the first time we had tried doing a play we hadn't created ourselves. And we were no good. We've got to originate the characters and situations ourselves."[21]

Room Service Corridors

For all its weaknesses, *Room Service* illustrates aspects of the history of the late 1930s. Most New Yorkers would have associated the fictional White Way Hotel with Manhattan's Theatre District, a 12-block section of Midtown between 42nd and 53rd Streets. That area was dubbed the Great White Way early in the 20th century, possibly by *New York Morning Telegram* columnist Shep Friedman. The name gained popularity after appearing in a 1902 *New York Evening Telegram,* the paper's late edition.[22]

"White" refers to electric illumination. In 1880, parts of Broadway removed gas lamps and replaced them with electrical lighting, making it one of the first places in America to do so. This made theater-going much safer. It was calculated that the average theater lasted just 13 years, as they were so frequently destroyed by fire. An 1875 conflagration in Brooklyn killed 278 theater patrons; in 1903, Chicago's Iroquois Theatre burned with the loss of more than 600 lives.[23]

It is easy to forget that in 1938, electricity was relatively new for many Americans, especially for country dwellers. The 1936 Rural Electrification Act began delivering electricity to farms, ranches and small communities at a time when a mere 11 percent of rural households had such amenities. It was even spotty in parts of major cities, as electrical grids were as yet underdeveloped. Times Square—as it was dubbed in 1904—sits in the middle of the Great White Way and its bright lights began attracting visitors in the 1890s.

Once the film gets underway, Binelli utters an amusing line that could have been used as the movie's epitaph. He greets his "boss," producer Gordon Miller, and tells him, "The rehearsal, she's-a wonderful.... I still think it's a terrible play, but it makes a wonderful rehearsal." This is followed by a gag in which Faker arrives shirtless. Binelli explains, "He just don't believe in shirts," and Miller retorts, "Oh, he's an atheist, eh?" For purposes of the plot, Faker's shirtless appearance aids one of Miller's schemes.

With Wagner downstairs about to discover $1,200 worth of unpaid bills in Miller's name, Miller decides to abscond so that his cast can't be evicted. Miller reasons that the minute he leaves, Joe can say he skipped, the "cast can reregister under their own names," and it will look to Wagner as if they had no part in Miller's scheme. But first Miller, Binelli and Faker must pack. They don layer upon layer of Miller's clothing so that when Wagner reclaims the room and seizes his trunk, it will be empty. The Marxes look like they are competing for the role of the Michelin Tire Man, but they quickly shed the extra clothes and remain in the room when Christine arrives to tell them that she has found a backer.[24]

Playwright Leo Davis arrives with hopes of being housed, fed and given an advance, none of which Miller can offer. Miller tries to convince Davis to go home, but Davis insists he can't. Miller makes an appeal to his lonely mother: "At this very moment, she may be sitting at the fireside, wringing her hands." "But we have no fireside," Davis protests. An incredulous Miller responds, "You have no fireside? How do you listen to the president's speeches?"

That quip references Franklin Roosevelt's "fireside chats," a series of radio broadcasts in which the president discussed issues of the day. Calvin Coolidge was actually the first president to speak on the radio, but FDR was truly the first president of the electronic age. Over some 50 broadcasts, Roosevelt aimed remarks directly at the American public in which he distilled, but mostly avoided "dumbing down," content. Roosevelt masterfully explained policies, economics and world affairs through plain language and deliberate pacing. They were called "fireside chats" because FDR either addressed radio audiences from a White House living area, or cast the illusion that he was doing so. He held court in ways that made listeners—as many as 60 million— feel as if they were part of the conversation. This was part of Roosevelt's strategy of improving morale during both the Great Depression and the rising crises in Europe. Media have changed, but his success on the radio inspired presidential candidates to duplicate FDR's stratagem of folksy charm and populist appeal.

Davis' rude awakening gets worse when Harpo-Englund attempts to pick his pocket and relieve Leo of the last 67 cents he has to his name. Englund also rifles through his possessions and comes upon a picture of Davis and his mother. Binelli remarks, "You know, I think he's reforming. He didn't steal the picture." Miller agrees it's "an encouraging sign," until Englund abruptly punches through the picture and steals the frame. Miller can only comment, "Now I know how Gypsy Rose Lee feels."

Gypsy Rose Lee was the stage name of Rose Louise Hovick, one of the most famous strip tease artists in entertainment history. Although she occasionally bared all, Lee tended to be suggestive rather than salacious. As a child, she had a song-and-dance vaudeville act with her sister June, both having been pushed onto the stage by an ambitious stage mother who made Minnie Marx seem like an amateur. It's possible the Hovicks met the Marx Brothers on the Pantages circuit, though the latter would not have paid much attention to a child act. Louise and June also appeared in a few films directed by Hal Roach, an important director of early silent comedies. June eloped in 1928 and subsequently launched a solo acting career under the name of June Havoc, while Louise gravitated to the burlesque stage and changed her name to Gypsy Rose Lee.

Originally, the lines between vaudeville and American burlesque were thin. Both had musical numbers, skits, parodies and variety acts. Many future vaudevillians got their start in burlesque and moved up; vaudeville usually billed itself as the "clean" alternative to "dirty" burlesque with its undressed female bodies and ribald jokes. Those, however, help explain why burlesque outlasted vaudeville. Burlesque was a perfect format for Lee, who wisecracked, made suggestive comments, shimmied and doffed articles of clothing. Vaudevillians seldom went further than stripping to pasties covering the areolas and a G-string over the pubic region. Lee's form of burlesque dominated the 1930s, a time in which several strippers gained celebrity status.

When it ran afoul of moralists and local obscenity laws, burlesque began to wane. Lee parlayed her renown into movie roles, a TV talk show and a 1957 memoir. Two years later, that memoir became the basis for the Broadway musical *Gypsy: A Musical Fable.*[25] No one in 1938, including Lee, could have predicted her enduring fame, but the *Room Service* joke was timely in that Lee's name was instantly recognizable. It would not have required much thought to get the punchline; the frame, devoid of its picture, was suggestive of Lee *sans* clothing.

Miller delivers another nice punchline as he awaits the arrival of Jenkins, backer Zachary Fiske's representative. Wagner's incessant threats lead Gordon to tell Joe, "My backer's on his way up now. Now go down and tell Wagner if he doesn't behave himself, I'll buy this hotel and make him a bellhop. No, that's too good for him. I'll make him a guest."

Jenkins promises that Fiske will invest $15,000 on the condition that his beneficence remains a secret. It seems there's a "young lady involved" who should get a part in the play, the inference being that she is Fiske's mistress. If you've seen enough comedies, you know that keeping Fiske's name a secret is the *last* thing that will happen. There's a name for such a device: Chekhov's gun. It comes from Russian playwright Anton Chekhov, who argued that plays and stories should be stripped of elements that are irrelevant to the action. If a prop or idea is introduced, it needs to be used in some fashion. Of course, the Marxes needed little reminding to do the opposite of what they were told to do; Fiske's secret gets out faster than you can say "jumping butterballs."

Wagner doesn't believe that Gordon's backer really exists, but how can he expel a sick man? Miller cooks up a ruse in which Leo is sprayed with iodine to pose as a measles victim. Next up is dealing with hunger by, as noted, convincing Sasha to divert another guest's order to Miller's room. Sasha's head is filled with dreams of becoming the next Russian actor to become famous in America, like Gregory Ratoff, an actor-director who fled Russia in 1922, or "Ginger Rogervitch," Gordon's punning allusion to actress-dancer Ginger Rogers. A highlight of the ensuing gluttony at the groaning board comes when Christine arrives with sandwiches that are no longer needed, though that doesn't deter the ravenous Faker. He unwraps a sandwich, checks its contents, rewraps it and devours it, wax paper and all.

Miller thinks he's cleared the last hurdle after convincing Hogarth from the We Never Sleep Collection Agency that Davis was taken away as a lunatic after tearing up all of his money and taking his typewriter with him to the asylum because he "likes to hear the little bell ding." When Hogarth asks where he was taken, Miller responds he was taken to a maternity hospital. "Maternity hospital?" Hogarth exclaims. "I thought you said he was crazy." Somehow, Miller's explanation makes sense: "Well, if he wasn't crazy, he wouldn't go to the maternity hospital, would he? You can't miss him. Second straitjacket to the left."

Davis lets Miller down by refusing to continue his sick man charade, opting instead to rendezvous with Hilda, so Faker is hastily placed in the bed instead. Miller insists that the patient's measles have passed and that a suddenly developed tapeworm is being treated by "Doctor" Binelli. On Wagner's orders, though, a real physician, Dr. Glass, arrives to examine the patient. Faker lives up to his name by squeezing a small squeaky doll to feign moaning, but Glass pronounces the patient well and is about to spill the beans to Wagner. Instead, the Marxes gag him and lock him in the bathroom.

This sets the stage for two scenes whose manic energy are the most Marxian in the picture. Wagner bursts in to evict Miller at exactly the moment Jenkins is in the room finalizing the deal. Jenkins is ruffled by all the commotion, and it gets worse when Glass extricates himself from the bathroom and tells Wagner to butt out because he overheard that Zachary Fiske is backing the play. Wagner is repentant, but Jenkins seeks to renege because his client's name has been revealed. The room erupts into bouts of pleading, a turkey flies around, and the overall pandemonium strains the heart of the string-bean–like Jenkins. Philip Wood is superb as Jenkins, a man whose sanity and physical health come undone before our eyes. He is so befuddled that he signs the check, staggers from the room and Wagner is happy. It's only after both leave that Miller discovers that Jenkins never signed the contract and has no intention doing so.

With Fiske's withdrawal, Miller must conjure a way to keep Wagner at bay until the curtain goes up. Why not a double redux of the sickness dodge? The central players are locked in the room until they can be taken away. They are certain they are going to jail for fraud, but then a scheme springs to mind. Leo takes "poison," and "dies" from "suicide." This gives Miller an opportunity to commiserate with a temporarily chastened Wagner and hold an informal bedside funeral for the departed. It doesn't buy as much time as he hoped, though, because Wagner insists on calling the police, a possible scandal to the hotel notwithstanding. After all, you can't just dump a corpse in the alley, as Miller suggests. Or can you?

Wagner begins to dial the police when Miller asks him not to use the phone in the room, as it was the one Davis used to call his mother in Oswego. Wagner exits, which is just enough time for Faker to stick a stage knife in his chest with a note that says, "Wagner drove me to my death, just as he drove Leo Davis." This time the desperate Wagner takes Miller's suggestion that they leave the body in the alley. When they encounter a policeman, they prop Faker against a wall and tell the officer that he is a drunken actor.

This wins enough time for the play to finish. We see from the final scene of *Hail and Farewell* that Sacha has wowed the audience and that the play's political content is evocative of agitprop productions associated with the WPA Federal Theatre Project. The curtain drops with the cast singing "Swing Low, Sweet Chariot," the very song Miller crooned during Leo's faux funeral. Wagner faints when Leo taps him on the shoulder and says, "It's going great guns, isn't it, Mr. Wagner?" Thunderous applause closes the show, implying that sold-out houses will ensue.

Room Service Laundry

Here are several things that might escape attention.

- **Bed in the wall:** Early in the film, Binelli arrives to lodge with Miller after leaving his room at the Metropol, which he calls a "schlock house." Among his complaints is that he couldn't get the bed out of the wall. The reference is to a Murphy bed, named for Irish immigrant William L. Murphy, who maximized space in his one-room San Francisco apartment by hinging the bed to a supporting wall so that it could be raised when not in use. Some rooming houses and hotels installed models that fit into an alcove behind the head of the bed. Murphy beds are still sold, though they are dangerous if misused. That, of course, is why they are a staple for comedians.
- **Why a moose?** A running sight gag is that everywhere Binelli lodges, he brings a stuffed moose head with him. He refuses to hock it, even when hungry. The only explanation is that Binelli shot the moose himself and ate it up to the neck!
- **Ipecac:** There are several references to Ipecac, a syrup whose active ingredient induces vomiting and was once used to help poison victims vacate their stomachs. It is rarely used nowadays, as it doesn't purge all poisons from the stomach and can have harmful side effects.
- **Who is Fiske?** It's not clear if playwrights Murray and Boretz had a particular individual in mind, but the play's "Zachary Fiske" would not have been the first to use his wealth to advance a mistress's career. One possible template was Gilded Age financier and playboy James Fisk Jr., though a better bet is newspaper baron William Randolph Hearst. In 1902, Hearst married Millicent Wilson, who bore him five sons. They remained married, but were estranged after 1926, when Hearst's affair with model and struggling actress Marion Davies came to light. After she and Hearst became lovers, he took an active role in promoting her career, even to the point of forming Cosmopolitan Pictures and casting her in roles.

Bombs Away Revisited

In addition to the play's unsuitability for the Marx Brothers, there are other reasons it bombed. The overall flatness to *Room Service* compounds our basic discomfort with the Marxes dressed in semi-legitimate garb. One wonders if Groucho's part would have been sharper had Lucille Ball had not appeared and the role had been rewritten for Margaret Dumont. Maurice Charney thought that many of the wisecracks pricked instead of stung because Groucho had no one "of sufficient stature to work them off on."[26] I agree. We should not be blinded by what Ball became; she was not a vital force in *Room Service*.

The film's fate was in the hands of history, too; 1937 and 1938 were tough years for the economy. New Deal programs took the edge off of the Great Depression, but they did not end it. In early 1937, unemployment tumbled from an official high of nearly 25 percent in 1933 to under 15 percent. By spring of 1938, though, it crept upward to at 19 percent, with manufacturing output in decline. Economists debate why this occurred, their rationale often aligning with their political views, but the bottom line is that disposable income dropped, which is seldom good for box office revenues. Roosevelt came up with new programs—largely updates of existing initiatives—that aided in recovery in 1939, though much of the surge was linked to increased defense spending in response to tensions abroad. Global uncertainties may have softened ticket sales for *Room Service*.

Some viewers might wonder why there are "Nazi salutes" on the screen. That's not what they are. A right arm thrust into the air has been so thoroughly identified with fascism that it has obliterated all other possible meanings of the gesture. Context matters; it is absurd to think that three Jewish actors would promote Nazism on the screen. Recall that Harpo traveled through Germany in 1933 on his way to Russia and was horrified by what he saw, even before Adolf Hitler fully consolidated power.

Some have claimed that the Nazi gesture was an appropriation of the ancient "Roman salute" used to honor military heroes and emperors. The historical basis for this is thin and rests upon interpretations of gestures found on ruins. Those owe more to the imaginations of French painters of the late 18th and early 19th-century, especially Jacques-Louis David and Jean-Léon Gérôme. Some Americans might have associated the gesture with the "Bellamy salute," which was later used to discredit the utopian ideals of Edward Bellamy, though it was the brainchild of his cousin Francis Bellamy, who used it to honor the American flag during recitations of the Pledge of Allegiance, which he wrote in 1892. It was commonly known as the "flag salute" as a consequence.

Room Service used the Roman salute because previous movies had done so, whether historically accurate or not. This was especially so during the silent era, when dramatic gestures helped convey meaning. As we have seen, Lew Wallace's 1880 novel *Ben-Hur: A Tale of the Christ* had an enormous impact on how the ancient world was imagined. By 1900, stage adaptations routinely used the Roman salute, as did the 1907 and 1925 film versions of *Ben-Hur*. The "hail and farewell" right-arm thrusts we see in *Room Service* are certainly derived from *Ben-Hur*.

By the time *Room Service* debuted, though, the gesture had taken on new meanings. Germany was thoroughly militarized, Hitler's dictatorship was firmly established, and Nazi Party policy had taken anti–Semitic and bellicose turns. It was also the year of the Munich Agreement, a treaty that became synonymous with the term appeasement. On September 30, 1938, British Prime Minister Neville Chamberlain—along with officials from France and Italy—agreed to accept Germany's annexation of the Sudetenland, German-speaking parts of Czechoslovakia, in exchange for Hitler's pledge that he had no further territorial ambitions. An ebullient Chamberlain returned to Britain to proclaim "peace in our time." Eleven months later, World War II began. In just over 27 months, America would be drawn into the fray.

In early November 1938, Hitler's rhetorical hatred of toward Jews took physical form in an event known as *Kristallnacht*, the night of broken glass. Jewish-owned shops were smashed, synagogues were burned, and some 30,000 Jewish men were sent to internment camps.[27] Most historians date the beginning of the Holocaust to Kristallnacht. No one should accuse RKO, *Room Service* writers or the Marx Brothers of insensitivity; none were prognosticators.

In essence, *Room Service* fell prey to forces such as the Roosevelt recession, a poorly chosen project, a bloated budget and gathering war clouds. Hector Arce wrote that, after *Room Service*, "RKO gladly allowed [the Marx Brothers] to perform in anything they wanted, as long as it wasn't another RKO picture."[28] Luckily, they had signed a new three-picture deal with MGM. Thirteen months after the release of *Room Service*, the first of those MGM movies hit the screens. *At the Circus* was worse than *Room Service*, but it was decidedly a Marx Brothers film. Like it or not, Groucho was forced to play Groucho, a role that fit him like a greasepaint mustache.

TEN

At the Circus (1939)

It seemed like a good idea. What could be funnier than turning three great comedians loose in a circus? After their RKO fiasco, the Marxes returned to MGM for the first of three movies in which they played characters written for and developed by themselves. The first was *At the Circus*, which was wooden enough to make one pine for *Room Service*.

Jeff Wilson (Kenny Baker) has walked away from Newport society to own a circus. His rich aunt, Suzanna Dukesbury (Margaret Dumont), has disowned him and he owes $10,000 to John Carter (James Burke), who calls in the loan a week early. Jeff has the money hidden in a lock box inside the cage of Gibraltar, the circus' gorilla. Unluckily for Jeff, three circus performers are in cahoots with Carter: strongman

The Marxes went back to MGM for *At the Circus*. Pictured: Groucho, Florence Rice, Kenny Baker (MGM, via Wikimedia Commons).

Goliath (Nat Pendleton), midget Professor Atom (Jerry Maren) and Perilous Pauline (Eve Arden), an "anti-gravity walker." Goliath sneaks up on Jeff, knocks him out and steals the cash.

Jeff now has 24 hours to pay up or he'll lose everything, including his fiancée Julie Randall (Florence Rice), a singer and equestrian artist. Tony (Chico), a circus roustabout, contacts lawyer J. Cheever Loophole (Groucho) to help. Loophole, Tony and Punchy (Harpo) try to solve the crime without being broken in half by Goliath, outmaneuvered by Atom or outwitted by Pauline.

Loophole enters Dukesbury's mansion posing as her husband, which baffles the servants, as she is a widow. Dukesbury is initially appalled, but warms to Loophole's wooing. As he romances her, Tony and Punchy move the circus into the sprawling backyard of her home and waylay Jardinet (Fritz Feld), whose outdoor seaside concert is intended to be the crowning moment of the gala Dukesbury is throwing. Instead, her wealthy dinner guests are treated to a circus whose havoc is analogous to *A Night at the Opera*. The guests are thrilled, Jeff's money is recovered, Dukesbury's prestige is enhanced, she is smitten with Loophole, Jardinet and his oblivious orchestra drift out to sea, and all is well.

At the Circus has its moments, but not nearly enough good ones. But the film provides plenty of things to discuss.

Derailing the Circus Train

Joe Adamson was critical of all three of the Marxes' post–Irving-Thalberg MGM films. He asserted, "What comes between the punchlines ... are just plain old ordinary 1940s movies." He declared that "the Age of Heroic Comedy" had ended, leaving little in its wake except "disintegration, demoralization, heartbreak and Abbott and Costello."[1]

Historians are dubious of "golden ages," but it is certainly true that *At the Circus* is often ordinary, which is the last thing one expects of a circus. Who is to blame: MGM, the Marx Brothers or the screenwriters? English novelist and journalist Graham Greene blamed MGM. He felt that the Marxes were "imprisoned in the Hollywood world," his way of saying that they were constrained by formulaic convention.[2]

At the Circus has plot logic holes large enough for Gibraltar to knucklewalk through. How does Loophole end up on a train we see leave without him? Why is he a lawyer? If you wanted to solve a theft, wouldn't you consult a detective? Apparently, an early script called for a courtroom scene in which a lawyer would have made sense, but once that idea was jettisoned, all that remains is a name that lampoons the legal profession.[3] Historically speaking, Dukesbury's party was unlikely. Dukesbury was loaded, but even someone like she might have hesitated at throwing such a massive gala. The 1939 federal tax bracket imposed a 77 percent tax on incomes of over $1,000,000 and a whopping 79 percent for those above $5,000,000.

The Marx Brothers appear listless in *At the Circus*. That might have something to do with Groucho and Chico moonlighting during the filming. Hector Arce notes that they "liked the easy money in radio," and the pair was involved in *The Circle*, a 25-week broadcast sponsored by the Kellogg Company.[4] It was one thing to shuttle back and forth between projects as they had done in their early Paramount days, but that level of energy was more difficult to sustain a decade later. Simon Louvish noticed that the pacing of *At the Circus* was "appreciably slower than earlier films." This was true of most movies of the day, but it's easy to imagine that the aging Marxes lacked the stamina to maintain their frenetic pace.[5]

Perhaps, though, it's best to spread the blame around. Mervyn LeRoy, MGM's new production head, greenlighted a project that looked seductively good on the drawing board. His was certainly a prestigious name, but as the director of romances and of gritty crime dramas such as *Little Caesar* (1931) and *I Am a Fugitive from a Chain Gang* (1932). Moreover, he had produced just two films prior to *At the Circus*, and proved to be no Thalberg. Adamson charged that LeRoy "really had no idea what to do about broad, farcical comedies, but, like everyone else who doesn't make them, he thought of them as one big lark...."[6]

Nor could LeRoy command the independence or budgets of Thalberg. Irving Brecher was the sole scriptwriter. In 1939, the 24-year-old had exactly one screenwriting credit on his résumé, *New Faces of 1937*, and even that was a team effort that included veterans Nat Perrin and Philip G. Epstein.[7] Brecher's major qualifications were that he had written radio gags and was under contract to MGM. The Marxes got to shape their characters, but their sharpest comedies came when multiple writers, scripts and contributors were involved. This time, the only other figure associated with the script was Buster Keaton, who was tasked with coming up with material for Harpo. He was dismissed after suggesting an idea involving a camel that couldn't walk until Harpo removed straw from its back. An incredulous Groucho barked out, "Do you think that's funny?"[8]

Edward Buzzell was tapped to direct. He had 11 previous films to his credit, five of them comedies. Buzzell was also a former vaudevillian who befriended the Marxes in their mutual days on the circuit. Friendship was put on hold on the set, though. Adamson writes, "They didn't mesh well. There wasn't one scene, there wasn't one gag that didn't get argued over, sometimes bitterly."[9] Buzzell soon learned to don a poker face. He remarked, "Personally, I think the Marx Brothers are among the funniest people in the world, but, like all laugh-seekers of their type, they are always 'working' and if I was to prove a good audience...I would be sunk. So, I never laughed at their cracks and never tried to match repartee with them...." That was too bad; some of the on-the-set cracks were funnier than Brecher's script. For example, when Buzzell suggested Groucho needed more makeup on his nose, Groucho parried, "Don't quibble, what I need is a new nose."[10]

Groucho wrote to Arthur Sheekman that he thought *At the Circus* "will be much better than I thought. That isn't saying a hell of a lot, but, really, I think the scenes are going to be pretty funny...." He tellingly admitted he hadn't looked at the rushes, and talked about the radio show in which he and Chico were involved.[11] Perhaps Groucho should have checked the rushes, as the final print of *At the Circus* has the earmarks of laissez-faire direction.

Any on-the-set personality clashes were smoothed over, as both Brecher and Buzzell worked on the Marx Brothers' next film.[12]

Another fateful decision was MGM's insistence upon a tight shooting schedule and budget, which prevented the Marx Brothers from road-testing their material. Maybe studio heads felt that two MGM hits proved the studio's ability "to make a Marx Brothers movie" and secure a robust box office return.[13] *At the Circus* hit theater screens on October 20, 1939, and generated $3.4 million in ticket sales, but mixed reviews. In a year in which nearly 50 other films outgrossed the Marx Brothers, the mercurial Mayer could not have been pleased.

Under the Big Top

One of the most revealing things about *At the Circus* is its look inside of what was once an entertainment juggernaut. Today, the word "circus" conjures flashy spectacles involving aerial acts, gymnasts, mimes and novelty acts, with high-volume music and precise computer-programmed lighting setting the mood. This sort of circus was pioneered by Montreal-based Cirque du Soleil, which was founded in 1984 and has spawned imitators. As of 2021, there is no federal law banning the use of wild animals in circuses, but with the 2017 demise of Ringling Bros. and Barnum and Bailey Circus, it is rare to attend a circus employing any animals other than human beings.

As we have seen, phonographs, radio and especially movies homogenized American culture in the early 20th century. By the late 1950s, television was well on its way to becoming an even more powerful popular culture delivery device, and once the Internet went viral in 1995, millions of Americans had unlimited entertainment options at their fingertips. This was not the world of 1939, when *At the Circus* was released. It is easy to forget that popular culture did not always spread at lightning speed, or that where one lived determined how much access one had to it. Traveling minstrel shows, vaudeville circuits and railroad circuses were among the first forms of entertainment in which legions of Americans experienced the *same* content.

The circus has ancient roots—the word derives from the Latin for circle, and Romans enjoyed ovular chariot races. The American circus can trace its origins to Scottish immigrant John Bill Ricketts. He was a trick horseback rider whose 1792 show in Philadelphia is often regarded as the first American circus. Ricketts inspired similar displays of equestrian skills. It was not until around 1825 that circuses became mobile by placing acts under a collapsible tent that was hauled from town to town. Dan Rice didn't come up with that idea, but his clown act and comedic take on Shakespearean characters, popular songs and self-parody made him—to use an anachronistic phrase—the first American circus superstar. Rice is credited with coining the phrase "Greatest Show" and its counterpart "one-horse show," a reference to an inferior spectacle. He also dabbled in politics, mostly unsuccessfully, but his involvement with Zachary Taylor's 1848 presidential campaign gave us the idiom "jump on the bandwagon," a reference to the circus wagon carrying musicians. It now means an unreflective adoption of a trend, fashion or movement.

Circuses were small at first, but in 1864, Adam Forepaugh assembled a large circus by purchasing two others, including Dan Rice's. Forepaugh shows were known primarily for daring equestrian acts. The modern circus, Les Standiford observes, combined acts that took place inside a ring—"riding, tumbling, juggling," plus clowning—and later added animals, sideshows and parades.[14]

Phineas Taylor ("P.T.") Barnum reshaped the circus before he was formally involved in one. His American Museum in New York City exhibited wild animals and oddities—some real and many fake—that became staples of sideshows and "freakshows." In 1871, Barnum joined forces with performer Dan Castello[15] and Wisconsin entrepreneur William Cameron Coup to create an extravaganza that included wild animals, high-wire acts, clowns, a hippodrome and sideshows. Barnum one-upped Rice by dubbing his the "Greatest Show on Earth." He and Coup also get credit for the self-defining three-ring circus, a non-stop whirl of visual imagery for viewers and a phrase now often used to describe chaos or sensory overload.

Coup's push to build a "railroad circus" was the most revolutionary idea of all, though it was probably not an original thought.[16] In 1869, the first transcontinental railroad linked the trans–Mississippi West to the rest of the nation. Coup's vision of moving circuses from town to town via the railroad made them a portable form of national culture. There were many circuses, but the largest ones tended to have comparable entertainment. Inside the big top (the main tent), one saw an assortment of aerialists, clowns, gymnasts, horseback riders, jugglers, strongmen, wild animal handlers and thrill shows such as balancing acts, human cannonballs, sword swallowers and tightrope walkers.

No circus worth its salt failed to procure monkeys and at least one elephant.[17] In 1882, Barnum purchased an African elephant from an English zoo and dubbed it "Jumbo," another word that became part of the American lexicon. Jumbo was an example of ballyhoo, another word traceable to the circus. Courtesy of Barnum's hype, people saw Jumbo as extraordinarily large, though he was not appreciably bigger than other elephants. Smaller tents held sideshows that appealed to sensation-seekers who wished to see ape men, bearded ladies, contortionists, escape artists, midgets, heavily tattooed men and women, and all manner of people with physical abnormalities (Siamese twins, those with encephalitic heads, three-legged men, those missing limbs, the grossly obese, "human pincushions," etc.).[18]

By 1890, railroad circuses were the norm for at least seven large circuses. Between 1871 and 1900, the amount of railroad mileage nearly quadrupled; in 1916, it reached its peak of 266,381 miles. Smaller circuses ventured further into the hinterlands, as it was hard to compete with the giants on their own turf. In 1888, Barnum merged his circus with that of James Bailey. Barnum's main competitor was Ringling Bros. Greatest Show, which was founded in 1884 by four siblings. They absorbed most of Forepaugh's assets in 1889, and in 1907, the Ringlings bought Barnum & Bailey. When the two circuses merged in 1919 to create Ringling Bros. and Barnum & Bailey Circus, it made it even harder for anyone wishing to compete. The American Circus Corporation, which managed Sells-Floto, Hagenbeck-Wallace, Al G. Barnes and several others, was also absorbed by Ringling Brothers in 1929.[19]

In 1939, Ringling Bros. and Barnum & Bailey was America's largest circus by far. It probably inspired the *At the Circus* script, as the Great Depression forced numerous circuses to close. Those that remained contracted and moved performers and props by truck rather than rail. In hindsight, 1939 could be viewed as a collapsing peak for American circuses. World War II put most shows on hold, and not all survived. Ringling Bros. continued to draw large crowds, but even it packed its tents in 1956, and performed only in exhibition halls and sports arenas.[20] Liability issues also impacted circuses. Train wrecks, fires and accidents were frequent.[21] In addition, animal-rights groups turned their ire on circuses. In 2017, Ringling Bros. and Barnum & Bailey went out of business.

These things lay in in the future when *At the Circus* debuted. Then, circus performers such as clown Emmett Kelly, animal trainers Clyde Beatty and Mabel Stark, high-wire acts like the Wallenda family, and trapeze artists Antoinette Concello, Lillian Leitzel and Alfredo Codona were well-known names.[22] There was a tantalizing parallel between circuses and the Marx Brothers film in 1938, when Ringling Bros. president John Ringling North was bitten by a gorilla named Gargantua the Great. The name similarity between Gargantua and the film's Gibraltar is suggestive of a connection.

Circuses played a big role in advancing popular culture. Imagine the excitement of Barnum & Bailey arriving in a town or city, unloading railcars, and parading elaborately carved circus wagons carrying performers and exotic animals through the town, and trailed by lines of elephants. Readers under the age of 50 would have been lucky to see such a phenomenon but can catch the vibe of such a spectacle by visiting places such as Circus World Museum in Baraboo, Wisconsin, the Circus Museum in Sarasota, Florida, the Barnum Museum in Bridgeport, Connecticut, and the International Circus Hall of Fame in Peru, Indiana. At Vermont's Shelburne Museum, they can even see an entire parade laboriously carved in miniature by Edgar Kirk.[23] Such has been the appeal of circuses, which were an integral part of the Marx Brothers' world. It seemed logical to put them in one.[24]

Marxes in the Circus Parade

But it wasn't! Early on, a decision loomed whether to place the Marx Brothers in a circus or at the World's Fair. The latter opened in New York City on April 30, 1939, and before it closed on October 27, 1940, more than 44 million people visited. Adamson nailed it when he wrote, "LeRoy decided that the Marx Brothers belonged in a circus. And he was right. The Marx Brothers *do* belong in a circus. Which is why they shouldn't be put there." It was the very incongruity of placing the Marxes where they did not belong that explains why earlier films worked and *At the Circus* was forgettable.[25]

We expect clowns and funny men at a circus, but we don't expect to find Groucho as head of a college, a nation or an opera agency. Chico is funny as a clueless auction bidder, a spy or a bouncer, but you might expect him to be hanging around a circus or carnival. Harpo is the character most likely to thrive in a circus, yet he doesn't have much to do in the film, and his best gags could have been adapted for other storylines. The film's working title was *A Day at the Circus*, a clear attempt to recreate *A Day at the Races* in a different setting.

Metaphorically speaking, the best reason to watch *At the Circus* today is to savor the sideshows. The movie's opening establishes Jeff's dilemma and provides Julie (Rice) with a musical number. "Step Up and Take a Bow" is a clever piece of choreography between Rice and a trained horse that captures some of the magic of the circus. The song is slightly cheesy, but a lot of music from splashy productions such as opera, Broadway or Las Vegas is overwrought when divorced from the total sensory experience. "Step Up" was one of three songs written for the film by composer Harold Arlen and lyricist E.Y. "Yip" Harburg. By 1939, Arlen had scored standards such as "Get Happy" and "Stormy Weather," while Harburg had penned lyrics for "April in Paris" and "Brother, Can You Spare a Dime," the latter widely considered the quintessential

Great Depression song. In partnership they produced "It's Only a Paper Moon" and "Last Night When We Were Young." They collected Oscars for their contributions to *The Wizard of Oz*, including "Somewhere Over the Rainbow," one of the most famous songs in musical history. Arlen and Harburg did not duplicate their success in *At the Circus*, though they did come up with one real winner. More on it in a moment.

Early on, the film's only humor comes from Tony trying to con the telegraph operator into giving him a cheaper rate. It's more amusing than side-splitting, but it's much better than listening to "Two Blind Loves," an Arlen-Harburg dud that makes you punch the fast-forward button rather than coo over the Jeff-Julie romance. The movie picks up when Loophole arrives and stiffs the cab driver. By 1939, there was a lot of mileage on Groucho's cheapskate schtick, though some comics—Jack Benny, for instance—milked that affectation for their entire careers. Plus, in real life, Groucho *was* a cheapskate.

A rainy-night cab ride is the prelude to Loophole's reunion with Tony and a brou-haha over the need for a badge to board the circus train. It's a funny scene even if it's a reworking of *Horse Feathers'* speakeasy password exchange. Even though Tony knows Loophole and sent for him, rules are rules. Loophole stands outside getting soaked as Tony puts forth several impossible solutions. Loophole muses, "It was awfully nice of you floating this case my way.... If you hadn't sent for me, I'd probably be home now in a nice warm bedroom in a comfortable bed, with a hot toddy." Tony's observation that if Loophole doesn't get out of the water, "you're gonna get wet," induces Loop-hole's comeback: "Nonsense. If I was any drier, I'd drown."

Stringing together words with visual non sequiturs is usually good for a laugh, and we get another when Punchy arrives. When Tony asks for his badge, Punchy opens his coat to flash a lining full of them. He is traveling with Celia, a seal, and even she has a badge. Tony finally decides to give Loophole his own badge if he promises not to tell anyone. Just as Loophole seeks to board, Tony snaps, "What are you, a wise guy? That'sa last year's badge," and pushes Loophole into a puddle.

Somehow, Loophole gets on the train and tries to finish dressing, but his coat is filled with small animals. "Takes a magician to get into this coat," Loophole remarks. "That's who I took it from," Tony explains. As a rabbit appears, Loophole puns, "Don't split hares." Tony promises to introduce Loophole to Jeff, and though Loophole mis-takes Punchy for Jeff, he utters a line that leaves no doubt about which impresario scriptwriter Irving Brecher had in mind: "Always wanted to meet you, sir. I think you're the greatest circus owner since P.T. Barnum."

Have You Seen Lydia?

Shortly thereafter, Loophole and Tony and muse over "childhood days, lemon-ade, romance" at the circus, the prelude for Loophole to pull up his sleeves and strut about singing "Lydia, the Tattooed Lady." Harburg and Groucho shared a love of Gil-bert and Sullivan; "Lydia" is clearly inspired by them. We are treated to a cockeyed history and geography lesson as viewed through the ink etched on Lydia's body.

There are touches of suggestive naughtiness: "She has eyes that men adore so/ And a torso even more so." As he sings, Loophole's fingers trace an airy figure of a shapely female. Later, Loophole does an upper-body shake and sings, "When her muscles start relaxin'/ Up the hill comes Andrew Jackson/... For two bits she will do a mazurka in jazz / With a view of Niagara that nobody has...."[26]

There are numerous delightful groaners that make Groucho's performance of "Lydia" the highlight of *At the Circus*. Let's explore some of the song's references. It mentions Thaïs, du Barry and Garbo. Greta Garbo's name is instantly recognizable, but not the first two. Thaïs was a fourth-century courtesan, if we're being polite, and a prostitute if we're not. She was one of Alexander the Great's lovers and, in legend, instrumental in convincing him to lay waste to Persepolis in 330 BC. Legend also holds that Thaïs had frivolous reasons for wanting Alexander to destroy the city. This suggests her tale may be linked to others, such as Old Testament villainess Salome, who demanded of King Herod II the head of John the Baptist. Upon Alexander's death, Thaïs married his chronicler and future pharaoh of Egypt, Ptolemy I Soter.

Jeanne Bécu transitioned into Madame du Barry by becoming the official mistress—yes, there were such things in the French court—of King Louis XV (1710–74). She was a renowned beauty who had a frosty relationship with Marie Antoinette, the wife of future King Louis XVI. When Louis XV died in 1774, newly crowned Queen Marie Antoinette convinced her husband to exile Madame du Barry. Ironically, all three were guillotined in 1793 during the phase of the French Revolution known as "The Terror."

If the point was to invoke past beauties, why Thaïs and du Barry rather than someone more instantly recognizable such as Cleopatra or Helen of Troy? Du Barry is easiest to explain. The Marx Brothers had long been fascinated with her and had initially considered a costume ball for *Animal Crackers* in which one of them would dress as she. Mainly though, historical figures have a way of going in and out of fashion; in 1939, du Barry was in. Six movies had been made in which du Barry was a character, including the 1938 MGM film *Marie Antoinette* with Norma Shearer in the title role and Gladys George as du Barry. Prior to that, famed actresses Caroline Dudley, Theda Bara, Pola Negri, Norma Talmadge and Dolores del Rio stepped into that role.

Harburg was the likely source for Thaïs. *Thaïs* was a 1917 silent film, based on an 1890 Anatole France novel that tells of Saint Thaïs, a prostitute who converted to Christianity. This Thaïs allegedly lived in the fourth century AD, but her very existence is questionable and her story is similar to that of the woman who lived seven centuries earlier. Four years after *At the Circus*, Harburg collaborated with Roger Edens on a song titled "Salome," whose biographical details are also similar to those of Thaïs. Harburg chose Salome rather than Thaïs because he and Edens were writing for the film version of the Broadway show *Du Barry Was a Lady!* To add further irony, Lucille Ball played du Barry in that movie.

The *Hesperus* was a real ship that wrecked off the coast of Gloucester, Massachusetts, in 1839, with a loss of 20 lives. "The Wreck of the Hesperus" is the title of an 1842 poem by Henry Wadsworth Longfellow and also the name of 1927 and 1948 movie adaptations.

Kankakee is a town in Illinois. The Marxes performed their vaudeville act in the Kankakee Majestic Theatre on May 15, 1912. It's probably mentioned in "Lydia" because it rhymed with "Paree," a nickname for Paris. Kankakee is also a word favored by comics because it simply sounds funny. Walla Walla, Washington, gets the same treatment.

A mazurka is an energetic dance—usually in triple time—native to Poland. Mazurkas were so popular in the 19th century that they spread from Poland to the rest of the globe. Even classical composer Frédéric Chopin wrote mazurkas, though his were mostly folk dances with a tempo similar to a fast waltz. Today, mazurkas are popular in Celtic, Cajun, Filipino and American old-time music.

There's also a mention of Mendel Picasso, a name that baffles Marx Brothers scholars. It may have been chosen at random as a joke that Lydia's tattoos are not Pablo Picasso masterpieces. It might, though, be a subtle dig at Picasso, the inference being you'd need a geneticist like Gregor Mendel to figure out his abstract offerings.

Grover Whalen's name is dropped into the song. He is a largely forgotten figure. In early adulthood, he was a New York City Tammany Hall politician who served in numerous offices, including police commissioner. In the 1930s, he chaired Mayor Fiorello La Guardia's Committee on Receptions to Distinguished Guests. This made Whalen the city's official greeter. As such, he spoke at the opening of the 1939–40 New York World's Fair, after having taken part in its planning. The Trylon was the fair's signature building, a 610' modernist spire that connected to the ball-like Perisphere. Designed by Wallace Harrison and J. Andre Fouilhoux, the structures sported what was then the world's longest escalator. The fair's theme was "The World of Tomorrow" and it depicted a future utopian city. That idea was revived for the 1964–65 New York World's Fair, whose Futurama also depicted a utopian city.[27]

Western star Buffalo Bill, born William F. Cody, is one of several figures to cameo in "Lydia the Tattooed Lady." He was a frontiersman in his youth but, after 1883, was known for his "Wild West" show, his own version of a circus, which I will discuss in the next chapter. Captain Spaulding "exploring the Amazon" also makes an appearance as a lead-in rhyme to "And Godiva with her pajamas on." Spaulding was Groucho's character in *Animal Crackers*.

The reference to Godiva is a bit of double wit. It sports a deliberately forced rhyme and a subversive allusion to Lady Godiva, an 11th-century Mercian (Anglo-Saxon) countess. Godiva supposedly rode naked through the town of Lincoln in solidarity with town commoners burdened by excessive taxation. She allegedly had long hair that she draped over her breasts, but we also get the term "peeping Tom" from the Godiva tale. Thomas was allegedly a local seeking to gaze upon Godiva's nude body. In the song, the idea of Godiva wearing pajamas undermines the entire legend.[28]

The final song cameo: Polish-born Vaslav Nijinsky, one of history's most acclaimed ballet dancers. The idea of Nijinsky doing the rumba was not farfetched; he enjoyed and excelled at all manner of dance, modern as well as classical.

Jokes in Search of Coherence?

"Lydia the Tattooed Lady" concludes with Harpo swinging back and forth from a light fixture as Groucho ducks, rises, ducks and rises. Would that the rest of *At the Circus* were as cleverly written and choreographed. There are sharp puns sprinkled throughout, including Loophole's snide, "Let's not jump to concussions" rejoinder to Tony's not-so-brilliant deduction that the person who hit Jeff on the head and knocked him out "didn't like him." But the next truly amusing sequence comes after Loophole takes one look at Goliath's muscles and decides he won't pursue him as a thief. Instead, he looks for another clue, which is provided by Punchy, who found a cigar at the site where Jeff was assaulted.

Instead of Goliath, Loophole chooses a smaller target, Little Professor Atom, a cigar-smoking midget. Loophole suspects that the cigar belonged to Atom, so all they need to do is match the smell of the stogie with one of Atom's to prove he is in cahoots with Goliath. They pay a visit to Atom's trailer with the plan of bumming a cigar from him. There are banged heads and stooped bodies inside Atom's child-sized dwelling, but these set up one of Chico's patented missing-the-whole-point routines. When Atom wants to know why the three of them have come calling, Tony blurts out, "We just want to trap you into a confession." Loophole holds up the found cigar butt and asks if Atom happened to have lost it, which he denies. He then tells Tony, "This man is undoubtedly innocent." He *un*-subtly turns to Atom and says, "By the way, I'm all out of smokes. Do you happen to have a spare cigar on you?" Instead, Tony reaches into jacket and announces, "Here. I got one," and hands it to Loophole. This happens four times before Loophole realizes Tony has ruined any chance of a confession. The skit offers mirth, especially Groucho's exasperation, snappy insults directed at Chico, and Harpo's improvised matches to ignite the cigars.

Next, Loophole investigates Peerless Pauline, Carter's girlfriend. She actually has Jeff's money; Carter asked her to hide it for him. When Loophole enters her room, she asks, "What brings you here?" He replies, "Lots of reasons. Ten thousand reasons.... Don't mind me. I'm just a talent scout for Alcatraz." Loophole spots the stuffed wallet on several occasions, including when it's stuffed into Pauline's bosom. That leads to a great Groucho line directed at the audience: "There must be some way of getting the money without getting in trouble with the Hays Office." Loophole's interrogation takes an odd turn when Pauline convinces him to don a circus outfit and a pair of anti-gravity shoes and walk on the ceiling with her. They grapple a bit, the wallet tumbles, and Pauline leaves Loophole literally stuck in place. She flees, leaving Punchy to rescue him by untying his shoelaces; Loophole crashes to the floor headfirst.

Loophole hatches still another plan when he learns that Dukesbury is Jeff's aunt. Loophole decides to romance her rather than implore her to help Jeff. It helps that she's in the Social Register, indicating that she's both rich and prominent. The Social Register was an annual—now semi-annual—list of upper-class families in the Northeast. The first

Groucho and Eve Arden in *At the Circus,* before she out-wits him as Peerless Pauline (MGM, 1939, via Wikimedia Commons).

was published in New York City in 1887 but, by 1925, had expanded to 25 cities. Those in the Social Register were the very pinnacle of the upper crust, and no Jews or Catholics were allowed on it. It was thus a way for the top of the upper class to identify each other. For a fortune-seeker like Loophole, the chance to tap into wealth was irresistible.

Before Loophole leaves to call on Dukesbury, he utters another amusing line. He turns to a cage filled with simians, shakes hands with one, and says, "Goodbye, Mr. Chimps." This is a pun on *Goodbye, Mr. Chips*, a novel written by James Hilton. It is the bittersweet saga of a man named Chipping, nicknamed "Chips," an aging Latin teacher in an English public (private) school.[29] The novel was made into an MGM movie earlier in 1939, with Robert Donat winning an Oscar in the title role. Once again, Groucho's pun is both funny and timely. Incidentally, *Goodbye, Mr. Chips* was directed by the not-so-beloved (by the Marx Brothers) Sam Wood.

Loophole's overtures to Dukesbury meet with surprising success, though one might count Dukesbury's sudden and unwarranted change of heart as among the film's continuity problems. Loophole cracks another wicked insult as he pretends to be her husband back from the grave: "You have forgotten those June nights on the Riviera when we sat underneath the shimmering skies moonlight-bathing in the Mediterranean. We were young, gay, reckless. The night I drank champagne from your slipper. Two quarts. It would have held more, but you were wearing innersoles."

Loophole is also buying time so that Jeff, Tony and Punchy can get the circus set up in the backyard. First, he has to get rid of Jardinet, the conductor hired to entertain Dukesbury's dinner guests the next evening. Loophole places a call to the steamship scheduled to dock and tells them to arrest a Jardinet imposter whose real name is O'Connor, the head of a large dope ring.

The circus tent goes up and the guests are shuttled in. They laugh and applaud heartily, thinking that everything they see has been planned. Actually, the mayhem under the big top is score-settling time. Among the craziness, we see Dukesbury being fired from a cannon, and a trapeze act with Gibraltar the gorilla, Punchy, Carter and Dukesbury flying back and forth. Loophole narrates the action as he did the *Monkey Business* barn fight. The money is recovered, the bandshell in which Jardinet and his orchestra are playing has been unmoored, and once again the Marx Brothers have rescued young lovers. It's just like Thalberg intended, except he would have insisted upon a better script.

Unwanted Elephant in the Room:
Swingali Strikes Out on Race

In Harpo's best sequence, he tears the stuffing from Goliath's mattress and plows through his room as if the feathers were snowflakes. He even has a feathery, Santa-like beard at one point. But as Punchy, his role is underwritten, which might be why LeRoy and Buzzell tried to catch lightning in a bottle a second time with a sketch reminiscent of *A Day at the Races*.

Readers will recall that the most discussed part of that film was the song-and-dance routine instigated by Harpo and infused with energy by African American singers and dancers. *At the Circus* returned to that formula. Mark Bego praised the Marxes: "While other 1930s films were featuring black performers as either servants or in minstrel numbers, the Marx Brothers were depicting them as friends, co-workers and music partners." By contrast, Adamson wrote, "You would think that the last thing they would *want* to copy ... would be that silly and patronizing Negro business...."[30]

Both writers are correct. Once again, we should differentiate what is acceptable now from what was commonplace then. Bego is correct that Marx Brothers films showed African Americans in a better light than most other 1930s films. He is wrong, however, to overlook aspects of minstrelsy in those portrayals. Adamson is on target with calling those representations patronizing, but when writing in 1973, his views were influenced by the black activism (and terminology) of his day.

The *At the Circus* routine begins when a black zookeeper is terrified by the roaring of the lions and runs off screen screaming. Just then, four black children peek under the tent and watch Punchy lull the lions to sleep by playing a lullaby on a small slide trombone. He then plays a jazzier tune on what looks to be a clarinet built into his bulb horn. The children fearlessly wander in through a line of elephants and launch a rap-like patter that includes the lines

> Well, button my lip and send me quick.
> That man's got a voodoo in that stick.
> When he voodoo raki-saks he can hypnotize an elf.
> That man must be Swingali himself.

As "Swingali," a play on mesmerist Svengali, Punchy instigates another black production number.[31] He conducts a music bandwagon filled with black youngsters, and dances boogie-woogie style with black children and adults in a sequence briefly interrupted by song snippets. Then he plops down behind the harp and plays "Blue Moon," a famous tune written by Richard Rodgers and Lorenz Hart and vocally covered by everyone from Frank Sinatra and Billie Holiday to Elvis Presley and Cyndi Lauper. In 1939, the song was just five years old.

Had Harpo never performed with black performers in *A Day at the Races*, his Swingali number in *At the Circus* might have looked better than it now plays, once we get past the stereotype of a screaming, bug-eyed black man—probably Willie Best—fleeing from caged lions. Or perhaps not. None of the children are credited, nor are the two black singers, Dudley Dickerson and Lillian Randolph. From the standpoint of 1939, though, there are several subversive things in the sequence. First, Harpo violated the unwritten rule about interracial touching. He is hoisted into the air on several occasions and black hands are upon him in several others. Second, Harpo gets up close and personal, especially with the kids, with whom he faces off just inches away. Perhaps that doesn't sound radical, but it was in its day.

To add another historical note, it wasn't unusual for black personnel to work in circuses, though in diminished roles. In many parts of the country, audiences sat in segregated sections and disproportionate numbers of African Americans appeared as "exotics" (as alleged Arabs, African "princes" and sideshow freaks). Black minstrel acts made their way into American circuses, as did the occasional singer and musician, but *At the Circus* more accurately depicts African Americans in work clothing. There were many black circus workers, including children, mostly laboring as roustabouts, janitors and animal tenders. It was certainly unusual for a white performer like Harpo to immerse himself in a sea of black faces and yield (even briefly) the limelight.

Nonetheless, the Swingali production is limp, as if it were mere padding of the script. Today we might use the term "tokenism" to describe what we see. More charitably, we might simply say it was a bad idea to try to duplicate something that was done far better in *A Day at the Races.*

Sideshows: *At the Circus* Miscellanies

- **Visual joke:** Nat Pendleton, who played the strongman, was one of the ringer Darwin football players in *Horse Feathers.* He was stiff in that role and stiffer still as Goliath. His character is, however, a visual pun. He wears a curly wig and looks like Harpo on steroids and with a mustache.
- **Professor Atom:** Jerry Maren—then known as Jerry Marenghi—was indeed a midget, not a child actor. He played one of the Munchkins in *The Wizard of Oz* and was the last of them to pass away. He enjoyed a long movie career, even if most of his roles came in B-movies. He also really smoked cigars.
- **Harpo speaks! (Sort of...):** We hear Harpo's voice in *At the Circus,* though just "ka-choo," when he sneezes from all the feathers ripped from Goliath's mattress.
- **Chico's solo:** Chico plays "Beer Barrel Polka" as his solo. It was a hit in 1939 and has since has become a standard. It was originally written in 1927 by Czech immigrant Jaromír Vejvoda.
- **Wagner:** As Jardinet and his orchestra drift out to sea—into the shipping lanes, no less—they play a suitably dramatic piece. It's from composer Richard Wagner's *Lohengrin,* an opera based on the Arthurian legend of Percival.
- **Ouch!** Parts of Harpo's solo sound atonal. Harpo was suffering from bursitis and couldn't play with his usual range of motion.[32]
- **The suit unmakes the man:** Gibraltar is makeup artist Charles Gemora in a gorilla suit. He had a second career as a Hollywood gorilla and appeared in many films dressed as one. According to Adamson, the suit rented for *At the Circus* was so poorly ventilated that its occupant fainted. There are two stories about how that problem was solved. Groucho claimed that a smaller orangutan skin was procured.[33] That's possible, as Gemora was less than 5'5" in height. A more plausible story is that Gemora used an awl to punch holes in the suit to provide easier breathing. It appears, though, that a smaller costume is at play in the trapeze scenes, so perhaps both tales are correct.
- **Sharing time:** In one of the film's more charming scenes, Groucho and Margaret Dumont share a soda at the circus with straws in the same bottle.
- **Code problems:** Writers and directors were often frustrated by uneven applications of the Code. The Hays Committee nixed a funny line in which Loophole encounters an old man sitting with a young woman and wisecracks, "Just mail them a dollar and they'll send you a monkey gland in a plain white envelope. If you mail them five dollars ... they'll mail you the whole monkey."[34] This joke is a reference to Dr. John Brinkley, whom we met in an earlier chapter, though his specialty was goat glands. Brinkley was exposed as a fraud in 1938, so the most likely explanation for cutting the joke is that

censors thought it inferred that the old man planned to bed the younger woman.

- **Another weird cut:** Another curious cut was a Hitler reference in "Lydia, the Tattooed Lady." Although World War II did not begin in Europe until September 1, 1939, there were few illusions left about Hitler's true nature. Perhaps no one wished to enrage the German American Bund, a pro–Hitler, anti–Semitic American Nazi organization formed in 1936. A February 1939 rally attracted an estimated 20,000 supporters. It is too bad that the Jewish Groucho didn't get to sing the original lines "When she stands, the world gets littler / When she sits, she sits on Hitler."
- **Left on the floor:** Glenn Mitchell details some scenes that were cut from *At the Circus* that suggest a much better film was left on the cutting room floor.[35]

Cleaning the Zoo Cages

At the Circus is unlikely to snag a place in the pantheon of great Marx Brothers films. In October 1939, Groucho remarked that he didn't like it and vowed never again to watch it.[36]

Only *Variety* lavished praise on it. *Life* saw it as formulaic, and *The New Yorker* damned it with faint praise by saying it was "only for their fans who must see [the Marxes] in everything." The *New York Times* saw more "perspiration than inspiration," though it may have gotten the formulation reversed; it often looks like the Marxes were just going through the motions.[37]

Groucho was in a disconsolate mood after the film. Ruth's alcoholism had deepened, he worried about taxes, and was keenly aware of world perils. He confided to Sheekman,

> You probably ask, "Why can't he sleep? He has money, beauty, talent, vigor and many teeth"—but I see Bund members dropping down my chimney, Commies under my bed, Fifth Columnists in my closets, a bearded dwarf called Surtax doing a gavotte on my desk with a little lady known as Confiscation. I'm setting aside a small sum for poison, which I'm secreting in a little sack under my mattress.[38]

Groucho was being cheeky with his friend, but not entirely so. He was aware that the 1940 Revenue Act was about to take a huge bite out of future movie paychecks. By then, America was exiting the Great Depression, largely because President Roosevelt had launched preparedness defense spending. It was to be funded through massive surtaxes on incomes. Surcharges were placed on incomes above $4,000 that accelerated quickly and dramatically. A $20,000 income, for instance—more than $370,000 today—incurred a 24 percent surtax on top of the existing tax rate. Once one got into Groucho's bracket of over $200,000, two of every three dollars ended up in federal coffers. It's hard to feel too badly for Groucho, as $200,000 is more than $3.7 million in 2020 dollars, but he never really got over the experience of being wiped out by the 1929 stock market crash. He again talked of retiring from movies.

Eleven

Go West (1940)

Go West is set in 1870. A young couple, Terry Turner (John Carroll) and Eve Wilson (Diana Lewis), dreams of settling a long-simmering dispute between their families by marrying. Terry has convinced the New York and Western Railroad that the best route to the West is through Dead Man's Gulch, a wasteland that his grandfather hoodwinked Dan Wilson (Tully Marshall) into buying.[1] Dan is a kind man, but he's poor and fatalistic. He's been prospecting and has no idea that Terry's deal would pay him $50,000 for Dead Man's Gulch—more than a million dollars by today's reckoning.

S. Quentin Quale (Groucho), an Easterner heading West, needs $10 more for a train ticket. He runs into Joseph (Chico) and Rusty (Harpo) Panello, whom he hopes

Poster for *Go West*. Not your average Western (MGM, via Wikimedia Commons).

to bilk out of the money by selling them useless items such as a big hat and a tattered buckskin coat. The Panellos' plan is for Rusty to head out on his own, pick up gold nuggets, and send money back East for Joe to join him. Chico is once again cast as a trickster who smells a way of relieving Groucho of his money.

The film heavies, gun-toting saloon owner Red Baxter (Robert Barrat) and railroad official John Beecher (Walter Woolf King), have a vested interest in making sure the railroad sticks to the original plan of skirting a mountain range via land they just happen to own. If the railroad buys Wilson's land, they stand to lose a small fortune. Determined to prevent the Dead Man's Gulch deed from reaching New York, they enlist the mixed-blood "Indian Pete" (Mitchell Lewis) to locate Wilson and get the deed.

Joe and Rusty are prospecting in the hot sun and having no luck. Dan tells them there's no gold to be found and that he's moving on once he comes up with a grubstake (provisions). Joe is moved by Dan's plight—he's supporting his granddaughter—and pretends that he and Rusty have plenty of money. They give him their last ten dollars, but Dan insists on giving them the deed to Dead Man's Gulch as security for the "loan." That deed will end up in the drawer of Baxter's saloon when Rusty is caught pilfering a beer. Joe writes an IOU for ten cents on back of the deed to get Rusty out of trouble. When they later learn that the railroad wants Beecher to purchase Dead Man's Gulch, they realize they need to reacquire the deed. But first, they head for the rail station, meet Beecher and pretend to have the deed so they can stall for time.

The Panellos and Beecher board a stagecoach that's also carrying Quale, Baxter's girlfriend Lulubelle (June MacCloy) and a woman with a bawling baby.[2] On the journey, Beecher offers $500 for the deed, but Quale is sharp enough to recognize a con man and promptly outbids him. Back at the saloon, a diversion allows Rusty to rifle the cash drawer and locate the deed. Quale, after a dangerous flirtation with Lulubelle, tries to broker a deal to sell the deed for $10,000, but Beecher and Baxter outfox him, lock the deed in a safe, and refuse to pay him a dime. Quale threatens to sue, but changes his mind when Baxter displays his sharpshooting talents. Instead, he endures a boot down the stairs and peals of laughter from saloon patrons.

Quale and the Panellos plan to break into the safe, but Lulubelle overhears them, sends word to Baxter, and enlists several dance hall girls to entertain Joe and Quale until Red arrives. In the adjacent room, Rusty is "quietly" trying to crack the safe, which is hard to do when you're using a small cannon! It works, but Baxter shows up with his gun drawn. The deed eventually ends up in Terry's hands and he vows to take it to New York personally. Baxter and Beecher shift tactics to make sure that doesn't happen. There's a lot of mayhem leading to a happy ending.

MGM Meddles

MGM conceded that audience-testing was a good idea. During April and May 1940, the Marxes visited Chicago, Detroit and Toledo and endured five-a-day shows. They gave an astonishing 103 performances in just three weeks, a grueling pace considering that all three were over 50.[3] Groucho remarked that they "were ready for the sanitarium," though the brothers enjoyed being back on stage.[4] Maxine Marx added,

"The only happy experience from this period right before the war was the tour of *Go West*." The Marxes were at ease enough for some improvised joking. On day four, Chico and Harpo switched parts to see if Maxine would notice, only to learn that she skipped the show to go to a party with friends![5]

Go West shooting was slated to begin on July 1, but script and financial squabbles largely independent of the Marxes caused delays. In late June, Groucho expressed the concern that dialogue sharpened on the road would be forgotten.[6] Shooting didn't get underway until the middle of July, leaving Groucho in a sarcastic mood. To Arthur Sheekman, he wrote, "*Go West* is being constantly postponed. I read the script and I don't blame them. If they [MGM] were smart, they'd pay us off and get three other fellows or take all that money and open up a big, gaudy cat house."[7] Around the same time, he wrote to his son Arthur:

> I don't know why the studio doesn't come right out and say they are afraid to make [the movie]. All I get from them is a weekly announcement to come to the wardrobe department and be fitted for a pair of early American pants. The writers have been taking some big hacks at the story, and from what I hear, once we begin, we should be able to shoot the whole thing in three days, and get the Academy Award.... Well, it doesn't bother me. My attitude is, take the money and to hell with it. I had my hair darkened to match my grease-paint mustache, but it has been so long since the scheduled starting date that the dye has faded and now, I will have to have it done all over again. So, you see my theatrical career has dwindled to being fitted once a week for a pair of early American pants and having my hair dyed every three weeks. This is a fine comedown for a man who used to be the Toast of Broadway.[8]

Given that much of the crew from *At the Circus* was back, *Go West* should have been easy to sort out. Eddie Buzzell returned as director, Irving Brecher wrote the script, Leonard Smith was again in charge of the camera crew, and old hands Bronislaw Kaper and Gus Kahn contributed half of the musical numbers. Chico contracted strep throat, which pushed the schedule back, but just for a few days. Nat Perrin also caused a short slowdown: He attended several *Go West* stage performances and, though he was not credited, contributed some new material. All of these were minor setbacks; MGM needlessly delayed matters. For example, one executive had to be talked out of cutting gags from the film's final scene, which is now considered one of the strongest in the picture.

It was ultimately a case of too many MGM hands on the throttle. Nepotism reared its ugly head. In September, Groucho complained, "Our picture has become a garbage can for the studio. The ingénue, who is no Helen Hayes, happens, by odd coincidence, to be William Powell's wife." Producer Jack Cummings was Louis B. Mayer's nephew, the unit manager was Cummings' nephew, and the assistant unit manager was Mayer's son-in-law. The goal of the road tour was, in Simon Louvish's words, "to avoid the flatness of the previous pictures. But the script kept changing."[9] Joe Adamson was blunter: "By August the poor script was a hacked-up chaos...."[10]

Ultimately, Louis Mayer's poor judgment bore rotten fruit. As noted in the last chapter, in 1936 Irving Thalberg had charged Bert Kalmar, Harry Ruby and William Slavens McNutt with producing a *Go West* script.[11] Had Thalberg lived, *Go West* would have been the next Marx Brothers film rather than *At the Circus*. Instead, Mayer halted the *Go West* script when Thalberg died. The original idea would have placed the Marx Brothers in a rodeo rather than the 1870s West, but Brecher nixed that idea and hammered out a completely new script.[12] He was a solid gag writer, but he was no Harry Ruby. One wonders what could have been salvaged from the original material.

Eyles, who disliked *Go West*, declared it "a great shame" that Ruby and Kalmar didn't write the script and songs.[13] George Seaton and Nat Perrin were critical of Buzzell's direction; Seaton held that he ignored Thalberg's belief that comedy had to serve the story, and Perrin felt the film lacked "a strong hand" and was overly invested in poorly integrated "individual scenes."[14] Of Buzzell's direction, Adamson wrote, "He had calmed his comedians down ... and he had gotten the scenes shot, and ... kept all three in the viewfinder range. That was about all you could say for it."[15]

Go West is uneven, but it's still a far better film than *At the Circus*. Wes D. Gehring pointed to a few inspired moments, but also noted: "[W]riting would have made the difference."[16] Perhaps the best script would have been one reined by Ruby and Perrin, with Brecher riding in the back of the buckboard wagon.

The Imagined Wild West

There are three noteworthy things about *Go West*. First, it is not a film about the historical American West; it's a spoof of *films* made about the "Wild West." Second, the Marxes borrowed heavily from previous Westerns send-ups. Third, the Wild West was more mythical than real, but railroads really were prone to crooked deals.

As noted previously, Westerns were quite the rage in Depression-era America. At least 222 were produced between 1931 and 1939, and some of Hollywood's biggest stars made appearances in them, including Gary Cooper, Marlene Dietrich, Errol Flynn, Henry Fonda, Olivia de Havilland, Tyrone Power, Randolph Scott, Barbara Stanwyck and James Stewart. The 1930s saw John Wayne rise from the B-list to star status through Westerns; he made an astonishing 46 Westerns in nine years.

Several Westerns are now considered classics. *Cimarron* won the 1931 Oscar for Best Picture. Other highly regarded films include *Riders of Destiny, Annie Oakley, Destry Rides Again, Dodge City* and *Stagecoach*, the last of which was nominated for seven Oscars and won two.[17] The 1930s was also the decade of singing cowboys such as Gene Autry, Bob Baker, Smiley Burnette, Tex Fletcher, Ken Maynard, Tex Ritter and Roy Rogers. Even Bing Crosby got in on the act in *Rhythm on the Range* (1936). MGM didn't make many Westerns, but it did release the successful 1937 Laurel and Hardy lampoon *Way Out West*.

Go West is loaded with comic twists on themes gleaned from Hollywood Westerns. Harpo wears a cowboy hat, but an outrageously oversized one that Martin Gardner describes as looking like "it would actually hold ten gallons of liquid."[18] Harpo also has a swaggering bowlegged pace-off with Red Baxter that ends in laughter when he pulls a gun loaded with a whisk broom. Other standard Western movie tropes included loners, unexpected rescues, saucy dance hall girls, lots of bandanas, the triumph of good over evil and, yes, a singing cowboy: John Carroll does the honors, with Harpo on harmonica. The Roger Edens–composed "Ridin' on the Range" doesn't do Carroll any favors, but it helps us remember we are watching a parody, hence Groucho's nasal New York–accented harmonies.

Three specific Hollywood films inform *Go West*: First, *The General*, an iconic

1927 Buster Keaton silent that inspired the train dismantlement scene. *Go West* also shares similarities with director Cecil B. DeMille's 1939 *Union Pacific* that, like *Go West*, featured a self-interested character seeking to manipulate the railroad's route. *Union Pacific* also depicted the joining of the eastern and western halves of the first transcontinental railroad by driving a golden spike into the connector at Promontory Summit, Utah. That scene is lampooned at the end of *Go West*, though the Marxes do so anachronistically. The film is set in 1870, which meant the Marxes would have been a year late to the party: The historical golden spike was planted on May 10, 1869.

MGM's *Way Out West* was the biggest inspiration. This confirms the charge leveled by Graham Greene quoted in the previous chapter: The Marx Brothers were "imprisoned in the Hollywood world."[19] *Way Out West* also involved a pilfered deed, a duplicitous dance hall singer, an attempt to remove the deed from a crooked saloon owner's safe, and singing cowboys. *Go West* is funnier, however.

Film Westerns helped invent the very idea of the "Wild West." They and pulp novels laid the foundation for myths and legends later reinforced by cowboy movies and the Western-themed TV shows that dominated viewing habits in the 1950s and 1960s. Collectively, they shaped popular perceptions that persist to the present of what the 19th-century West was like.[20] This is especially true of depictions set during the open-range cattle drives, a relatively short period of time. Until an extensive network of railroad trunk and branch lines crisscrossed the West, grazing cattle had to be driven to railhead towns such as Sedalia, Missouri, or Kansas railroad corrals in Abilene, Dodge City or Wichita. Cowboys were mostly hired hands akin to today's "gig" workers, not the rugged individualists of legend. Nor were they all white; roughly a third were either Mexican American or African American. They worked around the clock when they could, as it was imperative to get their stock to the railhead as quickly as possible; owners were compensated by the pound, and pay was adjusted accordingly. Cowboys also had to find grazing lands and water in areas that were often arid, not to mention populated by Native Americans.

The first drives began when free-range Texas longhorns were rounded up, though given that Texas was not part of the Union until 1845, it wasn't until the 1850s that large drives began in earnest. These were interrupted by the Civil War, at which time there were just 34 states. (Kansas had been added just two and a half months before hostilities began on April 12, 1861.) Although beef production did not cease entirely, the large drives were curtailed until 1866. That year saw Armour and Company open a meatpacking plant in Chicago, which in turn saw the Union Stock Yards swell with thousands of cattle and sheep. Swift and Company opened in 1875, flooding the market with even more beef. By the late 1880s, most of the cattle drives were over, victims of bad weather that decimated herds, railroad expansion, the invention of the refrigerated railcar, land consolidation, and barbed wire that made open grazing for cattle difficult. By 1890, most cowboys were hired hands on ranches, and it was a buyer's market for their services. Altogether, the open-range cowboy era was roughly 25 years long.

That quarter-century did not correspond with the West presented in popular culture. The U.S. added nine more states after the Civil War—West Virginia and Nevada were added during the conflict—swelling the total to 45. Of these, eight could be considered "Western" in the Hollywood sense: Nebraska (1867), Colorado (1876), the Dakotas (1889), Montana (1889), Idaho (1890), Wyoming (1890) and Utah (1896).[21]

In the movie version of the Wild West, civil authority was either non-existent or in the hands of U.S. marshals, rangers and hastily deputized heroes. Statehood, however, required organized government and the rule of law, not that of a six-gun or vigilante rule. Moreover, territories only became states when they attained a sufficiently large population. The 1862 Homestead Act opened vast tracts of land for settlers, but population increases mostly coincided with railroad expansion.

George MacDonald Fraser observed that the West was sometimes violent, "but brigandage and shoot-outs and Indian fighting were a drop in the ocean of hard work—clearing, planting, building, mining, cattle-raising and driving—which was the thing that really won the West."[22] In Fraser's words, "Hollywood's practice is to shape and adapt ... events and people to make them conform to romantic legend," which is why the term "horse opera" is sometimes applied to popular culture looks at the West. In such productions, farmers, mothers, shopkeepers, schoolteachers and ministers are given short shrift.[23] These, though, were the ones who transformed the West from scattered makeshift settlements into places ready for statehood.

It is conceivable that *Go West* could have taken place in some isolated locale conforming to Wild West perceptions, though such a destination probably would not have had rail access. Even then, the gap between Hollywood invention and reality would have been considerable. The real violence of the West was embodied in government policy toward Native Americans, the period between 1862 and 1890 being the height of the Great Plains Indian Wars that made land safer and more available for white settlers.[24] White-on-white violence was most evident, though exaggerated, in scattered locations. Christine Bold offers the illustrative example of Dodge City, Kansas, where the murder rate was 1:996 in 1880. That sounds high until one realizes that 996 was the total population of Dodge City. Marco Patricio and Randolph Roth note that Western data are often skewed by rates based upon incidents per 100,000 people. If one adjusts the data, the murder rate in the Dodge City of the Earp brothers, Doc Holliday and Bat Masterson was far lower than that of San Francisco, where one had a 1:203 chance of being murdered.[25] Similarly, lynching was rare in the West. Again, *Go West* was a send-up of Western movies, not the actual American West.

One aspect of *Go West* is historically sound. Railroad-building decisions often involved chicanery and bribery. In *Go West*, Turner meets with railroad officials and convinces them that routing their tracks through Dead Man's Gulch rather than Cripple Creek is a less-expensive option. Beecher is a railroad official, but he doesn't care about efficiency or cost; he and Baxter only want to line their pockets. Once Baxter has Wilson's deed in his safe, that's where he intends it to stay. There were plenty of similar opportunities for real-life Beechers and Baxters.

There was no such railroad as the New York and Western, but the film accurately alludes to longstanding dreams of connecting New York to the West Coast by rail. The United States had an unusual settlement pattern. It expanded west of the Mississippi River through the Louisiana Purchase (1803), the annexation of Texas (1845), the Mexican Cession (1848) and settling the border of the Oregon Territory (1848), but most white Americans lived east of the Mississippi River. That changed dramatically after gold was discovered in California's Sutter Creek on January 24, 1848, in an area that technically was still part of Mexico, as the Treaty of Guadalupe Hidalgo formally ending the Mexican War wasn't signed until February 2. Once word got out, fortune-seekers rushed to the West Coast. California became a state in 1850 and Oregon in 1859, but relatively few whites wished to settle in the Great Plains or Great Basin.

An individual starting from New York connected with a wagon train in Missouri, or boarded a ship that circumnavigated South America. The first took roughly five months once one got to Missouri, and entailed arduous and dangerous travel across lands populated by Native Americans; the second took six months and was more expensive.[26] The first transcontinental railroad reduced travel time to 83 hours, which seemed miraculously fast in 1869. It linked Sacramento to Omaha, where lines carried passengers further east, though it did little for those living distantly south or north of it.

As noted, a railroad-building surge began around 1871, and demand was high for new transcontinental lines. The Southern Pacific, completed in 1881, connected New Orleans to San Francisco via Texas and the Arizona and New Mexico Territories. In 1883, the Northern Pacific linked Chicago to Seattle. By 1900, the nation sported an estimated 170,000 miles of track, five transcontinentals and scores of webbing branch lines.

As homesteaders, prospectors, ranchers and farmers settled in the trans–Mississippi West soon found out, the value of their lands and the viability of towns were directly correlated to proximity to railroads. As in *Go West*, there was heated competition over planned routes. Bribery frequently occurred, quite a lot of it involving Congressmen and other high officials. By the late Gilded Age, Midwestern farmers and Western ranchers held railroads in contempt, as they were completely at the railroads' mercy for getting crops and animals to market. From this was born social movements such as the Farmers' Alliance movement and the Populist Party.

The true Wild West outlaws were railroad executives. Maps of Western railroad lines appear chaotic and illogical because they often were. As in *Go West*, the best route wasn't necessarily the one chosen, especially if there was a financial reason to divert it. During a period of breakneck expansion, railroads often went bankrupt, either because they floated watered stock or because they fell to stronger competitors. In such feverish times, shoddy construction was common. Those seeking an explanation for why today's American railroads are in such a sorrowful state could do worse than begin their investigations in the post–Civil War period.

Beginnings, Endings and the Stuff in the Middle

Let's return to the sequence in which Groucho is a flimflammer who gets out-conned. The film opens with two short segments that alert us that J. Quentin Quale is a cheapskate hustler. He charges into a train station trailed by black porters. Quale asks if any of them have change for ten cents and when they don't, Quale tells them, "Well, keep the luggage." Then he walks up to a ticket booth and orders a ticket for the West. The price is $70. Quale forks over a wad of cash and says, "There's your $70. Don't bother counting it." He does, and Quale is $10 short. That's why he sizes up the Panello brothers as the rubes he needs to secure another ten-spot.

Rusty (Harpo) allegedly has $70, but he indicates that his brother Joe (Chico) spent all of it except for $10. Rusty's remaining sawbuck has strings attached—literally. Quale circles like a shark. All he has to do is relieve Rusty of the bill, which he attempts by telling the two that in his Eastern duds, Rusty will be shot as a "tender-foot." There are jokes about Rusty's looks, but Quale appeals to Joe's altruistic side: "You love your brother, don't you?" He replies, "No, but I'm used to him."

This is the prelude to a cross-swindle reminiscent of *Day at the Races'* tootsie-fruitsie ice cream scam. Quale pawns off a few articles of clothing he insists Rusty will need, each of which just happens to cost $10. Joe tells Rusty to buy each item after talking Quale down to $1. Rusty hands over his $10 bill and Joe demands $9 in change, which Quale forks over. Rusty's ten has a cord attached to it, so each time Quale pockets it, the bill flies back into Rusty's pocket. Soon Quale is so befuddled that he's an easy mark. Rusty takes advantage of Joe's banter, slits Quale's pants, snips off the bottom of his pocket, and pilfers the rest of Quale's money.

The scene is hilarious, with quips and illogic flying about higher than the *Room Service* turkey. It's an opening that inspires hope that the Marxes have returned to the rapid-fire comedy of their Paramount days. Alas, no. The Paramount comedies used star-crossed lovers as filler between the skits; the Marxes' MGM movies reversed the formula. Although they have tighter narratives, it's hard to dispute Thomas H. Jordan's assertion that it's not a good thing when the Marxes "explicitly cancel their free spirits and irreverent characters and align themselves in a good guys-bad guys confrontation."[27] Eyles called the Marx Brothers "diminished" by "'an insipid potpourri of misunderstanding' in *Go West*."[28]

Those assessments are overly harsh, but Brecher's script is indisputably uneven and requires prospecting to separate the gold from the pyrite. After the big opening, *Go West* slows the pace to ground us in the railroad route question, the Turner-Wilson feud, Dan Wilson's encounter with Rusty and Joe, and the IOU written on the back of the deed. The last is a touching moment, but not the best material for two sharpies like the Panello brothers. We expect something edgy to follow, but instead there is a saccharine love scene between Terry and Eve, followed by just nine lines from Joe, then more exposition, this time Baxter berating Indian Pete for not having located Dan.

Only then do we get more Marxian hijinks. A parched Rusty intercepts a beer the publican slides down the bar and is caught in the act. This has promise, but Joe apologizes for his brother and writes an IOU for ten cents on the deed Wilson gave them. This is necessary for the plot, but since when does Chico resort to sweet talk instead of chicanery? The pace again lags until Joe reads a telegram intended for Eve, realizes the Dead Man Gulch deed has value, and decides to meet railroad executive John Beecher at the train station in hopes of shaking the money tree.

There is a short exchange between Beecher and the Panellos before boarding a stagecoach bound for Birch City that's already occupied by Lulubelle and a woman with a crying baby. They pick up Quale along the way and the interior compartment becomes cramped, as if it were a miniature version of Driftwood's *Night at the Opera* stateroom. It's not as expertly done, but it produces a funny moment. When Quale asks why the baby continues to cry, the mother replies, "He can't stand the jerks in the coach." She means the bumpy ride, but Joe and Rusty open the coach door and prepare to jump out before Quale stops them: "Now wait a minute, boys. It was nothing personal. She didn't mean anything by it." That would have been sharper without the third sentence, but it's a good setup.

The fumbling around in confined space that ensues is overkill as that schtick was played out moments earlier. Then comes the bidding war for the deed between Beecher and Quale before a redux of the hat-exchange routine done much more brilliantly in *Duck Soup*. When the scene shifts to the saloon, Quale lets loose with a line that makes one wonder if anyone still had a pulse at the Code Administration. He walks into the barroom, spies Baxter's girlfriend and cracks, "Lulubelle, it's you. I didn't recognize you standing up." Did the censors think that this line harked back to Lulubelle sitting in her stagecoach seat?

This is the best moment of the saloon sequence. It provides a backdrop for retrieving the deed from the cash register, Lulubelle's feigned interest in Quale, his attempt to sell the land before he has the money in hand, and Baxter's double-cross. There is a mildly amusing running joke concerning an almost comatose drunk, but mostly everything is a prelude for Chico's piano antics—including rolling an apple across the keys—and Baxter's humiliation of Quale. This is followed by a sentimental meeting between our three bumbling heroes and Eve. Quale assures her that her grandfather is well, but he also spills the beans about the deed. Her response was a mere: "Don't worry. You couldn't help it." She asks only that they don't mention it if they see Dan again.

This leads the crestfallen trio to sneak into Baxter's office with safe-cracking in mind. They agree that the job must be done quickly, before Baxter returns, though Joe tells Rusty not to worry because, "If any trouble starts, we'll telephone for help." Quale retorts, "Telephone? This is 1870. Don Ameche hasn't invented the telephone yet." The first part of the joke is historically correct. There was no such thing as a telephone in 1870; it first appeared in 1876. But Don Ameche? Didn't Alexander Graham Bell receive the patent for the first workable prototype of the telephone?[29] This joke within a joke escapes viewers who do not know that the pencil-mustached Ameche was once one of Hollywood's leading stars. Groucho's joke refers to a big 1939 film success: Ameche played the title role of *The Story of Alexander Graham Bell*.

Of course, whenever Harpo tries to be quiet, he makes a big racket. Lulubelle and two other saloon girls are in the adjoining room plying Quale and Joe with drinks until Baxter returns. In past Marx Brothers films, the jokes and sight gags would come fast and furious but in *Go West*, it's just an obvious plot device ornamented with contrivances whose humor falls flat. It does, however, preface an amusing serial stickup routine that places the deed in Terry's hands.

The only way to Birch City is either stagecoach or by horseback. Terry, Eve, Quale, Joe and Rusty poke along the trail, an excuse to insert a song and spend the evening at a Native American village. Next, Quale, Joe and Rusty commandeer a locomotive by bypassing Baxter's intended ambush, taking a shortcut to the next stop, hopping aboard, and tying up the crew. Small problem: None of the three knows how to operate a train or how to stop one once it's in motion, especially after Rusty pulls off the brake and tosses it away. Baxter and Beecher make their way to the engine and a chase ensues. The villains think they've rid themselves of the three by chasing them to the rear of the train and uncoupling the cars. They didn't count on Rusty having expandable legs that allow him to grab onto the escaping front half of the train as Joe and Quale cross the human bridge and pull Rusty across. Is that funny, or just insipid? The latter, I think.

There remains the problem of getting Baxter, Beecher and the liberated train crew off the train and Terry and Eve onto it. The first is accomplished by dumping the wood car with the bad guys in it and the second by dousing the engine. Beecher and Baxter think their troubles are over and leisurely ride off in a buckboard; after all, the wood was dumped so there's no way to fuel the train. Imagine their surprise when they hear a train whistle and see it hurtling by. Now it's their turn for a hell-bent-for-leather chase. You might wonder how horses can run ahead of a train and the short answer is that they can't. Trains seldom exceeded 25 miles per hour in 1870, but that's still blinding speed compared to the four or five MPH of a horse-drawn wagon on level ground. Then again, human legs aren't expandable, so let's call all of this movie logic.

Our heroes get the train moving by feeding the boiler with anything that burns, including wooden boxes filled with popcorn. That prompts Groucho to pun, "Pop goes the diesel," which amuses because they are on a steam train and there were no diesel engines until 1925. Movie logic comes into play several more times in how the train manages to get past attempts to derail it. Those who enjoyed the Marxes' dismantlement of the scenery in *A Night at the Opera* might find what they do to the train even funnier. At least they left the theater standing in *A Night at the Opera*, which is more than can be said for the skeletal remains of the passenger train in *Go West*. What's left arrives in time for the Marxes to mess up the driving of the golden spike.

Elephant in the Room: "Red man, you're a white man."

Maurice Charney writes, "*Go West* is full of the ethnic stereotypes of 1940."[30] Once again, we must take material from a Hollywood film and strain it through the (white) filters from the past. As Terry and company are about to leave the Indian encampment, Quale remarks to the chief, "Red man, you're a white man." This is a play on "That's awfully white of you," a now-offensive remark that originated in the 1890s. It meant to be treated fairly, but it is certainly shot through with the presumption that whiteness conveyed higher levels of trustworthiness.

In Hollywood movies, often even the Natives were white. Indian Pete, allegedly a mixed-blood individual, was played by former silent-film icon Mitchell Lewis. If Lewis had any Native ancestry, it was remote. Because of his ambiguously ethnic face, Lewis was often cast in roles such as Indians or Arabs. Hollywood's casting of white actors in such parts, was so common that "whitewashing" took on a new meaning in the early 20th century. For instance, in the 1929 film *China Bound*, both of the "Chinese" leads were Caucasian. Throughout the 1920s and '30s, Swedish American Warner Oland played Chinese or Chinese American characters such as Dr. Fu Manchu and Charlie Chan. Upon Oland's death in 1938, the role of Chan passed to other non–Asian actors, including Sidney Toler, who appeared on screen as Chan at least 22 times.

It was a given that the extras appearing as "Indians" in Westerns were mostly whites who donned red face for their parts. Major roles were usually played by whites or those pretending to be Native American. Chief Thundercloud is another example. He was Victor Daniels, who often claimed to be of Cherokee and Creek descent. That was probably a fabrication, but he nonetheless played a Native American many times, including the title role in *Geronimo* (1939). It is more likely that Daniels was of Hispanic descent; Social Security records list his parents as Jesus and Tomaca Daniels.[31]

Hollywood frequently used Latinos as substitutes for Natives; in *Stagecoach* (1939), famed Mexican singer Elvira Ríos appeared as Yakima. Often, even this subterfuge was ignored; a cowboy hat, a feather in the band and some dark makeup easily made whites into "Indians" in black and white films. As in *Go West* and scores of other films, the illusion of an Indian "camp" was easily created. Start with a few stern-looking, bare-chested, long-haired "braves" in buckskin trousers. Add a few pigtailed "squaws" in fringed costumes busy making blankets, and insert a taller man wearing a war bonnet posing as a "chief." Images of what has been dubbed the "white man's Indian" were seldom authentic.[32]

In 1939, America remained a nation in which either legal or customary Jim Crow practices held fast. Native Americans had long sought social justice, but that search was even less advanced than that of African Americans or Latino-Americans.[33] *Go West* is set in 1870, which is why we hear this query when Terry, Eve, Quale, Joe and Rusty decide to stop over at an Indian village: "Do you think it's safe to stay here tonight?" Terry assures everyone that the Natives are friendly, if treated well. Remember that the film's historical setting would have coincided with the Great Plains wars. These passed into lore to form images of what Native Americans looked and acted like.

Go West also has a connection to *At the Circus* in that perceptions of Natives were also mediated by traveling circuses. The life of William F. "Buffalo Bill" Cody is the stuff of Western legend in both shades of meaning. Cody was a Pony Express rider, a prospector and a soldier. In the last role he fought Indians in the 1850s, battled for the Union during the Civil War, and returned to the Great Plains Indian Wars after a brief stint (1867–68) in which he gained his nickname for his prowess in killing buffalo for sport and feeding railroad crews.

In 1872, Cody began to appear on vaudeville stages. Eleven years later, he launched the venture that cemented his legend: Buffalo Bill's Wild West Show.[34] For the next 30 years, Cody's circus contributed to how legions of Americans, especially Easterners, imagined Western life. Buffalo Bill's Wild West Show featured trick riding, rope tricks, shooting exhibitions and reenactments of dubious historical accuracy such as buffalo hunts, robberies and Indian attacks. A favored tableau was Custer's Last Stand, an exaggerated take on General George A. Custer's bloody 1876 defeat at the hands of Sioux, Cheyenne and Arapaho Natives. Sitting Bull later appeared in Cody's show, as would Geronimo, Chief Joseph, and others.[35]

Wild West shows were a bridge to early 20th-century Westerns. Much of what modern movie audiences see as racist was, in their day, rooted in different beliefs, not the least of which was a presumption of barely tamed Native savagery. The 1890 massacre at Wounded Knee Creek was viewed as the culmination of a 400-year effort of whites (and many uniformed African Americans) to "civilize" Indians and bring them the "benefits" of Euro-American culture. As open warfare faded, Native Americans were reinterpreted as vanquished peoples whose best fate was to be assimilated. Their past, however valiant, became fodder for novels, shows and movies, with Natives viewed through a prism of inherent inferiority.

Not everyone accepted these assumptions. A small number of white scholars and writers celebrated the nobility of Native Americans and decried their mistreatment. A larger number of Native American activists, advocates and writers challenged white exploitation in ways ranging from lobbying efforts and legal challenges to civil disobedience and open resistance.[36] Theirs was an uphill struggle; Native Americans were not even recognized as full citizens until 1924. Two years later, a group of Native actors formed the War Paint Club—later called the Indian Actors Association (IAA)—to help members secure roles and equal pay, but that effort was also painfully slow. It was not until the 1940s that the IAA was fully merged into the Screen Actors Guild.

This brings us back to *Go West*. Native Americans were decidedly a foil for now-cringeworthy comedy. In its defense, *Go West* is a parody of Westerns and there are few pre–1940 movies in which Indians were viewed as heroic. Under the Production Code, that would have been as difficult to justify as a gangster film in which the criminals triumphed.

Go West is an uncomfortable blend of offensiveness and in-jokes intended to bypass ethnicity. Joe and Rusty eye several comely Indian maidens, and the best that can be said is that at least Harpo wasn't chasing blondes. But Quale's question, "Are you the chief that runs from Chicago to Los Angeles in 39 hours?" is only tangentially linked to Native Americans. His reference is to the *Super Chief*, a route on the Atchison, Topeka and Santa Fe Railroad. (It is sad commentary that today's Amtrak successor, the *Southwest Chief*, now takes 43 to 68 hours!) That question irks the Native chief, and Joe offers to smooth things over. A surprised Quale queries, "Can you talk Indian?" Joe assures him he can: "I was born in Indianapolis."

That's amusing, though Chico's mumbo-jumbo and translation of the chief's response—"He wants to know if you want starch in your shirts"—is insulting. So, too, is an exchange in which Quale doesn't think the bonnet-wearing chief is actually an Indian and Joe retorts, "If he's no Indian, why is he wearing a chicken for a hat?" Quale continues to doubt the chief's authenticity and insists, "Stop trying to pass yourself off as a red man. Why, you can't even speak the language. Let me hear you recite 'Hiawatha' by Henry Wadsworth Longfellow."

"The Song of Hiawatha," published in 1855, was once standard reading in American public schools.[37] It is not as popular now for two reasons. First, Walt Disney made a 1937 cartoon titled *Little Hiawatha* that is even more politically incorrect than *Go West*. Second, Longfellow's poem exoticizes a Mohawk man and invents a backstory. He was a historical figure, but almost nothing found in Longfellow's poem corresponds with what is known of the historical Hiawatha.

Quale's remark leads to another outburst from the chief, translated by Joe. "He said first they'll give us a fair trial, then they kill us. White man talk too much. Make chief heap mad." This, however, is followed by an exchange that could be seen as a dig at white Americans:

> **QUALE:** Are you insinuating that the white man is not the Indians' friend? Who swindled you out of Manhattan Island for $24?
> **JOE:** White man.
> **QUALE:** Who stood your wooden statue in front of a cigar store?
> **JOE:** White man.
> **QUALE:** Who put your head on a nickel and then took the nickel away?
> **JOE:** Slot machine.

When Quale offers a cheap necklace to an attractive maiden, she dismisses it with, "No like. Me want Cadillac sedan." Quale can only marvel that she's been off the reservation. He is desperate to make amends, so Joe tries once again to talk to the chief. That prompts Quale's insult, "It's stimulating when two giant intellects get together," which he follows with a crack on the village medicine man: "Can you imagine taking a teaspoon of him every three hours?" Rusty saves the day with his music, despite Quale's "Red man, you're a white man" remark.

None of this will win awards for advancing Caucasian-Native understanding, but not much in American movies would improve for the next six decades. Whitewashing and donning red-face remained staples of both movies and television in post–World War II America. During the Cold War, Native Americans often were stand-in metaphors for Soviet Communists and cowboys for Americans. A short list of white actors who slathered on makeup to pass as Native includes Rock Hudson, Burt Lancaster and Victor Mature. It wasn't until 2020 that the Washington Redskins yielded to pressure to drop their offensive team nickname. In the long view, *Go West* didn't do much to counter racism toward American Indians, though perhaps its broad humor draws attention to the absurdity of it.

Miscellaneous Stops Along the Stagecoach Route

- **Look alike:** Irving Brecher and Groucho looked similar enough that Brecher stood in for Groucho for one of the film's publicity shots.[38]
- **Jail bait:** Groucho's full character name is S. Quentin Quale. In slang, a "San Quentin quail" is the equivalent of today's term "jail bait," an underage sexual partner or prostitute whose lovers risked arrest.[39]
- **That pesky fourth wall:** *Go West* features still another breaking of the fourth wall. It comes when Quale, Joe and Rusty tie up the train's engine crew. Groucho turns to the camera and pronounces, "You know, this is the best gag in the picture."
- **Musical chops:** *Go West* again features Groucho playing his guitar. Also, Harpo shows off his harmonica prowess.
- **War chant?** In 2017, the University of Illinois discontinued the use of a "war chant" tune played by its band during key intervals of home football games. Sources often mislabel that chant as the theme from a 1950s cartoon titled *Pow Wow the Indian Boy.* That cartoon didn't air until 1956, so how does it show up in *Go West* during the scene in the Indian village? Harpo wins the chief's trust by converting a rug loom into a harp and playing a harp-flute duet with the chief. Harpo's prelude is an echo of the University of Illinois "war chant." In 1910, students Howard Green and Harold Hill won a contest for penning a melody thought to be appropriate for the university's Fighting Illini sports team. The moniker derives from the Illiniwek confederation that gives Illinois its name. Recent reappraisals prompted scrapping the tune.
- **Another non–Native tune:** At the Indian village, Harpo segues from the war chant to "From the Land of Sky and Blue Water," which has also been mislabeled as a Native American tune. Not so! It was a 1909 composition by Charles Wakefield Cadman with lyrics from Nellie Richmond Eberhart. It

enjoyed later popularity—with an "s" added to "Water"—as the theme song for Hamm's Beer.

Post-Film Views

Go West made $2.6 million, a so-so return. Most reviewers thought it better than *At the Circus*, which wasn't saying much. Although the *New Yorker* and the *New York Times* disliked the film, they praised the train scenes; the *Times'* Bosley Crowther called the dismantling of the train one of the greatest comedy sequences ever done.[40] Marxian scholars are split on it. Charney likened it to earlier Paramount offerings, whereas others damned it with faint praise. Several noted that its material was better suited for Laurel and Hardy, from whom the Marxes mercilessly pirated. Adamson remarked, "For the Marx Brothers, rehashing all this warmed-over stew [was] simply a mistake."[41] Eyles added that some of the jokes were more appropriate for Bob Hope than the Marx Brothers.[42] He did not cite the Indian village sketch, but it certainly looks like something from a Hope-Bing Crosby film.

Groucho announced his intention to retire after their next picture, which he was contractually obligated to make for MGM. He again toyed with radio offers, though he initially turned down a project titled *You Bet Your Life* on the grounds that he disliked quiz shows. (He changed his tune in 1947.) He was more interested in *The Flotsam Family*, a radio show written by Brecher, but that didn't pan out, as the Blue Network—later renamed ABC—did not like the idea of Groucho in a straight role. William Bendix was recruited and the title was changed to *The Life of Riley*, which became a smash hit on radio and television.[43]

Groucho didn't know exactly what he would do after his next film; he also contemplated doing straight comedy on Broadway or perhaps writing a play. He was serious about his intentions to quit the motion picture business, though. The December 18, 1940, *Variety* noted, "Although the three Marx Brothers will make one more film for Metro next spring ... Groucho states that the trio will be no more thereafter."[44]

TWELVE

The Big Store (1941)

The Big Store is often panned by purists, but it has my vote for the most underrated Marx Brothers film. We've seen the Marxes wreck a college football game, a war, an opera, a horse race, a circus and an entire train, so why not a department store?

We are introduced to Ravelli (Chico) and Tommy Rogers (Tony Martin) at the Gotham Conservatory of Music. When founder Hiram Phelps died, he left half of a department store to his unmarried sister Martha (Margaret Dumont) and half to Rogers, his former star pupil, Martha's nephew and her sole heir. A professional singer, Rogers plans to sell his half.

This is bad news for store manager Grover (Douglass Dumbrille), who has been skimming money from the store. He warns one of his flunkies, Fred Sutton (William Tannen), to keep an eye on his (Fred's) sister Joan (Virginia Grey), who is smitten with Tommy. Fred doesn't yet know it, but Grover's plan is to have Tommy killed so that his half of the store goes to Martha. Then Grover intends to marry Martha and have her done away with. Time is of the essence, as Tommy's sale to the Hastings brothers is imminent and an audit would uncover Grover's graft.

Tommy is clobbered in an elevator after the power is cut. Luckily, it comes back on before Grover's thugs can finish the job. Tommy doesn't know what hit him, and thinks he inadvertently bumped into something—an elbow perhaps—and that nothing is amiss. But Martha decides to hire detective Wolf J. Flywheel (Groucho) to act as Tommy's bodyguard while posing as a floorwalker. Flywheel will also try to court Martha. Harpo plays Ravelli's brother Wacky, Flywheel's assistant.

With the Marxes loose in Phelps Department Store, what could possibly go wrong? Everything, of course, but somehow anarchy saves the day. But not before they dishevel and smash half the store. The film is marred by too much music and too few comedy sketches. This makes their announced last film akin to the Marxes' first, *The Cocoanuts,* though *The Big Store*'s production values are far superior. But a sign that times have changed was that the Marxes shared top billing with Tony Martin.

The World in Crisis

While *Go West* was in production, the Marx Brothers announced their intention to disband. Long before *The Big Store* opened on June 20, 1941, most people's minds were on other things. World War II had been underway in Africa, Asia and Europe for quite some time, and the outlook appeared bleak. Poland fell in September 1939;

Poster for *The Big Store* (MGM, via Wikimedia Commons).

German troops invaded Norway in April 1940; the Low Countries collapsed under Nazi assault in May; France fell in June; and Britain was in the grip of the Blitz.[1] European Jews were forced into concentration camps that opened during the spring and summer of 1940. Two days after *The Big Store* premiered, German troops rolled into the Soviet Union.

The situation was equally dire elsewhere. Italy annexed Ethiopia in 1936, and used it as a base of operations to conquer other parts of East Africa. Attempts to liberate the region led by Britain and allied Commonwealth nations[2] failed in December 1940, as did efforts to roll back German gains in North Africa. In the Pacific, Japan had been launching attacks on China. By September 1940, Japan controlled enough of China to use it as a staging platform to invade British-controlled Burma, Siam (Thailand) and French Indochina.[3] Southern Asia, Indonesia and Pacific Island nations were soon drawn into the war.

On December 7, 1941, Japan bombed U.S. naval installations at Pearl Harbor, Hawaii; four days later, America declared war on Japan, which prompted Japan's ally Germany to declare war on America.

This begs the question of whether a comedic romp was irresponsible or a needed diversion for a nation on the cusp of war. My vote goes for the latter, but don't look for consensus on this. Joe Adamson hated *The Big Store*. He called it a "mess" and compared it to the sort of thing the Three Stooges would do. Blogger Trav S.D. declared it the "worst" of the Marx Brothers films.[4] Martin Gardner felt that its script's many revisions wrung all the humor from it, an opinion shared by Simon Louvish.[5] Roy Blount, Jr., brushed aside all of the Marxes' later films with a succinct, "Thalberg died. The Marxes grew older. The romantic subplots grew sappier. Their madness went downhill."[6] Very few had nice things to say about *The Big Store*'s musical numbers.

By contrast, Maurice Charney declared the film "a nostalgic revival of old Marx Brothers comedies," which he found refreshing. Allen Eyles delivered a mixed verdict. He wasn't deeply impressed, but he did declare it a "recovery from the depths touched by parts of *Go West*."[7] In my view, *The Big Store* is overstuffed. It is 83 minutes in length, but could have been tighter and funnier by trimming starts and stops that harmed the flow.

As for the Marxes, only Chico showed much enthusiasm for the project, and he might have been faking it. On March 11, 1941, Groucho wrote to Arthur Sheekman, "We are starting our next picture this week and it stinks."[8] In June, Groucho lamented that MGM had made a mess of the film and was irked that segments that went over well with test audiences were excised from the movie. When the revamped script thudded before for a second test group, Groucho declared, "[MGM] imagines the audience hasn't laughed because the plot wasn't understood. The fact of the matter is, the audience hasn't laughed because they didn't understand the jokes."[9]

MGM was apparently sick of the Marxes as well. Groucho complained to Sheekman, "We have been ejected from MGM and are now conducting what little business we have from a barnlike building cater-cornered from the Bank of America. It's very convenient, especially for Chico, who now has only to cross the street to stop payment on checks he's written the night before."[10]

Mostly, Groucho had ceased caring. Son Arthur's book had little to say about *The Big Store*, an indication that it was not a topic of much discussion at home beyond his father's complaint of being in the studio re-shooting a scene on a day he planned to attend one of Arthur's tennis matches.[11] In his autobiography, Harpo devoted the entire time period *The Big Store* was in production to recounting his life of domestic bliss.

Maxine Marx was surprised that the brothers' oft-repeated threats to retire were finally coming to fruition, though she knew it would be hardest on her father Chico, who had no money in the bank and "couldn't afford to sit back leisurely." She called *The Big Store* a letdown "for the aging team," though she had few quarrels with Groucho's assessment that they "were indeed past their collective prime."[12] Groucho added an exclamation point in an April interview in which he told readers, "When I say we're sick of the movies, I mean the people are about to get sick of us.... Our stuff simply is going stale. And so are we."[13]

Once More into the Breach

How stale? So stale that the Marxes simply went along with most of the pre-filming creative process. Had they been their old combative selves, a better picture might have resulted. Except for Nat Perrin, an entirely new production crew worked on *The Big Store*. In their heyday, that alone would have assured battles over every detail. Not this time.

Charles Reisner directed the movie. He had captained 18 previous films, but the only ones of note were Buster Keaton's *Steamboat Bill, Jr.* (1928) and *Politics* (1931).

Reisner played second fiddle to producer Louis K. Sidney, who had exactly one production credit before *The Big Store*, which proved to be his last. MGM's first choice for the producer's job was Irving Brecher, but he declined. Sidney's main task was to safeguard the bottom line. He told the Marxes that their last two films had lost money and that he intended to make certain that didn't happen again. It's not clear they *had* lost money, which might explain why only Chico greeted Sidney's chat with any enthusiasm. He pledged he'd do whatever it took to make the film a success, but according to Adamson, that lasted only into the read-through of the script: "By the time they got to page 15, Chico was sound asleep and snoring."[14]

In the credits, it says, "From a story by Nat Perrin." The preposition is telling, because there wasn't much left of Perrin's concept by the time Sid Kuller, Hal Fimberg and Ray Golden finished tinkering with the script. Years later, Perrin still bristled over their doctoring: "I had a legitimate mystery story. Good, bad or indifferent, it was more of a story than any of the Marx Brothers films had except those with Thalberg...."[15] One wonders how Kuller, Fimberg and Golden managed to mess up material that Perrin, Groucho and Chico had already fleshed out on a radio episode of *Flywheel, Shyster and Flywheel*.

Kuller had been a vaudeville joke writer and also did some uncredited work with the late Al Boasberg, whom Groucho admired. That was a nice start, but he was not yet 21 when he signed onto *The Big Store* along with Ray Golden, who was a bit older and had more experience. This wasn't necessarily a virtue, though, as five of his eight writing credits were for the Ritz Brothers. Al, Jimmy and Harry Ritz were talented, but their schtick was very different from the Marxes'. They sang and danced wonderfully, but theirs was a synchronized act in which they usually dressed, moved, danced, joked and sang in unison. By contrast, the Marxes had three distinct character personalities to consider. Golden's other credits involved performers Don Ameche, the Andrews Sisters, Gene Autry, Kenny Baker, Bing Crosby, Jimmy Durante, Bob Hope and Ann Miller. During the weakest parts of *The Big Store*, one suspects Golden and Kuller had someone other than the Marx Brothers in mind.

Fimberg's résumé had just one movie writing credit: additional dialogue for a non-memorable mystery. He had a successful post–1941 career, but his later credits suggest he was most comfortable with song-and-dance performers such as Bing Crosby, Donald O'Connor and Danny Thomas. Questionable chemistry suggests why, in Adamson's words, musical director Georgie Stoll "had his hands full."[16] *The Big Store* sometimes seems as if another musical number was inserted whenever the creative team couldn't come up with anything for the Marx Brothers to do.

Yet only once did Groucho's hackles rise. There is a scene in which Groucho has won the heart of Martha Phelps, though she frets that after they marry, "a beautiful young girl will come along and you'll forget all about me." Groucho retorts, "Don't be silly. I'll write you twice a week." That's a good line, but Reisner ordered it struck from the script. Groucho countermanded him and Reisner was livid. He was overruled by Louis B. Mayer, who declared Groucho's comeback the "greatest line in the picture." The joke stayed.[17]

The Marxes did some of their best comedy off the set. When Mayer was negotiating with Hays Office censors who wanted to change a scene in another MGM film in which Lana Turner was showing too much cleavage, Harpo hired a stripper to run around the room. In another off-stage incident, Groucho and Perrin stepped into an elevator car with a woman wearing a very large hat. Groucho puckishly tipped the hat from her head and received a frosty look. Groucho cracked, "I beg your pardon. I thought you were a fellow I once knew in Kansas City." He was mortified to learn he had just raised the ire of Greta Garbo.

Overall, the Marxes were on relatively good behavior, but it still took ten months to gut Perrin's story and come up with the final script. The movie's first title was *Bargain Basement* and it was changed to *Step This Way* before *The Big Store* won out. At each juncture, the script changed. There was some discussion of releasing it in 3-D, another idea that went by the wayside.[18] Adamson speculates that *The Big Store* became the title mostly because Hollywood was obsessed with the word *big*. That sounds far-fetched until one reads an exhaustive list of titles he offers as evidence.[19] Perhaps *Bargain Basement* might have been a better title. *The Big Store* is very funny in places, but shoddy material is mixed in with the high-quality goods.

When Big Stores Ruled

Hollywood's obsession with the adjective *big* notwithstanding, such a term was apt to describe American retailing in 1941. Today's department stores—even those bearing venerable names—are pale remnants of past giants.

The idea behind department stores lives on in namesake "departments" in which distinct types of goods have separate sections: menswear, women's clothing, small appliances, toys, hardware, etc. Departments came, went, expanded or contracted depending upon availability, fashion and sales performance. This hasn't changed, but an early scene from *The Big Store* showcases two things that are now rare: service and staff expertise.

An older woman comes into Phelps and asks for the new record by Tommy Rogers. Joan tells her that, alas, she has just sold the last one. Luckily, Tommy is in the music department and tells the disappointed woman that he will *make* her a record. There is a piano, microphone and recording disc-cutting device in the department. In the film, this scene establishes a burgeoning romance between Tommy and Joan, but instant service and in-store recording actually did take place in some stores. So did many other things in well-staffed stores. In 1911, Macy's had a payroll of more than 5,200 workers. As Jan Whitaker notes, "A big store's population in daytime hours was greater than most of the towns in the United States." It was not unusual for more than 100,000 people to pass through a major department store in a single day.[20] Such stores stood in stark contrast to today's self-service discounters such as Kohl's, Walmart and Target.

There is debate over which American retailer warrants being called the first department store; New York City's Arnold Constable (1825) or A.T. Stewart & Co. (1847) are often cited. Most observers agree that modern department stores enjoyed their peak popularity between 1880 and World War II.[21] Their proliferation was directly linked to the growth of American cities and an expanding middle class. This made them competitors to discounters for those of lesser means and specialty stores for the so-called "carriage trade," that is, wealthy patrons.

Successful department stores often opened branch stores elsewhere, but most metropolitan areas had at least one establishment that was synonymous with that city. Below is a short list of cities and department stores associated with them. Some of the names continue, though many are now part of large chains. For example, Federated Department Stores now owns once-independent retailers such Macy's, Bloomingdale's and the May Company.

Atlanta: Rich's
Baltimore: Hecht's
Boston: Filene's, Jordan Marsh
Chicago: Carson Pirie Scott & Company, Marshall Field's, A.M. Rothschild and Company
Cleveland: Halle Brothers, May Company
Detroit: Crowley's, Frank & Seder, Hudson's
Hartford, Connecticut: G. Fox & Company
Houston: Foley's
Kansas City, Missouri: The Jones Store
Los Angeles: Blackstone's, Bullock's, Coulter's, J.W. Robinson & Company
Miami: Burdines
Milwaukee: Boston Store, Gimbels
Minneapolis: Dayton's
Newark, New Jersey: Bamberger's, Hahne & Company
New York City: B. Altman & Company, Bonwit Teller, Arnold Constable, Lord & Taylor, A.T. Stewart's
Omaha, Nebraska: J.L. Brandeis and Sons
Philadelphia: Strawbridge & Clothier, Wanamaker's
Pittsburgh: Kauffman's
Portland, Oregon: Olds, Wortman & King
San Francisco: I. Magnin & Company, Joseph Magnin Company

ST. Louis: Famous-Barr; Scruggs, Vandervoort and Barney; Stix Baer & Fuller
WASHINGTON, D.C.: Garfinkel's, Woodward and Lothrop

During their golden era, numerous department stores were very big indeed and marketed themselves as such. Wanamaker's once bragged that its Philadelphia flagship was one block long, one block wide, and one block high. It was so large that, in Whitaker's words, "it could have held an entire 125,000-square-foot big box store of today on each its 12 above-ground floors, and two more in its basement and subbasement." Hudson's in Detroit featured 16 floors of retail space.[22] Shoppers—mostly women in the first 60 years of the 20th century—sometimes spent all day shopping.

Stores were also quite grand and were adorned with marble, filigree, gilding, statuary, ornate stairways, carved columns, elaborate display windows and rotundas large enough to serve as concert halls. Today's functional interiors would have repulsed middle-class shoppers, who would have associated them with discounters for the lower classes. Even during the Great Depression, customers complained bitterly when cost-cutting measures resulted in cutbacks on the physical frills of stores.

One could find a little bit of everything in cavernous stores such as Wanamaker's or Marshall Field's. Many were analogous to the ancient Greek *agora*, public spaces in which urban life took place. To quote Whitaker:

> In the 1920s, larger stores were likely to offer alterations, banks, barbershops, beauty parlors, bridal consultants, caterers, charge accounts, check rooms, childcare, custom drapery and upholstery making, dressmaking salons, fashion shows, fur cleaning and storage, gift wrapping, interior decorators, lessons in sports and hobbies, lost-and-found departments, mail and telephone orders, meeting rooms, parcel delivery, parking garages, personal shoppers, photography studios, post office branches, restaurants, restrooms, telephones, theater ticket bureaus, travel bureaus, waiting rooms, watch and jewelry repair and Western Union offices. A smaller number of stores also provided chemical-testing laboratories, children's theaters, chiropodists, doormen, dry cleaners, employment bureaus for domestic help, fashion magazines, interpreters, manicurists, message boards and paging services, notary publics, optometrists, pharmacies, public library branches, radio stations, real estate agencies, rental libraries, shoeshine stands, smoking lounges for men, steam baths, stenographers, stockbrokers and utility payment stations.[23]

This is just a partial list. Some department stores manufactured many of their own goods; others had site-specific power stations in the basement. Politicians used department store spaces for speeches; symphonic orchestras held concerts in their rotundas. All manner of public events took place there, from circus acts and dog shows to showcases of Parisian fashion and screenings of experimental films. One could even view things such as Lindbergh's *Spirit of St. Louis* or famous works of art. Store roofs sported playgrounds, amusement parks and tennis courts.[24]

We get a sense of what even a smaller department store might sell from *The Big Store*. Some of the scenes fly by very fast, but among the things for sale are antiques, beds, bicycles, bolts of fabric, china and glassware, cotton goods, cookware, desks, exercise equipment, irons, men's hats, mirrors, musical instruments, nursery supplies, photographic equipment, radios, sporting goods, toys, washing machines and women's gloves. You might notice that there is an in-house ladies' hatmaker or that clothing departments seem rather understocked. The latter is no mistake; a lot of clothing was made to order. There are other surprising elements: a room decked out as a baroque tableau, a fashion show and salon, a large in-store security force, and a full orchestra with choir and crooner.

It would be easy to romanticize all of this, but *The Big Store* also makes us aware of the gender and social dynamics at work. Notice that most of the sales force was female, while men were supervisors, floorwalkers and administrators. The female staff was mostly often drawn from the working class, though the target clientele was middle class. Clerks worked long hours, were poorly paid, constantly scrutinized, and could be dismissed for trivial reasons. In many cases, sales staff did not handle money. In the film, we see cables stretched across the ceiling that connect a small trolley-like box to upper floors. These cables (or pneumatic tubes) sent sales slips and payments to male accountants and clerks trusted with financial transactions.

By the 1960s, the golden age had passed and most department stores began to shed staff, frills, money-losing offerings and personalized service. Ready-to-wear clothing, the entry of women into jobs outside their homes, busier lifestyles, changing tastes, the decline of public transportation and the building of suburban shopping malls all sapped vitality from department stores. Some persist, but discounters and online sales have supplanted them in popularity, with a smaller number of specialty stores catering to the wealthy.

Few *Big Store* viewers would have imagined such a decline. If anything, department stores enjoyed resurgence as the Great Depression drew to an end. One of the best ways to appreciate *The Big Store* is to forget about most of what you associate with modern retail and enter a world in which shopping was a total lifestyle option.

Inventory: Good and Bad Comedy in *The Big Store*

The Big Store opens with promise. At the Gotham Conservatory of Music, Ravelli puts a group of children through their piano lesson paces. This includes learning to shoot the keys Chico-style. The scene is especially funny because the young actors involved have Chico's techniques down pat.

Workers show up to take Ravelli's piano, as the conservatory is allegedly closing. Ravelli pleads that his friend Tommy Rogers is on his way to make matters right, and that's exactly what happens. Tommy also shares with Ravelli his intention to sell his half of the department store and use the money to build a new conservatory. Ravelli instructs the kids to practice: "But remember, no boogie-woogie."

Grover tells Fred Sutton to work on the books, with the implication that much needs to be hidden. When Sutton leaves, another subordinate questions whether Fred can be trusted, as his sister Joan has a crush on Tommy. Grover reveals a master plan in which both Tommy and Martha will suffer deadly misfortune, and he will assume total control of the store.

Part one of the plan fails when Grover's henchman muffs Tommy's murder. Because it was botched so badly, Tommy has no idea he was a target and objects to his aunt's insistence that he needs protection. Grover forestalls Martha's plan to call the police by convincing her that bad publicity would jeopardize the sale of the store. This sets up Martha's decision to hire detective Flywheel.

Flywheel's office apparently doubles as his home. His assistant Wacky is busy with domestic duties such as cooking Flywheel's breakfast on a desk that converts to a stove. When Flywheel sees Phelps approaching, he and Wacky quickly transform the room into an office via strategically placed curtains, wires and pulleys worthy of a Rube Goldberg machine. There was, however, no time to put out the fire in the desk-range. Phelps recoils when she sits on the edge of the desk. Flywheel pretends to be very busy, but agrees to take the case, though his fee of $2000 becomes $500. Phelps tells Flywheel that no one, including Tommy, should know that he is a detective.

Flywheel and Phelps set off for the department store. Wacky doubles as Flywheel's chauffeur, though the car would be better served by a junk dealer. We get a sense of the vintage of Flywheel's car in that it has a sign on the back that says, "Welcome Home Admiral Dewey." It's a visual anachronism; George Dewey, the victorious commander of the 1898 Battle of Manila Bay during the Spanish American War, returned to America and a hero's welcome in 1899, and the car looks to be a 1920s roadster. We get the sense, though, that passengers would be safer in a wartime battle cruiser than in Flywheel's clunker. Luckily, Flywheel has an explanation for everything. When Phelps' seat collapses, Flywheel insists, "I had that seat built below window level. Makes me safe from bullets." He also muses that he can't make up his mind if he should buy the car, but proclaims he probably won't when the door and several other parts fall off. Wacky has a nice sight gag: He pulls up in front of the store, removes a dummy fire hydrant, and parks.

Flywheel enters and Grover protests that the store doesn't really need any more floorwalkers. When Martha insists Flywheel should be employed, Grover enquires about his retail experience. Flywheel snaps, "I was a shoplifter for three years." Grover then wants to know how he'd deal with certain crises on the selling floor: "Assume I am a customer. I'm returning a baby carriage." Flywheel asks, "Are you married?" When Grover tells him he's not, Flywheel pounces: "Then what are you doing with a baby carriage?" Flywheel has already begun to woo Martha and turns to her to proclaim, "This man's a cad, a yellow cad," a pun on yellow "cab."

When Ravelli shows up, Flywheel's cover is blown in the wink of an eye. No matter; Flywheel brags that he's the greatest detective since Sherlock Holmes. Martha swoons, "I'm crazy about Sherlock Holmes," which prompts another wisecrack: "It won't do you any good. He's got a wife and kids." Martha isn't happy that Wolf has been revealed as a detective, but he wins her back by quoting lines from a Lord Byron poem and she is smitten when he recognizes the Shelley lines she quotes.

Groucho flirting by quoting poetry? Charney casually remarked that in *The Big Store*, Groucho courts "with less lascivious energy."[25] That's certainly true; he is much better as a smart-aleck shyster, which we observe when he "solves" the case of Martha's missing purse. (Wacky took it and also inadvertently smashed antiques in the store.) There are several droll lines in the sequence. When Grover makes the mistake of saying that if Flywheel is a detective, "I'm a monkey's uncle," Flywheel snaps, "Keep your family out of this." Flywheel is so self-assured that Martha is practically giddy in her affections. "You make me think of my youth," she gushes. Flywheel counters, "Really? He must be a big boy by now."

At this point in the film, all is well and good. Then comes a lavish but wildly uneven production number "Sing While You Sell." It's actually a pastiche of musical set pieces loosely strung together. These have energy, but the linking song from Hal Borne, Kuller and Fimberg is lackluster, as are cheesy gags such as Wacky charming what is obviously a rubber snake and an odd fashion show segment featuring Flywheel's dancing and spoken patter. At one point, he has his pants legs rolled up and his hair pomaded, making him look like a maniacal Smurf. The subsequent swing dancing is exciting, and both Judy Matson and a vocal group called Six Hits and a Miss professionally add vocals. Alas, there is also a problematic sequence involving the African American quartet the Four Dreamers.

Grover's associate Peggy (Marion Martin) is charged with luring Tommy to a roadhouse where assassins await, but Tommy has eyes only for Joan and this plot device is dumped shortly after some mischief from Wacky. The snobby Peggy asks a clerk for fabric to match her dress. There isn't any in stock, which prompts Peggy to berate the clerk. As Peggy fumes, a scissors-wielding Wacky cuts a swath of cloth from the back of her dress and hands it to the embattled clerk.[26] Peggy, though, is a jerk to the end: "I've changed my mind. I don't want the thing at all. It's awful."

There is a rather clumsy setup for the next major comedy sketch, but once we get to it, it's quite amusing. The setting is the bed department, where Flywheel is napping and Ravelli and Wacky are reclining. An Italian man named Giuseppe (Henry Armetta) and his substantial wife Maria (Anna Demetrio) arrive with their 12 children in tow. Giuseppe explains, "We live in a three-room apartment and all I can see is beds, beds, beds." He's looking for "something that no look like a bed." Inspired bedlam ensues. The store has several hideaway beds that appear at the push of a button, including a multi-tiered bunk bed that descends beneath the floor. Six of the kids pile onto the bunks and sink out of sight. Ravelli tries to assist, though Giuseppe thinks he's making fun of how he talks. Ravelli assuages him: "I no make fun. I'm the same national as you. Is you was born in Naples?" It turns out they once knew each in the days in which Giuseppe was "the best grape presser in all Italy." That puts him at ease, but where are his other six kids?

In the sort of coincidence that can only occur in a Marx Brothers film, three other families arrive, one Swedish, one Native American and one Chinese. Each has a dozen children. Other fanciful beds appear, including one that looks like a bookcase and another like a bank vault. In an elaborate variation of their mixed-up hat routine, the Marxes try to give Giuseppe and Maria six kids from the other families. Flywheel doesn't help matters any by suggesting that maybe six got drafted, and that a man who only makes $25 a week can't afford to have 12 kids. Soon Flywheel has Giuseppe so flustered that he believes he only has six kids, then 18. Maria flies into a rage, but her missing brood reappears and all is well. Needless to say, they didn't buy a bed!

There's no easy way to segue from such pandemonium, so we get more exposition: more of Grover's scheming, Joan's acceptance of Tommy's marriage proposal, the arrival of new thugs who don't know what Rogers looks like, and Ravelli's discovery that the men out to get Tommy are wearing gray topcoats. That's true, but so are the Hastings brothers, the store's prospective buyers. For contrived reasons, Ravelli asserts that if he plays the piano, people will gather around, and they can catch the would-be killers. Flywheel mistakenly places the Hasting brothers in handcuffs, but his ineptitude temporarily saves the day; the police arrive and recognize the thugs as Austin Benny and the Snapper, wanted criminals whom they arrest.

Grover has still another stratagem up his sleeve. Since it's Saturday and the doors close at one p.m., he convinces the Hastings brothers to sign the purchase agreement during an all-store party.[27] The media have been invited, and Grover plants a gun in one of the cameras that he hopes will finally put an end to Tommy. At this juncture, obvious plot padding interrupts the pace. The store celebration is another glitzy production number crammed with ideas irrelevant to the plot. Cut to Ravelli telling Wacky he can't perform at the party because his clothes are too shabby. This is an excuse for Wacky to wander into a department decked out in baroque themes. He opens a music box, which induces a daydream that he is wearing French court finery and sitting behind an ornate harp. Harpo's solo takes place in front of a series of mirrors that allow him to fantasize that he is accompanying himself in different guises, like playing a cello. It's expertly done, though we notice that Harpo's wig fits poorly. But the solo seems like a roughly stitched-in afterthought when Ravelli reappears and tells Wacky he can play at the party after all.

Riesner's hopscotch direction feels like he's killing time before the big climactic chase scene. Flywheel courts Martha some more, which produces some of the film's sharpest dialogue. He tells her, "Martha, dear, there are many bonds that will hold us together through eternity.... Your government bonds, your savings bonds, your Liberty bonds." It culminates in the great line that Reisner inexplicably wanted to cut; Flywheel's pledge that he'd write to Martha at least twice a week if a beautiful young girl sweeps him off his feet.

This is followed by Rogers singing "Tenement Symphony," a number whose heart was in the right place as it invoked "common man" themes (discussed in earlier chapters). Unfortunately, it is so over-the-top that Adamson called it "horrifying."[28] That's a bit vitriolic, but the number *is* overdone. In "Tenement Symphony," there is a full orchestra, a choir and musical snippets from Chico and Harpo. Martin's vocals border on the histrionic, plus common-man evocations would have worked better had social-class distinctions been drawn more clearly in the rest of the film. The store's upscale furnishings, the elaborate costumes and the opulence of the party make "Tenement Symphony" seem ironic rather than sympathetic. Mostly, it's another halting point in the film's stop-and-go narrative, one of several instances when we wonder what it has to do with anything.

Next comes more lights-out confusion, this time involving another failure to bump off Tommy, but also proof of Grover's perfidy: a photograph of him kidnapping Joan. It builds to the big chase in which Grover seeks to get the photograph and have Flywheel, Ravelli and Wacky arrested (or preferably shot) as thieves and would-be murderers. The helter-skelter chase through the store is playful, even when the slapstick is more Keystone Kops than Marx Brothers.

The scene is best remembered for a chain of events that begins when the Marxes land in the sporting goods department, don roller skates and zip through the store to avoid Grover, a security officer and a rather timid janitor (John Berkes in an uncredited role). Groucho, Chico and Harpo appear to be very good skaters, though there's a sloppy cut in which stuntmen skate across the tops of tall display cabinets. They don't look a thing like the Marxes.

One can scarcely imagine Thalberg allowing such slapdash filmmaking to see the light of day. Later, Harpo escapes from the top of the elevator by magically springing up the cable, complete with "boing!" sound effects. This marks a big difference between the Marxes in their Paramount and Thalberg films. Improbable things happened in those films, but the Marxes seldom resorted to cartoonish effects to pull them off; they relied upon words and manic energy to mask the unbelievable. The

Marxes are good at wrecking things, so you can imagine the swath of destruction through a store filled with mirrors, exercise equipment, stockroom boxes and other obstacles.

It looks like the smirking Grover has won: He has possession of the photo, which is aflame as police take Flywheel, Ravelli and Wacky into custody. When newspaper cameramen gather to snap Grover's picture, though, he panics as one of the cameras has a gun inside. Wacky clobbers Grover, who is taken away. In the end, Martha sells her half of the store, having given her heart to Flywheel. Wacky and the happy couple pile into Flywheel's car, and a tow truck drags them away.

Elephant in the (Stock) Room: Ethnic Humor

Joseph Boskin and Joseph Dorinson wrote that ethnic humor is "one of the most effective and vicious weapons in the repertory of the human mind." This strikes most people as profoundly correct, but the authors followed with this: "In time, ironically, the resulting derisive stereotypes were adopted by their targets in mocking self-description, and then, triumphantly, adapted by the victims as a means of revenge against their more powerful detractors."[29] To understand two problematic scenes from *The Big Store* more fully, both halves of the Boskin-Dorinson quote must be considered.

The first troublesome scene occurs during "Sing While You Sell." Flywheel has what appears to be a forked stick in his hand, from which he plucks fluffy spheres. It's not clear what he is doing until, moments later, we see four African American men dressed in straw hats and bibbed overalls going through the same motions and realize they are mimicking the picking of cotton.[30] They even croon a piece of "Old Folks at Home," an 1851 Stephen Foster song popularly known as "Way Down Upon the Swanee River." (These days, Foster songs are often dismissed for romanticizing Old South plantation life.) Flywheel also references plantations in his brief cotton-picking moment.

In 1941, the scene would have induced chuckles among whites consciously asserting the viciousness noted by Boskin and Dorinson. But first, let's note that America remained a global leader in cotton production well into the 1930s, most of it plucked from Southern soil. "Plucked" is the correct verb; mechanical pickers were notoriously unreliable and did not entirely supplant human labor until after World War II. The period between 1910 and 1970 saw large-scale movement of African Americans northward, a shift known as the Great Migration; the black population of the North swelled by 40 percent. It did not, however, mean that African Americans abandoned the South; millions lacked the opportunity, means or inclination to migrate. In 1940, 77 percent of all African Americans continued to reside in the South, and many were involved in cotton production.[31]

The African Americans on the screen are dressed as field hands. As such, they are a visual stereotype of unskilled black agricultural workers. Those young men were actually a talented 1940s harmony group known as the Four Dreamers. Were they embodying or subverting racial stereotypes? The first option is unlikely. As we have seen, some moviegoers were upset by the appearance of African Americans in *A Day at the Races* and the Marxes did not care about that. They certainly commanded enough star power to veto such decisions if they had.

Groucho is the first to be seen picking cotton. Does this mean he saw himself on par with the four field hands? Probably not, but his action infers some easily overlooked social-class commentary. The Four Dreamers don't belong in Phelps Department Store, but neither do Groucho, Chico and Harpo. Not much about the Marxes' screen characters conforms to standards of the 1940s white middle class. That's because they weaponized their assumed personae. Groucho's outrageous greasepaint mustache gave him license to finagle and insult, Chico's ethnic transplant allowed him to engage in all manner of impolite behavior, and Harpo's shambolic coat was a Pandora's box of mischief.

One could argue the Marxes could afford to play with stereotypes because they had whiteness to fall back on once the film ended. In their offscreen lives, Groucho and Harpo were wealthy, but they were also Jewish, which trumped wealth and skin color for much of the white Protestant majority in 1941. As noted previously, Marx Brothers films are more intent on dismantling the middle class than in promoting it. It should not escape notice that *The Big Store* frequently lampoons those values and that "Sing While You Sell" parodies consumerism.

As for the Four Dreamers, the joke was on any white person who viewed them as actual field hands. They are dressed in spotless attire that included straw hats, ties and carefully pressed overalls. They also appear as South Asian sedan-chair carriers, but they are wearing some rather fancy threads. The Four Dreamers were Clifford Holland, Carl Jones, James Shaw and General White. They made several recordings in the 1940s and had uncredited roles in two other films. Jones and Holland later performed with the Delta Rhythm Boys, who were highly successful: They appeared in 15 films, toured the world and made a movie in Sweden. The Rhythm Boys got their start at Langston University in Oklahoma and were the brainchild of Dr. Horace Mann Bond, the father of civil rights activist and politician Julian Bond. General White also continued in music as a baritone with the Basin Street Boys, who had a major hit, "I Sold My Heart to the Junkman," in 1946. In other words, three members of the Four Dreamers led lives that surpassed those of most whites who laughed at their field hand costumes.[32]

The second troublesome film scene is funnier, though it arguably has fewer redeeming qualities. It takes place in the bed department where Giuseppe and Maria need beds that convert into usable daytime space. The exchanges with Giuseppe and Maria let Chico play his Italian character to the hilt. The implied joke is that Italians, most of whom were Roman Catholics, have big families because of the church's stance against birth control. Flywheel implies the same when he looks at Giuseppe's brood and naughtily asks, "What other hobbies have you got?" Giuseppe was played by Henry Armetta, who was Sicilian rather than Neapolitan, but at least the film had him in the correct general region. Maria (Anna Demetrio) was born in Rome. Armetta and Demetrio, like Chico, played stereotypical Italians. Armetta came to the States as a stowaway in 1902 and had made dozens of films by the time of *The Big Store*. Armetta was a plus-sized performer whose specialty was portraying a comedic, loud Italian speaking in fractured English. Demetrio spoke accented English and also traded in caricatures.

The beds sequence involves several other ethnic gags. Flywheel thrice corrals six children from other families and try to palm them off on Giuseppe and Maria. There is a jarring contrast between them. A family of towheaded Swedes ventures in, with boys and father alike wearing suits. The humor of Flywheel's attempt to pass them off as Italian trades in troubling assumptions of Aryans vs. Southern Europeans. The Swedish parents quickly usher their children out of the room. Enter a family whom we instantly identify as Chinese since they are wearing elaborately designed two-piece silk outfits. The father is played by Eddie Lee, an American-born actor of Asian descent. When the Chinese family leaves, a family of Native Americans arrives, each wearing Great Plains costumes of deerskin, moccasins, feathers and headdresses. The paterfamilias was Mitchell Lewis, who played the chief in *Go West*.

At best, the ethnic depictions in *The Big Store* send mixed messages. At worst, they are offensive from a modern perspective. That's precisely why we should view them from the vantage point of 1941.

From the Stockroom: Miscellanies

- **Artie Shaw:** "If It's You," sung by Tony Martin, was co-written by Artie Shaw, arguably the most renowned musical talent associated with the film. Shaw, born Arthur Jacob Arshawsky, was a jazz clarinet wizard, big band leader, and friendly rival to Benny Goodman. In musical history, Shaw—though infamous for being difficult to get along with—was the first bandleader to hire a black female lead vocalist for a tour of the Jim Crow South: Billie Holiday. Shaw often had African Americans in his bands, including Lena Horne and Roy Eldridge. Many other musicians cut their teeth in Shaw ensembles, including legendary drummer Buddy Rich.
- **Poetry joke:** Flywheel woos Martha Phelps with a snippet of Byron's poetry, but adds a sneaky insult when he tells Martha that Byron "was thinking of you when he wrote it." Given that Byron died in 1824, it would have made Phelps at least 117 years old!
- **Burma Shave:** In the same sequence, Flywheel spouts a trite rhyme. When Martha asks, "Wolf, where did you learn to write such beautiful poetry?" he replies, "I worked five years for Burma-Shave." Groucho's joke references an early example of roadside advertising for the automobile age. In 1926, Burma-Shave, a brushless shaving cream, spread doggerel over numerous signs, the last of which read "Burma-Shave." These attracted public attention because they were humorous. One from 1930 read: "Does your husband / Misbehave / Grunt and grumble / Rant and rave / Shoot the brute some / Burma-Shave."[33] These signs could be found along highways into the 1960s, which made Burma-Shave ads a form of popular nostalgia and fodder for comics.
- **Consumerist irony:** *The Big Store* features consumerism just months before the government's Office of Price Administration began rationing programs. The first wave came on August 28, 1941, more than three months before the bombing of Pearl Harbor and American entry into World War II, and lasted into June 1947, nearly two years after the war's end. Everything from fuel (gasoline, oil, coal, kerosene, firewood) and foodstuffs (including coffee, cooking grease, fruit and meat) to nylon stockings and rubber were rationed. Families were issued allocation books into which stamps were pasted. Rationing hurt department stores by reducing available stock, but

also because gasoline was limited to eight gallons per week at a time when the average mileage of automobiles was just 10 to 15 miles per gallon.

• **Classical humor:** "Sing While You Sell" features puns on classical composers such as Chopin and Verdi.

• **Celebrity dress-up:** The Four Dreamers dressed as cotton-picking field hands was less unusual than you might presume. The recording industry was only in its third decade of featuring performers over composers and often resorted to costumed gimmickry. For example, Jimmie Rodgers, a country music pioneer, was packaged as the "Singing Brakeman" and dressed in the quintessential garb of his earlier work in the railroad industry. In his youth, Kentucky-born country music star Merle Travis performed in overalls with his face smudged with coal dust, though he had never been a miner.

   An extreme case was African American folk music icon Huddie Ledbetter, who had spent time in prison as a young man. When he was released in 1935 and began performing under the name Lead Belly, record companies advertised him as a dangerous convict and dressed him in striped penitentiary clothing. He soon rebelled and thereafter usually took the stage in a suit and tie. Matching outfits were a staple of 1950s doo-wop groups and pop and rock groups of the 1950s and 1960s. In more recent times, many of the rappers and hip-hop performers who assume the swagger, dress and gestures of gang members have no such associations in their past.

• **Gumshoe parody:** Martin Gardner asserts that the character of Wolf J. Flywheel was intended as a satire on the era's fictional gumshoe detectives such as Raymond Chandler's Philip Marlowe and Dashiell Hammett's Sam Spade.[34]

• **Farewell to Maggie:** *The Big Store* proved to be Margaret Dumont's final role in a Marx Brothers movie.

• **Joke recycling:** Groucho's joke about Giuseppe's large family—"What other hobbies have you got?"—was sharpened and repeated on his TV quiz show *You Bet Your Life*.

• **Stolen skates?** The roller skating is very good in *The Big Store*, though Charney charges that the Marxes lifted the idea from Charlie Chaplin's 1936 *Modern Times*.[35]

Accounting and Other Assessments

The Big Store is no one's favorite Marx Brothers film, but each time I watch it, the more I like it. The swing dancing is exciting. I'm still baffled why Tony Martin shared star billing, though it might be because his song "It's a Blue World" reached #2 on radio charts in 1940.

The Big Store brought in $2.5 million, which meant it just about broke even. That isn't too bad, considering that the total box office for 1941 was around $95 million for 220 films, which put it far above the average take of $431,818. Only one film, *Sergeant York*, made more than $10 million. Ticket sales for *The Big Store* work out to an adjusted take of nearly $83 million in today's dollars, which is respectable.

Reviews were generally positive. The *New Yorker* called it a "pleasure" even if it was "one of their more offhand efforts," and the *New York Times* chipped in that *The Big Store*, "as the last remnant on the counter, is a bargain."[36] The *Motion Picture Herald* gushed, calling the picture "one of the funniest ever made by the Marx Brothers." It even liked the musical numbers, though those judgments must be tempered by the fact that it was a trade publication aimed more at promoting the industry than in dispassionately evaluating quality. British reviewers were less restrained; several found *The Big Store* a desultory effort.[37]

In my estimation, *The Big Store* is a lot like *Go West*, a mix of sharp humor and substandard material. It mostly signaled that the old act either needed to fade gracefully into the sunset or undergo an update. The Marxes did not stay in retirement and, by now, readers know why: Chico needed the money. The trio made two more films, though neither was particularly memorable.

Thirteen

A Night in Casablanca (1946)

Five years after their official "farewell," the Marxes made *A Night in Casablanca*. The intent was to parody the beloved 1942 Humphrey Bogart-Ingrid Bergman romantic drama *Casablanca*. When Warner Brothers threatened legal action, a semi-original script emerged.

In November 1942, Casablanca, Morocco, was one of the first North African cities retaken by Allied troops. Details such as a 1946 release date and Nazis seeking refuge in South America suggests a setting in the late spring of 1945. As the film opens, a man sitting in the outdoor café of the Hotel Casablanca keels over, poisoned. The victim is the hotel's manager and, as police prefect Brizzard (Dan Seymour) laments, the third hotel manager in six months to be murdered. Brizzard tells his assistants to "round up the likely suspects," a nod to Captain Louis Renault's similar command in the original *Casablanca*.

Rumors abound of covert Nazi activity in the city but, somehow, it never occurs to Brizzard to question Count Pfferman (Sig Ruman),[1] who is obviously German and wanders about with henchmen Kurt (Frederick Giermann) and Emile (Harro Meillor) and a German nightclub singer, Beatrice Reiner (Lisette Verea). Pfferman is actually Heinrich Stubel, a top Nazi official in charge of art works smuggled out of Germany and France. He wears a toupée to hide a distinctive scar on his head, though no one notices he has another running across his jaw toward his "hairline." He is a brutish man who beats his fun-loving valet Rusty (Harpo), whom he calls *du schweinehund* (often translated as "son of a bitch.").

Pfferman hopes to become the new head of the Hotel Casablanca and use it as a base from which he can transfer art works to South America. That goes awry when he misses his appointment with Governor-General Galoux (Lewis Russell) because his toupée has disappeared (Rusty sucked it into a vacuum when cleaning). Without it, he fears being identified as Stubel.

A subplot involves Lt. Pierre Delmar (Charles Drake), a French pilot commandeered by Nazis to fly stolen artwork out of Europe. Instead, he crashed his plane near Casablanca, though local police think he is a disgraced collaborator seeking to avoid prosecution. Although he is no longer in the military, Pierre still wears his uniform because he has no other clothing. How he has kept it so clean for six months is left to viewers' imaginations. Only Annette (Lois Collier) believes in Pierre. Or, as Patrick Bergan put it, Drake and Collier are our "obligatory insipid young lovers helped by the [Marx Brothers]."[2]

Stubel's plans suffer another blow when Galoux hires Ronald Kornblow (Groucho), the former manager of the Desert View Hotel, to run the Hotel Casablanca.

Stubel must now engineer a fatal "accident" for Kornblow. He tells Beatrice to lure Kornblow to a street corner rendezvous, where he is supposed to be hit by a car. This too goes haywire, though the clueless Kornblow thinks nothing more than bad driving forced him to scurry up a palm tree.

Chico appears as Corbaccio, who runs a camel-taxi stand, but becomes Kornblow's bodyguard in time to mess up both Kornblow's planned seduction of Beatrice

The Marxes are showing their age in the poster for *A Night in Casablanca* (United Artists, via Wikimedia Commons).

and Stubel's scheme to shoot Kornblow for seducing his fiancée. Rusty's role is to help Corbaccio keep Kornblow and Beatrice apart. Rusty sabotages the elevator and inadvertently discovers the stolen art in a room between floors, plus a beautiful harp upon which he plays a solo.

Pierre learns about the existence of a toupée with Stubel's name inside, but still doesn't know Stubel's assumed identity. He discusses this with Lisette in a café, where a furtive spy (David Hoffman) overhears him and offers to "help." This plotline doesn't really add anything other than echoing Peter Lorre's role as Ugarte in *Casablanca*. Mainly it establishes Pierre's need to raise money to pay the spy, an excuse for a casino scene that lands Pierre, Lisette and the Marxes in jail for cheating at roulette and as suspects in the earlier murders. Pierre is slated to be flown back to France to stand trial for wartime collaboration with the Nazis who occupied France.

Stubel finally takes over the hotel and prepares to fly the art out of Casablanca. Our heroes escape from jail and Beatrice switches sides when she overhears Stubel's plan to abandon her. She and the jailbreak crew rush to Brizzard's office to tell the prefect of Stubel's perfidy, but he isn't there. Instead, Kornblow pretends to be Brizzard and orders the police to gather in the courtyard, a dodge that allows Lisette and Pierre to escape while Kornblow, Rusty and Corbaccio search Stubel's rooms. As it turns out, Beatrice also had the same idea, but she must hide in a trunk when Stubel returns. There is a funny scene in which the Marxes befuddle Stubel by unpacking everything he packs.

As Stubel, Kurt and Emile speed toward a secret air strip, Pierre, Lisette, Kornblow, Rusty and Corbaccio are in hot pursuit. There are chases on the runway, hijinks aboard the plane, some not-so-expert piloting by Rusty, and a crash landing at, conveniently enough, the jail. Stubel's deception is revealed, the young lovers kiss, and there is an ending gag. At no point could Groucho be mistaken for Humphrey Bogart, nor Harpo for Ingrid Bergman. Warner Brothers worried about this?

Domestic Bliss and Things Amiss

After MGM and the Marx Brothers parted ways, the plans of the latter were swept away by World War II. When Pearl Harbor was bombed on December 7, 1941, Chico was 54 years old, Harpo 53 and Groucho 51, which placed them well beyond draft age, but wartime was not a great time to consider new careers.

Harpo was best situated for happiness. His late-in-life marriage to Susan Fleming was a spectacular success. Beginning in 1938, the couple adopted four children: Bill, Alexander, Jim and Minnie.[3] Harpo happily dubbed himself "the most normal man in Hollywood."[4] He was prepared to golf with friends, occasionally drop in on his old pals from the Algonquin Round Table, play his harp, and act when the mood struck.

In July 1941, he trudged off to the Bucks County Playhouse in New Hope, Pennsylvania, to appear in the George S. Kaufman–Moss Hart comedy *The Man Who Came to Dinner*. The original play—made into a film in 1942—was based on the life of Harpo's best friend Alexander Woollcott. His character Banjo was based on himself, except that he was *not* silent. As Louvish writes, "Harpo had spoken. Nothing would ever be the same way again."[5] Other than the war, the only thing marring Harpo's happiness was Woollcott's fatal heart attack on January 23, 1943, at the age of 56.

Groucho appeared regularly on radio's *The Rudy Vallée Show* in 1941 and on *Pabst Blue Ribbon Town* during 1943 and '44.[6] He wanted to do legitimate theater, but few offers were forthcoming. To his frequent sounding board Arthur Sheekman, he wrote, "I had an offer from Berlin (Irving, not Hitler) to star in a Music Box Revue but that would mean the black mustache again and I'm ducking it as long as it is economically feasible." In January 1943, he half-heartedly joked, "I have a couple of radio things brewing but the heat under them is very low and God knows what will become of me."[7] Mostly Groucho indeed found it "economically feasible" to don the hated black mustache. He published *Many Happy Returns* in 1942, an ill-timed and not very amusing satire on the woes of income taxes.[8] It didn't help his finances when, in 1942, he and Ruth divorced. In 1945, he married again: Kay Marvis Gorcey was just 21 and he was 54. Their daughter Melinda was born 18 months later.[9]

Chico was, as usual, gambling heavily. According to Maxine, Groucho showed up at her mother's door shortly after she and Chico separated. He handed Betty $300,000 worth of securities that he, Harpo and Gummo put aside "before Chico had a chance to squander it." It was a veritable fortune—more than $5.5 million by today's reckoning—and he told her, "Your husband is a confirmed bum, and I don't want to have anything to do with taking care of him any more."[10] Alas, Betty still loved Chico and foolishly gave him access to half of the money, which he lost in just three months.[11] The marriage collapsed in 1940, after Chico had an affair with one of Maxine's friends.

Chico pursued a dream of fronting his own orchestra, one variously called Chico Marx and the Chicolets, Chico Marx and His Ravellies (or Ravellis) and simply Chico Marx and His Orchestra. He made several 78 rpm recordings for Hit Records in 1942 and enjoyed being on the stage.[12] Maxine recalled, "Band life attracted Chico. The schedule was tough ... but Chico found his name packed the house every night.... He would come on stage, tell a joke or two, and then introduce the show." Chico conducted his band, told more jokes, and ended with a solo of "shooting the keys and singing the old songs." Nonetheless, "He refused to trim his style of living to suit his cut in salary. Too many years of doing exactly what he wanted were taking their toll on him physically as well."[13] His charm level remained high—not many performers could delight an audience in Italian dialect at a time in which the nation was at war with Benito Mussolini—but irresponsibility took its toll. Chico began to have chest pains and was diagnosed with heart problems.[14] Groucho and Harpo broke their pledge not to take care of Chico, and agreed to make another film. It was likely also the case that Groucho's less-than-stellar success on radio was also a factor.[15]

The Marxes also contributed to the war effort morale. Just before Pearl Harbor, Groucho and Harpo took part in a benefit for the United Jewish Appeal and, in early 1942, took part in a coast-to-coast tour promoting the purchase of war bonds. In 1945, Harpo took part in a film with the same aim.[16] A highlight was meeting Eleanor Roosevelt when the actors were in Washington, D.C.[17]

Groucho and Harpo also took part in USO shows on military bases. Chico delighted military personnel with his piano antics and Groucho got to dance with someone shorter than he: actress Veronica Lake.[18] The Marxes were sometimes not recognized until they donned their trademark outfits. As Harpo recalled, though, once he was in character, "I never had any trouble getting a high-ranking officer to act as stooge in the knife-dropping act...."[19] Harpo got to renew acquaintances with Ivy Lee Litvinov, whom he had met on his tour of the Soviet Union nine years earlier.

Groucho dancing with Veronica Lake at a USO show (Groucho Marx Collection, Archives Center, National Museum of American History, Smithsonian Institution).

Harpo also recalled several sour notes. The first occurred at a military psych ward in Indiana, where he was set to play harp out of costume. Three soldiers carried the instrument to the stage in its coffin-like case. They looked like pallbearers, "the poor bastards in the ward started to yell and the event was scuttled." Harpo was on tour when he received word that his friend Alice Duer Miller was dying. He was there when she passed in July 1942.[20]

One of the Marxes' biggest wartime contributions took place in absentia. In May 1941, during one of the worst episodes in the German Luftwaffe's Blitz of London, Churchill was at Ditchley House in Oxfordshire. He recalled, "After dinner, news arrived of the heavy air raid on London. There was nothing that I could do about it so I watched the Marx Brothers in a comic film which my hosts had arranged.... The merry film clacked on, and I was glad of the diversion." Luckily, it was *Monkey Business*, not *Duck Soup*.[21]

It Was No *Casablanca*!

It's usually not a good idea to piggyback on a famous film. *Casablanca* is one of film history's landmark productions. No one will ever say that about *A Night in Casablanca*.

The planned *Casablanca* lampoon touched off an exchange between Groucho and Warner Brothers. It began with Groucho's feigned astonishment that the studio claimed exclusive rights to the name of an entire city. Groucho then dove into the absurdity of the situation:

> I just don't understand your attitude. Even if you plan on re-releasing your picture, I am sure that the average movie fan could learn in time to distinguish between Ingrid Bergman and Harpo. I don't know whether I could, but I certainly would like to try.
>
> You claim you own Casablanca and that no one else can use that name without your permission. What about "Warner Brothers?" Do you own that, too? You probably have the right to use the name Warner, but what about "Brothers"? Professionally, we were brothers before you were. We were touring the sticks as the Marx Brothers when Vitaphone was still a gleam in the inventor's eye, and even before us there had been other brothers—the Smith Brothers; the Brothers Karamazov; Dan Brothers, an outfielder with Detroit....

Groucho chided Jack Warner about others whose use of the forename "Jack" preceded his own, including Jack and the Beanstalk and Jack the Ripper. As for Harry Warner, Groucho noted that both "Lighthouse Harry of Revolutionary fame and... Harry Appelbaum" bore that name before him.[22]

Groucho puckishly assured, "I love Warners. Some of my best friends are Warner Brothers.... I have a hunch that this attempt to prevent us from using the title is the brainchild of some ferret-faced shyster, serving a brief apprenticeship in your legal department." He ended with a flourish of *faux* solidarity by pledging that the Marxes, Warners and all other brothers would stand united in fighting any "pasty-faced legal adventurer."[23]

Logic would suggest that Groucho's jocular letter would appease Warner Brothers and alert them that the *last* thing the Marx Brothers planned was a remake of *Casablanca*. Yet the studio legal department dashed off two more letters demanding information about the plot outline. It shows how little they knew about how the Marxes worked. First, there was as yet no final script and second, getting serious information out of Groucho was akin to peeling paint from a wall. Groucho wrote back the first time to say,

> In it I play a Doctor of Divinity who ministers to the natives and, as a sideline, hocks can openers and pea jackets to the savages along the Gold Coast of Africa.
>
> When I first meet Chico, he is working in a saloon, selling sponges to barflies who are unable to carry their liquor. Harpo is an Arabian caddy who lives in a small Grecian urn on the outskirts of the city.....
>
> There's a lot more I could tell you, but I don't want to spoil it for you. All of this has been okayed by the Hays Office, *Good Housekeeping* and the survivors of the Haymarket riots....[24]

Groucho followed with an even more ludicrous letter when the Warner Brothers legal department wanted still more information: "Since I last wrote you ... there have been some changes in the plot of our new picture *A Night in Casablanca*. In the new version I play Bordello, the sweetheart of Humphrey Bogart. Harpo and Chico are itinerant rug peddlers who are weary of laying rugs and enter a monastery just for a lark. This is a good joke on them, as there hasn't been a lark in the place for fifteen years." He peppered the rest of the latter with oblique references to William Gladstone, Lauren Bacall, and "apple-cheeked damsels, most of whom have been barred by the Hays Office for soliciting."[25] Only then did threats to sue stop, though apparently that had more to do with the Hays Office's refusal to accept the studio's complaint than Warner Brothers' realization that they were acting foolishly.[26] Wes D. Gehring correctly observed that *A Night in Casablanca* is "probably more famous for the series of letters Groucho wrote to the Warner Brothers legal department" than for its content.[27] Louvish speculates that the entire spat might have been an elaborate publicity stunt on the part of the Marx Brothers.[28] If so, it was such a brilliant one that suggests Groucho should have written the script! (He, Harpo and Chico did write some of it, uncredited.)

The working title was *Adventures in Casablanca*, and it's possible that Warner Brothers did force a change in tack. Character names such as Humphrey Bogus and Lowan Behold disappeared from Joseph Fields' first draft. When the film was finished, Fields and Roland Kibbee got screenplay credits, but numerous other writers came and went in the interim, with Groucho tossing out jokes and scenarios that simply didn't work. Alas, in the process some very funny setups were also jettisoned.[29] Ronald Bergan pegged the script well: "The only thing it had in common with *Casablanca* was its location."[30]

Joseph Fields was the son of famed vaudevillian Lew Fields, who appeared as half of the comic act (Joe) Weber and Fields. That legendary duo had just dissolved as the Marxes were starting out. Joseph Fields had written the book for several Broadway shows, but his previous movie script work was undistinguished. Kibbee had radio credits, including some writing for Groucho, but *A Night in Casablanca* was his first attempt at a screenplay. Mitchell notes that Fields and Kibbee mostly reshaped material fed to them by the Marxes. Frank Tashlin, who got an "additional material" credit, might have been the strongest outside contributor to the film. Prior to his involvement with the Marxes, he was known as an animator and cartoonist. This served well in his collaboration with Harpo.

The task of directing fell to Archie Mayo, who had gone from stage actor to gag writer to director. His directorial résumé is impressive in that he directed such stars as Joan Blondell, Humphrey Bogart, Gary Cooper, Bette Davis, James Cagney, Tyrone Power and Mae West. The Marxes initially liked him, though by January 1946, Groucho began to have doubts. He wrote to Sam Zolotow, a *New York Times* theater critic he knew well, to complain that he was beginning to feel like "one of the minor performers in Swain's Rat and Cat Act ... [which] consisted of rats, dressed as jockeys, perched on six cats, dressed as horses, [running] around a miniature race track." He confessed that he drew a bigger salary than the rats, whom "Swain paid off in cheese" because they "didn't have an agent." He added, "If *A Night in Casablanca* turns out disastrously, and there is no reason it shouldn't, I am going to look up Swain and ask him if he would be interested in reviving his act with me playing one of the jockeys."[31] As the film progressed, Groucho privately called Mayo "a fat idiot" and accused him of screwing up the picture.[32]

Groucho's assessments were acidic and unhelpful, but it was odd that a director as experienced as Mayo got so much wrong. At Harpo's insistence, a short tour was assembled—mostly on military bases—where he and Chico tried out scenes. (Groucho had just remarried and was unavailable.) It was clear that some things didn't work, but Mayo operated by addition rather than subtraction. Groucho's rant was prompted by a January 1946 preview of the film that ran 113 minutes. It would eventually be pared to 85. It needed to be shorter.

The final piece in the production puzzle was producer David Loew, one of the twin sons of MGM founder Marcus Loew (David left MGM in 1935). It was he who convinced the Marx Brothers to make another film. To that end, he set up Loma Vista Films. *A Night in Casablanca* was distributed by United Artists.

It's No *Duck Soup*!

In 1933, *Duck Soup* debuted against a backdrop of post–World War I cynicism over the need for it and its horrifying cost. By contrast, very few Americans questioned the necessity for World War II. Roughly 18 million individuals served in the military, ten million fought overseas, 25 million workers purchased war bonds, and just 43,000 draftees refused induction.[33] World War II was, after all, the war to rid the globe of fascism and liberate death camps in which some six million Jews were exterminated, along with untold numbers of Roma, Slavs, people of color, homosexuals and political enemies. Another 60,000 POWs died in Japanese camps, and its military committed countless war atrocities.

The phrase "the good war" was not in common use until 1984, when author-broadcaster Studs Terkel so titled his oral history collection of World War II memories. But many Americans had already expressed views in line with the philosophical ideas of a "just war." In the mid–1940s, American patriotism was at fever pitch, and returning military personnel were hailed as heroes. Cracks in the good-war thesis emerged later, but 1946 would not have been a good time to make a comedy that called the war into question or lampooned military figures.[34] Setting *A Night in Casablanca* in a French colony provided some cover, as did satirical echoes of *Casablanca*, but it was still necessary to tread lightly. The Marx Brothers simply could not turn back the clock 13 years and make a cheeky film like *Duck Soup*.

Allen Eyles writes, "*A Night in Casablanca* is incapable of dealing with the postwar era. In fact, its inspiration is the escapist cinema's own espionage cycle, including *Casablanca*."[35] His statement is correct, but many Hollywood films of the time followed similar patterns. George MacDonald Fraser noted, "Hollywood's most interesting war pictures, both before and after 1945, were those set in a shadowy half-world, usually ... far from the actual battlefronts." They were "peopled by tough American soldiers of fortune ... gorgeous Continentals whose wardrobes and coiffures seldom took account of wartime austerity ... and sinister men of mystery ... who exchanged messages in sleazy cafés, dark streets and sometimes quite popular nightclubs...." Such films were, in his estimation, "certainly not historical, but interesting as romantic propaganda of the war." Even movies depicting actual battles often fell short of historical fact.[36]

Propaganda tended to be more subtle during World War II, even though the Office of War Information (OWI) "won unprecedented control over the content of American motion pictures" for the war's duration.[37] As Peter Roffman and Jim Purdy observed, from 1942 to 1945, 28 percent of all Hollywood films dealt with the war.[38] They gravitated toward uplifting civilian morale, either by embellishing optimism or providing escapist thrills. War movies were also selective in their focus. Despite the OWI's efforts to dissuade filmmakers from trading in racial stereotypes, the Japanese were "uniformly shown as brutal, treacherous and subhuman." Tom Engelhardt notes that in this, "the movie industry reflected popular attitudes." He cites polling data from U.S. military personnel in which 38 to 48 percent said they hoped to kill a Japanese soldier.[39]

It was, of course, the Japanese bombing of Pearl Harbor that drew America into the war. Nazis became stock movie villains once hostilities ceased, but until the liberation of the death camps—a phenomenon previously unknown to most GIs and the American public—animus toward Germans did not parallel that of World War I. In the same aforementioned polls, just five to nine percent of American servicemen expressed a desire to kill Germans. Hollywood's focus remained skewed toward Japan—even in Bugs Bunny cartoons—as American and Allied troops invaded Italy and their bombers pounded Germany in 1943 and '44.[40]

There was something else missing: Africa. If I might digress, my father served during the war. He seldom spoke of it thereafter, but he spun a few tales about his first brush with conflict, which took place in Oran, Algeria. I mention this because, until I was in college, his were among the very few wartime references to North Africa that I had heard. High school history texts were full of information about Pacific theater island-hopping and the three-front war in Europe, but other than a brief mention of securing control over the Suez Canal by stopping the advance of Axis troops at El Alamein, Egypt, battles in North Africa got short shrift. This was partly because most of the fighting there took place before the U.S. entered the war, and partly because the U.S. originally favored an assault on Axis troops launched from Scandinavia rather than North Africa.[41]

Famed Scripps-Howard war correspondent Ernie Pyle complained that American policy was one of "soft-gloving snakes in our midst" by not challenging French Nazis: "Our enemies see it, laugh, and call us soft."[42] President Roosevelt ultimately authorized Operation Torch, wherein American troops helped invade Nazi-controlled French North Africa during late 1942 and into the spring of 1943. Americans specifically liberated Casablanca, Morocco, and Oran and Algiers, Algeria. For all the romance of the first and the comedy of the second, Hollywood movies such as *Casablanca* and *A Night in Casablanca* were among the few to concentrate on North Africa.[43]

A few words on Moroccan history in the first half of the 20th century casts some light on *A Night in Casablanca*. Morocco had long been a target of European powers, with France firmly establishing itself in the region by the dawn of the 20th century. Germany also sought influence, but the 1912 Treaty of Fez made most of Morocco a French "protectorate," a term that theoretically meant that France would defend it militarily but allow Moroccan officials to run their own affairs. In practice, France put into place a French-style bureaucracy, ceded land to French immigrants, exploited natural resources, and allowed French companies to gain enormous influence. This angered most Moroccans, but the French put down several rebellions and placed a governor general in charge of Casablanca and (by extension) the rest of Morocco except for the north, which became a Spanish protectorate. Casablanca was the locus of French authority, with the city swelling in population from 12,000 in 1906 to over 110,000 in less than 15 years. It became an international city open to just about anyone except Arabs, Berbers and mixed-blood Moroccans. In other words, most of the indigenous population.

World War II complicated matters. The Spanish Civil War (1936–39) ended with a Falangist victory that placed Generalissimo Francisco Franco at the head of a fascist-style right-wing government. On June 25, 1940, France fell to Hitler's armies. France was divided into two regions, a northern sector that it occupied directly, and a government in the south centered in Vichy. In theory, the south was "Free France," but that meant only that German control was indirect. The Vichy government was a collaborationist fiction in which Jews and other enemies of the German state were routinely rounded up.

Casablanca became a *de facto* center of French underground resistance. When *Casablanca* was made, the city was indeed a den of spies, shifting loyalties, independence movements, Nazi collaborators and anti-fascist activists. The Allied invasion of November 1942 supposedly ended Nazi control of Casablanca. It was pacified to the point that it was safe for President Roosevelt to travel there in January 1943, to discuss strategy with Winston Churchill and Free French leaders Charles de Gaulle and Henri Giraud, but the city remained a base of intrigue. Nazis could not operate openly, but Casablanca remained loosely controlled.

The Allied objective in Morocco, like that in Algeria and Tunisia, was to create a beachhead from which the invasion of Sicily could take place, not to police the area. "Operation Husky" commenced on July 9, 1943, and ended seven weeks later. The following month, Benito Mussolini was arrested and on September 8, 1943, Italy surrendered to Allied troops led by U.S. General Dwight D. Eisenhower. Mussolini tried to flee to neutral Switzerland, was captured, and was executed on April 28, 1945. Nine days later, Germany surrendered. All of this took place just weeks after President Franklin Roosevelt died of a cerebral hemorrhage. These events were fresh in the public's mind when *A Night in Casablanca* debuted on May 10, 1946.

Groucho's Film?

Several things stand out about *A Night in Casablanca*. First, Chico has a diminished role. He is once again a bodyguard, but mostly he's the proverbial "good guy" trying to do the right thing. Harpo has some good routines, though we've seen most of them before. The best jokes belong to Groucho, which means it's heavy on witty dialogue. There are some sharp insults and asides scattered amidst the film's uneven script.

Harpo supplies our first good laugh. When Brizzard orders a roundup of "likely suspects," Rusty (Harpo) certainly looks suspicious enough to be hauled in. He is idly leaning against a wall. A policeman barks at him, "Say, what do you think you are doing? Holding up the building?" Rusty nods slightly, the police officer grabs him, and the building tumbles into rubble. This gag bears similarity to one Buster Keaton used in *The General* and a few other films in which he's standing in front of an open door when a house collapses around him. Still, Harpo's take is laugh-inducing.

The next notable moment comes when Delbar tries to convince Brizzard that he was forced to fly stolen loot out of Paris during the Nazi occupation. Delbar is a movie fiction, but Nazi looting is historical fact. Thousands of precious works—including valuable books, drawings, jewelry, paintings and sculptures—were stolen from churches, museums, Jewish homes and synagogues throughout Europe. The toll would have been even worse had it not been for the courageous efforts of untold numbers of individuals who emptied art repositories and hid works from the Nazis. Nonetheless, works from art giants Sandro Botticelli, Jan van Eyck, Gustav Klimt, Michelangelo, Egon Schiele and Johannes Vermeer fell into Nazi hands.

Until recently, not many people outside of the art world knew about the Monuments, Fine Arts and Archives program in which 405 individuals from military and civilian ranks toiled to recover as many works as possible. It began in 1943 and ran through 1946, which means that for much of the time, their work literally took place under fire. More than a half million stolen items were recovered. No one knows exactly how many works are yet to be traced—estimates range from 100,000 to 300,000—and efforts at repatriation continue to the present. Some art appears at auctions, some is undoubtedly in private hands, some probably perished, and some is in Russia, as Soviet troops also engaged in looting when they liberated Nazi-held territory.[44] *A Night in Casablanca* doesn't delve deeply into such details, though it does remind us that Germans recently controlled Morocco.

Most of the rest of the film is less weighty. Rusty's dressing of Stubel involves amusing schtick. Or should I say "stick," which is what he inserts behind the arrogant Stubel's jacket and upon which his hat rests.

With Groucho's arrival, the one-liners begin to fly. Chico-Corbaccio gets off one of his few amusing bits of dialogue when he meets Groucho's Kornblow at the train station. When Kornblow learns that Corbaccio runs the Yellow Camel Taxi Company, he asks, "Aren't all camels in Casablanca yellow?" Corbaccio informs him, "You crazy. We got a Checker Camel Company too." If you've not taken a cab before 1999, you might not know that Checker Motors made taxi cabs adorned by a distinctive

No one looks like Bogart or Bergman in this publicity shot for *A Night in Casablanca*. Pictured: Groucho, Chico, Harpo (MGM, via Wikimedia Commons).

checked band. Checker cabs debuted in Chicago in 1922 and spread to other cities, especially New York City. New York retired its final Checker cab in 1999.

At the hotel, Kornblow meets Galoux and Brizzard, and insults the latter's beard. When informed that the staff has been assembled so he can tell them what he expects, he orders that the guests be assembled instead, so he can inform them what he expects of *them*. This is reminiscent of *The Cocoanuts* but luckily we don't endure anything as cheesy as that film's bellhop musical routine. Instead, Kornblow announces his intention to improve the hotel's efficiency: three-minute eggs are to be served in two, a two-minute egg in one, and if anyone orders a one-minute egg, "give him a chicken and let him work it out himself."

In his office, Kornblow lets loose with the lecherous line, "I'm a different man behind a desk, as any stenographer can tell you." Brizzard and Galoux lie to Kornblow that his predecessor died "a natural death." They lie again when he asks about the manager before that and they insist he was fired for stealing money. To that Kornblow replies, "You want a manager that doesn't steal? Good day, gentlemen." He is convinced to stay when he finds out he will be paid 500 francs[45] a week and that his laundry will be picked up once a month. Kornblow retorts, "If you wait that long, you won't be able to pick it up."

Rusty gets another funny turn when he hands Stubel a mop instead of his missing toupée. The count is so insulted that his flunky Kurt insists on teaching Rusty a lesson by challenging him to a sword fight. Rusty briefly flees, then reappears wearing one boxing glove and a baseball catcher's outfit. Kurt quickly strips Rusty of his protective gear, but he doesn't need it. Rusty is more than Kurt's equal with a blade; in fact, Rusty is bored, yawns and parries all of Kurt's thrusts while devouring food. It's a fun scene marred only by a clunky ending.

Kornblow gets in several zingers when Beatrice slinks into his office wielding a ridiculously long cigarette holder. Kornblow offers her a light and asks, "How are things down at the other end?" They flirt by blowing smoke over each other until Beatrice coughs. Kornblow blurts out, "This is like living in Pittsburgh. If you can call that living." If that sounds like a low-blow regional joke, it's only partially so. Pittsburgh was once America's "Steel City" and home to some 300 steel manufactories. Not surprisingly, it was also dubbed "Dirty Burgh" because of its soot- and pollution-fouled air. Two years after *A Night in Casablanca* debuted, the nearby town of Donora suffered a temperature inversion that trapped grimy air beneath a cold front. In three days, 70 people died and 6000 were sickened. Pittsburgh's air quality remained rank into the 1970s. It has improved since, mostly because of the decline of the steel industry.

Beatrice flirts with Kornblow as she tries to locate Stubel's toupee in the hotel's lost and found box under the guise that she lost a diamond clip. As Kornblow puts the moves on her, Beatrice quietly palms the toupée and remains long enough to make Kornblow think she's interested in him. Naturally, this is fodder for Groucho one-liners. Beatrice comments on his silky hair and he retorts, "Silky now, but next year I'm getting nylon." He tells her she's the most beautiful woman in the world and when asked if he means it, he responds, "No, but I don't mind lying if it will get me somewhere." Beatrice says she will sing at the club later and asks, "Will you join me?" His response: "Why? Are you coming apart?"

As she prepares to leave, Beatrice promises she will be singing only for him. This prompts a response that will be lost on those who haven't seen the heralded 1944 movie *To Have and Have Not*: "You don't have to sing for me. Just whistle." It's a sideways reference to the most famous line from *To Have or Have Not*. Marie Browning (Lauren Bacall) turns to Steve Morgan (Humphrey Bogart) and tells him to whistle if he needs anything. She embellished it with a nod and a wink: "You know how to whistle, don't you, Steve? You just put your lips together and blow."[46] Beatrice boards an elevator just in time to see Rusty aping her by smoking from a matching opera-length cigarette holder.

The middle part of *A Night in Casablanca* is its funniest. At the club, Kornblow soils Stubel's shirt and his apology doesn't assuage the enraged (fake) count: "You can hardly notice, unless you're looking for soup." As Stubel is led to the kitchen to clean the mess, Kornblow turns to Beatrice and comments, "Speaks excellent German." As Kornblow and Beatrice dance, Corbaccio and Rusty pull an amusing prank to raise money for Pierre to pay a spy for information on Heinrich Stubel. They do so by taking gratuities from those waiting to get into a club whose tables are filled. No problem; for a few francs, they set up another table. And another. And another. Soon, there is no room for dancers, waiters or anyone else, though it affords opportunities for Groucho to make wisecracks about the room's (non-) intimacy.

Chico plays his piano solo, which he introduces with his funniest line: "We gonna play a classical number. We're gonna play the second movement from the *Beer Barrel Polka*." That's followed by the unsuccessful attempt to knock off Kornblow, the sad tale of why Pierre and Annette can't yet be married, and the new plot to kill Kornblow, overheard by Rusty.

In the interim, Pfferman books a flight for Tunis. Kornblow is at the front desk and remarks, "Tunis? There are some beautiful women in Tunis." The impatient Stubel bellows that he's not interested in beautiful women, which prompts Kornblow to crack, "In that case, look up some of the women I've taken out." Kornblow is also tone deaf to Corbaccio's plea that there is a plot to kill him. He dismisses it by wisecracking, "I don't mind being killed but I resent hearing it from someone whose head comes to a point," a remark aimed at Chico's trademark hat. He isn't much happier when Corbaccio appoints himself his bodyguard.

Repartee ensues between Kornblow and Corbaccio, but it lacks the sharpness and vigor of classic Groucho-Chico banter. It also segues into another shop-worn routine: As part of his bodyguard duties, Corbaccio and Rusty grab Kornblow's lunch buffet on the pretext of making certain it's not poisoned. The best line comes when a bottle of bubbly is uncorked, but it's empty. Kornblow explains, "That's dry champagne." The scene ends with Rusty dusting off another old bit by eating a cup and saucer.

Groucho returns to the front desk to field a complaint from a guest who says his trunks have yet to arrive. Kornblow suggests, "Put your pants on. Nobody will know the difference." This segues into what is arguably the picture's best-remembered routine. It involves a haughty new arrival who makes the mistake of calling Kornblow a "clerk." His luggage is in transit from the airport, which provides opportunity for Kornblow to slap down pretension. When Kornblow is assured the bags are on their way, the following takes place:

> **KORNBLOW:** In all my years in the hotel business, that's the phoniest story I've heard. I suppose your name is Smith.
> **CLIENT:** No, it's Smythe, spelled with a "y."

KORNBLOW: ... Mr. and Mrs. Smythe and no baggage. Let me see your marriage license.
CLIENT: What? How dare you, sir!
KORNBLOW: How do you like that? Puts a "y" in Smith and expects me to let him in the hotel with a strange dame.
CLIENT: Strange dame?
KORNBLOW: She is to me. I've never seen her before.
CLIENT: Sir, you may not be aware of it, but I am president of the Morocco Laundry Company.
KORNBLOW [PULLING OFF SHIRT]: You are? Take this shirt and have it back Friday. Mr. Smythe or Smith, this is a family hotel, and I suggest you take your business elsewhere.
CLIENT: This lady is my wife. You should be ashamed.
KORNBLOW: If this lady is your wife, you should be ashamed.
CLIENT: You'll hear from me.
KORNBLOW: Do that, even if it's only a postcard.

This level of irreverence is reminiscent of the Marx Brothers' days at Paramount. The next scene, Kornblow's thwarted seduction of Beatrice, is a tepid variant of aborted trysts in *Horse Feathers* and *A Day at the Races*. The third time isn't a charm, but it has its moments. Rusty delays the would-be deadly seduction by sabotaging the elevator, climbing out the top trap door, discovering the Nazi loot, playing his harp solo, making off with a Rembrandt, and then cutting the cables with an axe. The sight of him and Kornblow bobbing up and down like sprung jack-in-the-boxes is quite funny.

Once again, Groucho is not the smoothest of Lotharios. His wooing of Beatrice is filled with asides, non-sequiturs and witticisms. Kornblow has been thoughtful enough to provide roses, but when Beatrice exclaims, "I shall keep them forever," Kornblow counters, "That's what you think. I only rented them for an hour." She then addresses him as "Mr. Kornblow," but he tells her, "Call me Montgomery." "Is that your name?" she asks. "No," he replies, "I'm just breaking it in for a friend." Corbaccio does his bit to make sure that Kornblow, Beatrice and Stubel are never in the same room together, but those efforts lack the maniacal energy and baffling Chico-speak found in *Horse Feathers* and *A Day at the Races*.

The casino scene has decent gags, but it's mainly there so Corbaccio, Kornblow, Pierre and Rusty can end up in jail. It's illogical in that Corbaccio and Rusty have already bilked diners to get the money Pierre needs, but it's needed to land them in jail so they can escape. In the cell, Rusty unveils the Rembrandt he took from the Nazi art trove—apparently prisoners were not searched in Casablanca—and then his face is lathered to make him look like a mad dog. The guard's fez is pulled over his head, he is relieved of his keys, and the heroes rush off to thwart Stubel.

Step one is to delay the trip. The packing and unpacking of Stubel's large cases is the film's best physical humor. Ruman is superb in this sequence—flustered, frustrated, and on the edge of nervous collapse. Even Kurt and Emile suspect that Stubel is losing his mind. Somehow no one notices the Marxes sneaking in and out of doors, from underneath tables, or inside trunks. Still, it's a delightful routine.

We next get a rather hackneyed chase scene with the Nazis in a car and the Marxes in hot pursuit inside a commandeered truck. The plane taxis on the runway, but must turn to gain lift as its heavy cargo precludes taking off into the wind. There are efforts to get onto the plane, struggles aboard the plane, and Kornblow stuck on a ladder between the truck and plane. Once again, such semi-slapstick humor is more the métier of the Three Stooges than the Marx Brothers. Not to mention its toll on aging bodies. Between scene retakes, Groucho asked Harpo if he too was sick of doing such strenuous material at their ages. Harpo's one-word response was, "Yes." It's hard to counter Louvish's assertion that it would have been "much funnier when they were younger [and] sassier."[47]

The denouement arrives when Rusty crashes the plane into the jail, where Brizzard arrests Stubel, Kurt and Emile. We rest assured that the stolen art will be recovered and Pierre's reputation cleared. Pierre and Annette smooch by the jail wall and Beatrice utters a line that provides an amusing ending.

Elephant in the Room: Orientalism

A Night in Casablanca is largely free of antiquated values that are now troubling. I earlier invoked the 1978 book *Orientalism*, in which Edward Said discussed the various ways in which non–Western cultures and peoples have been misrepresented. *A Night in Casablanca* was at best an exoticized look at Middle Eastern society and at worst, a soggy brine of imperialism, colonialism and (ironically) assumptions of racial superiority that were a central value of Nazism.[48]

A Night in Casablanca isn't an egregious flight into orientalism, in part because Moroccans are scarcely in evidence. It is Westerners who cavort about in fezzes and the few (implied) native peoples are often seedy and dangerous-looking. Pierre's barroom spy contact certainly falls into that category, though he's actually a Western actor. Corbaccio's camel-taxi service could also be considered mildly disrespectful. As noted, though, 1940s Casablanca was an international city with French infrastructure. Automobiles were certainly a more common feature on Casablancan streets than camels.

Several unsettling orientalist aspects of *A Night in Casablanca* disappeared during script revisions. One scene would have found Groucho smoking a hookah, with a cigar attached to the tube snaking through the water-filled bowl. Other discarded ideas include having Kornblow ogle Arab women and finding rooms for 27 women named Mrs. Abdulla. Even the camel-taxi scene was scaled back. Audiences in 1946 might have found such material funny, but it's probably best that it never made it to the screen.[49]

For the most part, the Marx Brothers and the writers deserve a pass against charges of orientalism. The film was, after all, intended to lampoon *Casablanca*, a box office powerhouse whose adjusted ticket take was a whopping $374.1 million. This made it an irresistible target for satire.[50] Neither film used Morocco for anything more than a backdrop for romance, intrigue, snappy lines and comedy. There is little attempt to replicate anthropological reality; North Africa is simply an excuse for establishing shots that situate and frame respective narratives.

Grains of Desert Sand

- **Dan Seymour**, who played Captain Brizzard, was also in *Casablanca*. In the earlier film, he was Abdul the doorman. Perhaps *that* deserves a charge of orientalism!

- **Lisette Verea:** Simon Louvish was not complimentary to Verea, who played Beatrice Rheiner. He writes that she "cannot really stand in for the combination Thelma Todd and Margaret Dumont she is called upon to play."[51] Perhaps, but Verea's performance is much stronger than those of Esther Muir (*A Day at the Races*), Eve Arden (*At the Circus*) and June MacCloy (*Go West*) in similar roles.

- **No room for Dumont:** As essential as Margaret Dumont was in Marx Brothers comedies, it's difficult to imagine a role for her in *A Night in Casablanca.* According to Maxine Marx, Dumont felt that association with the Marxes hampered her career. She reportedly said, "Nobody took me seriously as a dramatic actress. People always thought they saw Groucho peeking out from behind my skirt."[52]

- **Wigged out:** If Harpo looks different, it's more than age. According to Adamson, his wig was jettisoned and his actual hair was fluffed, curled and dyed blond. That was some feat, as Harpo's hair was short and receding by then. Adamson is correct that it made him look "more like an old man and less like a gremlin."[53] He returned to a stage wig for subsequent appearances.

- **Solo redux:** Harpo's solo is among the repeated elements in *A Night in Casablanca.* He played beautifully, but "Bohemian Rhapsody" was used in several other films.

- **Old gag updates:** Harpo came up with a variant of his knee-over-an-outstretched-arm gag. He pulls that trick as he walks through the Hotel Casablanca lobby with a broom, but when guests take offense, he points to his shoe. The sole flips up to reveal that he is sweeping trash and cigarette butts into it. The vignette ends with another twist: Harpo ogles an attractive woman. She looks frightened and runs away when Harpo beeps his horn. He does *not* chase her, perhaps because she was a brunette!

- **Mum's the word:** Harpo was offered a substantial bonus—allegedly more than $50,000—to utter the single word "Murder!" He reportedly claimed that he had spent decades building his silent character and did not intend to throw it away. Harpo never said how this squared with his speaking role in *The Man Who Came to Dinner.*

- **A song endures:** The Ted Snyder-Bert Kalmar-Harry Ruby song "Who's Sorry Now" had a successful pre– and post–*Night in Casablanca* life. Penned in 1923, it was recorded numerous times before and after 1946, and covered by artists as diverse as Bing Crosby, Ella Fitzgerald, Willie Nelson and Marie Osmond. In 1958, it sold more than a million records for pop singer Connie Francis.

- **Moroccan updates:** At the 1943 Casablanca Conference, Sultan Muhammad V pushed Moroccan independence. His overtures were tabled, partly because the Allies were focused on the war, but also because they were not committed to principles of self-determination. American officials told Free French leader Henri Giraud, "It is thoroughly understood that French sovereignty will be re-established as soon as possible throughout all the territory, metropolitan or colonial, over which flew the French flag in 1939." No doubt oil interests came into play.[54] As would be the case in Southeast Asia, the French were simply too weak to reassert colonial control. Moroccan nationalists regrouped after World War II. The next ten years saw two sultans replaced and several massacres of Moroccans by French forces. An agreement was struck in early 1956 for the return of Muhammad V and, on April 7, 1956, Morocco gained its independence.

Packing Up the Fezzes

The majority of *Night at Casablanca* reviews were positive, though quite a few remarked on how good it was to see the Marx Brothers again and said relatively little about the film. Almost no one saw it as one of their best efforts, nor did many echo the *New York Times* in calling the Marxes as "wheezy as an old Model T Ford panting uphill on two cylinders."[55] James Agee doubtless spoke for many when he declared that it wasn't a great film and added: "The worst [the Marx Brothers] ever make would be better worth seeing than most other things I can think of." Only *The Hollywood Reporter* and *Los Angeles Times* declared the film an unqualified success and raved over its content.[56]

Marx biographers have been more critical than the reviewers of the day. Eyles wrote, "There is a feeling of the routine about the film, a lack of ambition, a failure to explore new directions and explore new subjects."[57] According to Adamson, "The state of American comedy must have been on the verge of collapse to allow its heart to be gladdened by this sorry old film."[58] Groucho reportedly found everything about it such a chore that he returned home after each day's filming "to play guitar and try to forget the distasteful experience."[59]

A Night in Casablanca is mostly a decent, though not outstanding, Marx vehicle. One can easily imagine the thrill felt by legions of moviegoers to see the Marxes after a five-year hiatus. Novelist F. Scott Fitzgerald once said that there are no second acts in American lives. Not so. Comebacks have long been an American staple, especially in fields such as sports, politics and entertainment. But what about third acts? In 1949, the Marxes made *Love Happy*, and I so wish they hadn't.

FOURTEEN

Love Happy (1950)

Ronald Bergan states that *Love Happy* is "the only really bad Marx Brothers movie."[1] It's hard to disagree with that, unless one wishes to argue that it's not really a Marx Brothers film at all. The slang term "turkey" was coined in the 1920s to describe a show that flopped. *Love Happy* is one of the biggest gobblers of all time. There are lessons to be derived from *Love Happy*, but good filmmaking isn't among them.

Marilyn Monroe makes a brief appearance, though the movie is far less substantial than she. *Love Happy* can best be summarized as where schtick meets schlock. If you were underwhelmed by *Room Service*, you certainly won't like *Love Happy*. It's the same premise: a show with no money, performers needing food, and no chance of opening without a miracle. This time, Harpo—whose character is also called

Poster for *Love Happy*.

Harpo—is called upon to feed the cast. He does whatever he can to procure food, which is mostly steal it. Groucho is Detective Sam Grunion and he's on screen for just ten minutes, about 80 percent longer than he wished. Chico is Faustino the Great, a name that's more impressive than anything he does other than play the piano and interpret Harpo's whistles and gestures.

Love Happy plays like a diminished version of *The Maltese Falcon* (1941) in that its central device involves the pursuit of priceless jewels, shady characters looking for them, and the imperilment of those who get in the way. Mostly it's a series of sketches in search of a story and a chase scene that's an excuse for product placement.

Architects of a Mess

The film was Harpo's idea and was supposed to be a solo venture.[2] Groucho, usually Harpo's biggest defender, wasn't keen on his vision: "Harpo had [the] idea that he was Charlie Chaplin," meaning he wanted to channel Chaplin's Little Tramp. Chico finagled a part in the movie to collect a paycheck.[3] He had suffered a heart attack in 1947, but financial woes forced Chico onto the road a year later; that tour ultimately took him to Australia.[4] Once he joined the *Love Happy* cast, backers were reluctant to finance it unless Groucho also came aboard.[5]

Love Happy was a mess from the start, but don't blame director David Miller. His was a respected name with both feature films to his credit and wartime participation in Frank Capra's *Why We Fight* documentary series. Groucho liked Miller and recommended him to direct Bing Crosby's 1949 movie *Top o' the Morning.*[6]

Producer Lester Cowan was a different matter. He had produced two W.C. Fields films, but his Marx Brothers experience was bitter. *Love Happy* ran out of money on several occasions, which forced him to resort to product placements in order to complete the film. Even then, United Artists contemplated pulling out of its distribution deal. Harpo, known as one of the gentlest souls in Hollywood, called Cowan "the vilest man in the whole world" and allegedly spat on him.[7]

Publicity shot of the aging Marx Brothers on the set of *Love Happy*: Groucho (sitting), Chico, Harpo (photograph by Yousuf Karsh, Library and Archives Canada: Library and Archives Canada/Yousuf Karsh fonds/a207445).

Almost no one liked the film. Film legend Mary Pickford served as an executive producer, retired shortly after *Love Happy*, and never spoke of the movie. Joe Adamson noted, "You will notice that not one autobiography, not one biography, not one interview, not one straw vote, not one independent poll, not one Marx Brother ever admits to having anything to do with the picture."[8] Those words were written in 1973. Subsequent biographers *have* discussed *Love Happy*, but Harpo didn't mentioned it in his autobiography.

The World of 1950

Love Happy is often listed as a 1949 film, but it did not hit theaters until March 3, 1950.[9] By then, time had passed the Marx Brothers by. A sad reality of popular culture is that celebrities are routinely judged by their most recent work, not the sweep of their careers. Groucho enjoyed much success outside of the brother act, but that was up in the air as *A Night in Casablanca* was wrapping. In 1947, he was part of the cast of *Copacabana*, a film in which he played second banana to an actual banana. The film starred Carmen Miranda, the "Brazilian Bombshell," a salsa singer famed for wearing flamboyant headgear festooned with tropical fruit.

Copacabana was funny in spots, but Groucho's take on it varied according to whom he spoke. He disparaged Miranda to his daughter Miriam: "In addition to looking like a dressed-up bulldog, she sings each song the same as the preceding one, and to top it off, she is supposed to feed me [lines] ... and I didn't understand a ... damned word she said."[10] Yet he also claimed there was demand for more films with himself and Miranda, though it's hard to fathom how he came to such a conclusion; *Copacabana* was a thudding dud.[11] In 1948, he mockingly complained to critic Earl Wilson, "I found your reference to the picture *Copacabana* in shockingly bad taste. One doesn't speak despairingly of the dead."[12]

Groucho had no better luck with *Time for Elizabeth*, a play he co-wrote with Norman Krasna. It opened in New York on September 27, 1948, and closed after just eight performances.

Even radio seemed a dicey proposition. He was talked into hosting the radio quiz program *You Bet Your Life*, which first aired in October 1947, but was near the bottom of the ratings for the year. This led him to audition for roles he failed to land.[13] When asked why he so assiduously put himself through the auditions, he replied, "I knew I probably wouldn't make it as a quizmaster."[14] Groucho was spectacularly wrong about that. He won a Peabody Award in 1948, and when the show moved to television in 1949, he won an Emmy the next year, and was nominated for six others before the show went off the air in 1961.

Groucho had also begun to despair about the state of American comedy and could not have been happy with a 1949 Gallup poll in which the Marx Brothers were "consigned to the ranks of Hollywood's also-rans." They were ranked as just 13th on a list of the nation's 15 funniest comedians.[15] It would not be accurate to say that postwar American films lost their sense of humor, but the ground rules had changed dramatically. As Robert Sklar observed, during World War II, both military and civilian audiences showed a marked preference for escapist fare.[16]

That should have augured well for the Marx Brothers, but they faced new political realities. It is fair to ask why comedians such as Abbott and Costello, Milton Berle, Arthur Godfrey, Bob Hope, Danny Kaye and Red Skelton were suddenly deemed funnier than the Marx Brothers. Few today would agree with that assessment; after all, the Marxes made four of what the American Film Institute considers the 100 greatest comedies ever made. Some insight is embedded in the fact that Charlie Chaplin, who many consider history's greatest film comedian, ranked even lower in 1949.

Postwar American society was no longer as tolerant of those who challenged authority figures, lampooned its cultural heritage, or ridiculed institutions such as education, marriage, the medical establishment, military life or politics. Nor did the Marxes' penchant for anarchistic mayhem fit well within an emergent climate of social conformity. It was beside the point that there wasn't much controversial about more recent Marx Brothers fare such as *At the Circus* or *A Night in Casablanca*.

Love Happy represented an odd closing of the circle for the Marx Brothers. They made their first film in 1929, after the First Red Scare had ended, the Great Depression was about to begin, and it was perfectly acceptable—even expected—to question authority. They made their final feature film in 1949, when the Second Red Scare was about to supernova, the economy was booming, and it was dangerous to venture too far from mainstream values. One study reveals that the percentage of films dealing with "social problems" of any sort declined by more than 67 percent between the years 1947 and 1954.[17] As was discussed in the chapter on *Duck Soup*, wars have impacts on societies that linger far beyond the date peace treaties are signed. The Second Red Scare took the bloom off what Tom Engelhardt called "victory culture."[18]

The Second Red Scare, like its predecessor, targeted radicals real and imagined, even in Hollywood. "Red" was a broadly interpreted synonym for Communist. As early as 1937, conservatives created lists of those suspected of holding subversive views. The House Committee Investigating Un-American Activities—nicknamed the Dies Committee after its chair, Texas Democratic Martin Dies, Jr.—held hearings that year. Dies Committee members allegedly sought to ferret out Communists and fascists, though it was often a backdoor assault on New Deal programs, of which conservatives disapproved. Efforts were put on the back burner during the war, but were revigorated in 1945, under the name of the House Un-American Activities Committee (HUAC). It, a similar body in the U.S. Senate, and the FBI under the ideology-driven leadership of J. Edgar Hoover, cast suspicion upon thousands of Americans. Between 1940 and 1978, the FBI had an estimated 37,000 informants compiling dossiers on those suspected of disloyalty.[19]

Hollywood proved susceptible, in part because of labor strife in the industry, the Communist Party membership of a small number of entertainers during the Great Depression, and wartime movie content that cast the Soviet Union and Josef Stalin in a positive light. Films such as *Mission to Moscow* (1943), *The North Star* (1943) and *Song of Russia* (1944) were denounced as Communist propaganda, even though the Soviet Union was allied with the U.S. during the war and projects were produced in cooperation with the U.S. Office of War Information.[20]

Military leaders praised Hollywood's efforts during wartime, but what was heralded then was destined to be deemed un–American. In 1947, President Harry Truman issued Executive Order 9835, often called the Loyalty Order, as it required federal officials to sign oaths that they were not members of subversive groups. Some 20,000 employees were investigated and nearly 3000 either resigned or were fired.[21] Then it was Hollywood's turn. By one reckoning, just 50 or 60 actors, 15 or 20 producers, and no screenwriters had ever belonged to the Communist Party of the United States (CPUSA)—a legal political body until 1954—but HUAC went after the film industry anyway. Overnight, Hollywood was caught up in what historian David Caute called the "Great Fear."[22] Hollywood was rent into three distinct groups: "friendly witnesses" who revealed names of those they thought were disloyal, "unfriendly witnesses" who refused to cooperate with inquisitors, and those under suspicion who managed to avoid being called to the witness stand.

In 1947, HUAC subpoenaed selected writers and directors who were dubbed the "Hollywood Ten." They refused to cooperate and asserted First Amendment rights to free speech and association as their justification.[23] Each was cited for contempt of Congress and sentenced to a year in prison. This served to embolden Hollywood conservatives. The 1947 Waldorf Statement came immediately after the hearings and took the form of an agreement to blacklist those who should not be hired for any future projects.[24] Publications such as *Treason in Hollywood* and *Red Channels* kept up the pressure and expanded their reach to the new mass media phenomenon of television.

As would be the case during the sensational hearings held by Senator Joseph R. McCarthy between 1950 and 1953, no plots to overthrow the government involving anyone in Hollywood were unearthed. Nonetheless, blacklists and hearings of entertainment-industry figures persisted into the 1960s. Charlie Chaplin, an English citizen, left the States in 1952 and did not return for 20 years. Some of Hollywood's biggest stars, including Humphrey Bogart, Lauren Bacall, James Cagney, Melvyn Douglas, Fredric March and Edward G. Robinson found themselves under suspicion, though their A-list star power allowed them to continue working.

Hundreds with less stature in entertainment—singers, screenwriters, playwrights, directors and broadcasters—found themselves unemployable. One, Philip Loeb, who appeared with the Marx Brothers in *Room Service*, committed suicide in 1955 as a result of constant hounding. As one might suspect, many of those whose careers or lives were ruined by friendly witnesses such as Gary Cooper, Walt Disney, Elia Kazan, Louis Mayer, Ronald Reagan and Sam Wood never forgave their accusers.

Those looking for logic—if not justification—for what occurred during the Second Red Scare can find it in the tenor of the times. Events such as the Berlin Blockade and Airlift (1948–49), the Soviet Union's development of an atomic bomb (1949), the Communist revolution in China (1949) and the Korean War (1950–53) exacerbated fear. Celebrated spy arrests and/or accusations such as those leveled at Alger Hiss (1948), Klaus Fuchs (1950), Owen Lattimore (1950) and Julius and Ethel Rosenberg (1950) made credible the very idea of a widespread internal ring of subversives. Much of this was later discredited as Cold War hysteria but for legions of Americans, it did not appear so at the time.

Neither Hollywood nor television dared battle regulatory agencies or powerful politicians and hope to stay in business. Instead, they shifted with the political winds. The Nazis and ex–Nazi villains of mid–1940s films were supplanted by new malefactors, especially Communists and Native Americans. Safer still was to make mindless fare such as situation comedies or light-hearted fluff such as *Love Happy*.

Even then, the surveillance state was watching. Groucho was probably unaware of it, but the FBI compiled a 186-page dossier on him between 1953 and 1961, as Hoover suspected he might be an actual Marxist. Groucho was a frequent contributor to liberal causes and, back in 1934, was praised by *The Daily Worker*, a New York CPUSA newspaper. Mostly the FBI acted upon complaints about Groucho's wisecracks from those who saw Communists lurking behind every corner. Jerry Fielding, whose band played for Groucho's *You Bet Your Life* TV quiz show, later claimed he was fired when the FBI pressured the show's sponsor, DeSoto-Plymouth, to get rid of him as a "fellow traveler"[25] for refusing to name Groucho as a Communist. In a 1998 revelation of the accusations, *The Nation* quoted an apt Groucho line: "These are my principles. If you don't like them, I have others."[26]

How the Turkey Gobbled

Love Happy was the tamest movie the Marx Brothers ever made. Its working title was *Diamonds on the Sidewalk*. Wisely it was changed, as the film is devoid of precious jewels.

Let's return to Marilyn Monroe, as her brief appearance reveals a lot about the haplessness involved in trying to redeem *Love Happy*. Monroe's name appears on videotapes, DVDs and download graphics for the film as if she were a co-star. In some cases, her picture is bigger than that of the Marx Brothers. For pure hyperbole, though, it's hard to top come-ons that trumpet, "The Picture That Discovered Marilyn Monroe."

Hardly! Monroe was a relative unknown at the time, with *Love Happy* just her fourth walk-on, walk-off role. She had less than 60 seconds of screen time and her major contribution was to provide Grunion with one of the film's few funny lines. Monroe—whose character doesn't even have a name—walks into Grunion's office to plead for help: "Some men are following me." In a classic Groucho comeback, he arches an eyebrow and retorts, "Really? I can't imagine why." Years after she became a star, Groucho was asked what he recalled about her appearance in *Love Happy*. The best he could come up with was that she was "the most beautiful girl I ever saw in my life," and that for the few days she was on the set, she walked about bra-less.[27] That would have been unusual in a time in which women's bustlines were generally encased in architectural foundations.

When you watch the film, you understand why marketers directed our gaze away from the Marxes. Groucho's Grunion opens the film with a close-up in which recounts how he had long been on the trail of the disappeared royal Romanov diamonds and never expected his quest would take him to a "group of struggling young actors trying to put on a show." Was the name Sam a nod and a wink to Sam Spade, writer Dashiell Hammett's detective immortalized on the screen by Humphrey Bogart? Was Grunion chosen as a near rhyme with Runyon, as in writer-playwright-journalist Damon Runyon, famed for his stories of Broadway and the underworld? (Runyon wrote a short story that inspired the musical *Guys and Dolls*.) I'm not certain that the name Sam Grunion was intended as a semi-pun, but if that was the case, sadly, it was one of the film's better jokes.

Grunion's voiceover introduces us to the rehearsing singers and dancers trying to keep together body and soul, fend off bill collectors, and make it to opening night. Maggie Phillips (Vera-Ellen) is the principal dancer and the love interest of male lead Mike Johnson (Paul Valentine). Another cast member is big-voiced Bunny Dolan. She was played by Marion Hutton, sister of the more famous actress and musical star Betty Hutton, who matched movie hits with best-selling records. Marion's movie credits were more modest, but her vocal talents landed her a gig as a lead singer in the Glenn Miller Orchestra, the top swing band musician and conductor of his day.[28]

Love Happy contains glimpses of the show, including splashy musical numbers spotlighting Vera-Ellen and Valentine. Their performances received praise in some circles in 1950, a time when they were respected dancers. Now, though, their performances call attention to the fact that Valentine was no Gene Kelly, and Vera-Ellen wasn't the next Anna Pavlova. The film's musical numbers are most revealing today for the chorus line of dancing soldiers, another manifestation of post–World War II victory culture.

Harpo is connected with the show in a manner so ambiguous that he is variously described as its manager, a mascot, a tramp, a clown and a guardian angel (for feeding the cast). We first see him "helping" grocery shoppers into waiting vehicles by carrying their baskets to the curb, pilfering some of their purchases, and transferring them into his oversized coat.

He performs these feats outside of a grocery managed by Throckmorton (Melville Cooper), who also traffics in "hot" items. In this case, he is the middleman for the Romanov diamonds, which are slated to arrive to the store inside a sardine tin with a Maltese cross painted on the bottom. Throckmorton stands to collect a handsome sum once he hands them over to the mysterious Madame Egelichi (Ilona Massey).[29]

It is unclear who Madame Egelichi represents other than herself, but her role is in keeping with fortune-hunter, film noir movies, including the aforementioned *The Maltese Falcon.*

The search for missing Romanov jewels was a real thing. Romanov was the family name of Russia's last imperial family. They were deposed during the Bolshevik Revolution; Czar Nicholas II, Czarina Alexandra, their five children, and several others were executed by Communist partisans in 1918. Much of the Romanov fortune, including jewels and the royal crown, disappeared during the revolution. Some gems resurfaced and were sold at auction in 1927, with proceeds going to the cash-strapped Communist government. Some went on display as patrimony of the Soviet Union, other pieces subsequently reappeared, and some remain missing.

Harpo's shoplifting spree isn't quite over. He notices a food delivery truck arriving at Throckmorton's and hides behind boxes being unloaded to avoid a policeman. A freight elevator opens in the sidewalk and Harpo rides it to the basement storage room. He ducks into the shadows as boxes are unpacked and grabs whatever he can when delivery men are not looking. He even has an accordion-scissored grabber to lift goods from faraway shelves. Among the shipment items are cases of sardines. Throckmorton arrives in the storage room, locates the tin with the cross, and drops it into his suit jacket pocket. That's a dangerous place to keep things around the light-fingered Harpo: After a quick switcheroo, it's part of the haul he brings back to the hungry cast members. It remains backstage as the plot plods on.

Madame Egelichi is furious when Throckmorton produces a can of ordinary sardines. She orders her thugs, the Zoto brothers, to rough him up, assuming that Throckmorton has kept the jewels for himself. After a thorough thrashing, though, Egelichi is convinced he is innocent. She quizzes Throckmorton if he saw anyone suspicious near the store and he recalls seeing a "strange-looking creature" that looked like a tramp. This prompts Egelichi to ask the police to round up "bushy-haired" suspects and offers a $1,000 reward.

Chico makes his appearance as Faustino the Great, an alleged mind reader. He pleads for a job in the play and is present when Mr. Lyons (Leon Belasco), the producer, orders scenery and costumes to be collected in lieu of a promised $1,000 reimbursement by Yorkman, an underwriter Lyons now suspects doesn't exist. Faustino temporarily saves the day by telling Lyons he just left Yorkman's office and he still plans to bankroll the play. Faustino's quick thinking lands him a position, though no one stands to be paid until the play opens. When Harpo arrives in a coat bulging with food, the actors pounce on him like lions bringing down a wildebeest. In seconds, they empty his pockets and leave him dazed and crumbled in a corner.

Harpo knows Faustino and offers him his remaining can of sardines, which Faustino slaps aside because he was promised "something special." Harpo produces an ice cream cone from another pocket—tootsie-fruitsie, no less. Rehearsals resume with Bunny singing "Mama Wants to Know," an amusing ditty that turns ominous as Mama promises to "kick some teeth in" unless the child who stole the jam from her grocery bag confesses. The kids are represented by dolls that Bunny slaps and grabs. Mama isn't exactly making nice.

When we flip back to the grocery store, the police parade before Throckmorton a bunch of dodgy tramps with bushy hair—including Harpo. Throckmorton whispers to Egelichi that he's the one he saw and she saves $1,000 by telling the police they've not found the right man. She feigns concern and tells the cops to leave Harpo behind so she can help him. Throckmorton promptly threatens Harpo, but of course, he's not talking. Egelichi demonstrates another talent to go with treasure-hunting and cruelty: mesmerism. She removes her jacket to reveal a scandalously revealing décolletage, stares into Harpo's eyes, and places a "whammy" on him. Egelichi pulls Harpo to her breasts, but she can't get a word out of him. The Zotos take a crack at him. They begin to pull things out of his coat in perhaps the film's funniest silent sequence. Among the contents of his coat are a barber's pole, a welcome mat, the legs from a mannequin, a horse collar, a block of ice, sleigh bells, a sled and a live dog. But no necklace.

Harpo is subsequently spun upon a roulette wheel, subjected to food and water deprivation, and even has an apple shot from atop his head; he grabs and devours it like a crazed beast. He is placed in a locked room, and Egelichi listens on an extension line when Harpo calls Faustino. He communicates entirely in horn beeps and whistles, but Egelichi infers from Faustino's decoding that the sardine tin is at the theater. Harpo escapes by jumping out the window with a parachute he made from curtains.

These gags are pretty lame, but they're better than watching Maggie cavort about the stage as a ballerina, or dressed as a cross between a showgirl and a courtesan. Lyons again arrives to repossess the scenery and costumes, but this time he is only deterred long enough to play violin accompaniment to Faustino's piano on "Gypsy Love Song." In this small scene, Chico has his only good lines in the picture. Before he begins, he announces, "We play it allegro pizzicato.[30] That's what-a you call high-class Carnegie Hall stuff. You know allegro pizzicato?" When Lyons admits he doesn't, Faustino follows up: "You know Jimmy Pizzicato? ... None of the Pizzicatos, huh?" When pressed to name who he does know, Lyons gives his answer: "Er, I know pistachio." That's good enough for Faustino.

Lyons strips the show of all its props. Mike refuses to perform in street clothes on a bare stage, so all appears to be lost—and on Maggie's birthday, no less. Egelichi appears in the guise of a patron willing to underwrite the show so she can learn where the diamonds are hidden. Little does she know that the marked sardine tin has been set out in the alley for a cat's supper. Egelichi comes on to Mike, who takes her to dinner instead of Maggie. Maggie is crestfallen, and Harpo tries to cheer her up by giving her a necklace he found in the alley. It's the Romanov diamonds, though neither he nor she knows it.

More silly things happen, including the appearance of a small penguin in a tuxedo-like costume, Harpo's reversible mirror that allows him to comb first the front and then the back of his hair, a woeful scene in which Egelichi feigns interest in Faustino to gain access to the show's supply of sardines, and Grunion's brief encounter with Marilyn Monroe. As these things occur, Throckmorton finds the empty sardine tin in the alley, concludes the cat has eaten the necklace and sends it off to be examined. We hope it was treated better than Hutton's dolls. The crunch comes when Maggie is about ready to take the stage and Mike tells her to take off the necklace Harpo gave her because it looks "too phony." Maggie tosses it into an open piano but shortly thereafter is grabbed by Egelichi's henchmen because the fake jewels on the back of her costume look like the missing diamonds. She and others are freed by Faustino and Harpo. The show goes on and Egelichi notices the jewels bouncing off the piano strings when Chico plays forcefully.

All this rigmarole leads to a chase scene in which Harpo has the real necklace, but a fake one is also in play. Egelichi's hirelings chase Harpo to the theater rooftop. There are visual allusions to film noir in which lights flash on and off, thereby allowing Harpo to disappear into shadows at precisely the moment he is almost apprehended. As mentioned earlier, producer Lester Cowan turned out to be a real-life Yorkman, an underwriter without money who shamelessly sold as much advertising as he could. We watch Harpo cavort near big signs flogging Baby Ruth candy bars, Fisk tires, General Electric, Wheaties cereal, Mobil Oil, Bulova watches and Kool cigarettes. Mobil's logo was the flying horse Pegasus and Kool's was a cigarette-puffing penguin. Harpo rides a neon Pegasus and swings on the sweep second hand of a giant Bulova watch in ways reminiscent of Harold Lloyd's famed scene in the 1923 silent *Safety Last*. When Harpo is thrown into the mouth of the Kool penguin, he inhales enough smoke to exhale and overcome his pursuers.

Faustino appears holding the real jewels, but is felled by a door and drops them. Grunion reappears, only to be confronted by a gun-toting Egelichi. The existence of two sets of jewels is a quintessential Chekhov's gun scenario that requires uncertainty over who possesses the real ones. When the smoke clears, so to speak, Harpo waddles off with the real jewels in his pocket. Grunion informs us that Harpo was never seen again. Grunion's office phone rings and it's his wife, "formerly Madame Egelichi." An echo of the *Love Happy* theme song completes the trite ending.

Stage Paste

The best that can be said about *Love Happy* is that there weren't any elephants in the room.

- **Gimbel's basement:** In his opening monologue, Groucho tosses off a quick, amusing line. He says that his 11-year search for the Romanov diamonds has taken him around the globe, and ticks off the places he's been. He ends with "and into Gimbel's basement." Groucho's joke is that he searched for the Romanov jewels in the department store's bargain basement.

- **Going native?** Some might wonder why there is a brief rehearsal scene in which "natives" do a quick circle dance. They are clearly costumed actors, and there was no intent to pass them off as indigenous Asian people. They represent U.S. involvement in the Pacific Theater during World War II.

- **Raymond Burr:** The Zoto brothers were played by Bruce Gordon and Raymond Burr. Burr subsequently gained fame in television playing defense attorney Perry Mason in one of TV's top-rated shows. When *Perry Mason* went off the air, he took on the title role in *Ironside*. His character, Robert Ironside, was a police consultant who used a wheelchair. *Ironside* was what was then a rare portrayal of a physically challenged lead character.

- **Accents:** The only phony accent in the film is Chico's. Ilona Massey, who played Madame Egelichi, was Hungarian. That accent landed her numerous spy roles requiring a foreign *femme fatale*.

- **Look closely!** When Harpo's coat is emptied after Egelichi's double whammy, there are two subtle movie jokes take place, though you might need a magnifying glass to see them. The mailbox tumbling out of his pocket sports the name Moss Kaufman, a mash-up of playwrights Moss Hart and George S. Kaufman, friends of the Marxes. The sled bears the name "Rosebud," a nod to the final scene of *Citizen Kane*.[31]

- **Empty-headed:** Harpo clears his head by running a handkerchief through one ear and out the other and pulling the ends back and forth. This is an old sight gag used by the Three Stooges and many others.

- **Odd names:** Egelichi's name sounds odd, but several others are funnier, such as Mackinaw and Count Bouillabaisse. Mackinaw is a small city in Michigan, but also a felted material—often checked and called buffalo plaid—used in blankets, shirts and jackets as it is water-resistant. Bouillabaisse is a seafood-based soup popular in the Provençal region of France.

- **Zlotys:** We learn that Grunion was paid 100,000 zlotys to help recover the Romanov diamonds. The zloty was Polish currency, but the inside joke is 100,000 zlotys would have been about $525. That's not much incentive to locate $1,000,000 worth of jewels and certainly not enough to bankroll an 11-year global search!

- **Speaking Jolson?** The second time Faustino tries to figure out what Harpo is trying to tell him, Harpo goes down on one knee to get Faustino to come up with "Maggie" via the "ma" consonant. Chico guesses Al Jolson, and that's on the right track; Harpo is miming Jolson singing "Mammy" in the 1927 film *The Jazz Singer*.

- **Can't go there!** Grunion and Egelichi suspect each other of holding the diamonds. He reaches to search her, but that would have been a major violation of Hays Office guidelines. Instead, Grunion utters the aside, "If this were a French film, I could do it." Production codes were much looser in France, and nudity was sometimes depicted on the screen. Consider Groucho's remark a symbolic leer.

- **Dog's luck:** Near the end of the film, we see Faustino playing cards with a dog and losing. Given Chico's luck, it could have happened.
- **Promises, promises:** Groucho was promised $35,000 for what was supposed to be a two-minute cameo in *Love Happy*. He ended up with about ten minutes of screen time. For being a mensch, he had to sue Lester Cowan and Mary Pickford to get his salary.
- **Ben Hecht:** The film was briefly banned in Britain when it was discovered that Ben Hecht had an uncredited writing role. Hecht was a convert to Zionism and a harsh critic of British treatment of Jews in Palestine. He went so far as to support clandestine Jewish groups that attacked British soldiers and once made the intemperate remark of experiencing a "little holiday in my heart" when one was killed. Hecht was later praised for helping Jewish refugees settle in the newly created state of Israel. British authorities ultimately decided that Hecht's involvement in *Love Happy* was too small and too well-hidden to hold up the film.[32]

Final Reckonings

Love Happy took in $2.2 million, which wasn't as embarrassing as the film. It was clear, though, that audiences preferred to see stars such as Kirk Douglas, Van Johnson, Gene Kelly, Gregory Peck, Frank Sinatra, James Stewart and John Wayne. Comedies starring Lucille Ball, Bing Crosby, Cary Grant, Katharine Hepburn, Bob Hope, Jerry Lewis, Dean Martin, and Spencer Tracy raked in much higher grosses.

The *New York Times* liked *Love Happy* and *Variety* noted—with an arched eyebrow, one imagines—that the Marxes could "get away with almost anything."[33] It was not a good sign, though, that some reviewers commented more on Massey, Vera-Ellen and Hutton than the Marxes.

Allen Eyles felt that Harpo still exuded "youthful gaiety" and that his routines were "quite convincingly executed." Eyles also thought that Groucho's work "looks more like an afterthought, which is exactly what Groucho thought."[34] Because Cowan ran out of money, nothing got fixed or re-shot. As Arce noted, production values "were of the cheapest sort."[35] Thus, as Louvish observed, the film that reached the screen had "a plotline that made very little sense and appeared to have been hammered out by the Ritz Brothers on amateur night in the Catskills." With a gift for understatement, he noted, "The experience of shooting *Love Happy* was dire."[36]

Marx aficionados weighed in with verdicts similar to Louvish's. Ronald Bergan decried "the mistake of unbalancing a great three-man act [that] tried to force Harpo into sentimentality." Martin Gardner said that the film had "practically no satire to add spice...." As usual, Adamson pulled no punches. He called *Love Happy* one of the films that "conjure up horror, depression and nausea in the heart of any comedy fan."[37]

The Marxes had grown stale. Nearly everything that might have been funny was material that had been done much better previously. One might even say it had been done to death. Harpo stuffs things into his big coat. Check. Uses his flaming fingers to light candles. Check. Engages in acrobatics. Check. There are harp and piano solos. Check. Chico struggles to make sense of Harpo's whistles and beeps. Check. Has no money. Check. Groucho isn't in the movie for very long, but Sam Grunion is Wolf J. Flywheel with a more convincing mustache. And so it went until Harpo wanders into the fog at the film's end as if he were guilty exactly as Groucho charged: behaving as if he were Charlie Chaplin's Little Tramp.

The Marx Brothers made 13 films in 20 years, several of them comedy masterpieces, and with enough chuckles to make even their weaker films watchable. Alas, you would have to search harder than Sam Grunion to find uproarious humor in *Love Happy*. It was not the sort of departing gift one would have wished from comics of the Marxes' stature. In the entertainment world, final acts often disappoint. *Love Happy* disillusioned so thoroughly that not even Chico could convince his brothers to undertake another film.

This Is the End

Five, Four, Three, Two, One... Zero

Fade Away

As most celebrities can attest, time is a harsh mistress. The lucky ones enjoy second lives as commentators, producers, directors, media moguls and talk show guests. Most fade from public consciousness and exist in the murky realm where nostalgia occasionally intersects with the present: revival tours, retrospectives and late-night cable broadcasts. Rarer still, a new generation arises that finds their tastes simpatico with those of bygone legends.

By the time *Love Happy* opened in 1950, the Marx Brothers were already fading stars. Within a few years, audiences shifted their preferences to younger talents such as Marlon Brando, Audrey Hepburn, Rock Hudson, Grace Kelly, Jack Lemmon, Jerry Lewis, Elizabeth Taylor and, yes, Marilyn Monroe.[1] Younger Americans are generally the biggest consumers of popular culture and the Marx Brothers belonged to their parents' generation. By mid-decade, white youth had new icons, including Brando, Dick Clark, James Dean, Alan Freed, Bill Haley, Frankie Lyman, Sal Mineo, Ricky Nelson, Paul Newman and Natalie Wood. Black youth—and a considerable number of whites—idolized figures such as Harry Belafonte, Chuck Berry, Nat "King" Cole, Dorothy Dandridge, Ossie Davis, Sammy Davis, Jr., Ruby Dee, Bo Diddley, Little Richard, the Platters and Sidney Poitier. Above all others stood Elvis Presley and former Marx Brothers bit player Lucille Ball.

In 1957, Buddy Holly and the Crickets released a catchy love song titled "Not Fade Away." Metaphorically speaking, "fade away" is precisely what happened to the Marx Brothers as an ensemble act. Groucho enjoyed another 11 years of fame by adapting to the television, but even he was preferred more by parents than by their offspring.

It was hard to watch a Marx Brothers movie in the 1950s. Until the advent of cable during the 1970s, three networks—ABC, CBS and NBC—dominated programing. As noted in the introduction, most American homes relied on antennae to receive TV broadcasts. With an average range of under 60 miles, one had to live near a major city or transmitter to receive a signal, often not a very clear one. Televising a Hollywood film required either buying the film, negotiating broadcast rights, or waiting for its copyright to expire.

This—and changing values—explains why Marx Brothers films were not "rediscovered" until the 1960s. A new generation of young people shaped by civil rights protests, the Vietnam War and evolving styles and morals found consonance with the Marxes'

The brothers gather for *The Tonight Show*, circa 1961. Left to right: Harpo, Zeppo, Chico, Groucho, Gummo (Ethel Kirsner, NBC press employee, via Wikimedia Commons).

anarchic energy, irreverence and lampoons of authority figures. Until then, one seldom found the Marx Brothers on television, except as guest stars recounting past glories.

Not Fade Away: Post-Hollywood

The Marxes made no more Marx Brothers feature films, but they had not entirely faded away.

In 1957, they took part in *The Story of Mankind*, a film that makes *Love Happy* look like *Gone with the Wind.* Warner Brothers inexplicably greenlighted a picture directed and produced by Irwin Allen based on a 1921 children's book written by the wonderfully christened Dutch-American Hendrik Willem von Loon. That name is the best thing about the project. Its endlessly recycled premise is that humankind is on trial, with the Devil (Vincent Price) prosecuting its shortcomings and the Spirit of Mankind (Ronald Colman) defending its creativity and adaptability.

It's a collection of vignettes involving 28 major and numerous secondary actors spread across just 100 minutes, so no one was on screen for very long. Human history is sampled through figures such as Cleopatra, Hitler, Lincoln, Napoleon, Moses and Shakespeare.

The Marxes do not appear together. Chico is a nameless monk, but his affected Italian accent is appropriate for a chat with the Genoa-born Cristoforo Colombo, better known as Columbus. Chico tries to talk Columbus (Anthony Dexter) out of an "impossible" voyage that will end by sailing off the edge of the Earth. Columbus asks the monk to consider that the Earth is round, and from that point on, Chico doesn't do much except nod and say "buono." Just as Chico liked it, a paycheck without doing much.

Harpo is on screen for about two minutes. He sits under an apple tree, plays "Beautiful Dreamer" on the harp and whistles the same tune. An apple plonks him on the head and he angrily shakes his fist at the tree. It happens again and, as a voiceover informs us, Sir Isaac Newton has learned that "what goes up must come down" (the principle of gravity). The scene ends with Harpo pushing an apple through his harp strings to slice it. The best thing about it is that we see Harpo's red wig in full color.

Groucho got nearly four minutes on screen. His, though, was an embarrassing sequence. We see a group of Native Americans in Great Plains garb sitting under a tree when the cigar-smoking Groucho and several others drift into the shot dressed in stereotypical Pilgrim costumes. The chief says, "How!" and Groucho's Peter Minuet says, "Three minutes and leave it in the shell." The scene is reminiscent of the Indian village scene in *Go West*, this time with Minuet and the chief discussing the price for purchasing Manhattan Island.

The chief wants to sell so he can move West, which prompts Groucho's crack, "You're crazy to go West ... it's full of Indians." As they quibble over the sale price, a brave in the background says one thing and the chief another. Minuet intervenes to say, "One answer between the two of you, please," which those of the day would have recognized as the instruction Groucho gave to *You Bet Your Life* contestants. Minuet convinces the chief to accept $24 for Manhattan and begins to write a check using the back of the chief's beautiful daughter Laughing Water as a makeshift desk. Her fringed dress rides high on her thigh and she is strangely smitten with Minuet. The chief doesn't want a check and takes merchandise instead, per the legend that Minuet "bought" Manhattan for $24 worth of trinkets. Minuet gets both Manhattan and the girl.

Groucho got the girl in real life as well. Laughing Water—the term is slang for alcohol—was Eden Hartford, Groucho's third wife. She was a lovely young woman, *young* being the opera-tive word; she was 24 and he 40 years her senior. The chief could be said to be a tribesman, but not of the Native American sort. He was Burma-born Abra-ham Sofaer, a descendent of Iraqi Jews. The "brave" was Groucho's old friend, lyricist Harry Ruby. To complete the family saga, Melinda Marx, Groucho's 21-year-old daughter with Kay Gorcey, appeared as an extra in a different segment.

I wish I could say that these were the three worst sequences in the film. *The Story of Mankind* has been called one of the worst movies ever made. It invites descriptors such as bewil-dering, dreck and rubbish.

The three brothers

Harpo and Chico pull a heist in the *General Electric Theater* episode "The Incredible Jewel Robbery" (1959) (*General Electric Theater*, CBS television, via Wiki-media Commons).

appeared together in an episode of the CBS show *General Electric Theater* on March 8, 1959. *GE Theater* (1953–62) featured 30-minute segments that were mostly original takes on some work of fiction, play, or movie. Its host was future governor of California and president of the United States Ronald Reagan.

Chico and Harpo starred in "The Incredible Jewel Robbery," with Groucho in a cameo role. It is filmed as if it were a vintage silent movie. The film stock is deliberately scratchy and the episode features a "caper film"–worthy piano soundtrack. Harpo and Chico select paint and brushes as part of a plan to paint an automobile to look like a police cruiser. Harpo dons a disguise: a mask with spectacles and a mustache known then and now as "Groucho glasses." He enters Wayfair Jewels and, at gunpoint, relieves the manager of precious jewelry. Chico, disguised as a cop, enters to "arrest" Harpo, cuff him and place him inside the repainted car.

As they drive off, they continually encounter other police officers, though Chico nods, smiles and drives away. The boys would have pulled it off except for a small detail: They got the police logo wrong. They painted a black circle with white letters instead of a white one with black letters. They are arrested and placed in a lineup, and the manager identifies them. In some versions, Groucho simply joins them at the end to mug for the camera; in others, he speaks the only words heard in the film: "We won't talk until we see our lawyer." "The Incredible Jewel Robbery" was a clever throwback to the silent days.

When There Were Five

Even when the brothers were at the height of their popularity, each took part in projects beyond their 13 feature films. Sometimes just two of them teamed, as Groucho and Chico did on radio productions; sometimes they soloed. Groucho hosted or guested on many radio shows. Harpo turned up in *Stage Door Canteen* (1943) and occasional stage shows.[2] Chico was more suited for movie promos and radio, especially the latter. From 1932 through the 1940s, he was involved in several shows with Groucho, hosted one of his own (*Chico's Barber Shop*), and guested on at least nine others. Even Harpo did some radio work, usually with someone translating his non-verbal antics. There is, however, delicious irony in that he was the first Marx to speak on the wireless (in 1926).

These independent projects continued once they stopped making movies, thanks in large part to television. By 1951, there were 12 million TVs in American homes—up from fewer than 6,000 five years earlier.

Harpo came the closest to retirement in the conventional sense. He, Susan and their four adopted children moved to a new home near Palm Springs in 1957. There, the family enjoyed swimming, horseback riding and watching Groucho on *You Bet Your Life*. Harpo also played his namesake instrument, dabbled in painting, and golfed. Yet not even he avoided basking in celebrity fame. In all, Harpo made more than a dozen appearances on the small screen. He explained, "I hadn't moved to the desert to retire, not by a long shot.... I kept up a fairly busy schedule of concerts, benefits and guest appearances...."[3] As we have seen, he even recreated the *Duck Soup* mirror scene with Lucille Ball.

Harpo's tours with Chico underscored a comment Groucho made: "We all ended up supporting Chico until the day he died.... We would get angry with Chico for being such a schmuck and losing all his money, but that was the extent of it. We all loved Chico."[4] Maxine, who often harbored a grudge against Uncle Groucho, confirmed that fights with Chico were brief, and ventured that the brothers were often fonder of each other than of their respective wives and children. (That was an overstatement; Harpo was a devoted husband and father.) According to Maxine, "Chico persuaded Harpo, who really didn't need the money, to join him in an act consisting of bits and pieces from their pictures and ending with a piano and harp routine."[5] They performed a few times a year in resort areas such as Miami, Las Vegas and Reno, and occasionally in England. Sometimes those tours pushed Harpo to the limits of his tolerance. Bill Marx recalled that his father was "disgusted" by the "blue" (obscene) material in Chico's act when they went to England and didn't want to return to the stage with Chico, though the two overcame that obstacle. Harpo was usually offered a 75-25 money split to appear with Chico, but always insisted on a 50-50 split.[6]

Chico had fewer show business friends upon whom he could prevail, but he appeared on TV whenever he could. He was actually the first Marx to appear on television, as a guest on Milton Berle's show in 1948. He briefly starred in the comedy series *The College Bowl* in 1950 and '51, but it turned out to be the last time Chico had his own show. Thereafter—aside from "The Incredible Jewel Robbery"—he was relegated to a handful of guest appearances. His last was a 1959 sighting on *Championship Bridge.* In keeping with history, he lost.[7]

Groucho constantly complained that he disliked making movies, but you would never know it from the list of post–*Love Happy* films in which he appeared. These included *Mr. Music* (1950), *Double Dynamite* (1951), *A Girl in Every Port* (1952), *Will Success Spoil Rock Hunter?* (1957) and *Skidoo* (1968), in which he played God. Make of that what you will! Other than Gummo and Zeppo, who toiled on the agency end of movies, Groucho was the only member of the core three comedy team who had much to do with the silver screen.

Groucho worked constantly, though he certainly didn't need the money; his net worth was estimated at $12 million in 1977, the equivalent of nearly $51,800,000 in 2021. He also dabbled in stage productions, including summer stock revivals of *Time for Elizabeth* in the late '50s and 1960. He never really established himself as a dramatic actor, but he did indulge his love for Gilbert and Sullivan operettas. In 1960, he appeared in an NBC production of *The Mikado* that also starred veteran British comic actor Stanley Holloway, Broadway luminary Dennis King, and Groucho's daughter Melinda. Groucho played Ko-Ko, the tailor who becomes Lord High Executioner, but mostly he played Groucho. He wore a bald cap to simulate a Japanese *chonmage*, an Edo period hairstyle involving the shaving of the middle of the head, but he also wore his glasses, added Fu Manchu–like extensions to his mustache, sang in a New York accent, and danced with the leg gyrations showcased in Marx Brothers movies. In 1970, he helped promote the Broadway musical comedy *Minnie's Boys,* based on the Marx Brothers' early show business days. The book was written by his son Arthur.

Mostly, though, Groucho was a TV celebrity. He appeared many times on the small screen, in specials, as a talk show guest, and a host. He developed a late-in-life friendship with Dick Cavett and frequently appeared on his talk show. In 1969, Cavett did something nearly unfathomable by the standards of today's talk shows: He devoted all 90 minutes of his program to an in-depth interview of Groucho.[8] Cavett also introduced Groucho's one-man show at Carnegie Hall in 1972.

Groucho was an in-demand guest for virtually everyone, but he was best known for *You Bet Your Life*, a series that showcases Groucho's comedic timing. The format was simple: Producers chose a man and a woman to be on the stage with Groucho, who interviewed them before they took part in a quiz. A "secret word" was chosen in advance and if either of the guests uttered it, "Julius," a toy duck that sported Groucho's birth name and a pair of Groucho glasses, descended from above and the couple split $100.

The quiz part of the show allowed the couple to compete for more money, but Groucho's interviews were legendary. He recycled old lines and was rumored to have prepared material in reserve, but he mostly ad-libbed. When Groucho and/or his sidekick George Fenneman were amused or detected an avenue for humor, Groucho masterfully raised his brow and paused. His enigmatic Mona Lisa smile signaled that he was about to unload a zinger.[9]

When the show was cancelled after 13 seasons, Groucho hosted a 1961–62 show titled *Tell It to Groucho*, but it lasted just six episodes. By then, Groucho was again an icon instantly recognizable by his bow tie, glasses, cigar and a mustache that was all his own. For much of his remaining life, Groucho was famous for being famous. He reveled in the renewed popularity of Marx Brothers films during the 1960s and 1970s.

Groucho with sidekick George Fenneman on the set of TV's *You Bet Your Life* in 1951. Fenneman played the straight man to Groucho on both the radio and television versions (NBC Radio, via Wikimedia Commons).

Five, Four....

Chico divorced Betty in 1940, but she remained a presence in his life for years thereafter. By the 1950s, he was involved with Mary De Vithas—called "Mary Dee" by most—and married her in 1958. Despite her best efforts as lover and wife, Mary confided to Maxine, "I can't talk sense to your father. He just laughs at me, or worse, agrees to lay off wild nights and then goes ahead and does what he wants to do."[10]

He worked during the 1950s but, as usual, his wallet could not keep pace with his fast living. He owed $70,000 in back taxes. A 1958 appearance in an episode of the CBS series *Playhouse 90* netted him just $1,000, a far cry from the sort of paychecks he enjoyed during his film days. He later told Maxine that he lost about $2 million gambling, which was probably a lowball estimate. A well-traveled tale holds that Chico claimed that Harpo's net worth was how much he lost gambling.

Chico yearned for a lucrative project, but when that chance came along, he was too ill to cash in. Groucho and Harpo had preliminary discussions with director Billy Wilder to make a comedy caper whose working title was *A Day at the United Nations*. Chico suffered another serious heart attack just four days after Groucho's last broadcast of *You Bet Your Life* on June 29, 1961. The brothers visited Chico in the hospital and found his sense of humor intact. At one point he joked that he wanted to be buried with a deck of cards, a golf club and a blonde. The jokes ended on October 19, 1961, when various heart ailments silenced his voice forever.[11] He had lived to be 74, which was remarkable for someone who paid roughly the same amount of attention to his health as he did to his bank account.

The brothers were stone-faced during his funeral, an awkward affair given Mary's insistence that he have a religious service (Chico had shown little interest in such matters in life). Gummo procured a rabbi who never met Chico. When it was over, Groucho said he should have delivered the eulogy himself. Harpo told Maxine, "Listen, when I go, do me a favor and hire a mime."[12] The rites were well-attended, though, and included George Burns, Jimmy Durante and Buster Keaton. Later that night, Groucho, normally a light drinker, tossed back four whiskey sours and got drunk.[13] Maybe he wasn't quite as hard-hearted as Maxine suspected.

Four, Three....

Three years later, Harpo died after years of declining health. He said he hadn't moved to Palm Springs to retire, but he did so—at least four times. In 1953, Harpo spoke of how "lucky" he was to be "an old faun's ass of 65, the father of four children aged from 15 to 22, sitting in an air-conditioned house, admiring the spectacle of the California desert while I made music, with nothing to worry about other than whether I should keep on making music ... and then play nine holes of golf, or quit now and play 18 holes."[14]

In 1958, Harpo suffered a mild heart attack. In those days, doctors often prescribed complete rest. Harpo was told to retire, meaning, "No more work. No more engagements of any kind. No more golf. No more harp. Nothing but pure, full-time leisure."[15] Then it dawned on Harpo that this was a lousy prescription for someone whose joys in life included playing music and making others laugh.

Thereafter, he retired and unretired "three times ... after a total of three heart attacks."[16] His major concession to retirement was to take up painting. His son Bill thought his father quite talented with a brush, though Harpo was more modest (and realistic) about his own talents. According to Harpo, until he switched from watercolors to tempera and from realism to abstraction, "Every summer landscape I did turned into Vermont as seen from Neshobe Island. Every winterscape looked like Watertown, New York, as seen from a hotel window. Every figure I did turned into a guy in the rain under a black umbrella. The black umbrella had no significance except it was the best way to cover up the guy's face when it didn't turn out right—and it never turned out right."[17]

Harpo was a restless patient who tried and failed to follow medical advice. His new roundtable at the Hillcrest Country Club provided only partial diversion, as many of its members were working show business friends. Against orders, Harpo practiced the harp again and putted golf balls. Susan called Gummo, his agent, and told him not to accept any public appearance offers for Harpo. He was angry about that, but five days after taking up the harp again, Harpo suffered another heart attack. The result was, in the words of baseball great Yogi Berra, *déjà vu* all over again: He came home from the hospital, apologized to Gummo, and vowed he was truly retired.

He didn't mean it. Harpo found it hard to do nothing, and when his children visited, their offers to help him relax annoyed him. Even Susan lost patience and suggested that Harpo should take a trip. To get out of everyone's hair, Harpo flew to Las Vegas and had an amusing encounter with Milt Jaffe, the sports promoter whose $10,000 loan in 1929 saved Harpo's career. The trip revitalized him. In his words, "I had just recovered from the longest and most serious illness I ever had: retirement."[18]

Harpo dusted off his costume, bought new golf clubs, played the harp again, painted, gardened and made TV appearances. His last performance came at the Pasadena Theatre on January 19, 1963, when he appeared with his neighbor, comedy writer and song parodist Allan Sherman. Harpo announced his retirement and proceeded to give a speech—of sorts. It was actually his bar mitzvah speech![19]

Alas, Harpo's health again declined. Gummo convinced him to undergo heart bypass surgery, a procedure now considered a heart surgeon's equivalent of basic plumbing. In 1964, though, it was so new that it was considered by many as experimental. Harpo underwent surgery on September 26, 1964, and died of a seizure two days later. Groucho was inconsolable when Harpo passed. Arthur Marx claimed that it the only time he ever saw his father cry.[20] Harpo's daughter Minnie postponed her marriage to John M. Eagle, Jr., when her father died. When she finally walked down the aisle on November 28, 1964, Groucho gave her away. As Arthur noted, "there was something special" about the relationship between Harpo and Groucho.[21]

That's because there was something special about Harpo. His was a remarkable life built upon improbabilities. He and Chaplin were among the few performers to move from silent pictures to talkies and maintain their silence. (Or mostly so in Chaplin's case.) Consider also that Harpo held his own in the midst of two groups of wits and intellectuals, the Algonquin Round Table in New York and the Hillcrest Country Club clique in Los Angeles.[22] Not bad for a guy who left school at age eight and never looked back. Harpo was the ultimate autodidact.

Bill remarked that his father "died with no enemies."[23] Groucho claimed, "He inherited all of my mother's good qualities—kindness, understanding and friendliness. I got what was left."[24] Harpo has been called a clown, an imp and a mime, but I've always seen him as analogous to Shakespeare's Puck from *A Midsummer Night's Dream*: mischievous, but magical. Many others agree. More than five decades after his death, websites such as Harpo's Place[25] continue to see heavy traffic. For Marx Brothers newcomers, Harpo is usually the character to which they first gravitate.

2½ ... 2 ....

On March 6, 1965, another integral member of the Marx Brothers ensemble passed away: Margaret Dumont. She was not a blood relative, but Groucho dubbed her the *de facto* sixth Marx Brother. Dumont lived to be 82, never remarried after her husband's death in 1918, and worked infrequently after World War II. As previously noted, she once complained that the Marxes ruined her career by typecasting her as a clueless straight woman. In 1964, *Village Voice* writer Andrew Sarris took Groucho to task for treating her "shamefully."[26]

Both Dumont and Sarris were off the mark. Sarris inferred things that never happened and recoiled at sexist jokes that were the norm at the time. The sad reality is that a deeper form of sexism was at play than the one Sarris identified. In 1950, film legend Gloria Swanson appeared in the now-classic film *Sunset Blvd.* in the tailor-made role of Norma Desmond, a faded silent movie icon. When another character exclaims, "You're Norma Desmond. You used to be big," Desmond frostily replies, "I *am* big, it's the pictures that got small." It's a line that can be taken many ways, including a back-door mention of TV, but Swanson was just 50 when she uttered it.

In Hollywood, 50 was ancient for actresses. So was 40, for that matter. Dumont was 47 when she made her first movie with the Marx Brothers in 1929. As an "older" actress she was frequently cast as a dowager, and not just in Marx Brothers films. She was also almost always cast in comedies, though she longed for more dramatic roles. When *all* roles dried up, Groucho made discrete inquiries on her behalf through his friend Arthur Sheekman, who wrote plays and movie scripts. When Groucho received an honorary Oscar in 1974, he told the audience, "I only wish Harpo and Chico could have been here—and Margaret Dumont." He repeated the old canard that she didn't get his jokes, but called her "a great straight woman and I loved her."[27]

It was only fitting that Dumont's last public performance took place on February 26, 1965, on *The Hollywood Palace*, a variety show guest-emceed by Groucho. In a skit introduced by Melinda Marx, Groucho and Dumont recreated Dumont's *Animal Crackers* introduction of Captain Spaulding and the singing of "Hooray for Captain Spaulding." Dumont looked radiant in a full-length black gown and she laughed easily at Groucho's ad-libs.[28] Other than moving a bit stiffly, she appeared hale; eight days later, she died.[29]

On April 21, 1977, Milton "Gummo" Marx suffered a fatal brain hemorrhage. He was six months shy of his 84th birthday. Gummo was the brother who said no to his mother's plans, insisting that acting wasn't in his blood. Of that ability he joked, "For many years after I quit the stage, people referred to me as an actor, but during my career most people vehemently denied this."[30] As his son Robert recounted, a stuttering problem made him "very nervous on stage."[31]

During World War I, Gummo disappointed Minnie again by joining the Army.[32] He was not sent overseas, and his assessment of his acting skills notwithstanding, his status as a vaudevillian gained him special privileges that embarrassed him.[33]

Gummo married Helen (Theaman) von Tilzer in March 1929, nuptials accompanied by a nasty lawsuit. Helen had been married to R. Russell von Tilzer, who died on February 5, 1928. Helen assigned care of their daughter Kay to her in-laws, Jack and

Isabelle von Tilzer. In her 1929 lawsuit, Helen asserted that she was tricked into giving up custody via a document she thought was for temporary guardianship.[34] The courts found in her favor and Gummo adopted Kay. In 1930, Helen and Gummo welcomed a biological child, Robert.

Gummo struggled to find his way. He invented and patented a laundry-sorting system that used less cardboard, but his attempt at a non-skid tire failed.[35] His women's-garment business was moderately successful, but not enough to weather the Great Depression. When he closed shop in 1933, he headed a household of four but was more than $100,000 in debt.

The decision of Groucho, Chico and Harpo to select Gummo as their agent might have been an act of charity, but it proved a sound investment. In 1933, Zeppo also quit the act, and shortly thereafter Gummo joined his younger brother's talent agency. Gummo handled most of the Marx Brothers accounts, both as a team and as individuals. He continued to do so even after Zeppo closed his agency in 1949. Gummo's deal with CBS (moving *You Bet Your Life* from radio to TV) assured that Groucho remained in the public eye long after he stopped making movies, and Groucho responded with such generosity that Gummo continued as his brothers' unofficial agent even after closing his agency in 1953. He ostensibly quit because he didn't want Robert to get sucked into the craziness of show business management.[36]

Gummo also had the dubious distinction of making it into the FBI's files, officially because of suspicious Las Vegas hotel investments, but more likely because blackballed bandleader Jerry Fielding performed at those hotels. For the most part, Gummo enjoyed a quiet retirement. Robert compared Gummo's homebody temperament to Harpo's. He was content to spend time with Zeppo, who lived nearby, and to fade from the limelight. His wife Helen died on January 20, 1976, and Gummo descended into a period of prolonged grieving. He passed away 15 months later at the age of 83.

2 … 1 …

Groucho was not told of Gummo's death because he, too, was gravely ill. He survived Gummo by just four months and died on August 19, 1977, at 86. His *You Bet Your Life* sidekick George Fenneman said that he "was in total awe of Groucho" during their early years and remained so even after his passing. Groucho Marx, the king of wisecracks, insults and one-liners, left behind a fine legacy, though his immediate passing was underreported. Woody Allen complained to *Time* magazine, "Is it my imagination, or were you guys a little skimpy with the Groucho Marx obituary?"[37]

They were skimpy because the media was obsessed with Elvis Presley, who had died three days earlier. Arthur forgot to invite Groucho's old pals George Burns and George Jessel to the memorial service, and Zeppo stayed home out of pique for not having been named Groucho's conservator.[38]

A sordid dispute over Groucho's finances complicated matters. At its center was Groucho's "companion," Canadian actress Erin Fleming, with whom he spent the last seven years of his life. Depending upon whom one believes, she was either his loving nurse or a chiseler guilty of elder abuse. Fleming charged that Arthur, Groucho's previous conservator, had stolen from his father but in 1983, nearly six years after Groucho's demise, courts determined that Fleming had taken advantage of Groucho's decrepitude and they ordered her to pay $472,000 in restitution and damages to Groucho's estate.[39] This occurred even though Groucho left the bulk of his estate to his three children. In 2003, the 61-year-old Fleming committed suicide, years after being diagnosed as schizophrenic.

Groucho's legacy as one of the greatest comics in American history was and is secure, but his final years were difficult. At his best, Groucho was witty, shrewd and charitable; at his worst, he was sullen, vain, parsimonious and insecure. The Fleming imbroglio underscored Groucho's troublesome relationships with women. He was married three times. Only his first spouse, Ruth Johnson, was close to him in age; she was eight years younger. A 1933 home movie presents Groucho, Ruth and their children Arthur and Miriam as a happy family.[40] This was camera-ready fiction, as Ruth was already drinking to excess; their marriage crumbled long before they divorced in 1942. Groucho's next two wives also struggled with alcoholism. He married Kay Marvis Gorcey in 1945; he was 33 years older than she. Their union produced a daughter, Melinda, but lasted just six years. Groucho got custody of three-year-old Melinda.[41]

When Edward R. Murrow visited for TV's *Person to Person* series, Groucho played the role of a doting dad and no mention was made of Groucho as a single parent to nine-year-old Melinda.[42] That changed several months later when Groucho tied the knot with Eden Hartford, 40 years his junior. Against all odds, they stayed married until 1969, and Groucho was distraught when she left, despite rumors that she too abused alcohol and had been unfaithful. This was before he had to shell out a million dollars in the divorce settlement.[43] In 1971, Groucho took up with Erin Fleming, who stayed with him until his death.

Did Groucho drive his three wives to alcoholism? It is hard to say how much of their struggles was fueled by his mood swings and how much was due to the diminished roles for women at the time. In *The Feminine Mystique* (1963), Betty Friedan referred to middle-class marriage as a "gilded cage" for women. As noted elsewhere in this work, the social superiority of men was assumed in the days before second-wave feminism took hold in the 1960s. Wives were expected to take care of their households, be subordinate to their husbands, and give up non-homemaker careers.

Hollywood was (and is) notoriously hard on marriages. Elizabeth Taylor married eight times, for instance, and figures such as Clark Gable, Ginger Rogers and Stan Laurel each tied the knot five times. Heavy drinking was also a staple of the celebrity lifestyle, though Groucho hardly drank at all until later in life. Bill Marx asserted that Harpo's wife Susan was among the few women feisty enough to command his Uncle Groucho's respect.[44] Even his relationship with his daughters was complicated, and Miriam went through a bout of alcoholism. He also had strained relations with his niece Maxine.

Groucho often professed to dislike his stage and screen persona. One of his standard lines was that his get-up made him look like "George Washington with a mustache." In 1949, he wrote a piece for *The Hollywood Reporter* titled "Run for Your Career, Boys" in which he observed, "no American with a television set is ever going to go outdoors again."[45] He was only semi-joking; he believed that both movies and theater were already in decline. By 1955, when he wrote an essay titled "I Never Could Grow a Moustache," he was a television star whose only major concession to the role that he had inhabited for 49 years was that he *had* grown a mustache and dispensed with the greasepaint.[46]

The term *typecasting* is used to describe actors so associated with a particular type of character that writers, directors, producers and the public find it hard to imagine them as anything different. Some, however, melded into their fictional selves and lived as if they and their character were one. Samuel Clemens, for instance, *was* Mark Twain for the last decade of his life. Others have followed a similar path; both Mae West and Marilyn Monroe became the sexpots they played on the screen, and performers Herbert Butros Khaury, Vincent Damon Furnier and Stefani Joanne Angelina Germanotta disappeared into their assumed identities of Tiny Tim, Alice Cooper and Lady Gaga, respectively. Julius Marx slowly faded and the ad-libbing, irreverent and sometimes crude Groucho Marx took over. After 1962, he had no series of his own but whenever he showed his face, audiences prepared to laugh, even if he wasn't particularly amusing. Groucho endlessly recycled old tales, sometimes spinning them in ways that transformed hyperbole, legends and rumors into new "realities."

Measures of his insecurity can be seen in the pride he took in telling Johnny Carson that the Library of Congress asked him to donate his papers, and in letting Dick Cavett know that one of his books—*Groucho and Me*—was owned by the Library of Congress.[47] It was fitting for such an ill-educated individual to be amazed by those accomplishments, but it apparently did not occur to him that it was his celebrity, not his literary merits, that drew the library's attention. In total, Groucho penned four books, collaborated on three others, and published his letters. As a writer, he was no James Thurber.

An elderly Groucho commanded media attention. But who orchestrated it? (photograph by Bernard Gotfryd, Library of Congress).

Thurber was, however, a friend. Groucho envied Harpo's intellectual circles, but managed to cultivate his own. They were populated mostly by writers and stage figures, among them T.S. Eliot, Carl Sandburg, Max Gordon, Garson Kanin, George S. Kaufman, Norman Krasna, S.J. Perelman, Harry Ruby, Arthur Sheekman, E.B. White and Earl Wilson. Groucho had close show business friends—Burns, Benny, Jessel, Bob Hope, Jack Lemmon—but as he aged, others gathered around him. Most were

An ad for an event at O'Neill Ranch, October 6, 1974. Was Groucho even aware of it? (Howard Coy, Library of Congress).

hangers-on, but Groucho enjoyed the company of younger individuals such as Cavett, Elliott Gould and Marvin Hamlisch, the last of whom played piano for Groucho's triumphant *An Evening with Groucho Marx* at Carnegie Hall in 1972.[48]

Bill Marx observed that Groucho "let his guard down" late in life. The same man who once insisted that the Marx Brothers were always a clean act gave uncensored interviews in which he came across as a sex-obsessed "dirty old man." Robert Bader speculated that some of this may have been due to the medications he was taking, but one has only to peruse some of those interviews to detect Groucho's shift from clever innuendo to unfiltered raunchiness.[49]

A ribald 1971 interview with the *Berkley Barb* demonstrated that, in Arthur's words, "he needed more than a companion. He needed a manager and/or keeper to prevent him from saying things that got him into deep trouble." Among the opinions Groucho put forth was his hope that President Nixon would be assassinated.[50] Groucho's contempt stemmed in part from his opposition to the Vietnam War and Nixon's expansion of the war zone into neighboring Cambodia during 1969 and '70.[51] It also coincided with the release of *The Pentagon Papers*, which detailed how policymakers and presidents lied to the American public about the cause, tactics and results of the conflict. These stoked protests around the nation, but Groucho's comment was dangerous and possibly illegal.

Groucho met Erin Fleming shortly after his *Berkeley Barb* interview.[52] At that time, his celebrity ride on TV was ending, he perceived that he needed income (he didn't) and was approaching his 81st birthday. Groucho had a schoolboy-like crush on Fleming. It is open to speculation whether they were intimate, but it is unlikely; Groucho was an octogenarian with a serious bladder condition.

Whatever else might be true of Fleming, she certainly put Groucho back in the limelight. It was she who pushed for the 1972 Carnegie Hall show and probably also convinced him to journey to Cannes, France, in May, where he was honored as a Commander of the Order of Arts and Letters. Under Fleming's guidance, Groucho maintained a rigorous schedule throughout 1972, but suffered a stroke on September 12. She withheld news of the stroke, telling the media that Groucho was depressed by the September 5 murder of 11 Israeli athletes and coaches by Palestinian terrorists at the Munich Olympics.[53]

Such things would later be cited as evidence of Fleming's abusive treatment of Groucho, as were her frequent bouts of rage and her usurpation of Groucho's household staff. She screamed at Groucho and threatened to fire his accountant when Groucho wanted to send $200 to his ex-wife Kay, who said she needed dental work.[54] Arthur became persona non grata when he told Erin that he doubted Groucho's mental competency to depose him (Arthur) as conservator and appoint herself in his stead. Zeppo further divided the family by siding with Fleming, possibly because Groucho was sending his money-starved brother $1,000 per week with her blessing.

More galling were evenings at Groucho's home in which he was trotted out to tell a few jokes, spin a few tales, sing a few songs in his breaking voice.[55] Arthur began to suspect that he and his sisters had been written out of their father's will. That wasn't the case, but it seemed plausible.[56] Even Melinda came in for censure when she crossed Fleming. At one point, Fleming contemplated a harebrained scheme in which Groucho would adopt her!

By 1976, things were spiraling out of control and Groucho was declining. He made his final TV appearance that March on a Bob Hope special. His remaining 17 months of life were spent in such poor health that he was bedridden much of the time. More allegations that Fleming assaulted him verbally and physically set the stage for the battle royal that ensued after Groucho died.

The only thing critics and supporters of Fleming agreed upon was that she squeezed more life out of Groucho than he would have otherwise had. Hector Arce, Groucho's official biographer and a frequent visitor to his home, wrote, "Erin succeeded in showing [Groucho] how well loved he was," a sentiment echoed by others.[57] Even his nephew Bill, who distrusted Fleming, noted that Groucho was never really happy unless he had an audience. He thought that Fleming used him as a "trained seal," but also believed that she "kept Groucho alive for seven years by appealing to his ego ... for better or worse and believe me there was worse." Robert Bader made the trenchant observation that Fleming's influence on him paralleled that of Minnie. Call it a bittersweet closing of the circle. Two iron-willed women helped define Groucho Marx: Minnie when he turned 15, and Erin Fleming in his final years.

1 ... 0

The youngest Marx, Zeppo, survived Groucho by two years and three months, dying at 78.[58] Zeppo had no more desire to be an actor than Gummo did. He had once mused about doing comedy but, in his words, "I never did care about show business [and] with three boys doing comedy there wasn't room for another comedian. So, I played the straight man."[59] He did so in vaudeville and in five films with Groucho, Chico and Harpo before quitting the act.

Robert Marx once remarked, "Zeppo was tight like a string. He was constantly taut."[60] He compared Zeppo's temperament to Groucho's, though Zeppo was edgier and less concerned with his reputation. As a young man he carried a gun, drove fast cars, and cavorted with loose women, petty criminals and dope peddlers. Controversy followed him for much of his life, with allegations of ties to organized crime surfacing from time to time.

Zeppo's relationships with women were no better than those of Chico and Groucho. In 1926, he married actress Marion Ruth Bimberg Benda, who many sources confuse with a famed Ziegfeld starlet who also worked under the same name.[61] Marriage did not curtail Zeppo's womanizing, though he was possessive of Marion, flew into rages when she spoke to other men, and sometimes roughed up her conversation partners. Marion and Zeppo adopted two boys, Timothy and Thomas, in the mid–'40s, but divorced in 1954.[62]

Zeppo maintained a playboy lifestyle and, in 1957, was in the news for a punch-up in a Hollywood nightclub (in another jealous episode, he slugged a man he thought was flirting with his girlfriend du jour). Two years later, Zeppo married Barbara Blakeley, then best known for having been a Las Vegas showgirl previously married to bandleader Bob Oliver. She and Oliver had a son, Robert, who assumed the last name of Marx, though his biological father refused to sanction an adoption by Zeppo.[63] Zeppo and Barbara divorced in 1972, but remained friendly even though she jilted him for a neighbor who became her third husband: Frank Sinatra.

Zeppo's professional life was, for a time, more successful than his home life. His talent agency did well, though the deal he negotiated for Groucho, Chico and Harpo to star in *Room Service* (1938) made him forswear ever again representing them directly. As he told it, "I wanted to get away from the Marx Brothers anyway. I didn't want the feeling of them telling me what to do any more."[64] He left that task to Gummo, before closing his agency in 1949 and putting show business behind him for good.

Zeppo's highest calling turned out to be as a mechanic, engineer and inventor. In 1941, he opened a firm called Marman Products. The next time you see a photograph of the atomic bomb exploding above Hiroshima in 1945, think of Zeppo. He didn't invent the weapon, but his Marman clamp kept it in place so that it did not explode before being detonated.[65] In 1948, Zeppo built a motorcycle called the Marman Twin. He also patented the Vapor Delivery Pad for Delivering Moist Heat and an early cardiac pulse monitor. These and investments earned Zeppo millions, much of which he squandered.

Zeppo inherited his older brother Chico's love of gambling, but not his good-natured approach to it. Bader observed that Zeppo "had a bit of a gangster streak," and that while Chico actually bragged about losing money, Zeppo was a sore loser. Groucho added that Chico was "a rascal" at cards, but Zeppo was "just cold-hearted."[66] In 1952, Zeppo was involved a public fight with film producer Alex Gottlieb, who claimed that Zeppo wouldn't pay a gambling debt.[67] Gambling, tax problems, alimony, high living and lawsuits drained much of Zeppo's bank account.[68]

As noted, Groucho (via Fleming) provided Zeppo with a $1,000 per week income, a substantial sum, but not enough to maintain his errant ways or sustain lawsuits such as the $20,000-plus he was ordered to pay for a 1973 beating of a mobster's estranged wife.

He was ultimately diagnosed with lung cancer. Despite his divorce from Barbara, he spent his remaining days in the care of her family. With Zeppo's death on November 30, 1979, the final curtain fell on the Marx Brothers.

The Final Assessment

There's no need to belabor conclusions that should now be obvious. The Marx Brothers were among the greatest comics and most-flawed individuals in the history of American entertainment. Readers may not immediately think of them as path-blazing funny men at first glance, but a major goal of this book has been to interpret the Marx Brothers by the standards of *their* time, not ours. To return to one of the first foundations of this work, most humor is time-bound. Getting jokes often entails social archaeology. What were the prevailing values of the time? Who and what was ripe for lampoon? What people and events shaped what we see on the screen? Who were the in-groups and out-groups? In short, why did people laugh at things that elude us?

I have noted the various "elephants in the room" that modern viewers may find troubling. It has never been my goal to make persuade you to condone or ignore such

The Marx Brothers live on in a June 2021 *Zippy* cartoon (courtesy of *Zippy* creator Bill Griffith).

things, but it has *always* been my intent to ask you to put them in historical context. At the risk of ruffling some feathers, it is my fervent belief that those who wish to rewrite history by sanitizing it or making it more to their liking commit an injustice against truth. We can learn important lessons from things that perplex and/or distress.

What made the Marx Brothers brilliant despite their personal shortcomings is that they were simply funny. Harpo's silent clowning, Chico's good-natured sappiness, and Groucho's biting wisecracks, saucy wordplay and ratatat witticisms are amusing. If you know enough history to unravel them, the Marx Brothers' humor shifts from amusing to sidesplitting.

This is not merely my judgment. Name any entertainment delivery system of the past 120 years and the Marx Brothers can be found there: vaudeville, Broadway, movies, radio, recordings, websites, blogs, newsletters, fan clubs, VHS, laser discs, CDs, DVDs, YouTube, Pinterest, books, graphic novels, photo archives, animation, television, video games, spin-off merchandise. Who *hasn't* seen a pair of Groucho glasses? Why does the American Film Institute think so highly of the Marx Brothers?

I have been asked on numerous occasions which film is the Marx Brothers' best. Answering that question is too much like being at a party where people argue over the greatest rock band, the best TV show or the best place to live. "Best" is too subjective. It's like saying that blue is the best color; someone is bound to ask, "What do you have against red?"

Nevertheless, I list the films by *my* preference. If you disagree, great! That means you've been watching.

1. ***Duck Soup***: Freedonia goes to war and makes you think only quacks do so.
2. ***Horse Feathers***: Who can resist a lampoon of college life, Prohibition and football?
3. ***A Day at the Races***: A doc who's a vet, tootsie-fruitsie ice cream and amazing dancing.
4. ***Monkey Business***: Anarchy at sea and on land. And maybe Harpo sings.
5. ***A Night at the Opera***: Pretense, negotiating contracts and a theater destroyed.
6. ***Animal Crackers***: If Captain Spaulding is an African explorer, I'm a monkey's uncle.
7. ***Go West***: This parody of Westerns is underappreciated.
8. ***The Big Store***: Dumb stunt work, but I'll buy the rest.
9. ***A Night in Casablanca***: A spoof of *Casablanca*. Nazis lose again.
10. ***Room Service***: Weak supporting actors, but okay as a Marx Brothers film that isn't.
11. ***The Cocoanuts***: Crude early talkie, but insight into causes of the Depression
12. ***At the Circus***: Has "Lydia the Tattooed Lady," but this lion doesn't roar.
13. ***Love Happy***: Rhymes with sappy, and that's the best that can be said.

Glossary

Forms of Humor

It's hard to explain or define humor, but it's a bit easier to define some of its various forms. I've listed them in alphabetical order. This is by no means a complete list, but it touches upon most of those the Marx Brothers used. When forms overlap, I designate them in *italicized **bold*** letters for cross-referencing.

- **Absurdism** playfully stretches perceptions of what is normal. Absurdism can be expressed in ***jokes***, plays, art, illusion, literature, avant-garde film and many other media. It is a form of interpretation that can have political or social meaning ... or it can simply skew our senses.
- **Black humor** is a form of ***tragicomedy*** whose humor value is ***ironic*** in that it takes a "dark" subject and wrings laughs from it and defuses matters that would otherwise be depressing. It is also sometimes a form of ***satire*** that calls attention to the inherent ***absurdism*** of a situation.
- **Burlesque** mocks social conventions and seriousness in general. It is often associated with strip tease acts and sexual innuendo, but burlesque is also a variety act in which comedy sketches, ***slapstick*** and funny songs are interspersed with serious music, dance and other forms of entertainment. Most burlesque was (and is) mildly naughty rather than vulgar.
- **Caricature** is a form of ***parody*** that exaggerates physical or personal characteristics. It is a staple of political cartoonists, though it also shows up in song lyrics, art parodies, masquerades and protests using *papier-mâché* figures to lampoon public figures. It is sometimes used as self-deprecating humor, such as a plus-sized comic making fun of being overweight or a member of a social group addressing ***absurd*** and contradictory practices within the group.
- **Farce** relies upon unusual and/or improbable situations, especially those that place individuals in uncomfortable or socially gauche predicaments that produce unintended consequences. Many sitcoms are forms of farce. In the time of the Marx Brothers, farces known as screwball comedies[1] were a movie staple. Most poke fun at traditional romances by throwing together two people who, on the surface, are polar opposites. Witty banter and ***absurd*** events break down barriers and lead them to fall in love. There is a fine shading of difference between screwball comedies and today's romantic comedies, which have largely supplanted the former.[2]
- **Insults** are forms of ***ridicule***. They are a combative form of comedy. Those of

245

a delicate disposition often criticize insults as forms of cruelty. Some insults are cruel, but insult done well is an incisive form of *satire*.

- **Irony** emphasizes the gap between what is said or intended and contrary actions or interpretations. It can be expressed as cynicism, skepticism or *absurdity*. A lot of political humor is ironic and thrives on exposing human shortcomings related to lapses in behavior, values and character.
- **Jokes** are building blocks of humor. They are mostly individual comments or slices of dialogue, even though we could consider an entire movie as an extended joke. Other words used to indicate a joke include wisecrack, jest, gibe, taunt and *mockery*.
- **Mimicry** is usually more complex than simply imitating another person. Unless combined with *caricature, jokes, parody* or *satire,* there is little potential humor in mimicry. It exaggerates the personality of another person or type of individual for comedic or *ironic* effect. Ethnic humor is out of fashion these day—unless the comic is a member of the group being parodied—as are comedic accents; both are forms of mimicry.
- **Minstrelsy** involved white (and some black) actors rubbing burnt cork onto exposed body parts to *burlesque*[3] people of color. It is also a form of *caricature* and *ridicule* that today is problematic, though it persists to a greater degree than most people realize.
- **Mockery** is a form of *ridicule* that belittles a person, event or belief system (secular or religious). It can be done in jest, but it's mostly intended to sting. The implicit assumption is that whatever is held in high regard is unworthy.
- **Musical comedy** is a self-defining term. It expresses humor in tunes, songs and dance.
- **Parody** is a form of *mimicry* or *caricature*. It is so closely related to *satire* that the two terms are often used interchangeably, though parody is a more exaggerated form of imitation. Both are forms of *ridicule* directed at a person, group, situation, value system or idea.
- **Physical humor** uses the human body in amusing ways. It runs the gamut from funny faces and silly movements to deliberate buffoonery (clowning), pratfalls and *slapstick*.[4] It generally relies upon feigned physical violence or placing the body in inherently dangerous situations. Alarmists frequently charge that physical humor encourages real-life copycat behaviors. Physical humor is mostly seen as Dionysian. Clowns are often Dionysian *tricksters*.
- **Puns** are disparaged by some and revered by others. They twist language and make allusions that produce silly and distorted meanings. Malapropisms are a related form in which deliberate or accidental replacement of one word with another that sounds similar creates mirth when misused within a specific context. Spoonerisms accomplish that task by mixing letters from adjoining words or transposing them within a word.
- **Ridicule** is comedy whose intent is to belittle. Like *insults*, it is aggressive—and some consider it mean-spirited. Done well, ridicule is a *joke* or a form of *absurdism* that calls attention to human foibles and contradictions. Stand-up comics often use amusing banter to defuse its incendiary potential. *Mockery* is a form of ridicule.
- **Sarcasm** is closely related to *irony, satire* and *parody,* but is more barbed

and makes no claim of being harmless humor. It is acidic *mockery* that holds a person, group or happenstance in contempt. If inexpertly used, it lapses into cynicism.

- **Satire** is closely related to *parody*; both are forms of *ridicule.* Satire tends to be more original than parody in that the comic develops new ways to critique rather than engaging in *mimicry.* These distinctions are often ignored, however, and the terms are often used interchangeably. They can be unsettling, as they imply a judgment about superiority and inferiority.
- **Schtick** is basically a comedian's signature way of performing. It involves routines, characters and style that makes a comic unique.
- **Slapstick** has become a synonym for *physical comedy*, though it originally involved fake blows or controlled pratfalls accompanied by sound effects.
- **Topical humor** is considered a benign form of *satire*, especially when aimed at politicians, who are legally and socially acceptable targets. It pokes fun at well-known people and current events familiar to audiences. It is favored by many comics as it makes their material seem fresh and relevant.
- **Tragicomedy**—sometimes called **black comedy**—locates humor or consolation in situations otherwise grim or calamitous. It makes fun of hurtful, dangerous, inappropriate and/or unfair things. Grotesque humor is a variant that makes light of the horrific.
- **Tricksters**—figures who prank others—are among the oldest forms of comedy. In many cases, the trickster inverts power dynamics by besting those claiming social superiority. They are common within marginalized groups and abound in comedy, cartoons, comic books and stories featuring hucksters and con artists. Tricksters are so prevalent that Jungian psychologists identify the trickster as a basic archetype, a universal symbol linked to humankind's collective unconscious.[5]
- **Vaudeville** thrived in the late 19th and early 20th century. Vaudeville houses sought to differentiate themselves from *burlesque* theater, though both relied on a mixed slate of variety acts. Vaudeville claimed to be cleansed of objectionable material that amused rather than *mocked*. Often, though, the biggest difference was that vaudeville tickets were more expensive.
- **Wit** is a staple of stand-up comedians and comics engaging in funny banter. It involves clever wordplay, verbal exchanges and punchlines that expose incongruity, the stuff from which *jokes* are fashioned. Folklorists classify it as Apollonian, or cerebral comedy. Examples of wit include everything from deadpan tall tales, jests and double entendres that use language to allow for opposing meanings—preferably one of which is *absurd*. Another form, epigrams, is a lost art form that once thrived in European court culture and on vaudeville stages. Humor came from commentary that subverted proverbs or the usual meaning of words.

Chapter Notes

Preface

1. "Cardboard City" was a tract of homes in a section of Chambersburg where African Americans lived. They were old Army barracks designed to be temporary. Chambersburg was home to Letterkenny, a U.S. Army supply depot. During World War II, more military personnel were sent in than the depot could house, and additional barracks were hastily constructed in town. Cheap materials were used, including very thin wallboard that spawned the name "Cardboard City." Chambersburg is also located just a dozen miles from the Maryland border and was a Jim Crow town in the 1950s. Cardboard City became a *de facto* African American ghetto, as many area landlords refused to rent to people of color and no federal laws existed to ensure housing equity.

2. It's not at all clear that Goldman said it that way, but it has passed into popular culture as an irresistible slogan that can be found on posters, T-shirts, coffee mugs, and many other things.

Chapter One

1. Nancy Walker, ed. *What's So Funny? Humor in American Culture*, Wilmington, DE: Scholarly Resources, 1998, 4. Emphasis added.

2. A sixth son, Manfred, died at just seven months of age.

3. Groucho, Harpo, and Zeppo claimed that Sam never bothered to measure his clients. Though that assertion is unlikely, Sam wasn't successful as a tailor. His 1884 marriage to Minnie was his most astute financial decision. His birth name sometimes appears as Simon Marrix.

4. Details of Minnie's parents are sketchy. Two of the better sources are Hector Arce, *Groucho*, New York: Perigee Books, 1979; Simon Louvish, *Monkey Business: The Lives and Legends of the Marx Brothers*, New York: Thomas Dunne Books, 1999.

5. Vaudeville was so popular that a modicum of talent was often enough to get work. A 1900 issue of *Billboard* claimed that there were 67 vaudeville theaters in New York, a figure that's probably conservative. The same issue reports that in a given week, some 650–700 acts performed. Turnover was high, but one estimate holds that some 25,000 performers took the stage between 1880 and 1920. Joseph Csida and June Bundy Csida, *American Entertainment: A Unique History of Popular Show Business*, New York: Watson-Guptill Publications, 1978.

6. Louvish, *Monkey Business*.

7. Most accounts claim that Adolph (Harpo) was not a gifted vocalist. Nearly everyone agrees that Minnie and Hannah were lousy singers. Uncle Louis (Levy) also appeared with the Six Escorts on occasion.

8. Robert S. Bader, ed. *Groucho Marx and Other Short Stories and Tall Tales: Selected Writings of Groucho Marx*, Boston: Faber and Faber, 1993, 4.

9. Joe Adamson, *Groucho, Harpo, Chico and Sometimes Zeppo: A Celebration of the Marx Brothers*, New York: Simon and Schuster, 1973, 45–46; Louvish, *Monkey Business*, 66–67.

10. Note: This Edward Albee is the grandfather of the famous playwright.

11. The best work on the Marx Brothers during their vaudeville years is the meticulously researched Robert S. Bader, *Four of the Three Musketeers: The Marx Brothers on Stage*, Evanston, IL: Northwestern University Press, 2016. See also Charlotte Chandler, *Hello I Must Be Going*, New York: Citadel Press, 1993; Glenn Mitchell, *The Marx Brothers Encyclopedia*, London: B. T. Batsford, 1996.

12. Sherlocko led Arthur Conan Doyle to threaten legal action, which is why he was soon rechristened Hawkshaw the Detective.

13. Tom Wilson, "Of Groucho and Galesburg," *The Register-Mail* (Galesburg, IL), May 14, 2009, https://www.galesburg.com/article/20090314/NEWS/303149941 Accessed February 11, 2021. Some sources say Fisher's brainstorm occurred in 1916, though most say 1914.

14. There are conflicting reports of the change from Adolph to Arthur. One version is that he didn't want to appear too German. This seems unlikely, as U.S. involvement in World War One did not occur until 1917, which is when anti-German sentiments gathered steam. Another tale is that he disliked being called by the diminutive Ahdie. The most

likely explanation is that Adolph Marks was a well-known Chicago show business attorney and Harpo wished to avoid confusion. David Mikkelson, "Harpo Marx Name Change," *Snopes*, https://www.snopes.com/fact-check/harpo-marx/ Accessed February 11, 2021.

15. Robert W. Snyder, *The Voice of the City: Vaudeville and Popular Culture in New York*, New York: Oxford University Press, 1989, 44.

16. Adamson, *Groucho, Harpo, Chico and Sometimes Zeppo*; Mitchell, *The Marx Brothers Encyclopedia*.

17. Harpo Marx with Rowland Barber, *Harpo Speaks*, New York: Limelight Editions, 1985; Adamson, *Groucho, Harpo, Chico and Sometimes Zeppo*.

18. Associated Press, Seth Borenstein,"R2-D2 walks into a bar, doesn't get the joke," *Daily Hampshire Gazette*, April 1, 2019.

19. Emily Langer, "Dr. Robert Provine, 76, scholar of laughter and hiccups," obituary originally published in the *Washington Post* and reprinted in the *Boston Globe*, October 2, 2019. Robert Provine, *Laughter: A Scientific Investigation*, New York: Penguin Putnam, 2000.

20. Johan Huizinga, *Homo Ludens: A Study in the Play Element in Culture*, Translated from Dutch, New York: Random House, 1955.

21. Julia Wilkins and Amy Janet Eisenbraun, "Humor Theories and the Physiological Benefits of Laughter," *Holistic Nursing Practice*, November/ December 2009 23 (6), 349–354.

22. Provine, *Laughter: A Scientific Investigation*; Peter L. Berger, *Redeeming Laughter: The Comic Dimension of Human Experience*, Berlin: Walter De Gruyter, 1997.

23. Constance Rourke, *American Humor: A Study of the National Character*, Garden City, NY: Anchor Doubleday, 1931. The Yankee often appeared to be a simpleton but was actually a quasi-trickster who has the last laugh. The origin of "Yankee" is disputed, though a Dutch origin seems likely.

24. Enid Veron, ed. *Humor in America: An Anthology*, New York: Harcourt Brace Jovanovich, 1976; Louis Kronenberger, "The American Sense of Humor," in Veron, *Humor in America*, 266–271. Dionysius was the Greek god of wine, hence humor in this vein is akin to being inebriated. Apollo, by contrast, was the god of logic, music, and poetry.

25. Walker, *What's So Funny*. Haweis quote, 11.

26. To pick just one example, in Jan Harold Brunvand's *The Study of American Folklore: An Introduction*, New York: W. W. Norton, 1978, he draws upon Stith Thompson's magisterial *Motif-Index of Folk-Literature* (1955–58) to show how many tall tales, anecdotes, jests, and jokes are reworked versions of much older ones.

27. Arthur Power Dudden, *American Humor*, New York: Oxford University Press, 1987. Briggs quote, 17.

28. Peter L. Berger, *Redeeming Laughter: The Comic Dimension of Human Experience*, Berlin: Walter De Gruyter, 1997, chapter 5.

29. Robert E. Weir, "Vagabond Abroad: Mark Twain's 1895 Visit to New Zealand," *The Journal of the Gilded Age and Progressive Era* 8:4 (October 2006), 487–514.

30. Berger, *Redeeming Laughter*, 89.

31. Joseph Boskin and Joseph Dorinson, "Ethnic Humor: Subversion and Survival," in Dudden, *American Humor*, 97–117, especially 102–109.

32. Chandler, *Hello I Must Be Going*. Louvish also briefly touches on Judaism in *Monkey Business*.

33. Bill Marx is quoted in Louvish, *Monkey Business*, 94. For more on the *commedia dell'arte*, see Oscar G. Brockett and Franklin J. Hildy, *History of the Theatre* 10th edition, London: Pearson, 2007. See also "Commedia dell'arte," Wikipedia, https://en.wikipedia.org/wiki/Commedia_dell%27arte Accessed February 11, 2021. Note: Pierrot has held the fascination of numerous French film directors, including Marcel Carné, whose 1945 *Les Enfants du Paradis* is considered a landmark film; and Jean-Luc Godard, whose 1965 *Pierrot le Fou* is a stellar example of French New Wave cinema.

34. The *commedia dell'arte* is often conflated with *commedia all'improviso* (improvised comedy). Skilled improvisers mask the rehearsed parts of their acts. The Marx Brothers did so. Much of their mayhem was tested rather than made up on the set.

35. Berger, *Redeeming Laughter*, pp. 99–116.

36. Roger Abrahams, *Singing the Master: The Emergence of African American Culture in the Plantation South*, New York: Penguin Books, 1994. See also Lawrence Levine, *Black Culture and Black Consciousness: Afro-American Thought from Slavery to Freedom*, New York: Oxford University Press, 2007.

37. Alan Dundes, *Cracking Jokes: Studies of Sick Humor Cycles and Stereotypes*, Berkeley, CA: Ten Speed Press, 1987, vii, viii.

38. Paul Lewis, *Cracking Up: American Humor in a Time of Conflict*, Chicago: University of Chicago Press, 2006, 173–185.

Chapter Two

1. A 1926 film, *Don Juan*, was technically the first sound-on-film feature, though it featured a musical soundtrack and no spoken dialogue.

2. Warner Brothers was begun by four actual siblings: Harry, Albert, Sam, and Jack Warner.

3. An analogy can be made to the 2010s, when digital cinematography largely supplanted film stock. Many small cinemas went out of business because they had too few screens to justify the cost of digital projectors.

4. The last Hollywood silent was *Legong: Dance of the Virgins*. It was made in Bali and was

first released abroad. Its bare-breasted women got past censors because they were Balinese and their lack of attire was considered anthropological rather than salacious—a distinction not all attendees made!

5. "Feature" film is a subjective category, but the generally accepted standard is that it is a continuous narrative at least 40 minutes long. *The Story of the Kelly Gang,* a 1906 Australian film, usually gets credit for being the first. A handful of American features appeared before 1915, including *The Merchant of Venice* (1914) directed by Lois Weber, the first American woman to direct a feature. Many early features were adaptations of plays and classic novels. Thomas Dixon's novel *The Clansman* was the basis for *The Birth of a Nation* and is considered a cinematic breakthrough, though its content valorizing the Ku Klux Klan is problematic.

6. "Silver screen" is a time-honored synonym for movies. It comes from early projection screens in which silver or other reflective materials were embedded. Increased reflectiveness aided the weaker projectors of the early days and made the images brighter.

7. The Marx Brothers' first moderate success in New York was with *Home Again* in 1918, but this show was just 38 minutes long.

8. One estimate holds that more than half of all silent films were lost, either because stock was recycled for its silver content, or because they deteriorated. (Silver nitrate film was acidic and prone to catching on fire or dissolving.)

9. Hector Arce, *Groucho,* New York: Perigee Books, 1979, 156.

10. Helen Dudar, "Those golden years when Hollywood was back East," *Smithsonian Magazine,* November 1985, 111–123.

11. Martin A. Gardner, *The Marx Brothers as Social Critics,* Jefferson, NC: McFarland, 2009; Glenn Mitchell, *The Marx Brothers Encyclopedia,* London: B. T. Batsford, 1996.

12. Allen Eyles, *The Marx Brothers: Their World of Comedy,* London: Tantivy Press, 1974, 16.

13. Harpo Marx with Rowland Barber, *Harpo Speaks!* New York: Limelight Editions, 1985, 271.

14. Groucho Marx and Richard Anobile, *The Marx Brothers Scrapbook,* New York: Grosset and Dunlap, 1974, 117.

15. The term "book" is used in musicals in which skits and spoken words are links to songs and dance numbers. It is a (near) synonym for libretto and derives its name from *libro,* an Italian diminutive for book. A script—itself a diminutive of manuscript—is used for plays in which the directed action either has no music or is incidental to the overall production. Morrie Ryskind also wrote some of the music, but was not credited in stage or film production.

16. Theater or theatre? They are used interchangeably these days, with theatre considered a British spelling, but in some circles, theater is a film screening venue and a theatre is for plays.

17. Marx and Anobile, *Marx Brothers Scrapbook,* 116.

18. Groucho Marx, *Groucho and Me: The Autobiography of Groucho Marx,* New York: Fireside Book, 1959, 173.

19. Harpo Marx, *Harpo* Speaks! 189; Robert Bader, *Four of the Three Musketeers: The Marx Brothers on Stage.* Evanston, IL: Northwestern University Press, 2016, 309.

20. "When My Dreams Come True" did enjoy brief success. Paul Whiteman, Franklyn Baur, and several others recorded it. Once *Animal Crackers* was released, the song's association with the Marx Brothers caused "Dreams" to fade in popularity.

21. In one scene, a campy engagement party, Chico is introduced as Signore Pastrami, though inexplicably his character is allegedly Lithuanian.

22. Wop was/is a pejorative term for Italians. Its origin is uncertain, but most linguists believe it came from *guappo,* a Southern Italian term akin to "dude" or "dandy." Its Neapolitan pronunciation sounds a bit like wah'po.

23. Mitchell, *The Marx Brothers Encyclopedia,* 87; Joe Adamson, *Groucho, Harpo, Chico and Sometimes Zeppo,* New York: Simon and Schuster, 1973, 275.

24. Ayres, *The Marx Brothers,* 16.

25. Charlotte Chandler, *Hello, I Must Be Going: Groucho and His Friends,* New York: Citadel Press, 1993, 166.

26. Robert Horey interview in Marx and Anobile, *Marx Brothers Scrapbook,* 115–17. Marx Brothers ad-libs have been exaggerated, but there is no question that they were masterful at them. George S. Kaufman often remarked that every time he saw the stage show it was different. He allegedly once quipped from backstage, "I think I just heard one of the original lines." Mitchell, *The Marx Brothers Encyclopedia,* 58.

27. Once mastered, soundtracks became a staple, especially background music that set moods. This is why nearly all movies and television programs have them, though originally, they served to mask the motors of projectors and the clicking of film stock running through the sprockets.

28. Maurice Charney is especially praiseful of Harpo's work in *Cocoanuts.* See Charney, *The Comic World of the Marx Brothers' Movies,* Madison, NJ: Fairleigh Dickinson University Press, 2007, chapter four.

29. *The Cocoanuts,* Paramount Pictures, 1929.

30. T.D. Allman, *Miami: City of the Future,* New York: Atlantic Monthly Press, 1987; Kevin Kokomoor, "'In the Land of the Tarpon': The Silver King Sport, and the Development of Southwest Florida, 1885–1915," *Journal of the Gilded Age and Progressive Era,* 112: April 2012, 191–224; Thelma Peters, *Miami 1909: with Excerpts from Fannie Clemons' Diary,* Miami: Banyan Books, 1984, 111. Notes: In 1875, the nearest railroad station to Miami was 400 miles distant. Florida was not officially nicknamed the Sunshine State until 1970.

31. Chipley was also motivated to relocate to Florida because of his Ku Klux Klan activity in Georgia. He was implicated in a KKK murder of a Republican politician, and escaped conviction only because Georgia's readmission to the Union ushered in a racist Democratic government opposed to Reconstruction.

32. William Frazer and John J. Guthrie Jr. *The Florida Land Boom: Speculation, Money, and the Banks*, Westport, CT: Quorum Books 1995, 33. Biscayne Bay is the body of water associated with the Greater Miami area.

33. Gannon, *Florida: A Short History.*

34. Charles Tebeau, *A History of Florida*, Coral Gables: University of Miami Press, 1971, 379.

35. Frederick Lewis Allen, *Only Yesterday: An Informal History of the 1920's*, New York: Perennial Classics, 2000. Reprint of 1931 original.

36. Frazer and Guthrie, *Florida Land Boom*, 96.

37. Gannon, *Florida: A Short History*, 82–83.

38. Tebeau, *A History of Florida*, 384, 386.

39. Allman, *Miami: City of the Future*, Quote is from p. 224.

40. Allen, *Only Yesterday*, 244.

41. "Share of total music album consumption in the United States, by genre," *Statista*, https://www.statista.com/statistics/310746/share-music-album-sales-us-genre/ Accessed January 18, 2021.

42. As in most musical styles, many of the subgenres of jazz overlap. Big band swing and hot jazz are related. Sometimes the size of the ensemble is the major difference between them, with hot jazz tending to feature smaller lineups.

43. Lewis Erenberg, *Steppin' Out: New York Nightlife and the Transformation of American Culture, 1890–1920*, Westport, CT: Greenwood Press, 1981, 251.

44. Allen, *Only Yesterday*, 78. The *Telegraph*'s last line refers to houses of prostitution, though the writer might not have known that the term "flapper" had its origins in slang for a prostitute. Female sexual freedom should not be exaggerated; an unmarried young woman who got "caught," 1920s slang for pregnant, would find herself in dire straits in an age in which child-support laws were weak or non-existent. Nonetheless, a certain amount of sexual "treating" definitely took place in early-20th-century dance halls. See Kathy Peiss, *Cheap Amusements: Working Women and Leisure in Turn-of-the-Century New York*, Philadelphia: Temple University Press, 1986.

45. Ehrenberg, *Steppin' Out*, 226.

46. Nathan Belth, *A Promise To Keep: A Narrative of the American Encounter with Anti-Semitism*, New York: Times Books, 1979.

47. Michael Dobkowski, *The Tarnished American Dream: The Basis of American Anti-Semitism*, Westport, CT: Greenwood Press, 1979.

48. Belth, A *Promise To Keep*, 58.

49. Many reform laws were passed during the Progressive Era, but it was a very *regressive* period from an ethnic, gendered, racial, or social-class perspective. It was also a time of imperialism, repression of non-mainstream political views, the passage of Prohibition laws, arrests and forced-feedings of jailed suffragists, suppression of labor unions, and the revival of the Ku Klux Klan. Moreover, reforms were imposed from the top down and democratic processes led to what has been labeled the "cult of experts." Voting levels actually declined during the Progressive Era. Women did not get the right to vote until after World War I, and that was one of the few triumphs of mass participatory democracy until the 1930s.

50. Edward T. O'Donnell, "Hibernians Versus Hebrews? A New Look at the 1902 Jacob Joseph Funeral Riot," *Journal of the Gilded Age and Progressive Era* (April 2007), 209–25. O'Donnell argues that the riot was not a punch-up between Jews and Irish, as has been traditionally portrayed. Nonetheless, the events led to fear among many New York Jews.

51. Leonard Dinnerstein, *Anti-Semitism in America*, New York: Oxford Press, 1994; Hasia Diner, "The Encounter between Jews and America in the Gilded Age and Progressive Era," *Journal of Gilded Age and Progressive Era*, 11:1 (January 2012), 3–25; Digital Public Library of America, "Tragedy in the New South: The Murder of Mary Phagan and the Lynching of Leo Frank," https://dp.la/exhibitions/leo-frank Accessed January 18, 2021. B'nai B'rith is a Jewish civil rights and community service organization founded in 1843.

52. Simon Baatz, *For the Thrill of It*, New York: HarperCollins, 2009. Technically, Richard Loeb was only half Jewish, as his mother was a Roman Catholic. Leopold and Loeb poured acid on Bobby Franks' genitals in an attempt to hide that he was Jewish. In 1924, circumcision was rare among non-Jews.

53. Ronald Takaki, *A Different Mirror: A History of Multicultural America*, Boston: Little, Brown and Company, 1993; John Higham, *Strangers in the Land: Patterns of American Nativism 1860–1925*, New York: Atheneum, 1978; Dinnerstein, *Anti-Semitism in America.*

54. Belth, *A Promise To Keep*. Ford biographer Keith Sward quoted, p. 76.

55. *Ibid.*; Dobkowski, *The Tarnished American Dream.* The historical record shows that Ford's anti-Semitism was deep-seated and was manifest at least as early as 1915, long before he purchased the *Independent.*

56. For a portrait of the National Origins Act, see "Who Was Shut Out? Immigration Quotas, 1925–27," *History Matters*, http://historymatters.gmu.edu/d/5078 Accessed January 18, 2021.

57. Belth, *A Promise To Keep*; Dobkowski, *The Tarnished American Dream*; Marcia Synnott, "The Half-Opened Door: Researching Admissions Discrimination at Harvard, Yale,

and Princeton," *American Archivist* 45:2 (Spring 1982), 175–87; "Obstacles to Learning," Duke Center for Jewish Studies, https://sites.duke.edu/downhome/obstacles-to-learning-3/ Accessed January 18, 2021.

58. Maxine Marx, *Growing Up With Chico*, New York: Limelight Books, 1986, 53–54.

59. Chandler, *Hello, I Must Be Going: Groucho and His Friends*, 124–25.

60. Harpo Marx with Rowland Barber, *Harpo Speaks!* 162–90; Mitchell, *The Marx Brothers Encyclopedia*, 203; Chandler, *Hello, I Must Be Going*, 132.

61. *Ibid.*, 125.

62. The first joke is Chico's garbling of Swede and suite. Polack is an insulting term for Polish people. Its origins are disputed, but in English, Polack has been derogatory since at least the 19th century.

63. H.S. Linfield, "Statistics of Jews-1929," http://www.ajcarchives.org/AJC_DATA/Files/1930_1931_7_Statistics.pdf Accessed January 18, 2021.

64. I double-checked references to specific pieces of dialogue against those in Richard Anobile, ed. *Why a Duck? Visual and Verbal Gems from the Marx Brothers Movies*, New York: Darien House, 1971.

Chapter Three

1. Joe Adamson, *Groucho, Harpo, Chico, and Sometimes Zeppo*, New York: Simon and Schuster, 1973, 104.

2. Gerald Bordman, *American Musical Theatre: A Chronicle*, New York: Oxford University Press, 451.

3. Abe Laufe, *Broadway's Greatest Musicals*, New York: Funk and Wagnalls, 1997.

4. Simon Louvish, *Monkey Business: The Lives and Legends of The Marx Brothers*, New York: Thomas Dunne Books, 1999, 212.

5. Glenn Mitchell, *The Marx Brothers Encyclopedia*, London: B. T. Batsford, 12–14.

6. The Winchell send-up was cut either because screenwriter Morrie Ryskind didn't want to offend him, or because Winchell's reputation didn't extend much beyond New York City. Accounts differ.

7. Louvish, *Monkey Business*, 215.

8. *Ibid.*, 215.

9. Anderson is quoted in Mark Bego, *The Pocket Essential: The Marx Brothers*, North Pomfret, VT: Trafalgar Square Publishing, 2001, 50.

10. It's actually a parody of a parody, as Gilbert and Sullivan themselves made light of the affected weightiness of operas favored by the upper classes. The duo created such enduring works as *The Pirates of Penzance*, *The Mikado*, and *H.M.S. Pinafore*, which remain widely performed.

11. Those sold were usually either prisoners of war or from rival ethnic groups. Bargains were occasionally struck with kidnappers, but it would have been perilous (and expensive) for whites to venture into the interior as part of any organized slave-capturing expedition.

12. An exception was Zanzibar, a group of islands in the Indian Ocean off the coast of Tanzania, which was colonized by Portugal in 1503. Portugal tried to establish direct control, with mixed success. The French also tried direct-control models, which proved more successful in North Africa than in the Sub-Saharan west coast. The Indian Ocean colony of Madagascar also proved difficult to rule.

13. Toyin Falola, ed. *Colonial Africa 1885–1939, vol. 3*, Durham, NC: Carolina Academic Press, 2002; Adam Hochschild, *King Leopold's Ghost: A Story of Greed, Terror, and Heroism in Colonial Africa*, Boston: Mariner Books, 1999.

14. Jon R. Godsall, *The Tangled Web: A Life of Sir Richard Burton*, London: Matador Books, 2008. Burton was an unabashed racist and white supremacist. Before his search for the source of the Nile, Burton disguised himself as an Arab to enter Mecca during Ramadan. Had he been caught, he would have been executed. Burton also had what some have viewed as prurient interest in African sexual habits.

15. The reason Liberia was not attractive was quite simple. By 1822, much of the enslaved population was not African, but African-*American*. Many were not much more knowledgeable about African lands or cultures than their former masters.

16. Martin Dugard, "Stanley Meets Livingstone." *Smithsonian*, October 2003, 69–77; Richard Hall, *Stanley: An Adventurer Explored*, Boston: Houghton Mifflin, 1975. Stanley publicly disavowed having a role in the atrocities that occurred in King Leopold's indirect rule over the Congo. That was probably not the case. Stanley had very few positive views of Africans and was alleged to have acted with great cruelty toward them.

17. Phillips Verner and Harvey Blume, *Ota Benga: The Pygmy in the Zoo*. New York: St. Martin's Press, 1992. Note that Benga was enslaved long after the slave trade had officially ended. Pygmies remained in jeopardy more than a century later. See Paul Raffaele, "The Pygmies' Plight," *Smithsonian*, December 2008, 70–77.

18. You can find *Types of Mankind* at https://archive.org/details/typesmankindore01pattgoog Accessed January 19, 2021.

19. The script for *Strange Interlude* can be read through Project Gutenberg, http://gutenberg.net.au/ebooks04/0400161h.html Accessed January 19, 2021.

20. The script from *Animal Crackers* is not as widely available as those from other Marx Brothers films. I located it at: https://www.scripts.com/script.php?id=animal_crackers_2887&p=7 Accessed January 19, 2021.

21. Frederick Lewis Allen, *Only Yesterday: An Informal History of the 1920s*, New York: Perennial Classics, 2000, reprint of 1931 original, 85.

22. Jung later split with Freud over a variety of intellectual disagreements.

23. Allen, *Only Yesterday*, 172.

24. Coué (1857–1926) was a progenitor of what today is called "positive psychology." His methods, however, drew so heavily upon things such as hypnosis, belief in perfectionism, and the use of what he called "magical incantations," that he was dismissed by most social scientists as a fraud.

25. Allen Eyles, *The Marx Brothers: Their World of Comedy*, London: Tantivy Press, 1974, 47.

26. Mitchell, *The Marx Brothers Encyclopedia*, 113–14.

27. In some scripts and references, Hungadunga is written as Hungerdunger. The script I consulted clearly says Hungadunga, but this may be a mishearing of Groucho's New York accent.

28. Mitchell, *The Marx Brothers Encyclopedia*, 18. Groucho was fond of claiming that Zeppo was so good at being Groucho that he hurried his recovery for fear he'd be out of a job. Some sources also say that Harpo and Chico sometimes changed roles on stage and, again, no one noticed.

29. Eyles, *The Marx Brothers*, 54.

30. Michael E. Parrish, *Anxious Decades: America in Prosperity and Depression, 1920–41*, New York: W. W. Norton, 1992, 141.

31. Paula Fass, *The Damned and the Beautiful: American Youth in the 1920s*, New York: Oxford University Press, 1971, 264.

32. Allen, *Only Yesterday*, 101.

33. Robert S. and Helen M. Lynd, *Middletown: A Study in Modern American Culture*, New York: Harcourt Brace Jovanovich, 1955 reprint of 1929 original.

34. Fass, *The Damned and the Beautiful*, Quote p. 265; Barbara Ehrenreich and Deirdre English, *For Her Own Good: 150 Years of the Experts' Advice to Women*, Garden City, NY: Anchor Books, 1979. Ehrenreich and English speak of the "manufacture of housework" and also note the various "pathologies" attributed to motherhood.

35. Harpo Marx with Rowland Barber, *Harpo Speaks!* New York: Limelight Editions, 1985, 191.

36. *Ibid.*

37. In House of David thinking, long hair and unkempt beards drew "electricity" from the air, which was said to be as necessary for life as food, water, and air.

38. This part of House of David theology is based on the New Testament Book of Revelations. In it, the Apostle John has a vision in which he is given a scroll of revelations hitherto known only to God. Each seal John breaks unleashes one of those secrets, and the seventh leads to the Second Coming of Christ, which heralds the end of the world. In 1957, Swedish director Ingmar Bergman made *The Seventh Seal*, a film classic. The Book of Revelations lends itself to speculation as it is so enigmatic that early Christian councils doubted its authenticity. It was added to the New Testament in the 4th century, making it the last book accepted as canonical in the Christian Bible.

39. Ron Grossman, "A Cult in Benton Harbor: The good and (alleged) evil of the House of David," *Chicago Tribune*, July 16, 2017.

40. Shearer was the first actress to be nominated for five Academy Awards. She won a best actress Oscar for the 1930 film *The Divorcee*, which came out the same year as *Animal Crackers*.

41. "Abie's Irish Rose," https://en.wikipedia.org/wiki/Abie%27s_Irish_Rose Accessed January 19, 2021.

42. Adamson, *Groucho, Harpo, Chico and Sometimes Zeppo*, 115–16.

43. This witticism is a reference to Ravelli's frustrating attempt to get The Professor to know he wants a "flash" (light), not a fish, a flisk, a flush, or any of a number of like-sounding words in Harpo's coat pockets.

44. IMDB, "*Animal Crackers* Trivia," https://www.imdb.com/title/tt0020640/trivia Accessed January 19, 2021; Mitchell, *The Marx Brothers Encyclopedia*, 20–21.

Chapter Four

1. Adamson, *Groucho, Harpo, Chico and Sometimes Zeppo*, 145.

2. "Oh Yeah?: Herbert Hoover Predicts Prosperity," History Matters, http://historymatters.gmu.edu/d/5063/ Accessed January 21, 2021.

3. There is dispute over the date in which the recession became the "Great Depression," a capitalized compound noun. The *Oxford English Dictionary* credits British economist Lionel Robbins with using the term Great Depression in print during 1934, though it is uncertain whether it was an original formulation.

4. Hector Arce, *Groucho*, New York: Perigee Books, 1979, 188.

5. Martin A. Gardner, *The Marx Brothers as Social Critics*, Jefferson, NC: McFarland, 2009, 31–32.

6. Joe Adamson, *Groucho, Harpo, Chico and Sometimes Zeppo*, New York: Simon and Schuster, 121.

7. Groucho Marx and Richard Anobile, *The Marx Brothers Scrapbook*, New York: Grosset and Dunlap, 1974, 213.

8. Arce, *Groucho*, 189.

9. Alex Jay, Stripper's Guide, http://strippersguide.blogspot.com/2014/07/ink-slinger-profiles-by-alex-jay-j.html Accessed January 21, 2021. According to Jay, Pusey first came to the attention of the Marx Brothers because his strip *Benny* was about a little boy who didn't talk.

10. Simon Louvish, *Monkey Business: The Lives and Legends of the Marx Brothers*, New York: Thomas Dunne Books, 1999, 222–23; See also Arthur Marx, *My Life With Groucho*, Fort Lee, NY: Barricade Books, 1992, 41–42. Arthur Marx details the 1922 visit to London. Note: This Arthur Marx was Groucho's son, not his brother Arthur/Harpo.

11. Adamson, *Groucho, Harpo, Chico and Sometimes Zeppo*, 131. How much of this actually occurred, versus how much is a tall tale, is up for grabs!

12. Louvish, *Monkey Business*, 230.

13. Some sources say that the first movie trailer was for *The Pleasure Seekers*, a 1913 film that debuted in Loew theaters. There is disagreement over whether it was the first, or merely the first in North America. The term "trailer" comes from the original practice of showing them at the end of another picture, hence they "trailed" the feature being shown.

14. Films are often unfinished when a trailer is produced and sometimes use footage that is later cut. The official trailer can be viewed on YouTube. See "Monkey Business (1931) Trailer," https://www.youtube.com/watch?v=jh-yzc-k54U Accessed January 21, 2021. There have been several other films titled *Monkey Business*, hence it is important to use the 1931 date when doing any Internet search for the Marx Brothers film.

15. "The House That Shadows Built," https://www.youtube.com/watch?v=KUhaPEqV_Ao&t=7s Accessed February 15, 2021.

16. *Ibid.* The Marxes recycled a lot. The agent scene from *I'll Say She Is* was lifted from their 1923 show *On the Mezzanine Floor*.

17. Charlotte Chandler, *Hello, I Must Be Going: Groucho and His Friends*, New York: Citadel Press, 1993, 151.

18. Louvish, *Monkey Business*, 246.

19. Groucho Marx and Richard Anobile, *The Marx Brothers Scrapbook*, New York: Grosset and Dunlap, 1974, 17.

20. Robert S. Bader, ed. *Groucho Marx and Other Short Stories and Tall Tales: Selected Writings of Groucho Marx*, Boston: Faber and Faber, 1993, 30–33. The compromise, proposed by Chico, was that Wells would donate the $10 to the Salvation Army.

21. Gardner, *The Marx Brothers as Social Critics*, 16.

22. Chandler, *Hello, I Must Be Going*, 284.

23. Maurice Charney, *The Comic World of the Marx Brothers' Movies*, Madison, NJ: Fairleigh Dickinson University Press, 2007, 71.

24. I consulted an online edition of the *Oxford English Dictionary*, a password-protected site. Most academic and public libraries provide database access to students, faculty, staff, and cardholders.

25. James Cameron's 1997 film *Titanic* does a good job of showing social stratification on an ocean liner.

26. An excellent way to familiarize yourself with what it was like aboard a luxury liner can be found in the catalog for an exhibit on ocean travel that appeared at the Peabody Essex Museum in Salem, Massachusetts in 2017. See Daniel Finamore and Ghislaine Wood, eds. *Ocean Liners: Glamour, Speed and Style*, New York: Abrams Books, 2017.

27. Gardner, *The Marx Brothers as Social Critics*, 119–20.

28. A floorwalker, once a common feature of department stores, was a combination supervisor and customer-assistance expert. As the term implies, a floorwalker spent a lot of time in circulation throughout the store. Groucho ridicules the captain's status by comparing him to a retail worker.

29. Andrew Bergman, *We're in the Money: Depression America and its Films*, New York: Harper Torchbooks, 1972, xxi.

30. Internet Movie Database, "Feature Film, Released between 1930 and 1901–01 and 1930–12–31," Internet Movie Database, https://www.imdb.com/search/title/?year=1930&title_type=feature& Accessed January 21, 2021.

31. Bergman, *We're in the Money*, 5. Bergman also notes that the MPPDA code was widely ignored.

32. Crime Museum, "Jack Diamond," https://www.crimemuseum.org/crime-library/organized-crime/jack-diamond/ Accessed January 21, 2021. Diamond's colorful nickname was due to his prowess as a dancer. Though married, Diamond was a serial adulterer.

33. Gardner, *The Marx Brothers as Social Critics*, 59–61.

34. The term "A-list" references top stars in both box-office appeal and in salary. John Wayne's name was omitted from this list because in 1931, he was not yet a top draw.

35. Wes D. Gehring, *The Marx Brothers: A Bio-Bibliography*, Westport, CT: Greenwood Press, 1987, 58.

36. The song was written by Sammy Fain, Irving Kahal, and Pierre Norman. The first two were Jewish and Norman, the songwriting name for Joseph P. Connor, was a Roman Catholic cleric.

37. David R. Roediger, *Working Toward Whiteness: How America's Immigrants became White*, New York: Basic Books, 2005, 66.

38. Gehring, *The Marx Brothers: A Bio-Bibliography*, 59.

39. *Ibid.*, 58–59.

40. Adamson, *Groucho, Harpo, Chico and Sometimes Zeppo*, 154–56.

41. Perhaps his stiff performance explains why Romanoff was not credited.

42. https://www.pophistorydig.com/topics/tag/boxing-1920s/ Accessed January 21, 2021; Frederick Romano, *The Golden Age of Boxing on Radio and Television: A Blow-by-Blow History from 1921 to 1964*, New York: Simon & Schuster, 2017.

43. Frederick Lewis Allen, *Only Yesterday: An Informal History of the 1920's,* New York: Perennial Classics, 2000. Reprint of 1931 original, 142.

44. Michael E. Parrish, *Anxious Decades: America in Prosperity and Depression, 1920–41,* New York: W. W. Norton, 451–52.

45. Glenn Mitchell, *The Marx Brothers Encyclopedia,* London: B. T. Batsford, 1996, 95–97. Of their fee, $1,000 a week was paid to script writers.

46. Internet Movie Database, "Monkey Business: Trivia," https://www.imdb.com/title/tt0022158/trivia Accessed January 21, 2021.

47. Arce, *Groucho,* 167–69.

48. Gary Cooper was a movie heartthrob considered devastatingly handsome.

49. Bader, *Groucho Marx and Other Short Stories,* xiv–xvii; Groucho Marx, *Beds,* Indianapolis: Bobbs-Merrill, 1977 reprint of 1930 original. Note: I once had a hard-cover copy of this book and sold it in favor of keeping a paperback edition. Big mistake! A hard copy in good condition can command hundreds of dollars.

50. Chandler, *Hello, I Must Be Going,* 64–65.

51. Harpo Marx with Rowland Barber, *Harpo Speaks!* New York: Limelight Editions, 1985, pp. 359–414. Susan's poem in p. 476.

52. S. Elizabeth Bird, ed. *Dressing in Feathers: The Construction of the Indian in American Popular Culture,* Boulder, CO: Westview Press, 1996.

53. The 1928 Meriam Report detailed the horrendous conditions under which many Natives lived and the challenges faced on reservations.

54. David Grann, *Killers of the Flower Moon: The Osage Murders and the Birth of the FBI,* New York: Doubleday, 2017.

55. Ronald Takaki, *A Different Mirror: A History of Multicultural America,* Boston: Little, Brown & Company, 1997; Robert Hoxie, *This Indian Country: American Indian Activists and the Place They Made,* New York: Penguin USA, 2013; Roxanne Dunbar-Ortiz, *An Indigenous Peoples' History of the United States,* Boston: Beacon Press, 2015.

56. Gardner, *The Marx Brothers as Social Critics,* 7–8, 169.

Chapter Five

1. President Herbert Hoover initially used a lower-case "depression" to refer to the financial crisis because "recession" had a more serious connotation. Charles Michelson, a publicist for the Democratic National Committee, used "great depression" in advance of the 1932 presidential election to discredit Hoover's economic policies, again in lower-case form. Most historians believe the capitalized version came via British economist Lionel Robbin, who titled his 1934 book *The Great Depression.*

2. Paramount's movie division hemorrhaged $6 million and its theaters the remaining $12 million.

3. Hector Arce, *Groucho,* New York: Perigee Books, 1979, 194–98.

4. Wes D. Gehring, *The Marx Brothers: A Bio-Bibliography,* Westport, CT: Greenwood Press, 1987, 62; Arce, *Groucho,* 201.

5. Arce, *Groucho,* 199.

6. *Ibid.,* 206.

7. Maxine Marx, *Growing Up with Chico,* New York: Limelight Books, 1980, 71.

8. Arthur Marx, *My Life with Groucho,* Fort Lee, NJ: Barricade Books, 1992, 119, 121.

9. Joe Adamson, *Groucho, Harpo, Chico and Sometimes Zeppo,* New York: Simon and Schuster, 1973, 127. Parenthetical emphasis by Adamson.

10. Arthur Marx, *My Life with Groucho,* 121.

11. Perelman remained a good friend of Groucho's. He left the team to cultivate a burgeoning writing career. Like many writers, he worried about becoming identified as merely a gag man for a particular act. His style was also very literary and he sometimes clashed with Groucho, who complained that the average person would not understand his references. Perelman went on to a stellar career as a writer, humorist, and screenwriter. In 1956, he won an Oscar for his screenplay of *Around the World in 80 Days.*

12. Gardner, *The Marx Brothers as Social Critics,* 93.

13. National Center for Educational Statistics, "120 Years of American Education: A Statistical Portrait," https://nces.ed.gov/pubsearch/pubsinfo.asp?pubid=93442 Accessed February 17, 2021.

14. This was indeed fast work considering that Roosevelt was not yet in office when Congress took up the 21st Amendment. Until the passage of the 20th Amendment, newly elected presidents were sworn in on March 4. The crisis of the Depression prompted Congress to shorten the so-called "lame duck" interval between the outgoing and incoming presidents, but it was not applicable until the 1936 election. Amendments to the Constitution take time; they require the assent of 2/3 of both the Senate and the House of Representatives. Once that has been accomplished, ¾ of the states must approve the amendment. Contrary to popular views and political bluster, the president has no official role in the amendment process.

15. Daniel Okrent, *Last Call; The Rise and Fall of Prohibition,* New York: Scribner, 2010, 373.

16. W. J. Rorabaugh, *The Alcoholic Republic: An American Tradition,* Oxford, UK: Oxford University Press, 1979.

17. There were 48 states in 1920.

18. This was possible because the 21st Amendment recognized the power of individual states to regulate alcohol laws within their borders. The following states—in alphabetical order—remained dry, with the years in parentheses indicating when they finally allowed alcohol: Kansas (1948), Oklahoma (1959), Mississippi (1966),

North Carolina (1937), Tennessee (1939), and Texas (1935). Most states also have local-option laws that allow individual municipalities to ban the sale of alcohol. As of 2020, more than 500 towns and counties forbid alcohol sales.

19. Among the loopholes were provisions allowing "medical use" of spirits. The well-connected had little trouble finding compliant physicians willing to write "prescriptions."

20. Most nations consider their official border to be a certain distance out to sea from landfall. The U.S. today has a 12-nautical-mile boundary, though some states extend that. In 1932, the boundary was just three nautical miles. Alcohol could be served on boats beyond that mark. More significantly, smugglers anchored beyond the three-mile limit and waited for an opportune time to offload their wares without being detected.

21. Okrent, *Last Call*, 221. Note: In his 1943 book *Bound for Glory*, songwriter Woody Guthrie recounts a funny tale of his experience with adulterated "Jake," Jamaican ginger ale. Luckily, he lived to tell the tale.

22. Allen Eyles, *The Marx Brothers: Their World of Comedy*, London: Tantivy Press, 1974, 85.

23. Okrent, *Last Call*, 267.

24. "Prohibition," *Encyclopedia Britannica Online*, https://www.britannica.com/event/Prohibition-United-States-history-1920-1933#ref1215042 Accessed January 25, 2021; Marc Mappen, *Prohibition Gangsters: The Rise and fall of a Bad Generation*, New Brunswick, NJ: Rutgers University Press, 2013.

25. Larry Engelman, "Rum-running gave Detroit dim view of prohibition years," *Smithsonian Magazine*, June 1979, 113–25.

26. "How many speakeasies were open in New York City during Prohibition?" New York Historical Society, https://www.nyhistory.org/community/speakeasies Accessed January 25, 2021.

27. Speakeasy made its entrance into American slang in 1889, though it appears to have been in use in Australia since 1837. It is believed to have been a smuggler's term that's a short cut for either "Speaking softly shop," or perhaps "Speak easy! The police are watching." The term blind tiger dates to 1857, moonshine to 1877, barrel-house to 1883, blind pig to 1887, and bootleg to 1906.

28. The term "dive," meaning a seedy place to eat or drink, has been around since the 15th century. Dive bars were often those one "dove" into as they were under street level and were known for being dark, damp, and unsavory. Over time, a dive bar became any down-market drinking establishment, whether or not it was subterranean.

29. Maurice Charney, *The Comic World of the Marx Brothers' Movies*, Madison, NJ: Fairleigh Dickinson University Press, 2007, 75.

30. Okrent, *Last Call*, 373.

31. Groucho Marx, *Groucho and Me: The Autobiography of Groucho Marx*, New York: Fireside Book, 1989, 210.

32. *Oxford English Dictionary*.

33. Eyles, *The Marx Brothers*, 88.

34. Adamson, *Groucho, Harpo, Chico and Sometimes Zeppo*, 191. Adamson hated the song and remarked, "people are rumored to have *liked* [it] in 1932." [Emphasis his.]

35. Martin A. Gardner, *The Marx Brothers as Social Critics*, McFarland: Jefferson, NC, 2009, 97.

36. Groucho could indeed play the guitar.

37. National Center for Educational Statistics, "120 Years of American Education: A Statistical Portrait." The numbers were much lower for students of color; just 1.4 percent of males and 1.2 percent of females obtained a college degree.

38. Helen Lefkowitz Horowitz, *Campus Life: Undergraduate Cultures from the End of the Eighteenth Century to the Present*, New York: Alfred A. Knopf, 1987, 193.

39. *Ibid.*, 197.

40. *Ibid.*, 155.

41. *Ibid.*, 125; Paula Fass, *The Damned and the Beautiful: American Culture in the 1920s*, New York: Oxford University Press, 1977, Chapter 6.

42. Horowitz, *Campus Life*, 218.

43. "Thelma Todd," *Wikipedia*, https://en.wikipedia.org/wiki/Thelma_Todd Accessed January 25, 2021; Glenn Mitchell, *The Marx Brothers Encyclopedia*, London: B. T. Batsford, 1996, 231–32; Michelle Morgan, *The Ice Cream Blonde: The Whirlwind Life and Mysterious Death of Screwball Comedienne Thelma Todd*, Chicago: Chicago Review Press, 2015.

44. Brian Burnsed, "Athletic departments that make more than they spend still a minority," September 18, 2015, http://www.ncaa.org/about/resources/media-center/news/athletics-departments-make-more-they-spend-still-minority, Accessed January 25, 2021; Katharina Buchholz, Statista, "The Richest College Football Programs, https://www.statista.com/chart/20152/college-football-programs-earning-most-profits/ Accessed January 25, 2021.

45. Ethan Bauer, "Does high-level NCAA football have a graduation problem?" *Deseret News*, January 12, 2020, https://www.deseret.com/indepth/2020/1/12/21058607/clemson-lsu-championship-title-game-graduation-rates Accessed January 25, 2021.

46. Horowitz, *Campus Life*, 131.

47. Notre Dame's backfield was dubbed the "Four Horseman" because of a famed piece of prose from sportswriter Grantland Rice. In 1925 he paralleled their prowess on the field to the Biblical four horsemen of the Apocalypse.

48. Lily Rothman, "The Deadliest Football Seasons on Record," *Time Magazine*, September 18, 2014.

49. John R. Thelin, *Games Colleges Play:*

Scandal and Reform in Intercollegiate Athletics," Baltimore: Johns Hopkins UP, 1994; Allan Sacks and Ellen Staurowsky, *College Athletes for Hire*, New York: Praeger, 1998; Robert Ian Benedikt, "Analysis of the Modern Football Crisis: Historical Perspective and Recommendation, University of Texas at Austin Honors Thesis, 2017, https://repositories. lib.utexas.edu/bitstream/handle/2152/63615/ benediktrobert_3880563_44275389_Benedikt_ Analysis_of_the_Modern_Football_Crisis_2017. pdf?sequence=2 Accessed January 25, 2021.

50. Raymond Schmidt, *College Football: The Transformation of an American Sport 1919 to 1930*, Syracuse, NY: Syracuse University Press, 2007.

51. The other contender is Harriet Beecher Stowe's 1852 novel *Uncle Tom's Cabin*. Apparently, the debate rests in part upon how one counts sales outside the United States.

52. *The Story of the Kelly Gang*, an hour-long 1906 Australian film, is generally regarded as the first true feature film.

53. Adamson, *Groucho, Harpo, Chico and Sometimes Zeppo*, 198.

54. Wes D. Gehring, *The Marx Brothers: A Bio-Bibliography*, Westport, CT, Greenwood Press, 1987, 64–65.

55. Burr's was the first known copyright of a song originally used in hymnals. Its true author was probably Robert Lowry, and the song appears in print as early as 1877.

56. Dreiser sued to try to stop the film when Paramount reneged on promises he could review the script.

57. Louvish, *Monkey Business*, 249.

58. Margo Miller, "Losing Your Grip," *The New Yorker*, May 18, 2020.

Chapter Six

1. A reminder: The new (or newly re-elected) president took office in March until the passage of the 20th Amendment on March 2, 1933, which moved inauguration to January 20.

2. For those who don't know, alphabet soup is a vegetable and broth mix into which pasta in the shape of letters has been added.

3. Many businesses hated the NRA and rejoiced when it was struck down as unconstitutional in 1935. The joke was on them, as the NRA was rewritten and folded into the 1935 National Labor Relations Act, widely regarded as the strongest worker protection act in U.S. history. Other provisions showed up in the 1938 Fair Labor Standards Act.

4. Both the Communist Party and various socialist parties attracted tens of thousands of new members during the worst years of the Depression. Similarly, some Americans admired Mussolini, whose Italy was one of the few nations to ward off a depression. Others, including Charles

Lindbergh and Henry Ford, were initially enamored of Hitler.

5. Wes D. Gehring, *The Marx Brothers: A Bio-Bibliography*, Westport, CT, Greenwood Press, 1987, 66.

6. Joe Adamson, *Groucho, Harpo, Chico and Sometimes Zeppo*, New York: Simon and Schuster, 1973, 213–16.

7. Groucho Marx, *Groucho and Me: The Autobiography of Groucho Marx*, New York: Fireside Book, 1959, 239–40.

8. Adamson, *Groucho, Harpo, Chico and Sometimes Zeppo*, 222–23.

9. Hector Arce, *Groucho*, New York: Perigee Books, 1979, 212.

10. Maurice Charney, *The Comic World of the Marx Brothers' Movies*, Madison, NJ: Fairleigh Dickinson University Press, 2007, 80.

11. Arce, *Groucho*, 212.

12. Maxine Marx, *Growing Up with Chico*, New York: Limelight Books, 1980, 79–80.

13. Gehring, *The Marx Brothers*, 66.

14. Charlotte Chandler, *Hello, I Must Be Going: Groucho and His Friends*, New York: Citadel Press, 1993, 282.

15. Gehring, *The Marx Brothers*, 67.

16. Adamson, *Groucho, Harpo, Chico and Sometimes Zeppo*, 217.

17. Allen quoted in Arce, *Groucho*, 213.

18. Simon Louvish, *Monkey Business: The Lives and Legends of The Marx Brothers*, New York: Thomas Dunne Books, 1999, 270.

19. There is no mention of the Schwartz Brothers in Anthony Slide, *The Encyclopedia of Vaudeville*, Jackson: University of Mississippi Press, 2012. Tobias shows up again in a 1939 lawsuit in which he was unsuccessful.

20. Roy Blount, Jr. *Hail, Hail Euphoria!* New York: HarperCollins, 2010, 111–15; *Seven Years Bad Luck,* https://www.youtube.com/watch?v=_ 73nk6IYbB0 Accessed January 26, 2021. *The Hallucination of Baron von Munchausen* sequence is a nightmarish dream and bears little resemblance to the Marx Brothers routine.

21. Allen Eyles, *The Marx Brothers: Their World of Comedy*, London: Tantivy Press, 1974, 104. You can watch the hat routine from a 2001 production of *Waiting for Godot* at https://www. youtube.com/watch?v=1gnZN4SEhjA Accessed January 26, 2021.

22. Blount Jr. *Hail, Hail Euphoria!* Blount uses the phrase as the unofficial subtitle of his book.

23. Eyles, *The Marx Brothers*, 109.

24. Captain Alfred Dreyfus was sentenced to life imprisonment in 1894, allegedly for passing French military secrets to German intelligence officers. Evidence clearly pointed to a different individual, who was acquitted in a lightning-quick trial. Dreyfus won a new trial—courtesy of a public outcry—but was again found guilty, though his sentence was reduced to 10 years. Dreyfus' travails were clearly linked to his Jewish roots, though the trials stoked wider

outbreaks of French anti–Semitism. Dreyfus was not exonerated until 1906. It is worth noting that both Dreyfus and Marx were Alsatian Jews.

25. Louvish, *Monkey Business*, 38.

26. The full text of the 1917 Selective Service Act can be found at https://www.loc.gov/law/help/statutes-at-large/65th-congress/session-1/c65s1ch15.pdf Accessed January 26, 2021.

27. Louvish, *Monkey Business*, 102–03.

28. Arce, *Groucho*, 94.

29. Louvish, *Monkey Business*, 103.

30. Groucho Marx and Richard Anobile, *The Marx Brothers Scrapbook*, New York: Grosset and Dunlap, 1974, 174. Capital-letter emphasis in the original.

31. Martin A. Gardner, *The Marx Brothers as Social Critics*, McFarland: Jefferson, NC, 2009, 17. Gardner is among those postulating a connection between the Freedonian Rebellion of 1826–27 and the choice of the name Freedonia in *Duck Soup*.

32. Gardner, *The Marx Brothers as Social Critics*, 76–77.

33. Wilson was the president of Princeton from 1902–10.

34. Glenn Mitchell, *The Marx Brothers Encyclopedia*, London: B. T. Batsford, 1996,83.

35. Gardner, *The Marx Brothers as Social Critics*, 85.

36. The phrase "war to end war" actually comes from H.G. Wells, not Woodrow Wilson, who merely alluded to it.

37. Chandler, *Hello, I Must Be Going*, 271.

38. Gardner, *The Marx Brothers as Social Critics*, 83.

39. Louvish, *Monkey Business*, 278.

40. Louvish, *Monkey Business*, 270; Gehring, *The Marx Brothers*, 66.

41. Arce, *Groucho*, 215.

42. Gardner, *The Marx Brothers as Social Critics*,168.

43. Michael E. Parrish, *Anxious Decades: America in Prosperity and Depression, 1920–1941*, New York: W. W. Norton, 1992, esp. chapter 10.

44. Ultimate Movie rankings, https://www.ultimatemovierankings.com/1933-top-box-office-movies/; https://www.ultimatemovierankings.com/1932-top-box-office-movies/ Accessed January 26, 2021.

45. Maxine Marx, *Growing Up with Chico*, 83–84.

46. Actors and Artistes of America, an umbrella union for stage actors, musical artists (singers, producers, stagehands, dancers, and producers), variety artists, and—ironically given Chico's *faux* accent—the Guild of Italian American Actors. In 2012, SAG merged with the American Federation of Television and Radio Artists. It is now known as SAG-AFTRA and is chartered by the AFL-CIO.

47. Gehring, *The Marx Brothers*, 71. It was also a parody of a popular Time Inc. radio show,

The March of Time, which gained greater fame after 1935 when it added newsreel footage for short-subject reels shown in movie theaters before the feature film.

48. *Ibid.*, 70.

49. Groucho Marx and Richard Anobile, *The Marx Brothers Scrapbook*, 174–75.

50. Harpo Marx with Rowland Barber, *Harpo Speaks!* New York: Limelight Editions, 1985, 300.

51. *Ibid.*, 301.

52. *Ibid.* 307–08.

53. *Ibid.* 316–17.

54. *Ibid.*, 327.

55. *Ibid.*, 330–37. Harpo's "Exapano Mapcase" pseudonym came from what the Russian letters on his cases suggested to him.

56. "That Marx Guy, Again," in Robert S. Bader, ed. *Groucho Marx and Other Short Stories and Tall Tales: Selected Writings of Groucho Marx*, Boston: Faber and Faber, 1993, 103–04.

57. Charlene Mires, "I'd Rather Be in Philadelphia," *The Encyclopedia of Greater Philadelphia*, https://philadelphiaencyclopedia.org/archive/id-rather-be-in-philadelphia/ Accessed January 26, 2021.

58. Paul Wesolowski, "The Freedonia Gazette," https://www.marx-brothers.org/whyaduck/merchandise/gazette.htm Accessed January 26, 2021. The magazine's end date is considered tentative.

59. Adamson, *Groucho, Harpo, Chico and Sometimes Zeppo*, 211.

60. Blount Jr. *Hail, Hail Euphoria!* 141–42.

61. Chandler, *Hello, I Must Be Going*, 208–09.

Chapter Seven

1. Maxine Marx, *Growing Up with Chico*, New York: Limelight Books, 1980, 84–85.

2. Loew had an empire of amusement parks, theaters, music halls, film-production companies, etc., that lacked coordination and siphoned resources from movies. His deal with Mayer placed the latter in charge of MGM studios, and 24-year-old producer Irving Thalberg became chief of production.

3. Hector Arce, *Groucho*, New York: Perigee Books, 1979.

4. Charlotte Chandler, *Hello, I Must Be Going: Groucho and His Friends*, New York: Citadel Press, 1993, 172.

5. Arthur Marx, *My Life with Groucho*, Fort Lee, NJ: Barricade Books, 1992, 132.

6. *Ibid.*, 133–34.

7. Roy Blount, Jr. *Hail, Hail Euphoria*, New York: HarperCollins, 2010, 140. Blount reports that Zeppo negotiated a five-picture deal for his brothers. He confuses Gummo's role with Zeppo's. The only deal Zeppo directly negotiated for his brothers was 1938's *Room Service*.

8. Martin A. Gardner, *The Marx Brothers as Social Critics*, Jefferson, NC: McFarland, 2009, 21.

9. Arthur Marx, *My Life with Groucho*, 137; Gardner, *The Marx Brothers as Social Critics*, 176.

10. Simon Louvish, *Monkey Business: The Lives and Legends of The Marx Brothers*, New York: Thomas Dunne Books, 1999, *286*.

11. Glenn Mitchell, *The Marx Brothers Encyclopedia*, London: B. T. Batsford, 1996, 39.

12. Chandler, *Hello, I Must Be Going*, 172.

13. Louvish, *Monkey Business*, 291. Sam Wood died in 1949, two years after Hollywood bore the brunt of the Red Scare.

14. Arce, *Groucho*, New York: Perigee Books, 1979, 228; Louvish, *Monkey Business*, 288.

15. Arce, *Groucho*, 231.

16. Chandler, *Hello, I Must Be Going*, 352.

17. Robert Sklar, *Movie-Made America: How Movies Changed American Life*, New York: Random House, 1975, 182.

18. Steven J. Ross, *Working-Class Hollywood: Silent Films and the Shaping of Class in America*, Princeton, NJ: Princeton University Press, 1999.

19. Larry May, *Screening Out the Past: The Birth of Mass Culture and the Motion Picture Industry*, New York: Oxford University Press, 1983.

20. *Ibid.*, 179. Roscoe "Fatty" Arbuckle (1887–1933) was a popular silent film actor. In 1922, actress Virginia Rappe died from injuries sustained at a wild party thrown by Arbuckle. He endured three trials on rape and manslaughter charges. Two ended in hung juries, before Arbuckle was acquitted. His career suffered tremendously as he was (metaphorically) convicted in the court of public opinion, which made him essentially unemployable. He tried to direct under the name of William Goodrich, but died of a heart attack, allegedly the day after signing a contract to act in a Warner Brothers film.

21. *Ibid.*, 182, 205, 232–33.

22. The text of the 1927 and 1930 codes can be found in Steven Mintz and Randy Roberts, *Hollywood's America: United States History Through Its Films*, St. James, NY: Brandywine Press, 1993, 142–56. The 1930 code runs 10 pages.

23. Sklar, *Movie-Made America*, 189.

24. Richard Pells, *Radical Visions and American Dreams: Culture and Social Thought in the Depression Years*," Middletown, CT: Wesleyan University Press, 1984, 268.

25. Among them is Eyles, who called it "lamentable." Allen Eyles, *The Marx Brothers: Their World of Comedy*, London: Tantivy Press, 1974, 111.

26. Louvish, *Monkey Business*, 262–63.

27. Lyons used it in the title of his 1941 book. He was an ardent Stalinist during the 1930s and a Moscow-based correspondent for United Press International from 1928 to 1934. His enthusiasm for the Soviet Union waned as World War Two approached. Like numerous Communist Party of the United States members, he was disgusted by the 1939 the Molotov-Ribbentrop Pact, and the cooperation between Hitler and Stalin in dismantling Poland. Lyons became an anticommunist crusader.

28. "The New Deal is No Revolution," Colin Gordon, ed. *Major Problems in American History 1920–1945: Documents and Essays*, Boston: Houghton Mifflin, 308. Roosevelt also co-opted populism, whether expressed in reformist terms such as that of Francis Townshend, whose views were watered down and became the Social Security Act; the ambiguous populism of Huey Long; or the right-leaning appeals of Father Coughlin, who initially supported New Deal, but turned against it, drifted into anti–Semitism, and was banned from the radio by Pope Pius XI.

29. Rita James Simon, ed., *As We Saw the Thirties; Essays on Social and Political Movements of a Decade*, Urbana: University of Illinois Press, 1969, 111.

30. Melvyn Dubofsky, "Not So Radical Years: Another Look at the 1930s," Eileen Boris and Nelson Lichtenstein, eds. *Major Problems in the History of American Workers: Documents and Essays*, Boston: Houghton Mifflin, 2003, 308. See also Lizabeth Cohen, *Making a New Deal: Industrial Workers in Chicago, 1919–1939*, New York: Cambridge University Press, 1992; Seymour Martin Lipset and Gary Marks, *It Didn't Happen Here: Why Socialism Failed in the United States*, New York; W. W. Norton, 2000.

31. William Stott, Documentary Expression and Thirties America, Chicago: University of Chicago Press, 1986, 103–04. The terms "primitive" and "folk" art referred to creative expressions produced by those without formal academic training. "Primitive" is a more problematic term, as it often implied naiveté, especially when applied to art created by African Americans, immigrants, and Native Americans. Folk art—a term that embraced everything from painting and poetry to dance and music—is that which veered from expected conventions.

32. Lawrence Levine, *Highbrow Lowbrow, The Emergence of Cultural Hierarchy in America*, Cambridge, MA: Harvard University Press, 1990, especially Chapter two.

33. La Scala is the popular diminutive of Teatro alla Scala.

34. Marx, *My Life with Groucho*, 134.

35. Gardner, *The Marx Brothers as Social Critics*, 123.

36. Eyles, *The Marx Brothers*, 118.

37. Marx, *My Life with Groucho*, 137. Sources differ over how many people were in the cabin. Arthur says 20; others say 15. The scene is paced so well that it's hard to count how many food-bearing stewards entered the room.

38. *Ibid.*, 137–38; Arce, *Groucho*, 229.

39. Joe Adamson, *Groucho, Harpo, Chico and Sometimes Zeppo*, New York: Simon and Schuster, 1973, 291–92. Emphasis in original.

40. Paul Sann, *Fads, Follies and Delusions of the American People*, New York: Bonanza Books, 1967, 297–300.

41. Thanks go to my friend Chris Rohmann, a Western Massachusetts theatre critic, for helping me pick through farcical threads. He also reminded me that Michael Frayn's award-winning *Noises Off* (1982) drew upon Plautus. More recently, *One Man, Two Guvnors* (2011) drew inspiration from *commedia dell'arte* playwright Carlo Goldini.

42. Gardner, *The Marx Brothers as Social Critics*, 168.

43. A U.S. Navy crew made a transatlantic flight before Alcock in 1919, but in a seaplane that made numerous stops and took three weeks to reach its destination.

44. *Ibid.*, 65.

45. "List of accidents and incidents involving commercial aircraft," Wikipedia, https://en.wikipedia.org/wiki/List_of_accidents_and_incidents_involving_commercial_aircraft; "List of fatalities from aviation accidents," *Wikipedia*, https://en.wikipedia.org/wiki/List_of_fatalities_from_aviation_accidents Accessed January 28, 2021. The toll from airliner crashes today is much higher, even though flight is now a safe way to travel. Today's commercial flights carry hundreds of passengers in each flight on some 44,000 flights daily, whereas air flights were much rarer in the 1920s and '30s and a commercial plane seldom carried more than six to ten passengers and crew.

46. The Baltic Sea city of St. Petersburg, Russia, has undergone name changes since its founding by Czar Peter the Great in 1703. St. Petersburg became Petrograd in 1914, was renamed Leningrad upon Lenin's death in 1924, and reverted to St. Petersburg in 1991, when the Soviet Union was in dissolution.

47. Edward Said, *Orientalism*, New York: Pantheon Books, 1978.

48. Gardner, *The Marx Brothers as Social Critics*, 124.

49. Italian dressing was first made in Framingham, Massachusetts in 1941.

50. *"A Night at the Opera (1935) Official Trailer,"* https://www.youtube.com/watch?v=tu6COUl3fx8 Accessed January 28, 2021.

51. *Ibid.*, 135; Claire Suddath, "A Brief History of Suspenders," *Time Magazine*, December 16, 2010.

52. "The 'I want to be alone' quote," *Garbo Forever*, http://www.garboforever.com/I_want_to_be_alone.htm#Films, *Accessed January 28, 2021*.

53. Louvish, *Monkey Business*, 291; Arce, *Groucho*, 236.

54. Adamson, *Groucho, Harpo, Chico and Sometimes Zeppo*, 299–300; Wes D. Gehring, *The Marx Brothers: A Bio-Bibliography*, Westport, CT: Greenwood Press, 1987, 73–74.

Chapter Eight

1. Joe Adamson, *Groucho, Harpo, Chico and Sometimes Zeppo*, New York: Simon and Schuster, 1973, 310.

2. The overall setting is widely considered to be based on Saratoga Springs, New York. The horse track there is impressive, but the one in *A Day at the Races* looks more like Churchill Downs in Lexington, Kentucky. Both locations also have steeplechase racing.

3. Adamson, *Groucho, Harpo, Chico and Sometimes Zeppo*, 312.

4. *Ibid.*, 313.

5. Simon Louvish, *Monkey Business: The Lives and Legends of The Marx Brothers*, New York: Thomas Dunne Books, 1999, 305.

6. Adamson, *Groucho, Harpo, Chico and Sometimes Zeppo*, 313.

7. Charlotte Chandler, *Hello, I Must Be Going: Groucho and His Friends*, New York: Citadel Press, 1993, 347.

8. Adamson, *Groucho, Harpo, Chico and Sometimes Zeppo*, 311. Groucho claimed he was testing whether the lines worked, or if audiences were laughing at his facial gestures.

9. Hector Arce, *Groucho*, New York: Perigee Books, 1979, 247.

10. Chandler, *Hello, I Must Be Going*, 355–57.

11. Louvish, *Monkey Business*, 306.

12. Arthur Marx, *My Life with Groucho*, Fort Lee, NJ: Barricade Books, 1992, 140; Groucho Marx, *Groucho and Me: The Autobiography of Groucho Marx*, New York: Fireside Books, 1959, 248.

13. Some of this became *Go West*, a 1940 Marx Brothers film, but Ruby and Kalmar were not credited as scriptwriters.

14. Arce, *Groucho*, 251.

15. Chandler, *Hello, I Must Be Going*, 358. Pirosh incorrectly said that the Marx Brothers liked and respected Wood. They did not!

16. Arce, *Groucho*, 253.

17. Adamson, *Groucho, Harpo, Chico and Sometimes Zeppo*, 319.

18. Glenn Mitchell, *The Marx Brothers Encyclopedia*, London: B. T. Batsford, 1996, 73, 65.

19. Arce, *Groucho*, 244.

20. *Ibid.*, 252.

21. *Ibid.*, 251–52.

22. Adamson, *Groucho, Harpo, Chico and Sometimes Zeppo*, 320–23.

23. When President William McKinley was shot in 1901, his doctors did not trust x-rays. McKinley actually died of gangrene, not the gunshot wound. Had he lived, Theodore Roosevelt might not have become president.

24. Barbara Ehrenreich and Deirdre English, *For Her Own Good: 150 Years of the Experts' Advice to Women*, New York: Anchor Books, 1979, especially chapter three. To this day, 13 states refuse to license midwives.

25. Harvey Green, *Fit for America: Health, Fitness, Sport and American Society*, Baltimore: Johns Hopkins University Press, 1986, chapter six.

26. American health care remains saddled with "cures" that most physicians dismiss as

ineffective or fakery: anti-aging creams, Christian Science healing, copper bracelets for arthritis, crystal healing, diet pills, electric belts for weight reduction, homeopathy, rebirthing, etc. The medical establishment is also skeptical of numerous natural medicines, claiming there is no control over their quality or the manufacturing process. (The same has been claimed about drugs made in Canada, which are cheaper and undergo testing at least as good as that in the United States.) Many insurances refuse to reimburse for acupuncture or chiropractic care. Some AMA judgments are suspect given that medications it once opposed are now prescribed to patients. Similarly, doctors have been accused of prescribing drugs that companies paid them to endorse. In recent history, medical practitioners have been sued for over-prescribing opioids. The *Journal of the American Medical Association* did not endorse chiropractic care until 2017, even though the AMA lost a lawsuit in 1989, when chiropractors sued to be removed from practices deemed fakery by its 1963 Committee on Quackery. The line between public safety and turf wars is sometimes thin.

27. Pope Brock, *Charlatan: America's Most Dangerous Huckster, the Man Who Pursued Him, and the Age of Hucksterism*, New York: Crown Publishing, 2008. I recommend this book over the eccentric and uneven pseudo-biographical film *Nuts!* (2016).

28. "Mayo brothers" is now called the Mayo Clinic. It is named for its founders, William and Charles Mayo. Groucho's joke is that he studied with Horace and John Dodge, the brothers who started Dodge Motors.

29. The list of United States water spas is a long one that includes Saratoga Springs; Berkeley Springs, West Virginia; Hot Springs, Arkansas; Poland Springs, Maine; and Warm Springs, Georgia. The last of these was where President Franklin Roosevelt died on April 12, 1945. The town in which I live, Northampton, Massachusetts, once held two water spas: E. E. Denniston's Round Hill Water Cure facility, and another founded by famed blind abolitionist David Ruggles. When Ruggles died in 1849, German immigrant Charles Munde assumed control over the Florence Water Cure. The efficacy of drinking mineral water continues to be debated.

30. Wikipedia has an informative site on spas: https://en.wikipedia.org/wiki/Spa Accessed February 24, 2021.

31. Each spring—and there are 22 in Saratoga—contains different minerals. Many have high concentrations of silica, salt, and/or sulfur. Some have traces of radium.

32. Green, *Fit for America*, 141–154, 167–71.

33. Timothy Lavin, "The Sport of Kings," *The Atlantic*, May 2006, https://www.theatlantic.com/magazine/archive/2006/05/the-sport-of-kings/304911/ Accessed February 24, 2021.

34. Elliott J. Gorn and Warren Goldstein, *A Brief History of American Sports*, Urbana: University of Illinois Press, 1993, 54.

35. Many sources, including Wikipedia, incorrectly give an 1894 founding date for the AJC. That 1894 organization is a breeders' registry.

36. Steven A. Riess, *City Games: The Evolution of American Urban Society and the Rise of Sports*, Urbana: University of Illinois Press, 1989, 181.

37. Punter as a synonym for gambler is said to derive from the French *ponter*, meaning to bet against the bank. This may be more legend than fact. According to the *Oxford English Dictionary*, it was first recorded in *Phillips's New World of Words* in 1706.

38. *Ibid.*, 187–89.

39. There is some confusion about when the Triple Crown—the Kentucky Derby, the Preakness Stakes, and the Belmont Stakes—came into being. Sir Barton won all three races in 1919 and is regarded as the first Triple Crown winner, though few sports columnists used the term until 1923, and the *Daily Race Form*, which remains the go-to source for bettors, added Triple Crown to its lexicon in 1930, thereby elevating its status.

40. Paradoxically, gambling revenues usually rise during boom times rather than during lean ones. Lotteries and their poorer cousin "playing the numbers" are the only types of gambling that don't suffer during prolonged economic downturns.

41. Bettors can wager that a horse will win, place, or show; that is, finish first, second, or third. Place and show have lower returns than winning. These are also determined by the total amounts wagered. Payouts only work downward. That is, if you bet on a horse to show, you will receive the show payout even if the horse wins. If you bet on one to win and it finishes second, you get no payout unless you've also wagered a place wager.

42. Mitchell, *The Marx Brothers Encyclopedia*, 195.

43. Martin A. Gardner, *The Marx Brothers as Social Critics*, Jefferson, NC: McFarland, 2009, 180–81.

44. Stuffy's parody of Sherlock Holmes is actually based on actor William Gillette's portrayal; Holmes is not depicted as wearing a deerstalker cap in Arthur Conan Doyle's novels.

45. "Spike Lee's *Bamboozled*," https://www.nytimes.com/interactive/2020/09/25/opinion/blackface-tv-movies-race.html?campaign_id=9&emc=edit_nn_20200929&instance_id=22613&nl=the-morning&regi_id=93948453&section_index=4&section_name=play_watch_eat_baseball&segment_id=39290&te=1&user_id=58b20eb57046a0b9f6628eeb67918251 Accessed February 24, 2021.

46. *A Day at the Races*, Turner Entertainment Productions, Special Features, 2004.

47. Mitchell, *The Marx Brothers Encyclopedia*, 198.

48. The end of Reconstruction is generally

considered 1877, shortly after the disputed presidential election. Northern Republicans agreed to remove remaining federal troops from the South in exchange for the acceptance of Rutherford B. Hayes as the winner of the 1876 election over Democratic challenger Samuel J. Tilden.

49. Fay's first name is sometimes listed as Vivian. She was actually trained in ballet, though she also performed in vaudeville and in other productions that deemphasized classical ballet.

50. Eileen Southern, *The Music of Black Americans*, New York: W. W. Norton & Company, 1971. See also Roger D. Abrahams, *Singing the Master: The Emergence of African American Culture in the Plantation South*, New York: Oxford Press, 1992; Lawrence Levine, *Black Culture and Black Consciousness: Afro-American Folk Thought from Slavery to Freedom*, New York: Oxford UP, 1977, especially chapter 3. Various books from Howard W. Odum and Guy B. Johnson published in the early 20th century also delve into Black music and its themes. The same is true of 20th- and 21st-century offerings from the voluminous catalogue of Julius Lester.

51. Christopher Smith, *Dancing Revolution: Bodies, Space, and Sound in American Cultural History*, Urbana: University of Illinois Press, 2019, 91.

52. *Ibid.*, 85.

53. Anderson went on to record "All God's Chillun Got Rhythm." Alas, Ms. Anderson had chronic asthma, had to quit performing in 1942, and died seven years later. She was just 45. Herb Jeffries took over lead vocals upon Anderson's forced retirement.

54. Southern, *The Music of Black Americans*, 169.

55. Frederick Douglass, "The Hutchinson Family–Hunkerism," *The North Star,* October 27, 1848, http://utc.iath.virginia.edu/minstrel/miar03bt.html Accessed February 24, 2021.

56. Lee's *Bamboozled;* "List of entertainers who performed in blackface," *Wikipedia*, https://en.wikipedia.org/wiki/List_of_entertainers_who_performed_in_blackface Accessed February 24, 2021.

57. For more on blackface during the 1930s, see Peter Stanfield, "An Octoroon in the Kindling: American Vernacular and Blackface Minstrelsy in 1930s Hollywood," *American Studies* 31:3 (December 1997), 407–38.

58. Eric Lott, *Love & Theft: Blackface Minstrelsy & the American Working Class*, New York: Oxford UP, 1993. Quotes are from Lott, "The Seeming Counterfeit: Racial Politics and Early Blackface Minstrelsy," *American Quarterly* 43:2 (June 1991), 223–54, 228, 237, 247. *Love & Theft* evolved from the *American Quarterly* study.

59. W. T. Lhamon, *Raising Cain: Blackface Performance from Jim Crow to Hip Hop*, Cambridge, MA: Harvard University Press, 1995.

60. Such studies are too numerous to list. Micah Salkind's review of Miles White's *From Jim Crow to Jay-Z: Race, Rap, and the Performance of Masculinity*, Urbana: University of Illinois Press, 2011, is a succinct overview of several recent works. It can be viewed on H-Net Reviews, https://www.h-net.org/reviews/showpdf.php?id=37051 Accessed February 24, 2021.

61. Director Melvin Van Peebles is African American, and the film does deal with racism, but *Watermelon Man* is at best a mixed message film from a director soon to gain fame for Blaxploitation films that used racial stereotyping to make points about systemic racism.

62. Michael Rogin, "Blackface, White Noise: The Jewish Jazz Singer Finds His Voice," *Critical Inquiry* 18:3 (Spring 1992), 417–53, 447, 434. Rogin's study concerned itself mostly with jazz, which he called "musical miscegenation," and the 1927 film *The Jazz Singer*. See also Rogin, "Making America Home: Masquerade and Ethnic Assimilation in the Transition with Talking Pictures," *Journal of American History*, 79:3 (December 1992), 1050–77.

63. Daniel Lieberfeld and Judith Sanders, "Here Under False Pretenses: The Marx Brothers Crash the Gates," *The American Scholar* 64:1 (Winter 1995), 103–06.

64. Smith, *Dancing Revolution*, 90.

65. Arce, *Groucho*, 258–59; Scott Harrison, "From the Archives: Marx Brothers lose copyright case," *Los Angeles Times*, May 11, 2017, original story November 2, 1937, https://www.latimes.com/visuals/photography/la-me-fw-archives-marx-brothers-lose-copyright-case-20170323-story.html Accessed February 24, 2021.

Chapter Nine

1. *The Peter Principle* is the name of a 1969 book by Canadian educator Laurence J. Peter. In his study of management practices, Peter argued that they often erred by promoting successful individuals to positions beyond their ability. The Peter Principle has been extended to describe any situation in which individuals rise to levels of personal incompetence.

2. Joe Adamson, *Groucho, Harpo, Chico and Sometimes Zeppo*, New York: Simon and Schuster, 1973, 342.

3. Wes D. Gehring, *The Marx Brothers: A Bio-Bibliography*, Westport, CT: Greenwood Press, 1987, 79.

4. RKO emerged from vaudeville booking agents Benjamin Franklin Keith, Edward Albee II, and Martin Beck, the last of whom called his houses the Orpheum Circuit. The Keith-Albee-Orpheum merger took place in 1928, when vaudeville was in decline. RCA, a company formed in 1919, got involved with RKO Pictures in part because its head, David Sarnoff, pioneered in sound-on-film technology. RKO Pictures went bankrupt in 1959.

5. Hector Arce, *Groucho*, New York: Perigee Books, 1979, 257–58.

6. Reruns of both shows still appear on cable TV.

7. Simon Louvish, *Monkey Business: The Lives and Legends of The Marx Brothers*, New York: Thomas Dunne Books, 1999, 315; "Chico Marx Settles Check Suit of Bruneman Widow," *Los Angeles Times*, November 16, 1938. There was a complicated backstory in which Chico claimed Bruneman was a third party in a gambling debt. Chico produced a copy of a $1,000 check cashed by Bruneman. Note: Bruneman's name is sometimes spelled Brunemann.

8. Marx, *Growing Up with Chico*, New York: Limelight Books, 1986, 107–21. Quotes from pp. 112, 120.

9. Louvish, *Monkey Business*, 313.

10. Groucho Marx and Richard Anobile, *The Marx Brothers Scrapbook*, New York: Grosset and Dunlap, 1974, 150.

11. Arce, *Groucho*, 257.

12. Some sources dismiss the film's cost in the mistaken belief that eccentric billionaire Howard Hughes owned the studio. RKO was once owned by another wealthy man, Joseph Kennedy Sr., though he sold his shares in 1928.

13. Maurice Charney, *The Comic World of the Marx Brothers' Movies*, Madison, NJ: Fairleigh Dickinson University Press, 2007, 92.

14. Louvish, *Monkey Business*, 315.

15. Marx and Anobile, *The Marx Brothers Scrapbook*, 82.

16. *Ibid.*, 150.

17. Louvish, *Monkey Business*, 316.

18. Asro reprised the role of Sasha for the 1953 stage revival of *Room Service*.

19. The Hollywood production code wasn't the first to ban insults to things and words held sacred in the Judeo-Christian tradition. Such prohibitions are ancient and euphemisms in English date back at least as far as Middle English (1150–1470). Comedian W. C. Fields, a friend and contemporary of the Marx Brothers, used euphemisms such as drat and Godfrey Daniels.

20. Charlotte Chandler, *Hello, I Must Be Going: Groucho and His Friends*, New York: Citadel Press, 1993, 281; Arce, *Groucho*, 261.

21. Louvish, *Monkey Business*, 316; Gehring, *The Marx Brothers*, 79.

22. Most city papers published at least two daily editions at the time. The *Evening Telegram* began publishing in 1867, merged with the *New York Sun* in 1925, and with the *New York World* in 1931. It ceased publication in 1967.

23. Olivia Rutigliano, "Fire! A brief history of theatre fires in New York City—and the regulations that helped people escape them," *Lapham's Quarterly*, October 7, 2019, https://www.laphamsquarterly.org/roundtable/fire Accessed February 8, 2021.

24. Bibendum was a known advertising icon in 1938, having debuted in 1894.

25. Robert C. Allen, *Horrible Prettiness: Burlesque and American Culture*, Chapel Hill: University of North Carolina Press, 1991; Liz Goldwyn, *Pretty Things: The Last Generation of American Burlesque Queens*, New York: !t Books, 2010; Karen Abbott, *American Rose: A Nation Laid Bare: The Life and Times of Gypsy Rose Lee*, New York: Random House, 2010. Ironically, attacks on burlesque contributed to the emergence of seedier bump-and-grind strip clubs.

26. Charney, *The Comic World of the Marx Brothers' Movies*, 95.

27. Earlier pogroms took place, but were largely hidden from public view.

28. Arce, *Groucho*, 262.

Chapter Ten

1. Joe Adamson, *Groucho, Harpo, Chico and Sometimes Zeppo*, New York: Simon and Schuster, 1973, 349.

2. Greene quoted from Martin A. Gardner, *The Marx Brothers as Social Critics*, Jefferson, NC: McFarland, 2009, 82.

3. To read dialogue from the deleted courtroom scene, see Mikhael Uhlin, "At the Circus," *Marxology*, https://www.marx-brothers.org/marxology/loophole.htm Accessed February 9, 2021.

4. Hector Arce, *Groucho*, New York: Perigee Books, 1979, 263. *The Circle* was a flop. The idea was that America's top celebrities would have on-the-air gatherings filled with wit, chat, music, and sketches. It was meant to rival a variety hour sponsored by General Foods. *The Circle* debuted on January 15, 1939, with Groucho and Chico as original cast members. Ronald Colman and Noel Coward each tried hosting, before Basil Rathbone took over the role in February. The specifics of the show are so hard to pin down that some Marx scholars, including Glenn Mitchell, get its dates wrong and have it debuting in November, which was near the end of its run. Groucho and Chico apparently reworked older material and tried out gags that made their way into *Go West*. Only a few shows survive; Kellogg was happy to forget the entire experiment. Rathbone was reputedly unhappy with Groucho's ad-libs and wanted him to stick to the script, which simply wasn't going to happen!

5. Simon Louvish, *Monkey Business: The Lives and Legends of The Marx Brothers*, New York: Thomas Dunne Books, 1999, 319.

6. Adamson, *Groucho, Harpo, Chico and Sometimes Zeppo*, 350.

7. Brecher had an "additional dialogue" credit for *Fools for Scandal* (1938) and was an uncredited contributing writer for *The Wizard of Oz* (1939).

8. Adamson, *Groucho, Harpo, Chico and Sometimes Zeppo*, 352.

9. *Ibid.*, 351–52; Arce, *Groucho*, 267.

10. Arce, *Groucho*, 269.

11. Groucho Marx, *The Groucho Letters: Letters From and To Groucho Marx*, New York: Simon and Schuster, 1967, 20. Arce (p. 269) quotes Groucho telling Sheekman that Buzzell was "smarter than I had imagined" and reminded him of "a sort of Norman McLeod," but these remarks are not in *The Groucho Letters*. Note: Rushes are the raw footage from daily filming. All movies have more raw footage than can be used in the final cut, even when one discards multiple takes of the same scene. Good material but bad editing can sink what could have been a better film than the audience sees.

12. Brecher became good friends with Harpo and had a love/hate relationship with Groucho. He was particularly dismissive of how Groucho treated his wife. See Arce, *Groucho*, 268.

13. Adamson, *Groucho, Harpo, Chico and Sometimes Zeppo*, 353.

14. Les Standiford, *Battle for the Big Top: P. T. Barnum, James Bailey, John Ringling, and the Death-Defying Saga of the American Circus*, New York: PublicAffairs, 2021, Location 289 of 4548.

15. Many sources say that Castello, like Coup, was from Wisconsin, but he was actually from Kingston, Ontario, Canada.

16. A 1904 *Billboard* article credits the Spalding, Rogers, & Bidwell Circus with being the first to travel by rail, in 1850, though it mostly performed in theatres. Coup's big idea was one of scale. See Joseph and June B. Csida, *American Entertainment*, New York: A Billboard Book, 1978.

17. Standiford notes that in 1808, Hachaliah Bailey became the first American to display a circus elephant. Bailey's cousin Frederick was an early circus promoter and the employer of an orphan who took his surname. James Anthony Bailey became a circus entrepreneur and later partnered with P.T. Barnum.

18. Neil Harris, *Humbug: The Art of P.T. Barnum*, Chicago: University of Chicago Press, 1973.

19. Some of them retained their names and toured as stripped-down subsidiaries of Ringling Brothers.

20. Older New Yorkers recall that its professional basketball and hockey teams went on the road for two weeks every March when the circus took over Madison Square Garden.

21. In 1944, Ringling Bros. had a fire in Hartford, Connecticut, in which 167 people died and over 700 were injured. Though it may have been set, Ringling Bros. paid over $5 million in claims. See Stewart O'Nan, *The Circus Fire: A True Story of an American Tragedy*, New York: Anchor Books, 2001.

22. Leitzel died from injuries sustained from a fall caused by the collapse of her rigging. She was married to Codona, who subsequently committed suicide, allegedly despondent over Leitzel's death.

23. It took Kirk 40 years to complete his carved parade.

24. Joseph and June B. Csida, *American Entertainment*; Janet M. Davis, *The Circus Age: Culture & Society Under the American Big Top*, Chapel Hill: University of North Carolina Press, 2002; Harris, *Humbug: The Art of P.T. Barnum*; Ricky Jay, *Learned Pigs & Fireproof Women*, New York: Villard Books, 1986; Linda Simon, *The Greatest Show on Earth: A History of the Circus*, London: Reaktion Books, 2014.

25. Adamson, *Groucho, Harpo, Chico and Sometimes Zeppo*, 350.

26. The full lyrics of "Lydia" can be found at https://genius.com/Groucho-marx-lydia-the-tattooed-lady-lyrics Accessed February 27, 2021.

27. Parts of the 1964 exhibit were moved to Disney's EPCOT Center in Bay Lake, Florida, and operated from 1982 to 1996.

28. Godiva's name is an English rendering of the Saxon name Godgifu. Lincoln is located in England, where a veritable Godiva cottage industry now exists, despite scant historical evidence that her ride ever took place. Godiva is often misinterpreted as a tax protester. If it took place at all, Godiva's naked horseback jaunt was in protest of her own husband's unfair taxation of commoners, and was not any sort of justification for an 11th-century version of the trickle-down theory. Her husband, Leofric, was Danish and a descendant of Norsemen who conquered parts of Britain in the 9th century. By the 11th, Norsemen and Anglo-Saxons had long intermarried and many Danes had converted to Christianity. A vast swath of the eastern, southern, and northern parts of modern-day England were under Danelaw rather than Anglos-Saxon jurisprudence. Godiva's marriage was probably strategic rather than one of mutual attraction, as the Danelaw bordered the eastern edge of her Anglo-Saxon kingdom of Mercia. In case you're wondering, Godiva Chocolates, a Belgian firm now headquartered in New York City, was indeed named after Lady Godiva.

29. In the British educational system, a "public" school is anything but. Such schools are private and as exclusive as the American Social Register (though an occasional scholarship student is accepted). They were called "public" schools because in theory these endowed boarding schools were open to all. In practice, they were training grounds for the children of elites and stepping-stones into top-flight universities such as Cambridge, Oxford, and Edinburgh.

30. Mark Bego, *The Marx Brothers*, New York: Pocket Books, 2001, 67; Adamson, *Groucho, Harpo, Chico and Sometimes Zeppo*, 358. Adamson emphasis in original. When Adamson's book was published, the term "Negro" was an acceptable descriptor.

31. Svengali has passed into popular speech as a person who hypnotizes or casts a spell over others. There was no historical Svengali. He is

a character in George du Maurier's 1894 novel *Trilby*. *Trilby* also became a stage play and John Barrymore starred in a 1931 movie titled *Svengali*. Barrymore is largely responsible for the demonic, wide-eyed mesmerist image often associated with Svengali.

32. Adamson, *Groucho, Harpo, Chico and Sometimes Zeppo*, 359.

33. *Ibid.*, 354–55.

34. Louvish, *Monkey Business*, 321.

35. Glenn Mitchell, *The Marx Brothers Encyclopedia*, London: B. T. Batsford, 1996, 28.

36. Groucho Marx to Arthur Sheekman, October 27, 1939, Marx, *The Groucho Letters*, 21.

37. Adamson, *Groucho, Harpo, Chico and Sometimes Zeppo*, 360.

38. Groucho Marx to Arthur Sheekman, June 12, 1940, Marx, *The Groucho Letters*, 21–22.

Chapter Eleven

1. Dead Man's Gulch was likely inspired by the Gadsden Purchase, the remaining slice of land that completed the Continental United States as we now know it. Its 29,760 square miles are largely barren. The driving force behind the $10 million purchase from Mexico in 1854 was to provide easier access for a potential Southern transcontinental railroad.

2. Not that it matters much in a Marx Brothers film, but there is no explanation of how Quale got to the West after the Panellos took his money.

3. Technically, Groucho was 49, but he had his 50th birthday before *Go West* debuted.

4. Martin A. Gardner, *The Marx Brothers as Social Critics*, Jefferson, NC: McFarland 2009, 24.

5. Maxine Marx, *Growing Up with Chico*, New York: Limelight Books, 1986, 140. Out of costume, Harpo and Chico looked remarkably similar.

6. Groucho Marx to Arthur Sheekman, June 12, 1940, Groucho Marx, *The Groucho Letters: Letters From and To Groucho Marx*, New York; Simon and Schuster, 1967, 21.

7. *Ibid.*, Groucho Marx to Arthur Sheekman, July 1, 1940. Note: A cat house is slang for a brothel.

8. *Ibid.*, Groucho Marx to Arthur Marx, Summer, 1940. Groucho did not write a specific date, but filming began in mid-July, so one can safely date it sometime between July 1–15, 1940.

9. Simon Louvish, *Monkey Business: The Lives and Legends of The Marx Brothers*, New York: Thomas Dunne Books, 1999, 323. Groucho's letter to Sheekman was dated September 5, 1940. Note: William Powell was one of MGM's biggest box office stars.

10. Joe Adamson, *Groucho, Harpo, Chico and Sometimes Zeppo*, New York: Simon and Schuster, 1973, 369–70.

11. McNutt was the lesser known of the trio. Between 1922–35, he wrote seven screenplays, including *Lady and Gent* (1932), which received an Oscar nomination.

12. Mark Bego, *The Marx Brothers*, North Pomfret, VT: Trafalgar Square Publishing, 2001.

13. Allen Eyles, *The Marx Brothers: Their World of Comedy*, London: Tantivy Press, 1974, 155.

14. Groucho Marx and Richard Anobile, *The Marx Brothers Scrapbook*, New York: Grosset and Dunlap, 1974, 212, 214.

15. Adamson, *Groucho, Harpo, Chico and Sometimes Zeppo*, 371.

16. Wes D. Gehring, *The Marx Brothers: A Bio-Bibliography*, Westport, CT: Greenwood Press, 1987, 79.

17. Westerns were enormously popular, but *Cimarron* was the last to win a Best Picture Oscar until 1990, when *Dances with Wolves* was so honored.

18. Gardner, *The Marx Brothers as Social Critics*, 160.

19. *Ibid.*, 82.

20. Patricia Limerick, *Something in the Soil*, New York: W. W. Norton, 2000.

21. One could conceivably add Washington State (1889) to this list, though most of its economic activity was centered on its western coast and its cattle and sheep were largely contained in fenced ranches.

22. George MacDonald Fraser, *The Hollywood History of the World*, New York: Beech Tree Books, 1988, 191.

23. *Ibid.*, 187.

24. One of the best studies of the war on Plains Indians remains Dee Brown, *Bury My Heart at Wounded Knee: An Indian History of the American West*, New York: Holt, Rinehart & Winston, 1970. At Wounded Knee, some 300 Natives were killed. It is often considered the last "battle" of the Great Plains Indian Wars, though it was more accurately a slaughter. It occurred in South Dakota, which had obtained statehood just 13 months earlier.

25. Christine Bold, *The Frontier Club: Popular Westerns and Cultural Power, 1880–1924*, New York: Oxford University Press, 2013; Marco Patricio, "How Violent Was the Wild West?" August 26, 2019, https://medium.com/@marcodpatricio/how-violent-was-the-wild-west-a76783411462 Accessed March 1, 2021; Randolph Roth, *American Homicide*, Cambridge, MA: The Belknap Press of the Harvard University Press, 2009. See also Richard Slotkin, *Gunfighter Nation: The Myth of the Frontier in Twentieth-Century America*, New York: Atheneum, 1992; Roger McGarath, *Gunfighters, Highwaymen, and Vigilantes: Violence on the Frontier*, Berkeley: University of California Press, 1987; Eugene Hollon, *Frontier Violence: Another Look*, New York; Oxford University Press, 1974.

26. The Panama Canal did not open until 1914, which meant ships had to sail around the tip of South America and through the treacherous waters around Cape Horn.

27. Jordan is quoted in Gehring, *The Marx Brothers*, 79.

28. Eyles, *The Marx Brothers*, 154, 157.

29. Although it's not germane to Groucho's joke, debate rages to this day as to whether Bell or Elisha Gray deserves credit for the first telephone. Gray filed for a patent more than a year earlier, but a patent dispute lawsuit ended in a ruling that Bell demonstrated his model worked, but Gray had made no such claim.

30. Maurice Charney, *The Comic World of the Marx Brothers' Movies*, Madison, NJ: Fairleigh Dickinson University Press, 2007, 103.

31. "Chief Thundercloud," Wikipedia, en.wikipedia.org/wiki/Chief_Thundercloud, Accessed March 1, 2021.

32. Peter C. Rollins and John O'Connor, eds. *Hollywood's Indian: The Portrayal of the Native American in Films*, Lexington: University of Kentucky Press, 2003; G. M. Bataille and C.L.S. Silet, eds. *The Pretend Indians: Images of Native Americans in the Movies*, Ann Arbor, MI: Books on Demand, 1994.

33. Arguably, Asian Americans ranked even lower on the social-justice scale. Chinese restriction remained in place until 1943, and Japanese Americans on the West Coast were interned 1942–46.

34. Depending on how one defines it, author Ned Buntline's 1872 production *The Scouts of the Prairie* could be considered the first Wild West show, though it featured Cody and inspired him to continue on the stage despite negative reviews of his talents. Over time, *Buffalo Bill's Wild West Show* had competition from others, the most significant of which was *Pawnee Bill's Historic Wild West*. In 1908, the Pawnee Bill and Buffalo Bill shows were combined, though the merger didn't last long. In 1913, Buffalo Bill's show was folded into the Sells-Floto Circus in a deal Cody claimed was trickery. *Buffalo Bill's Wild West Show* fell victim to bankruptcy shortly thereafter.

35. *Buffalo Bill's Wild West Show* also spotlighted such famed Westerners as Wild Bill Hickok, Calamity Jane, Annie Oakley, and Will Rogers.

36. Frederick Hoxie, *This Indian Country: American Indian Activists and the Place They Made*, New York: Penguin Books, 2012.

37. "The Song of Hiawatha" can be read at: https://www.hwlongfellow.org/poems_poem.php?pid=296 Accessed March 1, 2021.

38. Adamson, *Groucho, Harpo, Chico and Sometimes Zeppo*, 369.

39. Charney, *The Comic World of the Marx Brothers' Movies*.

40. Adamson, *Groucho, Harpo, Chico and Sometimes Zeppo*, 379.

41. *Ibid.*, 372.

42. Eyles, *The Marx Brothers: Their World of Comedy*, 155.

43. Adamson, *Groucho, Harpo, Chico and Sometimes Zeppo*, 379.

44. Hector Arce, *Groucho*, New York: Perigee Books, 1979, 277.

Chapter Twelve

1. Blitz was short for the German *blitzkrieg*, which is usually translated as lightning war, as in striking quickly and furiously. The phrase "Low Countries" refers to Belgium, The Netherlands, and Luxembourg. They are also sometimes called the Benelux nations.

2. The British Commonwealth was/is the remnant of English colonialism. By the 20th century, many former colonies and territories had won or been granted sovereignty under the 1926 Balfour Declaration. These nations remained linked to Great Britain through the British monarchy, shared culture, the English language, legal principles, and preferential trade and immigration policies. At the time of World War Two, some of the Commonwealth nations that bore the brunt of war included Australia, Canada, India, Ireland, New Zealand, and South Africa. Irish participation was split, with some openly favoring the Axis powers as part of long-simmering resentment over centuries of English domination. (The Irish Republic left the Commonwealth in 1949). Today's Pakistan and Bangladesh were, at the time, part of India.

3. French Indochina included modern-day Vietnam, Laos, and Kampuchea (Cambodia).

4. Joe Adamson, *Groucho, Harpo, Chico and Sometimes Zeppo*, New York: Simon and Schuster, 1973, 380, 389; Trav S.D. "The Marx Brothers in Hollywood; The Slow Dissolution of the World's Greatest Vaudeville Act," October 2, 2013, https://travsd.wordpress.com/2013/10/02/stars-of-slapstick-5-marx-brothers/ Accessed March 2, 2021. Trav S.D.'s site was headed "Travalanche." For what it's worth, he reversed himself in a May 14, 2014, posting and declared *Go West* the worst. See "The Big Store: The Marx Bros. Descend to the Bargain Basement," https://travsd.wordpress.com/2014/05/17/marx-movie-madness-month-17-the-big-store/ Accessed March 2, 2021.

5. Martin A. Gardner, *The Marx Brothers as Social Critics*, Jefferson, NC: McFarland, 2009, 25; Simon Louvish, *Monkey Business: The Lives and Legends of The Marx Brothers*, New York: Thomas Dunne Books, 1999, 325.

6. Roy Blount, Jr. *Hail, Hail Euphoria!* New York: It Books, 2010, 141.

7. Maurice Charney, *The Comic World of the Marx Brothers' Movies*, Madison, NJ: Fairleigh Dickinson University Press, 2007, 105; Allen Eyles, *The Marx Brothers: Their World of Comedy*, London: Tantivy Press, 1974, 158.

8. Groucho's letter to Sheekman is quoted in Hector Arce, *Groucho*, New York: Perigee Books, 1979, 279.

9. Groucho Marx to Arthur Sheekman, June 23, 1941 in Groucho Marx, ed. *The Groucho*

Letters: Letters From and To Groucho Marx, New York: Simon and Schuster, 1967, 27–28.

10. Groucho to Sheekman, *Ibid.*, 28.

11. Arthur Marx, *My Life with Groucho*, Fort Lee, NJ: Barricade Books, 1992, 145–64.

12. Maxine Marx, *Growing Up with Chico*, New York: Limelight Books, 1980, 146.

13. Louvish, *Monkey Business*, 326; Wes D. Gehring, *The Marx Brothers: A Bio-Bibliography*, Westport, CT: Greenwood Press, 1987, 82.

14. Adamson, *Groucho, Harpo, Chico and Sometimes Zeppo*, 384.

15. Charlotte Chandler, *Hello, I Must Be Going: Groucho and His Friends*, New York: Citadel Press, 1993, 444.

16. Adamson, *Groucho, Harpo, Chico and Sometimes Zeppo*, 382.

17. *Ibid.*, 386.

18. Arce, *Groucho*, 277–78.

19. Adamson, *Groucho, Harpo, Chico and Sometimes Zeppo*, 380–83.

20. Jan Whitaker, *Service and Style: How the American Department Store Fashioned the Middle Class*, New York: St. Martin's Press, 2006, 159–60.

21. In economies of scale, a question arises of how big is big enough. In this case, how many "departments" are necessary to become a true department store? This is complicated by the fact that department stores evolved from soft-goods retailers, some of which grew quite large by the 1830s. Ready-to-wear clothing was rare, however, so those entering a dry-goods store generally bought fabric, not off-the-rack dresses, trousers, shirts, etc. These stores often departmentalized fabric, notions, collars, ribbons, and other accouterments, but most would not have carried non-soft goods.

22. Whitaker, *Service and Style*, 78.

23. *Ibid.*, 220–21.

24. *Ibid.*, 147–48.

25. Charney, *The Comic World of the Marx Brothers' Movies*, 105.

26. Careful observers will note very little headgear in the hat department, and that the cloth is wrapped around a wire frame. That's because hats were often bespoke goods, those made to order.

27. Saturdays were once "half days" for department stores, a welcome respite for clerks who worked nearly 60 hours a week during the 1920s. The New Deal reduced this to 40, and most city department stores stayed open beyond 1 p.m. There seems to be a blend of the 1920s and the late 1930s in *The Big Store*. Technically, this produces anachronisms.

28. Adamson, *Groucho, Harpo, Chico and Sometimes Zeppo*, 388.

29. Joseph Boskin and Joseph Dorinson, "Ethnic Humor: Subversion and Survival," in Nancy A. Walker, ed. *What's So Funny? Humor in American Culture*, Wilmington, DE: SR Books, 1998, 206.

30. Gene Dattel, "Cotton and Race in the Making of America: Global Economic Power, Human Costs and Current Relevance," Yale Colloquium, September 28, 2012, https://agrarianstudies. macmillan.yale.edu/sites/default/files/files/ colloqpapers/04dattel.pdf Accessed March 2, 2021.

31. The black population of 1940 was estimated to be 12.9 million, but was probably closer to 14.1 million as the Census Bureau undercounted Black Americans.

32. Clifford Holland was born in Kenosha, Wisconsin. He performed and recorded with Ella Fitzgerald, among others. He left the Delta Rhythm Boys before members moved to Europe in 1956. Carl Laemmle Jones, Sr., moved to Europe, though he left the Delta Rhythm Boys in 1960, and was living in Los Angeles at the time of his death. Major White was born in Dallas and died in Texas. The only member of The Four Dreamers whose musical career stalled was the Little Rock, Arkansas-born James "Jimmie" Shaw, who was listed as a musician in 1940, but was unemployed when he registered for the draft. I am indebted to the following individuals for help in tracking down The Four Dreamers: Tony Fournier of www.vocalharmonygroup.com, Marv Goldberg, who operates the online site "R & B Notebook," and Marlene Wong of the Werner Josten Library of Smith College.

33. "Burma Shave Slogans," http://www. skypoint.com/members/schutz19/burma2. htm#TOP Accessed March 2, 2021.

34. Gardner, *The Marx Brothers as Social Critics*, 159–60.

35. Charney, *The Comic World of the Marx Brothers' Movies*, 105.

36. Adamson, *Groucho, Harpo, Chico and Sometimes Zeppo*, 393.

37. Glenn Mitchell, *The Marx Brothers Encyclopedia*, London: B. T. Batsford, 1996, 38.

Chapter Thirteen

1. Ruman dropped the second n from his surname.

2. Ronald Bergan, *The Life and Times of the Marx Brothers*, 114.

3. William ("Bill") bore the middle name of Alexander Woollcott, and his second son was given Woollcott's first name. Minnie is named for the Marx Brothers' mother.

4. Simon Louvish, *Monkey Business: The Lives and Legends of The Marx Brothers*, New York: Thomas Dunne Books, 1999, 327.

5. *Ibid.*, 328.

6. Rudy Vallée is often seen as a quintessential 1920s singer but he was also was a saxophonist, band leader, actor, and a 1940s heartthrob for bobby soxers. (That term is derived from the short cotton socks worn by teenage girls who idolized singers such as Vallée, Frank Sinatra, and Bing

Crosby.) Note: Virginia O'Brien (*The Big Store*) was also a regular on Pabst Beer radio shows.

7. Groucho Marx to Arthur Sheekman, February 12, 1942; September 17, 1942; January 26, 1943. See Groucho Marx, *The Groucho Letters: Letters From and To Groucho Marx*, New York: Simon and Schuster, 1967, 30–33.

8. *Many Happy Returns* is not vintage Groucho witty. Most copies were allegedly pulped. Its publication was badly timed. As a wartime measure, Congress enacted and President Roosevelt signed into law the Revenue Act of 1942. It imposed income surtaxes to finance the war. These placed a heavy burden on those with large incomes, but was viewed by most as a patriotic sacrifice.

9. Ruth wanted 25 percent of Groucho's income until she died or remarried, but was in a rocky position given her alcoholism and her own infidelities. When Groucho counteroffered with 12.5 percent and no stipulation against remarrying, she took it. Ruth remarried on May 7, 1946, just six days after the divorce was finalized. Hector Arce, *Groucho*, New York: Perigee Books, 1979.

10. Maxine Marx, *Growing Up with Chico*, New York: Limelight Books, 1980, 146.

11. Arce, *Groucho*, 283.

12. Glenn Mitchell, *The Marx Brothers Encyclopedia*, London: B. T. Batsford, 1996, 202, 223. 78 rpm (revolutions per minute) records were roughly the size of current vinyl albums. Unlike them, the faster playback speed allowed just one song per side. The term "album" derives from the practice of gathering five or six 78 rpm records and placing them in sleeves inside a hard cover akin to how people collected snapshots in a photo album.

13. Maxine Marx, *Growing Up with Chico*, 148, 152.

14. In 1947, shortly after *A Night in Casablanca* was made, Chico suffered a heart attack. It did not reform him.

15. Louvish, *Monkey Business*, 346.

16. These bonds were interest-bearing notes that helped finance the war.

17. Arce, *Groucho*, 284–86.

18. Groucho was 5'7" tall, but Lake a diminutive 4'11".

19. Harpo Marx with Rowland Barber, *Harpo Speaks!* New York: Limelight Editions, 1985, 420–21. Note: USO stands for United Service Organizations, a morale-boosting organization that provides entertainment on military bases.

20. *Ibid.*, 424–32. Mrs. Litvinov's husband, Maxim, was the Soviet ambassador to the United States at the time.

21. Louvish, *Monkey Business*, 331.

22. Harry Applebaum was the name of a neighbor from Groucho's New York City youth. Warner Brothers would not have recognized his name.

23. "Groucho Marx to Warner Brothers," undated letter from 1945, *The Groucho Letters*, 14–16. Smith Brothers was a popular brand of cough drops. *The Brothers Karamazov* was a novel published by the Russian author Fyodor Dostoevsky in 1880. Several movie versions and TV series have been made of it. Dan Brothers is a misspelling of a star player Dan Brouthers, who played for various teams in the years 1879–1904. In 1945, he was posthumously inducted into the Baseball Hall of Fame. His lifetime batting average was .342, he knocked in nearly 1,300 runs, and slugged 106 homeruns though he played his entire career during the "dead-ball era" before baseballs had cork centers that allowed for greater flight. "Lighthouse" (actually Light Horse) Harry was Henry Lee III, who acquired his colorful nickname while serving as a cavalry officer during the American Revolution.

24. *Ibid.*, 16–17. *Good Housekeeping* has been published since 1885. Groucho's joke alludes to the Good Housekeeping seal of approval, created in 1909 and awarded to household products tested in the magazine's research lab. The Haymarket riot took place in Chicago on May 4, 1886. A bomb was hurled during a labor protest, killing seven and wounding 60. It was blamed on anarchists, though the evidence for that allegation was questionable. Eight anarchists were convicted in a trial that delved more into their political beliefs than material evidence. Although only two defendants were even at the protest, one defendant got 15 years in prison and the other seven were sentenced to hang. One man blew himself up—by biting down on an explosive cap smuggled into the jail—and the other six died on the gallows.

25. *Ibid.*, 17–18.

26. Joe Adamson, *Groucho, Harpo, Chico and Sometimes Zeppo*, New York: Simon and Schuster, 1973, 398.

27. Wes D. Gehring, *The Marx Brothers: A Bio-Bibliography*, Westport, CT: Greenwood Press, 1987, 86.

28. Louvish, *Monkey Business*, 347.

29. Mitchell, *The Marx Brothers Encyclopedia*, 182. Louvish shares the view that superior material was left out. See also Louvish, *Monkey Business*, 350.

30. Ronald Bergan, *The Life and Times of the Marx Brothers*, New York: Smithmark, 1992, 114.

31. Groucho Marx to Sam Zolotow, January 23, 1946, *The Groucho Letters*, 19.

32. Mitchell, *The Marx Brothers Encyclopedia*, 182.

33. Howard Zinn, *A People's History of the United States: 1492–Present*, New York: Harper Perennial Modern Classics, 2005, 407, 418. I am a great admirer of his work, but Zinn made far too much of the 43,000 war resistors. He noted that was three times the number of conscientious objectors (CO) in World War One, but there are several flaws in his assessment. First of all, 43,000 is less than ½ of one percent (.0043) of

all draftees. Although I once knew a gentle soul who was a CO, one could dismiss such a low percentage as statistically irrelevant. Moreover, the population of the United States in 1917 was an estimated 102.3 million; in 1940, it was 132.1 million. Second, Zinn's World War One resistance numbers involve only those who actively pursued CO status. In 1917, it was much easier to resist informally by hiding, going underground, moving, etc. Most estimates place the number of World War One resistors at over 3 *million*. Some 72,000 men filed for CO status in World War Two; most applications were rejected and some chose alternate non-military service such as the Civilian Public Service program. About 16,000 chose prison instead of fighting. There were other ways to avoid combat, but the total number of those resisting induction was no more than 373,000, a number that pales in comparison to World War One resistors. A more reliable source is John Whitely Chambers, *To Raise an Army: The Draft Comes to Modern America*, New York: Free Press, 1987.

34. Few scholars dispute the necessity of World War Two, but it is not hard to call simplistic moralism into question. American responses to the war include unsavory chapters such as the internment of Japanese-American citizens on the West Coast, the persistence of racism at home (though African Americans fought abroad), the recruitment of women to work in war industries who were shuffled out of the workforce once the war was over, the refusal of the United States to address colonialism in the postwar period, the decision to unleash atomic warfare against Japan, the abandonment of rapprochement with the Soviet Union, and the recruitment of former high-level Nazi officials and scientists during the Cold War.

35. Allen Eyles, *The Marx Brothers: Their World of Comedy*, London: Tantivy Press, 1974, 169.

36. George MacDonald Fraser, *The Hollywood History of the World: From One Million Years BC to Apocalypse Now*, New York: Beech Tree Books, 1988, 235–36.

37. Clayton R. Koppes and Gregory D. Black, "What to Show the World: The Office of War Information and Hollywood, 1942–1945," in Steven Mintz and Randy Roberts, eds.. *Hollywood's America: United States History Through Its Films*," St. James, NY: Brandywine Press, 1993, 169–77.

38. Peter Roffman and Jim Purdy, *The Hollywood Social Problem Film: Madness, Despair, and Politics from the Depression to the Fifties*, Bloomington: Indiana University Press, 1981, 219.

39. Tom Engelhardt, *The End of Victory Culture: Cold War America and the Disillusioning of a Generation*, Amherst: University of Massachusetts Press, 2007, 48.

40. *Ibid.*

41. The idea was to defeat Germany via a pincer movement in which Russian troops would advance westward, and Britain, Free French, and the United States troops would advance southward from Scandinavia and, eventually, eastward from somewhere along the English Channel. Instead, the U.S. was convinced to help liberate Northern Africa and launch a south-to-north assault in which Italy was conquered and used as a platform for liberating southern and central Europe. The famed June 1944 D-Day assault opened a front in France.

42. Donald W. Whisenhunt, "Ernie Pyle: From a 'Worm's-Eye View,'" in Whisenhunt, ed. *The Human Tradition: America Between the Wars, 1920–1945*, Wilmington, DE: SR Books, 2002, 221.

43. A few others include *Sahara* (1943), an action picture set in Libya, and the Bob Hope-Bing Crosby musical comedy *The Road to Morocco* (1942).

44. Robert M. Edsel, *Monuments Men: Allied Heroes, Nazi Thieves and the Greatest Treasure Hunt in History*, New York: Center Street Books, 2009; Michael J. Kurtz, *America and the Return of Nazi Contraband: The Recovery of Europe's Cultural Treasures*, Cambridge, UK: Cambridge University Press, 2009; Lynn H. Nicholas, *The Rape of Europa: The Fate of Europe's Treasures in the Third Reich and Second World War*, New York: Vintage, 1995. Note: Japan looted a smaller number of works.

45. The franc was French currency until 2002, when it adopted the Euro. In the 1940s, a French franc was worth about two cents, hence Kornblow's salary was roughly $10 per week. Today that would be about $26.30, which just goes to show that Kornblow could be bought—cheaply!

46. Bacall and Bogart later became lovers and married. When Bogart died in 1957, she placed a whistle in his coffin inscribed, "If you want anything, just whistle."

47. Mitchell, *The Marx Brothers Encyclopedia*, 182; Louvish, *Monkey Business*, 352.

48. Edward Said, *Orientalism*, New York: Pantheon, 1978.

49. Louvish, *Monkey Business*, 348–350.

50. Ultimate Movie Rankings, https://www.ultimatemovierankings.com/site-index-2-2/ Accessed March 3, 2021. The raw totals were that *Casablanca* earned $11.8 million in 1942, an adjusted $374.1 million. In 1946, *A Night in Casablanca* made $2.7 million for an adjusted $84.9 million.

51. Louvish, *Monkey Business*, 352.

52. Maxine Marx, *Growing Up with Chico*, 151.

53. Adamson, *Groucho, Harpo, Chico and Sometimes Zeppo*, 399.

54. Zinn, *A People's History of the United States*, 412–14. Quote from p. 412.

55. Mitchell, *The Marx Brothers Encyclopedia*, 183.

56. Eyles, *The Marx Brothers: Their World of Comedy*, 168.

57. *Ibid.*, 169; Adamson, *Groucho, Harpo, Chico and Sometimes Zeppo*, 403–04.

58. Adamson, *Groucho, Harpo, Chico and Sometimes Zeppo*, 403.

59. Martin A. Gardner, *The Marx Brothers as Social Critics*, Jefferson, NC: McFarland, 2009, 25.

Chapter Fourteen

1. Ronald Bergan, *The Life and Times of the Marx Brothers*, New York: Smithmark, 1992, 118.

2. Maurice Charney, *The Comic World of the Marx Brothers' Movies*, Madison, NJ: Fairleigh Dickinson University Press, 2007, 114.

3. Groucho Marx and Richard Anobile, *The Marx Brothers Scrapbook*, New York: Grosset and Dunlap, 1974, 251.

4. Simon Louvish, *Monkey Business: The Lives and Legends of The Marx Brothers*, New York: Thomas Dunne Books, 1999, 370–71.

5. Marx and Anobile, *The Marx Brothers Scrapbook*, 251. Martin A. Gardner, *The Marx Brothers as Social Critics*, Jefferson, NC: McFarland, 2009; Glenn Mitchell, *The Marx Brothers Encyclopedia*, London: B. T. Batsford, 1996.

6. Glenn Mitchell, *The Marx Brothers Encyclopedia*, 158.

7. Joe Adamson, *Groucho, Harpo, Chico and Sometimes Zeppo*, New York: Simon and Schuster, 1973, 407.

8. *Ibid.*, 404.

9. Some sources give a May release date instead of March.

10. Mark Bego, *The Marx Brothers*, North Pomfret, VT: Trafalgar Publishing, 76.

11. Nor was time on Miranda's side for another project with Groucho. She made just three more films before suffering a heart attack in 1955, and passing away at the age of 46.

12. Groucho Marx to Earl Wilson, October 18, 1949, Groucho Marx, ed. *The Groucho Letters: Letters From and To Groucho Marx*, New York: Simon and Shuster, 1972, 34. The same letter mentions that each day's shooting was preceded by pasting on a mustache. Some Marx scholars, including Eyles, claim he wore his own facial hair for the film, but that seems to be incorrect. Allen Eyles, *The Marx Brothers: Their World of Comedy*, London: Tantivy Press, 1974, 179.

13. Hector Arce, *Groucho*, New York: Perigee Books, 1979, 315.

14. *Ibid.*, 299.

15. *Ibid.*, 321–22.

16. Robert Sklar, *Movie-Made America: How the Movies Changed American Life*, New York: Random House, 1975, 252.

17. Peter Roffman and Jim Purdy, *The Hollywood Social Problem Film: Madness, Despair, and Politics from the Depression to the Fifties*, Bloomington: University of Illinois Press, 1981.

18. Tom Engelhardt, *The End of Victory Culture: Cold War America and the Disillusioning of a Generation*, Amherst: University of Massachusetts Press, 2007.

19. *Ibid.*, 119.

20. *Ibid.*, 124.

21. Paul Boyer, *By the Bomb's Early Light: American Thought and Culture at the Dawn of the Atomic Age*, New York: Pantheon, 1985, 103.

22. David Caute, *The Great Fear: The Anti-Communist Purge Under Truman and Eisenhower*, New York: Touchstone Books, 1979.

23. In 1950, director John Berry made a short documentary titled *The Hollywood Ten*. It is widely available and remains a powerful look at HUAC browbeating and intimidation.

24. Roffman and Purdy, *The Hollywood Social Problem Film*, 286.

25. The term "fellow traveler" was applied to those said to be sympathetic to communism.

26. Jon Weiner, "The Secret Word on Groucho," *The Nation*, September 28, 1998; Associated Press, "To FBI, Groucho was no laughing matter," October 13, 1998.

27. Marx and Anobile, *The Marx Brothers Scrapbook*, 251. Groucho made a few other remarks about Monroe that are too off-color to repeat here.

28. Miller's plane disappeared over the English Channel on December 24, 1944, and was presumably shot down or suffered engine failure. If you think conspiracy theories are new, there were numerous alternative explanations put forth for Miller's disappearance. Two of the odder ones are that General Dwight Eisenhower ordered his assassination, or that Miller actually died in a French brothel.

29. In some sources Ilona Massey's character is listed as Egilichi. It scarcely matters, as the name doesn't mean anything in particular.

30. This term infers that Lyons will pluck the strings of his violin and that the overall tempo will be fast and happy in tone.

31. Charney, *The Comic World of the Marx Brothers' Movies*, 115; Louvish, *Monkey Business*, 371.

32. Adamson, *Groucho, Harpo, Chico and Sometimes Zeppo*, 409–10.

33. Mitchell, *The Marx Brothers Encyclopedia*, 148–49.

34. Eyles, *The Marx Brothers: Their World of Comedy*, 180, 187, 179.

35. Arce, *Groucho*, 318,

36. Louvish, *Monkey Business*, 371, 370.

37. Bergan, *The Life and Times of the Marx Brothers*, 118; Gardner, *The Marx Brothers as Social Critics*, 26; Adamson, *Groucho, Harpo, Chico and Sometimes Zeppo*, 404, 406.

This Is the End

1. "Top Movie Stars of the 1950s," https://www.ultimatemovierankings.com/top-movie-stars-1950s/ Accessed March 4, 202.

2. I am indebted to Simon Louvish for compiling some of these. Louvish, *Monkey Business: The Lives and Legends of The Marx Brothers*, New York: Thomas Dunne Books, 1999. 426–34.

3. Harpo Marx with Rowland Barber, *Harpo Speaks!* New York: Limelight Editions, 1985, 457. In the same passage, Harpo called *A Night in Casablanca* the last Marx Brothers film, another indicator that he was prepared to forget all about *Love Happy*.

4. Groucho Marx and Richard Anobile, *The Marx Brothers Scrapbook*, New York: Grosset and Dunlap, 1974, 252.

5. Maxine Marx, *Growing Up With Chico*, New York: Limelight Books, 1986, 160–61, 170.

6. "Marx Brothers Round Table" with Robert S. Bader Josh Frank, and Bill Marx, *Gilbert Gottfried's Amazing Colossal Podcast*, https://podcasts.apple.com/ie/podcast/255-marx-brothers-round-table-robert-s-bader-josh-frank/id883308059?i=1000434932357 Accessed March 4, 2021.

7. Robert S. Bader, "The Marx Brothers on Television," https://marxbrothers.net/essays/the-marx-brothers-on-television/ Accessed March 3, 2021.

8. Parts of that interview are available on YouTube, as are other appearances on *The Dick Cavett Show* and several other talk shows. There is also a four-DVD set titled *The Dick Cavett Show—Comic Legends*, in which Groucho figures prominently.

9. Groucho's zingers became so famous that he was legendary for things he didn't actually say. The most famous tall tale is that he interviewed a man with 20 children who said that he really loved his wife. Groucho was alleged to have retorted, "I love my cigar too, but sometimes I take it out." That line would not have gotten past censors. Groucho appeared on *The Jack Benny Show* and spoke of quotes attributed to him that he never uttered. A list of known *You Bet Your Life* contestants can be found at https://www.imdb.com/title/tt0042171/fullcredits Accessed March 4, 2021, 2021. Most of the guests were non-celebrities, but some were famous or about to become so. They included movie personalities Francis X. Bushman, Jeanne Crain, Hoot Gibson, Edith Head, Vera Miles, Harry Ruby, and Johnny Weissmuller; sports stars such as baseball's Don Drysdale, boxers Rocky Marciano and Joe Louis, Olympian Bob Mathias, and tennis champion Pancho González; writers William Blatty, Ray Bradbury, and C. S. Forester; and TV entertainers Candice Bergen, Ernie Kovacs, Liberace, and Art Linklater. Then-unknown comedienne Phyllis Diller also appeared and her impromptu schtick bombed.

10. Maxine Marx, *Growing Up with Chico*, 170.

11. *Ibid.*, 171–75; Hector Arce, *Groucho*, New York: Perigee Books, 1979, 389–96.

12. Marx, *Growing Up with Chico*, 176.

13. Arce, *Groucho*, 397.

14. Harpo Marx with Rowland Barber, *Harpo Speaks*, 459.

15. *Ibid.*, 461.

16. *Ibid.*, 464.

17. *Ibid.*, 465. After one of Harpo's heart attacks, he was told to eat egg whites, but not the yolks. Tempera paint was traditionally made by mixing pigment with egg yolks and water. Harpo also used casein, which is milk protein combined with pigments. It has a quick-drying adhesive quality. Neshobe Island is found in the middle of Lake Bomoseen in Rutland County, Vermont. Harpo knew of it because Aleck Woollcott often summered there and invited Harpo and other friends to visit him. I am unsure why he mentioned Watertown, a city in upstate New York near the shores of Lake Ontario. Perhaps it was a memory of his vaudeville days; Watertown's Avon Theatre was a circuit venue.

18. *Ibid.*, 466–74. Quote p. 474.

19. Bill Marx on *Gilbert Gottfried's Amazing Colossal Podcast*. Allan Sherman was briefly a pop-culture phenomenon. His lampoons of folk music were done during the folk-music revival when performers such as Joan Baez, Judy Collins, Bob Dylan, The Kingston Trio, and Peter, Paul, and Mary rose to national prominence. Others, including Bart Barker and "Weird Al" Yankovic, followed in Sherman's footsteps.

20. Arce, *Groucho*, 396. For the record, Arce slightly misquoted Arthur. In Arthur Marx, *My Life with Groucho*, Fort Lee, NJ: Barricade Books, 1992, 219, Arthur actually wrote, "Groucho was more broken up than I'd ever seen him."

21. Marx, *My Life with Groucho*, 219.

22. Hillcrest was a Jewish club where golf and verbal jousting were the two major sports. Groucho was also a member, though he did not immerse himself in the roundtable to the degree Harpo did. Among those who dusted off their wits at Hillcrest were Milton Berle, Irving Brecher, George Burns, Eddie Cantor, George Jessel, Al Jolson, and Danny Kaye.

23. Bill Marx on *Gilbert Gottfried's Amazing Colossal Podcast*.

24. Ronald Bergan, *The Life and Times of the Marx Brothers*, New York: Smithmark Publishers, 1992, 122.

25. *Harpo's Place*, www.harposplace.com Accessed March 4, 2021.

26. Maxine Marx, *Growing Up with Chico*,151; Arce, *Groucho*, 254–55.

27. Arce, *Groucho*, 451.

28. In this re-creation, Groucho was carried in by muscular white men instead of "Africans," as in the movie.

29. *The Hollywood Palace*, February 28, 1965, https://www.youtube.com/watch?v=-eBembBcK-bE Accessed March 4, 2021.

30. Gummo recounted some of his discomfort on stage in an essay: Gummo Marx, "The

Fifth Marx Brother," *New York Tribune,* August 17, 1932. Parts of this essay have been reprinted in Louvish, *Monkey Business,* 250–52.

31. Louvish, *Monkey Business,* 75.

32. Minnie kept the rest of her sons out of the military by establishing them as "farmers." See Chapter Six.

33. Louvish, *Monkey Business,* 112.

34. "Wife of 5th Marx Brother Charges Baby Was Stolen," *New York News,* August 24, 1929. See also Arce, *Groucho,* 161.

35. *Ibid.*

36. Louvish, *Monkey Business,* 381.

37. Robert Kistler and Dale Fetherling, "Groucho Marx Dies; Kept Them Laughing 65 Years, *Los Angeles Times,* August 20, 1977; Woody Allen, "Letters to the Editor," *Time,* September 19, 1977.

38. Marx, *My Life with Groucho,* 284–86. Groucho's son Arthur was the first conservator, but a new document placed Erin Fleming in that role. A charge that Groucho was not competent to appoint her was among the charges aimed at Fleming. In the bitter legal clashes that both preceded and came after Groucho's demise, Arthur tried to void Fleming's conservatorship. A compromise was struck in which Arthur's son Andy assumed the role. This, in turn, angered Zeppo. In another who-do-you-want-to-believe scenario, Zeppo claimed he was barred from Groucho's memorial service rather than refusing to attend.

39. Aurelio Rojas, "Erin Fleming reduced Groucho Marx to a helpless, pathetic...," United Press International, January 28, 1983, https://www.upi.com/Archives/1983/01/28/Erin-Fleming-reduced-Groucho-Marx-to-a-helpless-pathetic-old-man/5044412578000/ Accessed January 6, 2021; Howard Markel, "How Groucho Marx fell prey to elder abuse," August 19, 2019, https://www.pbs.org/newshour/health/how-groucho-marx-fell-prey-to-elder-abuse Accessed March 4, 2021; Aurelio Rojas, "A jury ruled Wednesday that former showgirl Erin Fleming..." United Press International, March 30, 1983, https://www.upi.com/Archives/1983/03/30/A-jury-ruled-Wednesday-that-former-showgirl-Erin-Fleming/5483417848400/ Accessed March 4, 2021. See also Steve Stoliar, *Raised Eyebrows: My Years Inside Groucho's House,* Los Angeles: General Publishing Group, 1996. Stoliar was Groucho's secretary for the final three years of his life.

40. "Groucho Marx's Home Movie," 1933, https://www.youtube.com/watch?v=m5ty30NMgt8&list=PLkATTHDb-OZvUKRyw1KMp0V-6IDIPBLBi Accessed March 4, 2021.

41. In 1951, it was quite rare for men to gain custody of a child, even if they were famous. This suggests that Kay's drinking problem must have been severe.

42. *Person to Person,* April 9, 1954. https://www.youtube.com/watch?v=PhrbtU4fGfU &t=1188s Accessed March 4, 2021. Groucho and Eden married on July 17, 1954.

43. Arthur Marx, *My Life with Groucho,* 223–24. Arce, *Groucho,* 465.

44. Bill Marx, *Gilbert Gottfried's Amazing Colossal Podcast.*

45. Robert S. Bader, ed. *Groucho Marx and Other Short Stories and Tall Tales: Selected Writings of Groucho Marx,* Boston: Faber and Faber, 1993, 147.

46. *Ibid.,* 149–52. Controversy remained over Groucho's lip hair. He may have used paste-on enhancements during his TV years.

47. Groucho made his revelation to Johnny Carson on October 4, 1965, and to Dick Cavett on September 5, 1969.

48. A recording was made of that show, mostly Groucho croaking out versions of songs from Marx Brothers movies. It is now a collector's item.

49. Bill Marx and Robert Bader, *Gilbert Gottfried's Amazing Colossal Podcast.* Some of the late Groucho interviews are available in Charlotte Chandler, *Hello, I Must Be Going: Groucho and His Friends,* New York: Citadel Press, 1993.

50. Arthur Marx, *My Life with Groucho,* 235.

51. Air attacks on Cambodia—dubbed Operation Menu—took place between March 18, 1969, and May 28, 1970. Revelations of what were supposed to be secret precision raids led to massive protests, especially on college campuses. Nonetheless, bombing continued into 1973. The major impact of this was to weaken Cambodia to the degree that it fell to the brutal communist regime of the Khmer Rouge. The result was similar in Laos.

52. Groucho's comments appeared in the June 4–10, 1971 issue of the *Berkeley Barb,* an "underground" alternative newspaper. They were all the more ill-advised given that the FBI routinely monitored such publications.

53. Louvish, *Monkey Business,* 402. The attacks at the Olympics shocked the world. A Palestinian group called Black September carried out an assault at the Olympic Village. Five of the eight terrorists and a policeman died when West German police attempted to free hostages. This shocking raid poisoned Middle Eastern peace overtures for many years to come. Note: West Germany was not reunited with (formerly) communist East Germany until 1990.

54. Arce, *Groucho,* 465. Fleming asserted that Kay wanted the money to "go on a bender."

55. Bill Marx, *Gilbert Gottfried's Amazing Colossal Podcast.*

56. Arce, *Groucho,* 474.

57. *Ibid.,* 435.

58. Gummo lived to 83, making him second to Groucho in longevity.

59. Groucho Marx and Richard Anobile, *The Marx Brothers Scrapbook,* 174.

60. Louvish, *Monkey Business,* 384.

61. Rules were loose about assumed names for actresses. The more famous Marion Benda was born Marian Elizabeth Wilson and was a Ziegfeld Follies star reputed to be the most beautiful woman in show business. She was also said to be Rudolph Valentino's last paramour, and some said she was his secret wife. Zeppo's wife was the former Marion Bimberg. Because of the confusion, there are numerous biographical errors floating around. Her date of death is variously given as in 1951, 1954, and 1986. The last is correct. The confusion is reminiscent of how Minnie Marx once took the name of Minnie Palmer, even though there was another actress using that name.

62. When he was just 11, Timothy injured a 9-year-old girl by hurling a rock. This was the subject of a $300,000 lawsuit that was eventually greatly reduced.

63. Robert Oliver Marx should not be confused with Gummo's son, also named Robert.

64. Groucho Marx and Richard Anobile, *The Marx Brothers Scrapbook*, 175.

65. Justin Pollard, "The Eccentric Engineer," *Engineering and Technology*, July 2014, https://ieeexplore.ieee.org/stamp/stamp.jsp?arnumber=6863815 Accessed March 4, 2021.

66. Bill Marx, *Gilbert Gottfried's Amazing Colossal Podcast*; Groucho Marx and Richard Anobile, *The Marx Brothers Scrapbook*, 253.

67. Bill Marx, *Gilbert Gottfried's Amazing Colossal Podcast*; Louvish, *Monkey Business*, 381.

68. Oddly, Zeppo had to pay Barbara $1,500 per month for ten years, though Sinatra had more money than Zeppo could dream of.

Glossary

1. Legend holds that "screwball" comedies owe their name to baseball. A screwball is a pitch that is difficult to hit because its twisting trajectory is hard for a hitter to follow, hurlers to control, or catchers to receive. It's a good story that might be apocryphal. According to the *Oxford English Dictionary*, the adjective "screwy," as in crazy or eccentric, was in wide use by the 1880s and possibly derives from an 1820 synonym for being mildly drunk.

2. Some scholars use screwball comedy and situational comedy interchangeably. Technically, screwball comedies were used to work around censorship rules to which American movies conformed from 1934 into 1968. These rules regulated all manner of content, though clever writers, directors, and performers found ways to subvert regulations. Situational comedies are also constrained—movies carry ratings, for instance—but fewer barriers now exist.

3. Burlesque can be used as either a noun or a verb. As a noun, it references particular shows; as a verb, it is the act of mocking.

4. A pratfall was originally a form of comedy in which an actor fell onto his butt. Over time, it became any deliberate fall or tumble done for comic effect. Slapstick comedy owes its name to an early special effect. A slapstick was two wooden slats that were slapped together whenever one actor (or puppets such as Punch and Judy) pretended to hit another. The smacking noise added drama to the action and became a staple of comedy. Its usage probably came to vaudeville via English music halls.

5. For a quick look at the trickster archetype, see "Carl Jung's Archetype: The Trickster," https://schoolworkhelper.net/carl-jungs-archetype-the-trickster/ Accessed February 11, 2021. Note: Theories of a collective unconscious are controversial and not all psychologists believe such a thing exists.

Bibliography

This is an incomplete list of all the works that were consulted for this book. I have organized the sources into the categories shown. The last, "Other Sources," contains a few general sources that I consulted multiple times. General details can be found in any reputable U.S. history textbook.

Articles and books that were used only to supplement a single point or two are not listed here. Readers should consult the Chapter Notes for specific chapters for further documentation.

Primary Sources—Marx Brothers

Anobile, Richard, ed. *Why a Duck? Visual and Verbal Gems from the Marx Brothers Movies.* New York: Darien House, 1971.

Bader, Robert S. ed. *Groucho Marx and Other Short Stories and Tall Tales: Selected Writings of Groucho Marx.* Boston: Faber & Faber, 1993.

The Dick Cavett Show–Comic Legends. Four-DVD set, Shout Factory, 2006.

Groucho, Chico, Harpo: The Marx Brothers Collection. Warner Brothers Entertainment Inc./Turner Entertainment Co., 2004. 5 DVD set includes: *A Night at the Opera,* Metro-Goldwyn-Mayer (1935), *A Day at the Races,* MGM (1937), *Room Service,* RKO Radio Pictures (19380, *At the Circus,* MGM (1939), *Go West,* MGM (1940), *The Big Store,* MGM (1941), *A Night in Casablanca,* United Artists (1946).

The Incredible Jewel Robbery (1959). CBS, "General Electric Theater," YouTube, https://www.youtube.com/watch?v=2uW8lsjx8uU

Kanter, Stefan. *The Essential Groucho Marx: Writings by, for, and about Groucho Marx.* New York: Vintage, 2000.

Love Happy. Republic Pictures Home Video, VHS, 1988, United Artists (1949/50).

Marx, Arthur. *My Life with Groucho.* Fort Lee, NJ: Barricade Books, 1992.

The Marx Brothers. 3 VHS set of movie clips, television projects, newsreels, interviews, and home movies, Passport International, 1990.

The Marx Brothers Collection. 5 DVD set of film and radio clips, interviews, TV shows, and "You Bet Your Life" TV pilot, Passport International Entertainment, 2007.

The Marx Brothers Silver Screen Collection. Universal Studios Home Entertainment, 2011, 5 DVD set includes: *The Cocoanuts.* Paramount Famous Lasky Corporation (1929); *Animal Crackers.* Paramount Publix Corporation (1930), *Monkey Business,* Paramount Publix Corporation, 1931; *Horse Feathers,* Paramount Publix Corporation, 1932; *Duck Soup,* Paramount Productions, Inc., 1933.

Marx, Chico. *The Story of Mankind* (segment), Warner Bros. (1957), YouTube, https://www.youtube.com/watch?v=BPHeAql_0TI Accessed May 25, 2021.

Marx, Groucho. *Beds.* New York: Bobbs-Merrill, 1976. Reprint of 1930 original.

_____. *Groucho and Me: The Autobiography of Groucho Marx.* New York: Fireside Books, 1959.

_____. *The Groucho Letters: Letters from and to Groucho Marx.* New York: Simon & Schuster, 1967.

_____. *Love, Groucho: Letters from Groucho Marx to His Daughter Miriam.* Boston: Da Capo Press, 2002.

_____. *Many Happy Returns! An Unofficial Guide to Your Income Tax Problems.* New York: Simon & Schuster, 1942.

_____. *Memoirs of a Mangy Lover.* New York: Manor Books, 3rd edition, 1973.

_____. *The Story of Mankind* (segment), Warner Bros. (1957), YouTube, https://www.youtube.com/watch?v=EB6VGKccul8&list=PLaukiTt7wl8Aa9MYAZMhZlUfuXb9EqHx-

_____, and Richard Anobile. *The Marx Brothers Scrapbook.* New York: Grosset and Dunlap, 1974.

Marx, Gummo. "The Fifth Marx Brother," *New York Tribune,* August 17, 1932.

Marx, Harpo. *The Story of Mankind* (segment), Warner Bros. (1957), YouTube, https://www.youtube.com/watch?v=H7de1sTeD6w Accessed May 25, 2021.

_____, with Rowland Barber. *Harpo Speaks!* New York: Limelight Editions, 1985.

Marx, Maxine. *Growing Up With Chico.* New York: Limelight Books, 1986.

Monkey Business. Paramount Publix Corporation (1931), *Horse Feathers* (1932), *Duck Soup,* Paramount Productions (1933).

Project Gutenberg, https://www.gutenberg.org/ is a good source for scripts of plays and some films. This page is searchable.

Stoliar, Steve. *Raised Eyebrows: My Years Inside Groucho's House.* Albany, GA: BearManor [sic] Media, 2011.

YouTube, https://www.youtube.com/ contains many Marx Brothers film clips, interviews, movie trailers, and related material. This page is searchable.

Secondary Sources—Marx Brothers

Adamson, Joe. *Groucho, Harpo, Chico and Sometimes Zeppo.* New York: Simon & Schuster, 1973.

Arce, Hector. *Groucho.* New York: Perigee Books, 1979.

Bader, Robert. *Four of the Three Musketeers: The Marx Brothers on Stage.* Evanston, IL: Northwestern University Press, 2016.

Bader, Robert S., Josh Frank, and Bill Marx. *Gilbert Gottfried's Amazing Colossal Podcast.* https://podcasts.apple.com/ie/podcast/255-marx-brothers-round-table-robert-s-bader-josh-frank/id883308059?i=1000434932357

Bego, Mark. *The Pocket Essential: The Marx Brothers.* North Pomfret, VT: Trafalgar Square Publishing, 2001.

Bergan, Ronald. *The Life and Times of the Marx Brothers.* New York: Smithmark, 1992.

Blount Jr., Roy. *Hail, Hail Euphoria!* New York: HarperCollins, 2010.

Chandler, Charlotte. *Hello, I Must Be Going: Groucho and His Friends.* New York: Citadel Press, 1993. Chandler's book also contains primary source material in the form of interviews.

Charney, Maurice. *The Comic World of the Marx Brothers' Movies.* Madison, NJ: Fairleigh Dickinson University Press, 2007.

Eyles, Allen. *The Marx Brothers: Their World of Comedy.* London: Tantivy Press, 1974.

Gardner, Martin. *The Marx Brothers as Social Critics.* Jefferson, NC: McFarland, 2009.

Gehrig, Wes D. *The Marx Brothers: A Bio-Bibliography.* Westport, CT: Greenwood Press, 1987.

Harpo's Place. www.harposplace.com

Leaf, David, and John Scheinfeld, directors, writers, and producers. *The Unknown Marx Brothers: A Unique Look at Film's Most Original Comedy Legends.* DVD, Crew Neck Productions, 1993.

Lieberfeld, Daniel, and Judith Sanders, "Here Under False Pretenses: The Marx Brothers

Crash the Gates," *The American Scholar* 64:1 (Winter 1995), 103–06.

Louvish, Simon. *Monkey Business: The Lives and Legends of The Marx Brothers.* New York: Thomas Dunne Books, 1999.

Mitchell, Glenn. *The Marx Brothers Encyclopedia.* London: B. T. Batsford, 1996.

Pollard, Justin, "The Eccentric Engineer." *Engineering and Technology,* July 2014, https://ieee explore.ieee.org/stamp/stamp.jsp?arnumber= 6863815

Trav S. D. (Donald Travis Stewart). *Travalanche* blog. Observations of the Marx Brothers can be found at https://travsd.wordpress.com/ ?s=marx+brothers

Wesolowski, Paul. "The Freedonia Gazette." https://www.marx-brothers.org/whyaduck/ merchandise/gazette.htm

Secondary Sources—American Culture

Abbott, Karen. *American Rose: A Nation Laid Bare: The Life and Times of Gypsy Rose Lee.* New York: Random House, 2010.

Abrahams, Roger. *Singing the Master: The Emergence of African-American Culture in the Plantation South.* New York: Penguin Books, 1994.

Allen, Robert C. *Horrible Prettiness: Burlesque and American Culture.* Chapel Hill: University of North Carolina Press, 1991.

Bader, Robert S. "The Marx Brothers on Television." https://marxbrothers.net/essays/the-marx-brothers-on-television/

Bataille, G. M., and C.L.S. Silet, eds. *The Pretend Indians: Images of Native Americans in the Movies.* Ann Arbor, MI: Books on Demand, 1994.

Belth, Nathan. *A Promise to Keep: A Narrative of the American Encounter with Anti-Semitism.* New York: Times Books, 1979.

Berger, Peter L. *Redeeming Laughter: The Comic Dimension of Human Experience.* Berlin: Walter De Gruyter, 1997.

Bergman, Andrew. *We're in the Money: Depression America and Its Films.* New York: Harper Torchbooks, 1972.

Bird, S. Elizabeth, ed. *Dressing in Feathers: The Construction of the Indian in American Popular Culture.* Boulder, CO: Westview Press, 1996.

Bold, Christine. *The Frontier Club: Popular Westerns and Cultural Power, 1880–1924.* New York: Oxford University Press, 2013.

Bordman, Gerald. *American Musical Theatre: A Chronicle.* New York: Oxford University Press, 3rd edition, 2001.

Brock, Pope. *Charlatan: America's Most Dangerous Huckster, the Man Who Pursued Him, and the Age of Hucksterism.* New York: Crown Publishing, 2008.

Brown, Dee. *Bury My Heart at Wounded Knee:*

An Indian History of the American West. New York: Holt, Rinehart & Winston, 1970.

Chambers, John Whitely. *To Raise an Army: The Draft Comes to Modern America.* New York: Free Press, 1987.

Csida, Joseph, and June Bundy Csida. *American Entertainment: A Unique History of Popular Show Business.* New York: Watson-Guptill Publications, 1978.

Davis, Janet M. *The Circus Age: Culture & Society Under the American Big Top.* Chapel Hill: University of North Carolina Press, 2002.

Diner, Hasia. "The Encounter between Jews and America in the Gilded Age and Progressive Era." *Journal of Gilded Age and Progressive Era*, 11:1 (January 2012), 3–25.

Dinnerstein, Leonard. *Anti-Semitism in America.* New York: Oxford University Press, 1994.

Dobkowski, Michael. *The Tarnished American Dream: The Basis of American Anti-Semitism.* Westport, CT: Greenwood Press, 1979.

Dudden, Arthur Power. *American Humor.* New York: Oxford University Press, 1987.

Dundes, Alan. *Cracking Jokes: Studies of Sick Humor Cycles and Stereotypes.* Berkeley, CA: Ten Speed Press, 1987.

Edsel, Robert M. *Monuments Men: Allied Heroes, Nazi Thieves and the Greatest Treasure Hunt in History.* New York: Center Street Books, 2009.

Ehrenreich, Barbara, and Deirdre English. *For Her Own Good: 150 Years of the Experts' Advice to Women.* Garden City, NY: Anchor Books, 1979.

Engelhardt, Tom. *The End of Victory Culture: Cold War America and the Disillusioning of a Generation.* Amherst: University of Massachusetts Press, 2007.

Erenberg, Lewis. *Steppin' Out: New York Nightlife and the Transformation of American Culture, 1890–1920.* Westport, CT: Greenwood Press, 1981.

Fass, Paula. *The Damned and the Beautiful: American Youth in the 1920s.* New York: Oxford University Press, 1971.

Fraser, George MacDonald. *The Hollywood History of the World: From One Million Years BC to Apocalypse Now.* New York: Beech Tree Books, 1988.

Goldwyn, Liz. *Pretty Things: The Last Generation of American Burlesque Queens.* New York: !t [*sic*] Books, 2010.

Gorn, Elliott J., and Warren Goldstein. *A Brief History of American Sports.* Urbana: University of Illinois Press, 1993.

Green, Harvey. *Fit for America: Health, Fitness, Sport and American Society.* Baltimore: Johns Hopkins University Press, 1986.

Harris, Neil. *Humbug: The Art of P.T. Barnum.* Chicago: University of Chicago Press, 1973.

Higham, John. *Strangers in the Land: Patterns of American Nativism 1860–1925.* New York: Atheneum, 1978.

Hollon, Eugene. *Frontier Violence: Another Look.* New York; Oxford University Press, 1974.

Horowitz, Helen Lefkowitz. *Campus Life: Undergraduate Cultures from the End of the Eighteenth Century to the Present.* New York: Alfred A. Knopf, 1987.

Hoxie, Frederick. *This Indian Country: American Indian Activists and the Place They Made.* New York: Penguin Books, 2012.

Huizinga, Johan. *Homo Ludens: A Study in the Play Element in Culture.* Translated from Dutch, New York: Random House, 1955.

Internet Movie Data Base, https://www.imdb.com/ This page is searchable.

Jay, Ricky. *Learned Pigs & Fireproof Women.* New York: Villard Books, 1986.

Kurtz, Michael J. *America and the Return of Nazi Contraband: The Recovery of Europe's Cultural Treasures.* Cambridge, UK: Cambridge University Press, 2009.

Laufe, Abe. *Broadway's Greatest Musicals.* New York: Funk and Wagnalls Books, 1997.

Levine, Lawrence. *Black Culture and Black Consciousness: Afro-American Thought from Slavery to Freedom.* New York: Oxford University Press, 2007.

Levine, Lawrence. *Highbrow Lowbrow, The Emergence of Cultural Hierarchy in America.* Cambridge, MA: Harvard University Press, 1990.

Lewis, Paul. *Cracking Up: American Humor in a Time of Conflict.* Chicago: University of Chicago Press, 2006.

Lhamon, W. T. *Raising Cain: Blackface Performance from Jim Crow to Hip Hop.* Cambridge, MA: Harvard University Press, 1995.

Limerick, Patricia. *Something in the Soil.* New York: W. W. Norton, 2000.

Lott, Eric. *Love & Theft: Blackface Minstrelsy & the American Working Class.* New York: Oxford University Press, 1993.

May, Larry. *Screening Out the Past: The Birth of Mass Culture and the Motion Picture Industry.* New York: Oxford University Press, 1983.

McGarath, Roger. *Gunfighters, Highwaymen, and Vigilantes: Violence on the Frontier.* Berkeley: University of California Press, 1987.

Mintz, Steven, and Randy Roberts. *Hollywood's America: United States History Through Its Films.* St. James, NY: Brandywine Press, 1993.

Nicholas, Lynn H. *The Rape of Europa: The Fate of Europe's Treasures in the Third Reich and Second World War.* New York: Vintage, 1995.

Okrent, Daniel. *Last Call: The Rise and Fall of Prohibition.* New York: Scribner's, 2010.

Peiss, Kathy. *Cheap Amusements: Working Women and Leisure in Turn-of-the-Century New York.* Philadelphia: Temple University Press, 1986.

Pells, Richard. *Radical Visions and American Dreams: Culture and Social Thought in the Depression Years.* Middletown, CT: Wesleyan University Press, 1984.

Provine, Robert. *Laughter: A Scientific Investigation.* New York: Penguin Putnam, 2000.

Riess, Steven A. *City Games: The Evolution of American Urban Society and the Rise of Sports.* Urbana: University of Illinois Press, 1989.

Sklar, Robert. *Movie-Made America: How Movies Changed American Life.* New York: Random House, 1975.

Roediger, David R. *Working Toward Whiteness: How America's Immigrants Became White.* New York: Basic Books, 2005.

Roffman, Peter, and Jim Purdy, *The Hollywood Social Problem Film: Madness, Despair, and Politics from the Depression to the Fifties.* Bloomington: Indiana University Press, 1981.

Rollins, Peter C. and John O'Connor, eds. *Hollywood's Indian: The Portrayal of the Native American in Films.* Lexington: University Press of Kentucky, 2003.

Rorabaugh, W. J. *The Alcoholic Republic: An American Tradition.* Oxford, UK: Oxford University Press, 1979.

Ross, Steven J. *Working-Class Hollywood: Silent Films and the Shaping of Class in America.* Princeton, NJ: Princeton University Press, 1999.

Roth, Randolph. *American Homicide.* Cambridge, MA: The Belknap Press of the Harvard University Press, 2009.

Rourke, Constance. *American Humor: A Study of the National Character.* Garden City, NY: Anchor Doubleday, 1931.

Said, Edward. *Orientalism.* New York: Pantheon Books, 1978.

Sann, Paul. *Fads, Follies and Delusions of the American People.* New York: Bonanza Books, 1967.

Simon, Linda. *The Greatest Show on Earth: A History of the Circus.* London: Reaktion Books, 2014.

Slotkin, Richard. *Gunfighter Nation: The Myth of the Frontier in Twentieth-Century America.* New York: Atheneum, 1992.

Smith, Christopher. *Dancing Revolution: Bodies, Space, and Sound in American Cultural History.* Urbana: University of Illinois Press, 2019.

Snyder, Robert W. *The Voice of the City: Vaudeville and Popular Culture in New York.* New York: Oxford University Press, 1989.

Southern, Eileen. *The Music of Black Americans.* New York: W.W. Norton & Company, 1971.

Standiford, Les. *Battle for the Big Top: P. T. Barnum, James Bailey, John Ringling, and the Death-Defying Saga of the American Circus.* New York: PublicAffairs, 2021.

Stott, William. *Documentary Expression and Thirties America.* Chicago: University of Chicago Press, 1986.

Takaki, Ronald. *A Different Mirror: A History of Multicultural America.* Boston: Little, Brown and Company, 1993.

Ultimate Movie Rankings. https://www.ultimatemovierankings.com/site-index-2-2/ is a searchable page. Marx Brothers films can be found at: https://www.ultimatemovierankings.com/marx-brothers-movies/

Veron, Enid, ed. *Humor in America: An Anthology.* New York: Harcourt Brace Jovanovich, 1976

Walker, Nancy, ed. *What's So Funny? Humor in American Culture.* Wilmington, DE: Scholarly Resources, 1998.

Whitaker, Jan. *Service and Style: How the American Department Store Fashioned the Middle Class.* New York: St. Martin's Press, 2006.

Wilkins, Julia and Amy Janet Eisenbraun. "Humor Theories and the Physiological Benefits of Laughter," *Holistic Nursing Practice,* November/December 2009 23 (6), 349–354.

Other Useful Works

Allen, Frederick Lewis. *Only Yesterday: An Informal History of the 1920's.* New York: Perennial Classics, 2000. Reprint of 1931 original. (A classic that remains one of the more informative books on the 1920s.)

Boris, Eileen, and Nelson Lichtenstein, eds. *Major Problems in the History of American Workers: Documents and Essays.* Boston: Houghton Mifflin, 2003.

Gordon, Colin, ed. *Major Problems in American History 1920–1945: Documents and Essays.* Boston: Houghton Mifflin, 1999.

History Matters: The U.S. History Survey Course on the Web. http://historymatters.gmu.edu/ (A good source for those seeking short primary source documents. The site is searchable.)

Lynd, Robert S., and Helen M. Lynd. *Middletown: A Study in Modern American Culture.* New York: Harcourt Brace Jovanovich, 1955 reprint of 1929 original. (A classic sociological study still used by those delving into early 20th century America.)

Parrish, Michael E. *Anxious Decades: America in Prosperity and Depression, 1920–41.* New York: W.W. Norton, 1992.

Whisenhunt, Donald W. *The Human Condition: America Between the Wars, 1920–1945.* Wilmington, DE: SR Books, 2002.

Zinn, Howard. *A People's History of the United States: 1492–Present.* New York: Harper Perennial Modern Classics, 2005.

Index